# FROM
# LEXINGTON
## TO
# DESERT STORM
## AND
# BEYOND

SECOND EDITION

# / FROM LEXINGTON TO DESERT STORM AND BEYOND/

## War and Politics in the American Experience

Donald M. Snow and
Dennis M. Drew

*M.E. Sharpe*
Armonk, New York
London, England

**Library of Congress Cataloging-in-Publication Data**

Snow, Donald M., 1943–
    From Lexington to Desert Storm and beyond : war and politics in the American
experience / Donald M. Snow and Dennis M. Drew.—2nd ed.
        p. cm.
    Includes bibliographical references and index.
    ISBN 0-7656-0698-4 (alk. paper) — ISBN 0-7656-0699-2 (pbk. : alk. paper)
        1. Politics and war. 2. Sociology, Military—United States. 3. Military art and
science—United States—History. 4. United States—History, Military. 5. Civil-military
relations—United States—History. I. Drew, Dennis M. II. Title.

UA23.S5247 2001
306.2′7′0973—dc21                                                    00-038783

Printed in the United States of America

The paper used in this publication meets the minimum requirements of
American National Standard for Information Sciences
Permanence of Paper for Printed Library Materials,
ANSI Z 39.48-1984.

BM (c)   10   9   8   7   6   5   4   3   2   1
BM (p)   10   9   8   7   6   5   4   3   2

# Contents

# List of Maps

# Preface

This volume is a revision and expansion of *From Lexington to Desert Storm: The American Experience at War*, which in turn was an expansion of *The Eagle's Talons*, published by Air University Press in 1988. This new edition came about after conversations with Peter Coveney, our editor at M. E. Sharpe, and has two primary purposes.

The first is to expand the coverage to include critical changes that have occurred since the first book was produced. Writing for that edition was completed in 1992, and obviously things have changed since then: the cold war has conclusively ended, the United States has been involved in a number of minor conflicts in places like Somalia and Kosovo, and there has been a renaissance of professionalism and effectiveness in the American military establishment.

These changes are reflected in the text. The end of the cold war has meant that our emphasis on nuclear weapons has diminished, for instance. An added chapter on the post–cold war period talks broadly about how the United States is adapting militarily to a changing world since Operation Desert Storm. Sadly, we conclude that the United States still does not have it entirely right in connecting political and military objectives and in achieving the best possible postwar conditions (the better state of the peace).

The second reason for a new edition is to broaden our audience base. In the original volume, we identified three audiences we hoped to reach: civilian decision makers with a limited background in military affairs, military leaders with a limited background in political affairs, and citizens who lacked expertise but had an interest in the complex relationships between political and military affairs.

Air University Press proved a strong conduit for reaching the first two audiences but, due to the nature of government operations, was less than ideal for reaching the general public and an equally important fourth audience, students. For those audiences, a commercial press seemed more appropriate, and we are delighted that M.E. Sharpe concurred.

We have been the beneficiaries of a great deal of indispensable help in developing this volume. The staff of Air University Press was very helpful and patient in the production of the original volume. Our editor, John Jordan, labored long and hard to produce a unified text from our disparate writing styles. David MacIsaac, an eminent military historian, offered invaluable suggestions and corrected numerous errors of omission and commission. Our associates at M.E. Sharpe, notably Michael Weber, Patricia Kolb, and Peter Coveney and the production staff, were very helpful in transforming the original into this expanded effort.

Finally, we want to acknowledge the encouragement and support of two very patient wives and neglected families. The original volume required countless evening hours and weekend days that should have been devoted to them, and the revised effort was similar in its demands. We thank them for their patience and support. Also, we want to thank Mrs. Jan Pugh of the political science department at the University of Alabama for valuable editorial (including scanning) assistance that greatly facilitated preparation of this new edition.

Donald M. Snow
Dennis M. Drew

# Introduction

As we greet the twenty-first century, the United States finds itself at a cross-roads of sorts concerning the appropriate role of military force as an instrument of power to support the objectives of foreign policy. The debate over military power is part of a much larger disagreement over America's place in the world. The basis for the larger controversy is that although American military power has diminished relatively, we remain the most powerful country in the world. The poles of the larger debate about our power range from the expanded responsibilities the United States assumes as the remaining superpower in the world to the need to pull back and not be the world's police officer.

Future applications of American military might are clearly important elements of the the post–cold war world because military force is, and has been throughout history, a prominent means societies have used to settle their differences. One can decry or celebrate that observation, but one can ignore it only by the considerable application of selective perception. The overriding questions for Americans are where, if anywhere, and over what should they be willing to shed their blood and expend their treasure.

Three factors stand out and collectively define the issues underlying the debate. The first is the issue of limited war, a problem of adjustment to fighting less than World War II–sized conflicts and a problem the currency of which surrounds American limited intervention in places such as Somalia and Bosnia and Herzegovina. The second is the effects of the end of the cold war and hence the missions and ways of doing things that flowed from that competition. The third is the lingering legacy of America's most traumatic and unsuccessful adventure at arms, the Vietnam War and its aftermath.

The period since the end of World War II represents a watershed in the reasons and purposes for which the United States goes to war. For a period beginning with the American Civil War and ending with World War II, the significant uses of American force were in support of total political purposes: the overthrow of the enemy's regime, a purpose adequate to justify the large-scale mobilization of American society.

Such wars are not history's norm, but in popular (including the military's) thinking they became our norm. Total wars are simple and straightforward: the enemy must be vanquished and whatever means are necessary will be employed to that end.

In a world where total war could mean nuclear holocaust (which is still physically possible, even with the demise of the Soviet Union), such war has become inconceivable. Indeed, the only instance since World War II where the US entertained the unlimited goal of overthrowing an enemy regime was during the course of Operation Desert Storm, where there was some discussion of overthrowing Saddam Hussein of Iraq.

America and the American military have had to adjust to an era when force is used for more limited purposes, and it has been difficult. Wars with limited objectives are often fought with less than the total means available, which is frustrating to the military. Limited goals are also generally less morally lofty and uplifting; the enemy is not so evil that he must be exorcised. Particularly when the wars are confined to a single country, differentiating good from evil is difficult. Moreover, the purposes underlying limited war are often vague and poorly articulated and understood.

During the cold war, US–Soviet competition necessitated limits on any wars in which the US—or for that matter, the Soviet Union—was involved. Since military engagements generally pitted the United States against a Soviet ally—North Korea, North Vietnam—a concern always had to be whether some action might cause escalation to direct confrontation that could lead to nuclear war. Certainly such reasoning affected the way both the Korean and Vietnam conflicts were fought.

Since the end of the cold war, that inhibition no longer exists. American involvements, however, remain limited, but the cause of limitation has changed. The conflicts of the post–cold war period have been small, mostly internal affairs in third world areas where American interests are minimal by traditional definition. These wars, as in Bosnia and Herzegovina, Somalia, Kosovo, and the Kurdish enclaves in Iraq, do not demand maximum force, nor are they situations where large-scale force could achieve defined objectives.

The second factor is the end of the cold war itself. The central reality for the American military during the forty-four years between the end of World War II and the beginning of the end of the Soviet empire in 1989 was the menace caused by Soviet-led communism. As a military problem, it had two sides: the conventional balance between the North Atlantic Treaty Organization (NATO) and the Warsaw Treaty Organization (WTO) in central Europe, and the thermonuclear balance between the Soviets and the Americans.

This confrontation provided the conceptual framework from which all other thinking and planning derived. The purposes of military force were straightforward: to deter either kind of attack by convincing the opponent he could not succeed (deterrence) or to defeat an attack should deterrence fail.

Nuclear weapons played a special, evolving role in this regard. As nuclear arsenals grew and the calamity of their use became appreciated, they increasingly became the limiting factor for the whole competition. Everyone on both sides came to understand that a nuclear war would be catastrophic and could not be allowed to occur. Since any direct conflict between the superpowers had within it the potential to escalate to nuclear exchange, all confrontations had to be avoided.

The result was a "necessary peace" between the superpowers where the avoidance of mutual annihilation was the conceptual glue. In that circumstance, the whole competition gradually became more ritualistic than real: we planned, we organized, and we practiced for a war we knew could never occur. When that ritualistic nature was combined with the economic crisis of the Soviet system, the fate of the cold war was sealed.

The Soviets' losing the cold war, however, has meant the increasing irrelevance of the concepts on which it was premised. The new international system that succeeds the cold war system is not yet clearly in place. One component of that system will be a set of criteria defining when the United States will and will not use military force. One factor that continues to condition the evolution of thinking about that use is what remains of the Vietnam legacy.

The third concern is a product of the limited-war problem in general, and more specifically, the American experience in Vietnam. The war in Southeast Asia was a national trauma which, in many important ways, triggered the entire debate over the American role in the world and the utility of military force.

The Vietnam War was bewildering. The US effort inundated Indochina with a flood of American equipment, advisers, technology, and combat troops. Applied American military power dwarfed the physical efforts of the Vietcong and the North Vietnamese. Militarily, the American battlefield effort yielded an almost unbroken string of victories. American forces commanded the air and sea and could operate in any area with ground forces. On the one occasion in which the enemy stood and fought American forces in a conventional style, the Tet offensive in 1968, the enemy was so badly mauled that it could not launch another major offensive for four years. But despite all this "success," the United States could not prevail.

The Vietnam War was the first war in which none of the American political objectives were attained. Despite an enormous military effort, continual
success on the battlefield, and the sacrifice of more than 50,000 American
lives, the United States was unable to translate apparent military success into
success in the larger war. Perhaps worse, the controversy that eventuated
over American participation in the war ripped apart the fabric of American
society as private passions about the war erupted into massive demonstrations and occasional violence. Many became disillusioned with American
military and political leadership. In addition, the fiscal consequences of the
war were still being felt in the American economy more than a decade after
the end of US involvement. Finally, the struggle's end was as difficult as its
conduct. According to one point of view, the United States shamefully abandoned its South Vietnamese ally, thus making a mockery of the American
effort and of those who were sacrificed in that effort.

That the Vietnam experience was traumatic is unquestionable; the question that remains is what can be usefully learned from the experience—and
again, Americans have not achieved consensus. Purported lessons have included simplistic cries for "no more Vietnams" to equally simplistic pleas
demanding that the military be unfettered when prosecuting such struggles.
Other "lessons" span the gamut from geopolitical to technical and have been
equally diverse and contradictory. In short, the passions caused by the Vietnam trauma have generated considerable heat but little light by which Americans can guide future actions.

Confusion, bewilderment, anger, and simplistic solutions are symptomatic
of the vague and often myopic historical view of most Americans, including,
unfortunately, many civilian and military leaders charged with important national security responsibilities. The authors contend that current concerns about
the effects of the end of the cold war, limited war, and the Vietnam experience
are but threads in the much larger historical tapestry of American politico-military
experience. We believe that just as individual threads should be viewed as only
part of a whole tapestry, current politico-military concerns can be evaluated
accurately only if viewed in their historical context.

Simplistic approaches to politico-military problems are also indications
that Americans have not been forced to deal comprehensively with the role
of force. History, and especially military history, has treated the United States
kindly. Few countries share the American experience of carving a new state
from a vast wilderness only sparsely populated by aboriginal tribes and of
transforming that bountiful wilderness into a great democratic experiment.
As a result, Americans have had a legacy of optimism: despite obstacles,
Americans have expected to achieve their goals. The "can do" spirit has
been an indelible element in their collective psyche.

Much of this American optimism has stemmed from a reprieve from history's darker side, but history has shown another face to Europeans. Plowshares have been beaten into swords as often as the reverse and conquerors have regularly scourged the land. The result has been to breed caution, reserve, suspicion, and a belief that peace and prosperity may be only temporary interludes. In short, Europeans have a long tradition in which war is an integral, if not central, part of political activity.

The luxury of long isolation from the internecine struggles of Europe has molded the American view that war is an aberration, an unfortunate diversion from the normal course of events. Rather than a political instrument, war represents to Americans the failure of political policy—the failure to deal successfully with a direct threat to the essential virtue of the American experiment. When forced to arms, Americans view warfare as a great crusade to overcome a well-defined evil.

If war has touched Americans with less frequency and effect than others, it has also left Americans with a legacy of military success. That this legacy is partly mythology built on selective memory is almost beside the point. Thus Americans cherish the tradition that the United States is not only "slow to anger" and enters into war only with great reluctance but also wins when the crusade is mounted. Despite such contrary evidence as the American military performance in the War of 1812 and some isolated unseemly or embarrassing episodes, applied force and victory have been inextricably linked in the American recollection. Because Americans believed in their infallibility, the tarnish from recent experience (whether Vietnam or lesser debacles such as Beirut or Desert One) is all the uglier.

Because fortune has shielded Americans from some of the nastier realities of military force, most Americans have been able to avoid coming to grips with the central role military force has had and continues to play in an international setting where the recourse to force remains the "court of last resort" for achieving national ends. More specifically, American innocence has allowed us to avoid confronting war as a political act and learning the often harsh relationship between politics and military force. In a relatively uncomplicated world in which the United States was not a central player that innocence was affordable. In a world of increasing mutual dependency in which the United States is center stage that innocence is a too expensive luxury.

That it is now time to decide when, where, and why the United States should be willing or unwilling to use force in the future is obvious and compelling. The debate has been joined but remains jaundiced by proximate concerns and exacerbated by historical myopia. We believe significant insights into why and how the United States could and should use force in the future lie in understanding why and how America has done so in the past. At a minimum, an excursion into American military history may dilute the tendencies to separate political and military affairs and to treat all events as unique and discrete.

Given the complexity and breadth of the subject, the organization of this volume takes on considerable importance. Following an introductory chapter to provide the framework for our analysis, we have devoted an entire chapter to each of America's major wars—the exceptions being the War of 1812, the war with Mexico, and the Spanish-American War, which are combined in one chapter, the Persian Gulf War (and the post-Vietnam experience) and the post–cold war experience, each of which also has its own chapter. Each of these chapters is divided into sections titled (in order): Issues and Events, Political Objective, Military Objectives and Strategy, Political Considerations, Military Technology and Technique, Military Conduct, and Better State of the Peace. We have attempted to write each chapter so that it can stand alone and, at the same time, flow together with other chapters to form an integrated whole. Within each chapter, each section is written to stand alone and yet contribute to a coherent chapter. These objectives are somewhat mutually exclusive and could only be accomplished by a limited degree of repetition in the text. The result is a survey history of the American experience in war and individual surveys of political objectives, military strategies, military technology, and the other subjects that are treated discretely in each chapter and successively from chapter to chapter. The final chapter draws conclusions and delineates important trends evident in the broad sweep of the American experience.

# FROM
# LEXINGTON
## TO
# DESERT STORM
## AND
# BEYOND

# 1

# War and Political Purpose

"War is a continuation of political activity by other means," the great Prussian strategist Carl von Clausewitz wrote over a century and a half ago. His famous dictum, so disarmingly simple and straightforward, is mimicked constantly in discussions about the role of military force in accomplishing the goals of groups and states. Despite its obvious truth and power, it is a statement shallowly comprehended and constantly forgotten.

What Clausewitz meant, and what is at the very heart of understanding why countries go to war, is that military force is a tool, one among many, by which states (or groups of states or groups within states) seek to accomplish their ends. Those ends are defined politically in terms of imposing the policies of one group on another. Force is certainly not the only means by which countries seek to accomplish their political ends, but because it inevitably involves the taking of human life, it is the most extreme of the so-called instruments of national power. Other instruments of power are conventionally described as the economic and diplomatic instruments: the use of various forms of economic reward or deprivation and of persuasion to achieve ends. What should never be forgotten is that the instruments of power are ultimately judged and gain their entire meaning by the extent to which they serve national policies.

Despite its bestial and grotesque nature, war continues to be a tool of national policy. Americans must understand war and its purposes as clearly as possible to choose most intelligently when to use and when not to use the military instrument of power. That is our purpose in this volume.

The bulk of our concern is why Americans go to war. We must begin by looking at why people generally have gone to war as context for looking at why Americans have found and will find the use of military force necessary.

3

To begin to unravel that relationship, one must begin with two general questions. The first deals with the environment in which we find ourselves: How and why does the international system permit circumstances in which opposing states determine that only the use of armed violence will allow them to settle their differences? Once that question has been answered, the second question can be addressed: What is the role of military force in solving political differences?

The key concept in understanding how and why the structure of the international system permits and even sometimes encourages the use of armed force is *sovereignty*. Sovereignty means supreme and independent political authority, and it is a quality possessed not by the system itself but by its constituent members, the states. What this means in practice is that within the territorial boundaries of a country, the authority of the national government is supreme and knows no superior source of authority. In the relations among states, the implication is that there is no higher source of authority to regulate those relations and to resolve policy differences when they arise. The absolute nature of sovereignty is under attack in places such as Somalia, whose sovereignty has been violated by humanitarian military efforts.

This situation is utterly unlike the relations among individuals and groups within states (at least where national political authority is effective), because in that instance there is an arbiter, the state. All states have rules established to regulate internal conflicts of interest and, in the ultimate, the mechanisms of state (e.g., the judicial and legislative systems) provide forums for the authoritative settlement of policy disagreements short of the use of violence (which is uniformly proscribed in word if not in deed). A sovereign exists as the ultimate settler of differences.

There is no equivalent in the relations among states because the members of the international system are themselves the sovereigns. There is no authority superior to the state that can be called on to resolve the differences between the states. When states come into disagreement over policy, they cannot take the matter to court to gain a resolution, simply because there is no court with that kind of authority.

Why is this the case? The answer flows from the notion of sovereignty and finds expression in the idea of "vital national interests." Vital national interests are those interests about which the state is unwilling to compromise, will not submit to arbitration, and hence will seek to protect by all available means. The most basic of those interests are the territorial integrity of the state itself and the maintenance of sovereign control over that territory.

Should, for instance, Mexico decide to reassert its claims to the American Southwest, the United States would be unwilling to take the matter to the World Court (which gains authority over cases only when the states who are party to a dispute specifically give it jurisdiction for that particular matter). Why? The answer is simple in a world of sovereign states. The Southwest is a vital interest of the United States, and we would clearly be unwilling to relinquish sovereign control over it. If we went to court, we might lose. Since we would not honor the verdict, the simplest way to handle the situation is to avoid having a mechanism capable of rendering unfavorable authoritative judgments. And that is the way the system is.

In such a system, given that disagreements over policy will inevitably arise, how are policy differences resolved? The answer, once again, is straightforward: states can favorably resolve policy differences to the extent that they can impose their will on others. The principle is known as *self-help*, and it means that international politics are fundamentally an exercise in power. Power, in turn, can be defined as the ability to get people to do something they would not otherwise do, in this case to accept policies in opposition to those preferred.

Take the hypothetical case of Mexican irredentist claims on the Southwest as an example. Should such claims exist, there would be a clear policy disagreement between the United States and Mexico, with American policy based in continued sovereign control of the Southwest and Mexican policy demanding its return. The policy disagreement is total: only the United States or Mexico can exercise sovereign control over the territory. Since the current situation reflects American policy, the problem for Mexico is how to get the United States to change its policy. In the absence of authoritative mechanisms to resolve the dispute, the problem for Mexico thus becomes one of self-help, the effective exercise of power to achieve its political ends. This brings us back to the question of the instruments of national power and the ability to apply them effectively.

As stated earlier the instruments of power are conventionally divided into the three categories of diplomatic, economic, and military power. Diplomatically, the Mexican government might seek to engage in negotiations, using its most persuasive diplomats and framing its argument in historical or demographic terms, to convince us voluntarily to cede the territory because of a superior Mexican claim. Failing in that, the Mexicans might threaten or carry out economic sanctions or promise rewards if we would agree to the cession of the Southwest. They could, for instance, threaten to deny American access to Mexican oil reserves or, using a more positive approach, they could offer unlimited access to those reserves in return for the territory. The degree to which such a strategy might be effective depends on American dependence on Mexican oil. If we were highly dependent, the Mexican government might have an effective lever that would compel us to accept its policy. If not, the economic instrument of power would be ineffectual.

Should all else fail there is always the military instrument of power. Should Mexican claims be serious enough (considered a vital national interest) and should other instruments fail to achieve the purpose, then Mexicans might consider the use of military force to seize and control the Southwest. That may not be the way we like to think of things, but it is sometimes the way things are.

Force is thus a tool of political authority, and its purpose is either to guarantee that the inimical policies of others are not imposed on the political unit or to impose one's own policies on a recalcitrant adversary. Seen this way, military power gains its meaning as an agent for realizing the political purposes and objectives of the state (or whatever designation the political unit has). Unless this subjugation of military force to the political authority from which it flows is fully comprehended, the role of force cannot be adequately understood. Unless policy is made for military force starting from this ordering, the result is likely to be inappropriate policy and unnecessary friction between political authority and the military. Their roles may be distinct, but the military is an agent that implements the decisions of political authority.

Interestingly, it was Clausewitz who best understood this relationship. One level of this understanding is the Prussian dictum with which this chapter began: "War is a continuation of political activity by other means." The dictum is not an advocacy for using force to resolve political differences. Clausewitz, as a military man, understood that the decision to use force resides with political authorities; his role was to implement those decisions should that determination be made. The dictum merely states the relationship between war and politics. When the policies of two or more states become so incompatible that they cannot be pursued simultaneously, some means to resolve those differences must be found. Military force is one means to resolve those differences—it is another means to continue the political process of conflict resolution.

The relationship can be seen in another light captured by Clausewitz in an equally true but less cited observation that war has its own grammar but not its own logic. What he meant was that once the decision to go to war has been reached, the nature of conducting warfare—the so-called military art and science—dictates how war should be fought on the battlefield (the grammar, or as most people would say today, the language of war). The reason for going to war and the political objectives for which war is fought do not flow from that language, but derive from the overall political objectives (the logic of war) to which they are subordinate. In the heat of campaign that subordination is often blurred by the passion of the moment, but the Prussian was quite explicit that one should never lose sight of the relationship.

The language of war, quite clearly, is written in blood, and it is man's most extreme means of resolving differences. Because its consequences include the expenditure of human life and the destruction of the things people value, it is a political remedy *in extremis*. The use of force is the means chosen when the objective is vital and where other, nonviolent instruments of power have been ineffective in resolving political differences.

The purpose of force, thus, is to exercise power. "War is," as Clausewitz notes, "an act of force to compel our adversary to do our will." Doing "our will" is, however, a more complex matter than the quotation may suggest. A good deal of the misunderstanding about the role of force arises from over-simplifying how political and military aspects of war contribute to achieving the imposition of will.

In more contemporary terms observers often refer to the objectives of overcoming hostile will and ability. Hostile will contains at least two distinct parts. On one hand, hostile will consists of the willingness to continue to resist the imposition of hostile policies. What levels of cost, in terms of deprivation and suffering, are a people willing to endure, and at what point is the price of accepting the adversary's policies less than the cost of continuing to resist? Hostile will as willingness to continue to resist is well captured in the term *cost-tolerance:* what levels of cost are you willing to accept? On the other hand, hostile will also, and ultimately, is defined in terms of the willing acceptance or embrace of the originally objectionable policies. How does one go about convincing an adversary that the policies one seeks to impose are right and to the benefit of those who opposed them? The notion of hostile ability is more straightforward, referring to the physical ability of an adversary's armed forces and society to continue resistance.

Many practitioners and theorists have underemphasized the distinction between the two forms of hostile will and have consequently distorted the degree to which political authority and the military instrument contribute to achieving the ends of overcoming hostile will and ability. The assumption, implicit or explicit, has been that once the decision to use force has been made, it is the appropriate task of the military instrument to overcome hostile will and ability. We contend that it is more complicated than that.

Because hostile ability is represented by an adversary's armed forces, the military instrument is most clearly useful in removing that source of opposition. The classic method of defeating an enemy is to destroy his army, which is to say his hostile ability, although this is a realistic objective only part of the time. If one's armed forces are inferior to those of the enemy, then destroying those forces is usually an impossible way to achieve one's goals. In that case one may be forced to attack hostile will (cost-tolerance) by forcing the enemy to endure more suffering than his goals are worth. Sometimes one can pursue both objectives simultaneously; that is, break the enemy's will while destroying his army.

Overcoming hostile ability is clearly a military imperative and hostile willingness an ambiguous military or political goal. Overcoming hostile will (defined as acceptance of originally odious policies) is a political problem solvable only in the peace that follows hostilities. Obviously, the military aspect plays a part and there is a sequential relationship: until either hostile will or ability is overcome, one can neither impose nor convince the adversary to accept one's policies. At the same time, military victory does not ensure the later psychological acceptance of the outcome by the vanquished. Military victory may allow one to "compel our adversary to do our will," but in the long run, it is acceptance at the psychological level that renders the outcome totally successful.

This is a subtle but very important and often overlooked point. Victory or defeat in war has two distinct definitions. The most obvious is military victory because that aspect is easiest to view. The other, and ultimately more important, definition is the achievement of the political purposes for which war is fought in the first place, and that means acceptance by the adversary of the political objectives for which the war was fought. In turn adversaries must be convinced that the objectives for which they fought were wrong and that those for which you fought were correct. Military force may be able to enforce the terms of peace, but convincing the enemy population to embrace the peace is a political task of persuasion for which military force may be irrelevant or counterproductive. It is indeed possible to "win the war and lose the peace" if one assumes that once hostilities are concluded victory is complete. The lesson of World War I, when a punitive peace virtually ensured that the German people would not embrace the peace treaty, is only the most obvious example.

The purpose of this discussion is to establish the intimate, complex relationships between war and its political purposes. Americans tend to think of war primarily in its military aspects, but that is clearly not enough if we are to comprehend fully the dynamics of military conflict and where military force can and cannot be applied intelligently and effectively, especially in the contemporary context. Rather, the complex interaction between military and political affairs needs to be viewed systematically, and it is our purpose in the rest of this chapter to lay out a framework for organizing that relationship, which we will then apply to the American military experience in subsequent chapters.

The first element in that framework is what is often referred to as the causes of wars: those underlying issues that make the recourse to war an apparent solution and the proximate events which lead to the decision to go to war. The political objective that directs the war effort and gives it meaning emerges from these issues and events. Political objectives, in turn, lead to the determination of military objectives to achieve the political objective and military strategies that will accomplish the military task. We will then turn to the purely political considerations that affect the conduct and outcome of hostilities and in that context examine selectively the actual conduct of each conflict. Because technology has been such an enormous influence on the evolution of war, we will look at technological innovations—how they were or were not applied effectively, and how they affected the conduct and outcomes of wars. Finally, we will examine whether or how the political purposes were achieved, using Sir Basil Liddell Hart's "better state of the peace" and the notions of overcoming hostile will and ability as yardsticks.

## Issues and Events

The decision to go to war is seldom a casual matter. The road to war is generally a long one, and with the considerable assistance of hindsight, one can normally detect a gradual deterioration in the relations between what became warring units over underlying issues or sets of issues that were not resolved peacefully. Those underlying issues were transformed into events that serve as lightning rods that made the end result seem inevitable.

A caveat is in order here. One of the important concerns of historians and other social scientists is to speculate on the true "causes" of war and to devise elaborate theories about why there is war. We do not propose to add to that body of thought in the sense of proposing any grand scheme or overarching grand design to explain why men go to war. Our concern is more limited and descriptive. We begin from the more modest premise, supportable by evidence, that Americans from time to time make the political decision that armed violence is the way they must settle disputes. From that premise, it is our purpose to look at those instances and to see if there was commonality and to see how the decision chain led to and directed the political and military objectives. The decisions to make war will in all likelihood be made again. It is our hope that those determinations will be made wisely and will be translated into appropriate, supportable, and achievable political and military aims and objectives.

With that context, one can divide the road to war into two analytical distinctions. The first deals with the underlying issues (or causes) in the preceding peace that eventually led to war. What kinds of incompatibilities in policy fester to the point that differences appear solvable only by the sword? How did these come about, and were they resolvable by other forms of action? Were the issues fundamental, or did they simply devolve because of inattention or the inability of men to resolve them? How did these issues evolve into the political objectives for which the war would be fought (which is really the most important question of all)?

The second distinction arising from those underlying issues is the specific events (or proximate causes) that normally emerge to hasten the process toward war. Clearly, one is not always in control of these events because they can be precipitated by either antagonist. It is, however, those proximate events that either galvanize popular opinion behind the decision to go to war or fail to create that support. The important factor is the dynamic relationship between the underlying issues and the proximate events.

The distinction may best be demonstrated by example, contrasting two conflicts from the American experience—the Civil War and Vietnam. As we will argue in chapter 3, the underlying issue from which the Civil War arose was a fundamental clash of cultures. The North had gradually evolved from an agrarian to an industrial society while the South remained an agricultural society based around the plantation and the cultivation of cotton. The United States had become not a society but two distinct societies. The issue was fundamental and pervasive; two distinct socioeconomic systems could not coexist within one political framework indefinitely, and the differences gradually consumed more and more of the social and political fabric of the country.

The specific events that led to war flowed from this underlying incompatibility. Whether it was the debate over protectionist tariffs, the extension of slavery to the territories, or the election of Abraham Lincoln in 1860, all these events can be seen as reflections of the underlying issues. Within that context, the country could not survive as it was evolving. There were only two solutions available: either disunion that would allow each society to be represented by its own political system or union wherein one society triumphed and imposed its will.

Contrast the clarity and profundity of the issues and events leading to the Civil War with the parallels that led to American involvement in Southeast Asia. If there was a clear underlying issue (a point that remains contentious), it only indirectly involved the United States and North Vietnam. Rather, there were asymmetric issues: the American commitment to the policy of containment and the North Vietnamese desire to unite the country, by force if necessary. Ho Chi Minh cared little about the American policy, and the United States had little direct stake in the North Vietnamese objective. Rather, the Southeast Asian peninsula simply became a forum wherein quite different concerns would clash. Moreover, the underlying issues were of a different nature: the US policy was abstract (containing Communist expansion), whereas the adversary's goal was concrete (unification of a divided nation).

If the underlying issue was vague and less than pervasive from an American standpoint, the translation into specific events was also less than crystalline. At the beginning the events that would lead to American combat involvement had relatively little to do with Vietnam per se, but were instead part of a generalized response precipitated by North Korea's invasion of South Korea and a concern that the French economy was not recovering adequately due to the drain of the war against the Vietminh. Moreover, the road to war had an incremental flavor: relatively discrete decisions by a series of American presidents eventuated in a war they all hoped to avoid.

## Political Objective

The basic reason for war, which should provide the definitive guide for its conduct, is to attain its political objective. The definition of the political objective is normally framed in terms of the peace that ensues after war is complete, and is well captured in Basil H. Liddell Hart's concept that the object of war is to produce a better state of the peace. (The *better state* being defined in the victor's terms.) Broadly speaking, those political objectives can be either total or limited, depending on the extent of policy incompatibility between the antagonists. Although the instigator of war may have a clearer vision of the better state of the peace at the outset, both (or all) parties in a war ultimately justify their efforts in terms of what is and is not a satisfactory ensuing condition of peace.

The political objective serves two basic functions, at least in a democratic society such as the United States. The first function, to which allusion has already been made, is to provide a framework for directing the war effort. The political objective provides guidance for the proper conduct of hostilities, which should be aimed at attaining the political objective. The second function is to provide a rallying cry for public support of the war. Because modern war involves, to some extent, societal commitment and sacrifice, war can be conducted by democratic societies only if it has explicit and continuing support. The failure adequately to galvanize support through the political objective almost inevitably leads to a lagging willingness to continue the effort (or the exceeding of cost-tolerance).

This critical role of the political objective suggests some criteria for how the objective must be framed if it is to have broad support. At the risk of some oversimplification, a "good" political objective should have all or most of four characteristics. The more of these that are met, the more strongly supported the war is likely to be. Conversely, the more they are violated, the more unpopular (and hence unsustainable) the effort is likely to be.

The first characteristic of a good political objective is that it is simple, straightforward, and unambiguous. Given that war is an inherently complex business, the public needs a readily understood reason for supporting it. At best the objective should be reducible to a catchphrase that is widely acceptable. "Independence" (the political objective of the American Revolution) or "destroying the Hitler monster" met that criterion.

Second, the objective should be morally and politically lofty. This need is particularly important to Americans, who have always considered themselves a special, even morally superior, people. In the American experience support has always been most unwavering when the purpose resembled a crusade. "Making the world safe for democracy" had the kind of loftiness that gained broad American support; restoring the status quo in Korea did not.

The third and fourth criteria overlap somewhat. The third is that attaining the objective must be seen as vital to the interests of the United States. This, of course, is a difficult criterion to get a precise grasp upon and is difficult partially because of the subjective nature of what is vital to the United States. For instance, was the ending of impressment (War of 1812) vital enough to go to war over? The War Hawks thought so; others disagreed. Moreover, the expeditionary nature of American military adventures invariably creates a debate about whether vital interests are involved. Precisely which overseas threats are threats to core American interests will always be a point of de-bate. Reexamining what constitutes a vital interest will have a major impact on defining when to use force in the post–cold war world, since obviously vital American interests rarely seem at risk in places like Haiti and Kosovo, where American arms have been summoned.

The fourth criterion is that the interests of most Americans must appear to be served by the decision to go to war. This criterion was most problematical in the wars of the nineteenth century when sectionalism was an important concern. Support for the War of 1812, for instance, was far greater in some parts of the country than it was in others, and the Mexican War had very little appeal in either New England or the South.

Although wars of limited political purpose have been by far the more frequent through history, Americans have tended to show the greatest sup-port for unlimited wars. This is the case partly because total war most obvi-ously meets the criteria for a "good" political objective: total defeat of the foe is a simple and unambiguous goal; total defeat must be necessary be-cause an inherent evil requires eradication (loftiness); the vital interests of the United States must be threatened or a total effort would not be necessary; and most Americans can agree that the outcome is necessary. The destruc-tion of fascism and its symbols in World War II is the most obvious case.

Limited political objectives, on the other hand, are more likely to violate one or more of the criteria. The objectives may not be simple and under-standable, as was the objective of containment in Vietnam. There may be moral ambiguity in the cause (seizing the Southwest United States can be viewed as either manifest destiny of the American people or as naked imperialism). In a limited action vital interests of the United States may or may not be involved. (If they are, why would we not go all out to win?) Limited ends can divide the American people (regionally as it did in the nineteenth century, or as the limited political objectives in Korea or Vietnam have done in the second half of the twentieth century). Virtually all the political involvements of the United States in post–cold war conflicts will confront this problem.

A final point about the limited–total distinction should be made. Clearly, both sides in war have their own political objectives, which are in opposition (both cannot be achieved). That does not mean, however, that the objectives are necessarily symmetrical in limited–total terms. It can and does happen that one side may have limited political objectives while the other has total objectives. In the American case two examples come to mind. In the American Revolution, the purpose of independence was total and indivisible: you cannot be partly independent. The British objective of restoring control was, as it evolved, not total. Ultimately, the restoration of British authority was justified as exemplary to other parts of the empire (if the Americans won, other parts of the empire might get seditious ideas). The even clearer case is Vietnam. The American objective of containing Communist expansion and thus allowing the South Vietnamese to engage in self-determination was clearly a limited one. We did not seek the overthrow of the North Vietnamese government (although we would not have objected to that outcome). North Vietnam had the total objective of overthrowing the government of the Republic of Vietnam and of uniting the country by force.

## Military Objectives and Strategy

If war is politics carried on by other means, then the fundamental objective of all military operations in wartime is quite simple and straightforward. The military's basic task is to overcome the enemy's ability to resist our policies militarily. Although straightforward, this fundamental objective is so broad that it provides little practical meaning or useful guidance for military planners. It is, however, instructive to keep this fundamental objective in mind for two different reasons.

First, the fundamental military objective excludes certain specific objectives as legitimate pursuits for armed forces. For example, the battle for the "hearts and minds" of an enemy population would be an inappropriate undertaking for military forces. Such a battle is better reserved for civilian authorities who can make political, economic, and other nonmilitary policy decisions that will have a direct impact on the perceptions and attitudes of hostile populations. This is not to deny that successful military operations are often necessary prerequisites to winning "hearts and minds." Such was certainly the case in World War II. Complete military victory allowed the imposition of nonmilitary policies that has resulted in over 50 years of friendship and support from our former enemies. Nor does this deny that the military can often be the executive agent to implement these nonmilitary policies. Perhaps the most memorable instance of the military functioning as the executive agent is found in Japan following World War II. General of the Army Douglas MacArthur was the de facto dictator of occupied Japan responsible for imposing the enlightened nonmilitary policy decisions that resulted in a resurgent Japan friendly to American policy objectives.

Second, the enemy's ability to resist militarily is directly affected by the enemy's will to resist. Thus victory on the battlefield does not necessarily translate into victory in the war. Defeat on the battlefield does not necessarily mean that the cause is lost. America's experience in the Vietnam conflict provides conclusive evidence that one belligerent can win virtually all of the significant military engagements and yet lose the war. Conversely, America's enemies in the Vietnam conflict demonstrated that there are occasions when simply avoiding catastrophic defeat while exacting a high price in blood from the enemy can make a decisive contribution to the destruction of the enemy's will (and thus his ability) to resist militarily.

The objective of war is not military victory. Rather, the objective of war is to attain the political objectives which spawned the war. Military victory is merely one means to political ends.

One might assume that specific military objectives would flow naturally from political objectives, but such is not always the case. Although what follows is not an encyclopedic list, four situations have commonly caused conflict between political and military objectives.

First, one can confuse means and ends, particularly when deeply mired in bloody conflict. Such was the case for the belligerents in World War I, particularly those struggling in the trenches on the Western Front. As the casualties mounted along with the frustrations of a stalemated war, the declared objectives on all sides disappeared into the mud of Verdun and Flanders and were replaced with simple hatred and the desire for retribution. In many respects, the object of war became the war itself rather than the peace that followed. The result was unsatisfactory to all sides and formed the breeding ground for an even greater conflagration.

Second, political objectives can clash with military expediency. Sherman's famous march from Atlanta to the sea was a military expedient that surely shortened the American Civil War. The wanton destruction caused by his rampaging troops gutted the heart of the Confederacy and led to serious morale problems among Confederate troops. On the other hand, it led to long-lasting and deep-seated bitterness among the vanquished and postponed true reunion between the North and the South. This drives home the point that the manner in which a war is fought can have a significant effect on the peace that follows. Moreover, political objectives can frustrate prudent military operations. In the Vietnam conflict military operations were banned in certain areas for political reasons. These sanctuaries, however, ensured that the military security required to win the "hearts and minds" of the civilian population could never be achieved. In a sense, political objectives were hoisted by their own petard.

Third, political objectives can be so abstract that the military is left with little on which to base its objectives. For Americans, the political objectives for most wars have been concrete (although they may also have been simplistic and shortsighted) and military objectives followed easily. Such was the case in the Civil War and both world wars. Each was a great crusade against a clearly defined "evil." In Korea the political objectives were more obscure but were still definable because of an overt invasion. In Vietnam political objectives remained abstract and the resulting military objectives were nebulous and muddled. As a result, military strategy was often confused and inappropriate, interservice rivalry flourished as parochial interests came to the fore, and morale crumbled. In situations such as Somalia, it is difficult to determine what the objective was beyond interrupting the starvation. In contemporary situations like Bosnia and Kosovo, the military objective may be no more than suppressing the violence.

Finally, the military may be given the task of accomplishing political objectives that are inappropriate for military means. The Vietnam experience may be the classic case. Given the unrest in third world areas and the importance of those areas to the industrialized nations, this situation may be more common in the future. As will be described in later chapters, the principal American problem in Vietnam was not military. Rather, the problem was one of state building, an objective that requires vigorous nonmilitary action. Military actions in such a situation could only provide the security needed for other actions to succeed. And yet the military was the principal power instrument used by both the South Vietnamese and the Americans, while nonmilitary actions were given far less attention. The result was predictable. The South Vietnamese state was never built and, ironically, the proximate cause of its downfall was the failure of the South Vietnamese military. Many contemporary problems are comparable.

Although the most fundamental military task in war has remained relatively constant (at least in nonnuclear war), specific military strategy—the technique of developing, deploying, and employing military forces—has evolved. The two centuries of the American experience have witnessed rapid and fundamental changes in military strategy. The eighteenth century was the era of limited war, limited by the nature of the political objectives sought by the interrelated absolute monarchies that dominated all of Europe (the exception being Great Britain). They waged war for a province here, a city there, or control over royal succession in another kingdom, but rarely to overthrow a brother monarch. There was little passion involved, the objectives being the royal rather than popular interest. The armies that fought for these objectives were composed of the dregs of society and mercenary soldiers recruited from throughout Europe. In essence, the bulk of the population was isolated from both the objectives of war and those who waged it.

The linear tactics developed to use the limited-firepower technology of the day led to bloody but indecisive battles. Rather than risk their expensive and hard-to-replace armies in pitched battle, eighteenth-century generals sought to gain advantage through maneuver to cut the enemy's line of supply. The elaborate depot and magazine system required to support an army in the field presented a convenient vulnerability that could decide a campaign with minimum risk of pitched battle.

Near the end of the eighteenth century, the idealism of the American Revolution returned ideology to warfare. The common man had a political objective for which he would voluntarily fight and die. The trend continued during the French Revolution and Napoleonic Wars. Ideological objectives and the democratization of war eventually paved the way for mass popular armies, more flexible tactics and supply systems, and, finally, wars fought for unlimited objectives. By the time of the American Civil War, this drift toward total war was well under way.

In many ways, the American Civil War was America's first total war. For the Union, at least, the political objectives were unlimited. No compromise could be accepted; militarily, the Confederacy itself had to be crushed and forced back into the Union fold. Confederate political objectives were also unlimited (independence). However, its military objectives were limited as it sought only to repel Union invaders and maintain its independence. From these objectives flowed the strategy of each side. For the Union an annihilation strategy was in order: it needed to destroy the Confederate armies and overthrow the Confederacy's government to achieve reunion. Confederate strategy remained largely that of attrition, seeking not to destroy the Union Army and overthrow the Northern government, but to defend the Confederacy and inflict enough pain on the Union forces to discourage further attacks on the new Confederate state. The North had to destroy Confederate hostile ability; the South's objective was to exceed Northern cost-tolerance.

The Civil War was also a war of unlimited means. Mass armies took to the field. Maneuver was critically important but bloody battle was the decisive factor. Both sides attempted to mobilize their civilian populations and industrial bases for war. Finally, civilian populations and economies became military targets, at least for the Union forces. Thus the Union blockaded Southern ports in an attempt to shatter the Confederate economy and starve the Rebel population. The rationale for Gen William T. Sherman's march through Georgia and Gen Franz Sigel's less well-known but equally devastating attacks in the Shenandoah Valley were directed to the same end.

The Civil War also demonstrated for the first time the importance of mechanization in warfare. It was the first American war in which railroads played a major role. Mass armies were transported over vast distances with great speed and were kept well supplied. Rail transportation expanded the scope of the war, which was conducted simultaneously in widely separated theaters of operation. But with the opportunities of mechanization came limiting factors. Much of the military strategy revolved around rail lines themselves. Cutting the enemy's rail lines or protecting one's own became a major preoccupation of Civil War generals.

As the trend toward mechanization continued into the twentieth century, changes in military strategy continued apace. The internal combustion engine added greatly to military flexibility and the speed of maneuver. Combined with other technological gadgets, the internal combustion engine gave rise to armored war on land, undersea warfare, and war in the air. Each of these developments provided new opportunities for the military strategist, particularly when combined with the unlimited objectives of modern total war. Rapid and fluid maneuver, deep penetration, and increased firepower characterized modern warfare, culminating in the campaigns of World War II.

But increased mechanization presented vulnerabilities as well as opportunities. Supply lines became even more important (one cannot forage for spare parts and fuel) and thus were a prime target for attack. The same was true for the industrial base that supported mechanized forces in the field. Traditional naval blockade (and blockade by submarine) remained an exceptionally important tactic. The airplane offered the opportunity to attack the civilian industrial base directly and with more immediate effect than blockade. Thus direct combat operations ranged from the front lines to the skies over civilian industrial centers. Total war was all-encompassing, sweeping up civilian and soldier alike.

The nuclear weapons developed and used at the end of World War II significantly changed the way we think about war, particularly after other countries also developed nuclear weapons. Even the incredible cost of total war could, until then, be justified by unlimited objectives that seemed to be of greater value. But the advent of nuclear weapons raised the specter of total war involving total cost—the possible annihilation of civilization itself. Surely no political objective could be worth the all too real risk of mankind's extinction. Thus the concept of deterrence came to the fore along with its arcane language and arabesque logic.

The Clausewitzian dictum, it seemed, no longer applied, or at least it did not apply to nuclear war. Nuclear war, it appeared, could not be an extension of politics because the possible death of civilization served no rational political purpose. The fundamental objective of deterrence is to ensure that nuclear war never will serve any rational political purpose, that no one would ever risk the possible catastrophic consequences. And thus the paradoxical situation came about where incredibly powerful weapons are developed and fielded, their sole purpose being to ensure that neither they nor similar weapons possessed by any enemy will ever be used.

The nuclear stalemate has not been matched at lower and less threatening levels of warfare. Although both superpowers carefully avoided any direct military confrontation, even at lower levels of conflict, both fought lesser foes at these lower levels. Additionally, many countries in the third world have taken up arms against one another, often supported by one or the other of the superpowers. What has happened, in effect, is that we have returned to eighteenth-century limited war—but with two significant differences. First, the political objectives of these conflicts became ideologically based. They tend to arouse impassioned support and a considerable degree of fanaticism.

Second, and as mentioned earlier, at least when the United States has been involved in these conflicts, the political objectives of the belligerents have been asymmetrical. While America has waged limited war in these instances (limited objectives, limited means), its smaller opponents have waged unlimited war. Their objectives were unlimited in the sense they dealt with perceived vital interests that could not be compromised, and they used all means at their disposal to conduct the war. Such a situation places the United States at a distinct disadvantage.

American strategy has been only partially successful in this new situation. The Korean War was little more than a World War II–style conflict on a limited scale. American objectives at the time we intervened were clear and understandable. American attitudes were helped by the fact that this war involved an outright invasion without provocation. Although Americans (both military and civilian) chafed at fighting a war with less than the total means available, the war was brought to a conclusion that achieved our originally stated national objectives. The same cannot be said for the American venture into Southeast Asia. Protracted insurgent warfare using guerrilla-style tactics continues to frustrate American political and military strategists, and since guerrillas assume military inferiority, it would seem impossible to deter such conflicts.

Total war was more the product of unlimited objectives than the product of modern weaponry. In fact, it has been the terrible impact of modern weapons of mass destruction that forced a return to limited war by the superpowers. The limited wars of the post–World War II era, despite the availability of modern weapons of mass destruction, prove the point. American political objectives have been limited during this period, and the means by which America has fought have been constrained. Clearly, the primary influence on military objectives and strategy is the political objective, which is as it should be. It is also true that military technology and technique have also strongly influenced military strategy. In truth, military strategy is the result of the interplay of numerous factors. All of these interrelated factors play a significant role in determining how a war is fought and in doing so affect the peace that follows.

**Political Considerations**

Just as political concerns lead to war and the political objective defines its scope and purpose, there is a dynamic relationship between military and political considerations before and during the conduct of hostilities. Both domestic and international political concerns affect the way war is fought and, conversely, the ebb and flow of warfare influence political forces at each level.

Especially in a democratic society, when the use of the military instrument is contemplated, a major consideration must be the likely level of public support for the enterprise. In some cases, of course, the decision may be thrust upon one, as with Pearl Harbor. For a country whose primary military engagements are expeditionary, however, there will generally be some meaningful opportunity to consider the question. Public reaction to Vietnam paralyzed the use of force for a time, but a string of at least apparent successes in the last few years has reenergized support for the military instrument of power.

The question of public support has become increasingly important. While not attempting to exhaust all confounding influences on public support for American military adventures, at least four can be mentioned, each of which will arise as the odyssey through the American experience at war unfolds. They are presented in no particular order of importance.

The first, and perhaps least well-understood, factor is the impact of the media, and especially the electronic media. At the most obvious level, the electronic revolution permits coverage of military operations at a speed and with an intimacy heretofore impossible. Certainly, media coverage of the battlefield is not particularly new. In the American experience, close and rapid coverage of war goes back to the Civil War and the introduction of the telegraph, which allowed next-day reportage of engagements. What is unique about the electronic media, however, is that they bring a vivid, visual quality to coverage.

One obvious effect has been to deglamorize war. The blood, maimed bodies, and corpses that constitute the tribute of combat cannot be hidden from the camera's eye. It is an image difficult to ignore. Moreover, the television camera is most effectively used in capturing the discrete and dramatic event. Television coverage does not focus effectively on the long lulls between combat that make up the vast majority of war; instead, it trains on the spectacular—the maimed child, the firefight, the exploding bombs. At the same time, television reportage of violence and atrocity may have the opposite effect of creating public support for using force to relieve misery as in Somalia. As mass atrocity became commonplace during the 1990s in places like Bosnia and Rwanda, public tolerance of carnage may have increased as audiences become desensitized to the sights of war.

A second factor is the burgeoning expense of war. This expense is largely due to the increased sophistication of weaponry that makes equipment both more costly and more deadly, a phenomenon discussed in the section on technology. The result is that even fairly minor military involvements place great burdens on resource bases on which there are multiple competing claims. The Vietnam War, while certainly not a minor engagement, is estimated to have cost the United States $150 billion. Similarly, the British Falkland Islands engagement cost nearly $3 billion, and someone has to pay for it. The question is just what economic sacrifices will people be willing to make in the future?

A third problem is that likely future scenarios involve conflicts for limited political objectives in third world countries where American interests are minimal. As discussed earlier and as will be amplified in the pages that follow, developing and sustaining support for these kinds of wars is often difficult. The ramifications of that observation are explored in chapter 10 and in the final chapter.

Fourth and finally, there is the historical American aversion to things military—and particularly to the costs of military forces—that goes back to the birth of the country. Part of the American Anglo-Saxon heritage is to suspect military force and to look toward other instruments of power to solve problems. When the dollar ruled supreme in the world during roughly the quarter century after the end of World War II, the economic instrument could be used effectively to achieve American ends. That relative advantage has eroded, however, and Americans must contemplate the use of alternate instruments, one of which is military power. The end of the cold war enlivens the debate over military spending as well.

The interplay of politics and military force does not end once the decision to go to war has been reached. Rather, in some ways that relationship intensifies at essentially two levels, what one may call the high politics and low politics of war.

The high politics of war refers to the direction of military efforts to achieve political objectives and to ensure that the application of force does not alter the objectives beyond politically acceptable bounds. This latter problem is particularly acute in wars of limited political objective because purely military imperatives and political objectives most often come into conflict in these situations.

Clausewitz, once again, recognized the problem. The tendency in war, he observed, is to intensify and broaden the scope of action, a dynamic against which he warned political authorities to be constantly vigilant. The dynamic can occur whether one is winning or losing. If one is successful in achieving the objective through military means, there is a powerful temptation to broaden the objective and attempt to achieve even more. The decision to cross the 38th parallel in Korea in late 1950 exemplifies the point. At the same time, losing may cause one to intensify the effort, to up the ante, to avoid defeat. The gradual buildup in Vietnam and Gen William C. Westmoreland's ceaseless pleas for more troops represent this case.

The low politics of war refers to the direction and exploitation of military situations for personal political or other gain. In its seamier aspect, it may be the use of military activity to serve the ends of political figures. The image of President James Polk diligently watching the Washington press to see if either of his military commanders (both of whom were potential political opponents in the 1848 presidential election) was gaining too many headlines and then directing their campaigns to minimize such publicity comes to mind. Conversely, military victory or defeat can influence political outcomes. Lincoln, for instance, might well have lost the 1864 election had Atlanta not fallen to Sherman in the nick of time, just as stalemates in Korea and Vietnam helped drive two presidents into retirement.

The conduct of war affects and is affected by international concerns as well. Although there is really no such thing as international public opinion, the general opposition of America's NATO allies (largely reflecting public opinion in Europe) to our involvement in Vietnam weighed heavily on US decision makers. Likewise, military events may influence foreign powers in ways that can alter the situation. For instance, the American victory at Saratoga in 1777 (our first significant battlefield success) convinced the French to intervene openly and probably allowed the success of the American Revolution.

It is this dynamic interaction between military and political affairs during wartime that is most nettlesome to the military, and forms the basis for charges of political interference or derogations about political wars. Once again, the problem is greatest in limited-war situations, where concerns about remaining within the limited political objective may call for limitations on military actions that impede the effective application of force. Military art and science teach the virtue of maximum force to achieve the destruction of enemy forces wherever they may be. Within the confines of limited objectives, it may not be possible to unleash the full fury of military capability without running the risk of broadening the war and, implicitly, its political objectives. The granting of sanctuaries in Korea and Vietnam are examples, and they are the kinds of constraints under which the military is likely to be forced to labor in any future conflict.

**Military Technology and Technique**

Military technology is only one of many factors that influence the conduct and the character of war. However, it is the primary factor that determines how battles within a war are fought. The history of battle is, to a great extent, the story of military men struggling to cope with technology. The outcome of battle is often determined by the ability of one antagonist or the other to make the best use of available military technology. Thus to the extent that it actually influences the outcome of battles, technology directly influences the course of war and, more indirectly, the peace which follows.

Since the ancients first took up arms, one clearly identifiable trend has been constant. The power and destructive efficiency of weapons have become ever greater, as reflected in their explosive power, accuracy, and range. In the twentieth century, we may have reached the ultimate extension of this trend with thermonuclear weapons riding atop intercontinental ballistic missiles. Today weapons of previously unimagined power are only minutes away from any spot on the face of the earth. In essence, it has been changes in power, accuracy, and range of weapons that have caused the nature and technique of war to change over the 200-odd years of the American experience. These changes are reflected in the scale, intensity, tempo, organization, scope, and cost of battle.

The first change has been to increase the physical scale of conflict. The size of the individual battlefield began to expand in the eighteenth century as generals attempted to maximize smoothbore musket firepower by packing more men armed with these weapons onto the battlefield. However, instead of the densely packed formations of earlier ages, eighteenth-century warfare was characterized by linear formations. Formations spread laterally and were generally only three ranks deep. This allowed for fire by all three ranks while minimizing the possibility of muzzle-blast damage to one's own troops. Thus the frontage of individual units was vastly expanded as was the size of the battlefield.

In the nineteenth century, advances in transportation and communications technology expanded warfare far beyond the already swollen eighteenth-century battlefield. The railroad allowed mass armies to be transported rapidly over great distances and permitted the efficient resupply of these far-flung armies. The importance of rail transport first became obvious during the American Civil War. In that conflict separate armies operated throughout different theaters of war and yet did so with considerable coordination. Railroads made it possible to operate effectively in distant theaters and the telegraph made coordination of these operations both possible and practical.

In the twentieth century, globe-girdling warfare has become the norm. All modes of land and water transportation increased in both speed and carrying capacity, making overseas force deployments relatively commonplace. By mid-century, air transport added a new dimension to deployment speed while the advent of radio provided instantaneous communications without reliance on fragile wires. In addition to the worldwide breadth of twentieth-century military operations, the development of the airplane and the submarine expanded the battlefield vertically—beneath the sea and into the sky.

In essence, technology expanded the battlefield to proportions unimagined in the eighteenth century. Advances in transportation and communication solved the twin problems of logistic support and coordinated command. Modern military commanders have been forced to expand their horizons far beyond the confines of the immediate battlefield. During the same time period, however, technology also brought about rapid increases in the intensity of warfare and the speed of maneuver on and between battlefields. The ongoing applications of the fruits of the telecommunications revolution to warfare promise an ever-accelerating rate of technological change on the battlefield.

In the eighteenth century, warfare was conducted at a rather leisurely pace. Military campaigning seasons—when the weather was good and gunpowder could be kept dry—were relatively short, and armies regularly went into winter quarters during the cold and wet months of the year. Even during the campaigning seasons, little fighting or maneuvering occurred during hours of darkness. By the twentieth century, keeping one's powder dry was no longer a significant problem because of cartridge ammunition. The incandescent lamp facilitated night operations, as did electronic marvels such as radar and light amplification equipment. Thus, by the last half of the twentieth century, war had become an intense activity waged around the clock throughout the year.

The tempo of war increased along with its year-round intensity. In the twentieth century, wheeled and tracked self-propelled vehicles speed the maneuver of men and guns on the battlefield, just as railroads, fast ships, and even faster aircraft speed the transport of men and weapons to the battlefield. The organization and scope of combat has multiplied as well. At the same time that technology expanded the scale, intensity, and tempo of military operations, it also created significant problems. First, it complicated the structure of armed forces and placed a premium on quality staff work. The infrastructure required to command, control, and support a technologically sophisticated military force has expanded at a geometric rate and the logistic support required has assumed momentous proportions. Second, the coordination of ground, air, and sea forces in modern three-dimensional war requires large, complex, multiservice staff structures. These factors have combined to change radically the ratio of combat to noncombat troops in modern armed forces over the last 200 years.

However, it is more significant for our purpose to realize that technological sophistication has made the industrial base that supports armed forces in the battlefield vitally important. The production of modern military weapons, vehicles, aircraft, and ships requires a robust industrial base (or access to one). Naturally, this same industrial base has become an important target for military operations. Civilian populations that support a nation's industrial base have also become targets for attack either directly (physical attack, psychological operations, and deprivation) or as a by-product of attacks on industrial plants (so-called collateral damage). As technology made the home front an important target, that same technology also made it possible to attack home-front targets without first defeating armies and navies.

Last, but not least, is the economic cost factor, which is both a military and political concern. The cost of war has dramatically escalated during the American experience in terms of both blood and treasure. Although the ratio of killed and wounded to the total in uniform during a war has decreased since the eighteenth century, the absolute number of casualties has vastly increased. This is a natural product of larger armed forces and far more lethal weapons. At the same time, the survival and complete recovery rate for those wounded in action has increased dramatically because of rapid advances in medical science and military efforts to bring medical care to soldiers on the front line.

The treasure expended in war has escalated to mind-boggling proportions. In the eighteenth century, the village smithy could produce most of the kinds of weapons required by an army and could do so at a relatively low cost. Modern armies require weapons of great complexity and incredible cost. The lethality of these weapons means that battlefield attrition and consequent replacement demands add enormously to the total cost of a modern high-intensity war.

In essence, technology expanded the battlefield horizontally, vertically, and finally in depth to include the home front. Modern total war increased in intensity, in tempo, and in scope to include everyone, not just the soldiers on the front lines. Armed forces that had originally protected the home front can no longer do so. Factory workers have essentially become frontline soldiers without guns. Thus in many ways the unlimited involvement characteristic of modern total war has matched the unlimited objectives of ideologically based modern war.

The most recent development in warfare flies in the face of the trend of developments since the eighteenth century. In the face of total war with totally destructive nuclear weapons, the second half of the twentieth century has seen a resurgence of limited warfare reminiscent of the eighteenth century. Protracted insurgent and partisan warfare using guerrilla tactics allow the weak to compete on the battlefield with the strong. Forces using guerrilla tactics pick the time and place of battle, refuse to stand and fight unless they desire to do so, and melt away into a friendly (or at least neutral) civilian population when they do not. Guerrilla forces make no pretense of protecting civilian populations on which they depend for their survival. Rather, the guerrilla reverses the relationship and uses the civilian population as a shield to hide from the enemy. As a result, the terrible destructiveness of modern weaponry has only limited utility in combating the guerrilla. Where success in "conventional" warfare depends on the ability to kill people, success in combating guerrilla forces depends on the control of people. Only if the population is controlled and secure can guerrillas be ferreted out of the general population they use for protection.

**Military Conduct**

Much has already been said during the discussions of military objectives, strategy, technology, and technique about how wars have been and are fought. In the eighteenth century, war was, in effect, a battle of masses. Although the American Revolution was an exception, war in that era often held to Voltaire's observation that "God is always for the big battalions." By the time of the American Civil War, however, the situation began to change. More complex weapons and the use of mechanically powered transportation systems put a premium on industrial capability and capacity. By the time of the two world wars, this trend matured and war became a battle of factories. Industrial plants were so important that the factories themselves became military targets rivaling deployed forces in importance. Finally, the technological explosion during the last half of the twentieth century made warfare a battle of brains. It would seem that Voltaire has been turned on his ear as God now seems to favor the best technology. The exception to the modern trend, protracted warfare using guerrilla tactics makes much modern military technology irrelevant. Perhaps God is on the side of the smart battalions.

Although the evolution of warfare from a battle of masses to a battle of brains encapsulates the evolution of war fighting during the American experience, one important point remains to be made if one is to understand the nature of modern warfare and if one is to understand the difficulties of winning the peace.

Viewed broadly, warfare has become a progressively more desperate undertaking during the nineteenth and twentieth centuries. War has always been a desperate affair for the individual warrior. However, the increasingly ideological basis of warfare and its consequently unlimited political objectives have turned much of modern warfare into a death struggle between rival societies. Failure in such a war is catastrophic, and as a result, the struggle is fought with bitterness and desperation. War is no longer the glorious adventure to which men march with bands playing and flags waving. The glorification of war was a tradition buried beneath the mud of Flanders fields if not earlier. Any sense of chivalry has all but disappeared from battle as the unlimited ends sought seem to justify unlimited means. Naval blockades indiscriminately starve civilian and soldier alike. Civilian population centers have been routinely attacked and weapons of mass destruction have been used. Defenders have often used scorched-earth tactics and one finds many instances of fierce fighting when all hope of victory has clearly been lost.

One might be led to believe that the "limited" and "low-intensity" wars characteristic of the nuclear age would have a less desperate nature. However, one must remember that such terms as *limited* and *low intensity* are given meaning by one's perspective. For those on the battlefield, no war is limited and all wars are intense. On a larger scale, all of America's opponents in these types of conflicts (North Korea, China, and North Vietnam) were essentially waging unlimited wars. Only their relative military weakness (when compared with a superpower) and the secondary importance of our objectives in these conflicts have allowed us to characterize these conflicts as limited or low intensity.

The modern desperation in war produces a bitter legacy. Few, if any, are untouched by the horror of modern warfare. All sides harbor bitter feelings because of widespread death and destruction. The losing side agonizes over how much it gave and how much it lost. The winner resents the suffering endured in relation to the objectives achieved, which often seem hollow in the harsh light of war's aftermath. The bitter legacy makes the task of the peacemaker far more difficult than in any other age. Winning a better state of peace after a modern war may be the most difficult of all tasks.

## Better State of the Peace

"There is no substitute for victory," Gen Douglas MacArthur said in testimony about American conduct of the Korean War. It is a beguiling statement and so straightforward as to appear unimpeachable. But what does it mean? What exactly constitutes victory in war?

The most obvious answer, and the one to which Americans (including Gen MacArthur) are drawn, is that winning the war means military victory, but that is an incomplete answer. Military victory is only a part of winning wars, and although one tends to associate military triumph with victory, such is not always the case. Victory has another, more profound meaning. The other, ultimately more important, sense of victory is the attainment of the political objectives for which war is fought in the first place.

These two aspects of victory should not be confused. Although military victory on the battlefield is usually prerequisite to "imposing our will" on the adversary, such is not always the case. It is possible, for instance, to fight to a militarily inconclusive ending but still accomplish the political objective of war, as the American colonies did in the Revolution. At the same time, one can actually lose the military campaign and achieve at least part of the political objective, as the United States did in the War of 1812. Finally, it is also possible to win all the military campaigns in war and yet lose politically, a distinction demonstrated by the American experience in Vietnam.

To comprehend the two senses of victory, we need to return to the notions of hostile will and ability. As was argued earlier, the distinct task of the military is to overcome hostile ability, and military victory (or its absence) is normally determined on that basis. Overcoming hostile ability in the American experience has usually been equated (at least since the campaigns of Grant and Sherman in the Civil War) with the destruction of the enemy's armed forces and that is the most obvious, measurable, and observable outcome of war. The most vivid expression was the unconditional surrender of Axis armed forces at the end of World War II. But there is more to victory than that. One may also win wars militarily by overcoming hostile will, defined as exceeding cost-tolerance, which is the way the colonies defeated Great Britain and the North Vietnamese overcame the United States.

Victory in a political sense, however, is best equated with the notion of political will defined as acceptance by the vanquished of the political objectives of the victors. The political objective includes imposition and acceptance of policies and that forms the reason for going to war in the first place. Clearly at the outset, the visions of a better state of the peace are diametrically opposed, or there would be inadequate reasons to engage in war. In the end, one vision of the better state of the peace must prevail and the other must vanish (unless, of course, they are modified or compromised).

The question is how the better state of the peace is accomplished. The answer must begin with the realization that acceptance of policies is itself a political process, and one that must be accomplished by political authorities during the ensuing peace. It is a political, not a military, task.

Broadly speaking, there are two ways of implementing desired policies. The first way is through the simple imposition of the victor's vision of the better state on the vanquished in the form of a *punitive peace*. The terms of the peace can simply be imposed, and if the former enemy objects or tries to alter those terms, coercive means can be used to guarantee continued compliance. Punitive peace was the model for the settlement of World War I and, to a lesser degree, the American Civil War.

The other means is to engage in active efforts to convince former foes that one's policies are more enlightened than theirs were and that they are better off embracing this vision of the better state of the peace.

This form is known as a *reconciliatory peace* and requires intense political and psychological efforts to overcome the residue of hostile feelings. The process of reconciliation is inherently political and can be accomplished only by political authorities through political processes (although the military may serve as the agents for political authorities, as in the postwar occupation of Japan). The clearest case of a reconciliatory peace accomplishing the political objective occurred in Germany and Japan after World War II, and it was the path that Abraham Lincoln had charted for the Confederacy before his assassination.

As a general rule, a reconciliatory peace is preferable to a punitive peace because it involves acceptance and embracing of political objectives rather than sullen acceptance of imposition. As a result, the residue of hostile will (resistance to policies) is more likely to be overcome. Unfortunately, a reconciliatory peace is the most difficult to attain for at least two reasons.

First, the nature of war itself makes reconciliation difficult. War leaves physical and emotional scars in the forms of death, maiming, and the destruction of property. The result is a natural inclination, on the victorious side, toward vindictiveness as the caskets and maimed veterans come home and the rubble is sorted through. In those circumstances the impulse to punish is a powerful feeling that is difficult to overcome. The carnage and physical destruction of World War I had a powerful influence on French attitudes toward the peace negotiations. At the same time, the way war is fought may exacerbate the hostile feelings of the vanquished. Sherman's march to the sea and through the Carolinas, while militarily justifiable, undoubtedly inflamed lingering bitterness in the defeated South. The expanded nature and lethality of modern war exacerbate these problems.

Second, and this is particularly true in the American experience, there is a tendency to ignore (or at least inadequately consider) the task that remains after physical hostilities have concluded. This tendency is part of the classic American mobilization-demobilization pattern that says once the war is won (militarily), it is time to return as quickly as possible to the more normal condition of peace. It is a tendency against which one needs to guard. The physical conduct of war, as Clausewitz correctly noted, is instrumental, a means toward an end. The end is attainment of the political objective and that is a "battle" that can be won only in the ensuing peace. If we are to avoid winning the war but losing the peace in the future, that is a lesson that must be well learned.

# 2

# American Revolution

The American Revolution was this country's great formative act. Along with the Civil War, the Revolution stands as the most influential military event in American history in terms of its political purposes and political impact. Although it was not particularly recognized at the time it was being fought, the Revolution also marked an important turning point in international politics: it was both the first major war of independence against European colonial domination and the conflict that reintroduced ideology into the underlying causes and sustainers of warfare.

In purely military terms, the Revolution pales in comparison to the great struggles that began with the Civil War and continued into the twentieth century. The armies that contested the war were tiny by modern standards; at its apex, the British had a force numbering about 32,000 on colonial soil, and George Washington's Continental Army never numbered more than 20,000. Battles were relatively few and comparatively bloodless, reflecting the eighteenth-century style of warfare. In the climactic Battle of Yorktown (which is more properly the Siege at Yorktown) an army of 16,000 Continentals and French marines in about equal numbers faced a British force of about 7,500 under Lord Cornwallis. When the British surrendered, the battlefield toll was slightly more than 200 killed, of whom only 20 were American.

The Revolution also continued the American mythology about the American military tradition begun in the French and Indian War. Yorktown, Saratoga, Trenton, Princeton, King's Mountain, and other fields of battle have become symbols of the tradition of military prowess and the American self-image as winners. That most of these battles were not as successful as we remember them, nor as militarily significant, and that they were interspersed with a series of military reverses that were nearly decisive, (e.g., the battles of New York and Brandywine Creek) have faded from the popular mind. An objective evaluation of the war itself shows that militarily it was no better than a draw for the Americans, who were aided by mediocre British generalship.

In addition, the revolutionary experience did much to create the myth of the militia tradition in America. When the war began almost accidentally at Lexington and Concord, the only military forces available to the rebellion were militia units. Throughout the war's conduct, militia units played an important role (especially the so-called revolutionary militia, about which more will be said later). Colonial success created the myth that militia was effective against regular troops and that the United States did not need a standing armed force of any size during peacetime. The militia could be quickly mobilized and hold its own until a regular army could be fielded to carry the day. Once the war was over, demobilization could be rapidly accomplished (in 1784, a year after the peace treaty was signed, the standing army consisted of 80 regulars whose sole purpose was to guard military supplies). The performance of militia units in the Revolution, viewed carefully, hardly justifies that level of faith, but it created a tradition that still leaves Americans at least slightly uneasy about maintaining a large standing force during peacetime.

That the war was not exactly what we choose to remember does not depreciate the importance of the struggle. Although the American Revolution may not have been a major military struggle, it was a major political event. There were military lessons to be learned. Europeans would again be faced with the problem of attempting to retain control of colonial empires against determined indigenous resistance, and Americans would be confronted with parallel difficulties in Southeast Asia.

In some ways, our revolution was the harbinger of things to come for the European powers, first the Spanish and Portuguese in Central and South America and later other European powers in Asia and Africa. The British military problem of snuffing out a determined rebellion fought by unconventional methods far from home was one of those precursors. The cost and political unpopularity of such endeavors which, as much as the success of the Continental Army, drove the British from the field would be revisited by the French in Indochina and Algeria. That the parallel was well appreciated and the lesson well learned is doubtful.

The great irony and tragedy of the revolutionary experience is in its parallel with the American morass in Southeast Asia 190 years later. As one sifts through the Revolution, the parallels draw closer and closer, and the reader is encouraged to look for them. Great Britain was attempting to quell a rebellion far from home against a force and population largely hostile to it, just as the United States did in Vietnam. The war was fought by an enemy who usually refused to stand and fight in the accepted manner, preferring instead guerrilla tactics. Moreover, the British had to fight two wars, one against the revolutionary militia guerrillas who attacked from ambush and who suppressed loyalist support (leading one British commander to refer to the activity as "the dirty little war of terror and murder") and the other against Washington's regular army. The parallels with the Vietcong and the North Vietnamese army are striking. Finally, public opinion turned against the British cause at home as success eluded them, just as American support waned for the struggle in Vietnam. The British problem in America was the American problem in Vietnam. That the outcome for Britain in the Revolution and for the United States in Southeast Asia should have been the same is less than surprising. That the parallel was not seen nor the analogy drawn is tragic.

## Issues and Events

Like most momentous political events, the underlying issues that led to the first great modern revolution built up over a period of time. At heart the underlying issues were relatively moderate by comparison to a contemporary world that thinks in terms of the Iranian revolution of Ayatollah Khomeini or the Russian or Chinese Revolutions' bloodbath of the twentieth century. Many historians view the American Revolution as an essentially conservative revolt.

The most pervasive issue was the relationship between the Crown in London and the citizens of the colonies. The heart of the matter was the standing of the colonials: virtually all Americans of the 1760s and early 1770s considered themselves loyal British subjects. (With the exception of inhabitants of enclaves like formerly Dutch New York and settlements of persecuted religious groups from the European continent, most Americans were of British stock.) Because they viewed themselves as coequal British subjects, they believed they should have the same political rights as other English citizens. The core of their grievance was not that most wanted to be treated distinctly as Americans nor that they desired autonomy; rather, most aggrieved Americans (and by no means did all Americans feel aggrieved) simply wanted to be treated more like any other Britisher.

The matter boiled down to a disagreement over rights versus obligations. From the colonial viewpoint, the basic issue was the political rights adhering to them as British subjects from which obligations logically flowed. Most Americans did not so much mind obligations in the form of taxes and the like so long as they went hand-in-hand with the full rights of English citizenry. It was the imposition of duties without parallel rights that troubled them.

The Crown disagreed. From the royal viewpoint, the subjects of the colonies were, after all, *colonial* subjects, and the primary role and purposes of colonial subjects were to support the Crown. The fact that these particular colonials were of British descent might make one more sympathetic with them than with subjects one had conquered, but the fact did not alter the basic relationship between colony and mother country. Colonies had, in a word, obligations, not rights.

Constructed this way, the whole matter has the abstract quality of a debate over political philosophy, and through a good bit of colonial history the matter remained at that level. Political rights might have symbolic importance but were not basic as long as the mother country was in essence leaving the colonies alone, thus failing to impose obligations and granting rights indirectly. The debate became concrete and lively when the Crown began to impose obligations on colonial subjects without granting matching rights. The precipitating event was the French and Indian War and the debts that Great Britain ran up prosecuting it. The lightning rods after 1763 became the dual and interrelated issues of taxation of colonials and the permanent stationing of British troops on colonial soil.

Fairness dictates that one look at the issues from both sides. The Crown's position was straightforward. The British Crown had contributed heavily both in terms of manpower and treasure to defending the colonies during the French and Indian War (as well, of course, as kicking the French out of Canada and adding Canada to the British Empire). Moreover, after the war Great Britain was forced to maintain a garrison of about 6,000 troops along the frontier to protect against the Indians (who were often French inspired). All of that cost money and someone had to pay the bills. From the royal vantage point, it seemed entirely logical that those who were benefiting (the citizens of the colonies) should help pick up the tab.

In the Crown's view there were two ways that the colonials could contribute. The first, and most generally vexing to the colonials, was through taxation. Originally, most of the tax revenues were to be generated through import and export taxes (the taxes on tea and sugar), but other forms of taxation like the stamp tax were also included. Second, since the colonies were British colonies, it seemed entirely reasonable to the Crown that the home islands should have a special trading relationship with the colonies from which British private enterprise, and ultimately governmental coffers, would be beneficiaries. The result was restrictions on whom and with what the colonies could trade. The restrictions excluded colonial trade in some items with anyone but Britain (rum was an example), gave preferential access and treatment for goods produced in the colonies to the British, and required that a great deal of commerce be shipped on British ships.

Those colonial subjects who would ultimately lead the Revolution disagreed with this logic and the consequences it produced. The colonials appreciated neither the idea of permanent garrisons of British troops on their soil nor the idea of being taxed without their explicit consent. Obviously, the two issues were related since the costs of maintaining the troops created both the perceived need and the rationalization for taxation. Despite this linkage one can separate the two for analytical purposes.

The problem with having British troops on American soil in peacetime was twofold. First, it was an imposition that British subjects on the home islands would themselves not have tolerated, and hence was a reminder that the Crown did not consider the colonials as equals. Second, part of the Anglo-Saxon tradition is a deep and abiding suspicion of standing armed forces in peacetime, because British history had taught that such forces could be used for political repression. The Glorious Revolution of the seventeenth century had had as one of its major outcomes a specific banning of standing armies during times of peace. Despite the threat of Indian attacks, most colonials chafed at the idea of having these troops around. There was a suspicion that potential political repression was the real reason that the troops were there. The colonial militia, after all, was capable of defending against the Indians, so why were the Redcoats there? To many the question was rhetorical.

The second issue was the imposition of the various sets of taxes upon the colonials to help defray the costs associated with defense of the frontier. The colonials were unfavorably disposed to taxation in any form and for any reason, partially because they were unused to the idea and partly because it hit them in the pocketbook. The taxes added to the cost of goods, and restrictions on trade forced them to buy from British suppliers, generally at a higher price than they could obtain elsewhere. More specifically, however, they objected to the imposition of those taxes in an arbitrary manner without being consulted. Taxation, the imposition of burden, became the lightning rod that enlivened the debate about rights and obligations, and the rallying cry became "no taxation without representation."

As causes that would eventuate in revolution, these issues were relatively mild. The colonists were not crying "off with their heads," as the truly radical French revolutionaries would do more than a decade later. Rather, the heart of the matter was the request to be treated as British citizens. Had there been even nominal direct colonial representation in London (possibly even nonvoting observers in the Parliament) and had British troops not been called in from the frontier, there likely would not have been a revolution of any consequence.

It should be added that the disgruntlement of Americans with the Crown's acts was largely regional and that it affected different groups within the society differently. Objections were strongest in New England because that region was the most strongly affected. Most of the British soldiers on the continent were stationed in New England, and the merchant class most disadvantaged by the trade restrictions was largely based in that region, especially around Boston. As one moved farther south through the middle Atlantic and southern colonies, there was considerably less British military presence and a smaller trading class as well. Although the British restrictions were generally disadvantageous to colonies, they were more onerous to some than others, and some sectors, such as the indigo plantations in South Carolina, actually benefited from the Intolerable Acts. These differentiations in grievance would affect the general appeal of the Revolution regionally, as well as help to dictate the strategies of the combatants once the Revolution entered its military phase.

Thus the underlying causes of the Revolution were less than what we would now think of as radical, and the proximate events that led to the first shots at Lexington and Concord were gradual and more nearly accidental than carefully preplanned. The situation basically accumulated until a comparatively minor event triggered "the shot heard 'round the world." The evolution of each underlying cause reflects this gradual nature of the accumulation of events.

The various tax measures imposed on the colonies included the Sugar Act of 1764, the Stamp Act of 1765, and the new Tea Act in 1772. The taxes were levied sequentially and became a gradually irritating factor. The reason that new taxes had to be added was that each tax, which was supposed to meet British revenue needs, failed to produce the amount anticipated. The reason for the shortfalls was colonial resistance to paying the taxes.

The inefficiency of tax collection created, in the minds of the British monarchy, the need for more effective means for royal tax collection. The instruments selected were the very British forces the taxes were supposed to underwrite, and gradually those forces (who, it will be remembered, were there to protect the frontiers against the Indians) were moved from the frontier to the urban areas. Their presence, previously realized but unseen, became visible, particularly when troop contingents were moved into the urban areas, notably Boston. Matters were made even worse when the Quartering Act of June 1765 required that citizens open their homes to these troops. Now the Redcoats were not only in town, they were in private homes, and the cry against "quartering" of soldiers was heard across New England.

Tensions gradually increased and there were instances of hostility on both sides. As early as the winter of 1770, a group of Boston youths pelted a contingent of British troops with rock-filled snowballs. The Redcoats panicked and fired into the crowd, and the result was the famous Boston Massacre. In 1773 a group of the Sons of Liberty, disguised as Indians, sneaked aboard a British merchant ship in Boston Harbor and dumped its cargo in defiance of the Tea Act (the Boston Tea Party).

As acts of hostility and sedition increased and relations between colonial authorities and the citizenry became more strained, the Crown and its representatives became increasingly more concerned about the possibility of open rebellion. As these thoughts emerged, the size of the colonial militia, the only organized armed forces that could oppose the Crown, increased as well. Although the fighting capabilities of the militias were suspect, they did have considerable stores of arms in their armories without which armed resistance would be impossible. Disarming the militias became an appealing way to nip a potentially nasty problem in the bud.

It was this motivation that caused the British governor of Massachusetts to order British troops to march out of Boston to seize arms caches at Lexington and Concord. As word spread (carried by people like Paul Revere in his famous ride) of what the British were up to, militia units began to form along the road as the British column marched toward its destination. Tempers flared, names were called, and someone (no one knows on which side) fired the shots that signaled the beginning of the American Revolution. In the fighting that ensued, the British retreated into Boston, and the militia units, almost instinctively, followed them and took up posts at Bunker (Breed's) Hill on the Charlestown Neck, overlooking Boston. The British counterattacked at what is usually called the Battle of Bunker Hill, and the militia (which was gradually reinforced by units from adjacent areas) began the siege of Boston. The Revolution was joined, with very few having any real idea of what would follow.

**Political Objective**

Largely because of the largely accidental way in which it began, the American Revolution belies the neat depiction of a clear political objective defining the reasons for the outbreak of the war and then determining how the war would be fought. Rather, the Revolution began without a clear notion of a political objective shared by the majority who initiated it, and nearly a year of violence occurred before the larger purpose for which the Revolution was fought emerged.

At the time of the skirmishes at Lexington and Concord and the subsequent siege of Boston, the idea of political independence was not a widely shared vision. Indeed, even after the siege was laid, the Continental Congress was unwilling to make independence the goal of the colonies. Rather, in August 1775, four months after the initial battles, the Congress instead sent the so-called Olive Branch petition to King George III asking him to intervene in the colonials' behalf to protect them from the "tyrannies" (represented by the Intolerable Acts) of the Parliament. The Crown, however, rejected this offer of conciliation, instead declaring the colonies to be in a rebellion that would be put down. It is at least arguable that had the king responded favorably to the Continental Congress's request, the Revolution would have either died or become a small, isolated movement.

The military situation forced a defining of political purpose, rather than the other way around. The key event was the evacuation of British forces from Boston on 17 March 1776 to Halifax, New Brunswick. When the British garrison left Boston, there remained no British military presence in the colonies. De facto political independence had been achieved, and it was then a matter of declaring formally that independence was the goal of the revolution.

Even with independence militarily asserted, translating that circumstance into a formal political purpose was no easy task. Three months elapsed between the evacuation of Boston and the formal promulgation of the Declaration of Independence on 4 July 1776. At that, the Declaration, as an ideological statement, was a comparatively mild document that had as its basic features statements of grievance directed at violations of rights by the king and the assertion of largely commercial, mercantile rights. Once again, had the British monarchy embraced those principles and agreed that the colonials were entitled to them, it is questionable whether broad-based support for the objective would have been forthcoming.

Once political independence had been asserted as the goal and that purpose had been rejected by the Crown, the issue was joined and was central to the objectives for both sides in the following seven years before a peace treaty was signed. Political independence within the context of a free and, by the standards of the time, democratic polity became the objective of the revolutionary cause, reintroducing political ideology into warfare for the first time in over a century and setting the precedent for ideologically based warfare ever since. The objective was not embraced by all or even a majority of Americans. The Declaration did, however, galvanize enough support to recruit an army and to sustain the military effort to its conclusion.

The major feature of the Declaration of Independence as a political objective was that it placed an absolute purpose on hostilities. The issue of independence was indivisible: it is impossible to be partially independent. With the issue so defined, compromise was unlikely; the rebellion either had to succeed or be crushed. There were no alternatives.

The British objective, of course, was the obverse of the American purpose. Initially, the Crown viewed the purpose as a discrete matter of quelling a rebellion and reasserting British authority in the colonies.

This objective did not meet with great popular or parliamentary support, as there were sizable numbers of Britons who felt that the colonials' demands were either reasonable or at least not worth fighting over. Given this lack of enthusiasm, the Crown eventually evolved its own version of the "domino theory" by asserting that resistance to rebellion was a matter of precedent. If the Crown did not forcefully react to sedition in the American colonies, other parts of the empire would try the same thing.

## Military Objectives and Strategy

In the simplest terms, the fundamental British objective during the American Revolution was to regain sovereignty over the American colonies. As such, the British military objective was to provide the circumstances in which that sovereignty could be reclaimed. The problem was how to accomplish this goal.

By July 1776 British authority had been effectively removed from the rebellious colonies, although Canada remained firmly under British control. Looking at the situation at hand, the British saw the colonies as divided over the issue of independence and believed (rightly) that strong loyalist sentiment remained. They saw a rebel military force composed of ragtag militia, officered by a group of men with limited military experience and training. They viewed the colonies as a long, thin, disconnected string of outposts clinging to the edge of a great wilderness and, as such, vulnerable at innumerable points to dominant British sea power. The British also realized they could not occupy all of the colonies. Britain's traditionally small land army was not designed for such a task, especially considering that the American colonies were not Britain's only responsibility—or even her most important colonial possession.

What options did the British have? Three options presented themselves, to be used individually or in combination. The first was to destroy the rebel military force, which would eliminate the instrument of the rebellion—the means of military resistance. The second option was to occupy the decisive places that were the bases of the rebellion and thus to choke the rebellion to death. The third was to win over the "hearts and minds" of the uncommitted colonists who, combined with the Tory loyalists, would themselves put an end to the revolt.

The British results were also less than successful. Gen William Howe, leading the first British counterthrust at New York, attempted to combine all three possibilities. He desired to defeat Washington's small army while attempting to negotiate, since he was empowered to make concessions to the rebels. At the same time he would seize New York, which the British assumed to be a vital center, and was prepared to launch a two-pronged campaign to separate New England from the rest of the colonies. Unfortunately for Howe, he quickly discovered that Washington would not stand and fight a decisive battle. Rather, Washington fought and then retreated to preserve his army to fight another day. Howe also found the American rebels totally unwilling to negotiate; and although New York made an excellent base of operations, it was anything but a vital center in the European tradition.

This pattern was to repeat itself throughout the war. Rebels would not negotiate, Tory sympathizers were kept in check by the revolutionary militias, British victories came often but were indecisive, and there were no vital centers to capture.

American military objectives were much more complex. As Dave R. Palmer pointed out in his brilliant exposition on the subject, American military objectives were time dependent. The Revolution was actually in four phases, each with its own military objectives. Phase one, lasting from the battles at Lexington and Concord in April 1775 until July 1776, was the Revolution itself. The military objective was quite simple—throw the British out. Even if the long-term political objective was some sort of political settlement with the British retaining sovereignty, the rebels could not negotiate with the British in control or occupying a threatening position. The rebels could only negotiate from a position of strength. Such an objective dictated an offensive military strategy. Thus came the capture of Fort Ticonderoga (with its cannons), the siege of Boston, and the invasion of Canada in hopes of sparking an uprising by French Canadians.

The invasion of Canada was a failure, but by the summer of 1776 the Revolution was complete. The British had been thrown out of the 13 rebellious colonies. Now the rebels were almost prisoners of their successes. The revolt had been so successful and so complete that some sort of precipitous political action was a foregone conclusion. Thus came the decision by the Continental Congress for complete political independence.

The Declaration of Independence marked the beginning of phase two of the war and a new military objective. The rebel army now had to defend its newly won independence against the invasion by the British that was sure to come. With independence declared but not yet won, the Americans suddenly had everything to lose. It was clear at this point that Washington could not defeat a determined professional British army in a decisive battle. Thus Washington had two objectives. The first, and more important, was to prevent a decisive defeat. As long as he could preserve his army and keep it in the field, the Revolution probably could remain alive. The second objective was to make the British pay a high price for their invasion of the newly independent colonies. He must wage a war of attrition, hoping to wear the British down, hoping they would tire, and hoping the cost of imperialism would become too high. Then, too, there was always the hope that Britain's enemies would come to the aid of the struggling rebels.

Phase three began in February 1778 with the signing of a treaty between the rebels and the French. With the French as allies more troops and arms became available. More important, the French navy challenged British control of the American coast. The British navy no longer had a free hand in moving troops from one point to another. Washington could afford to take more risks. With new troops and newfound sea power he might, with luck, actually inflict a decisive defeat upon the British. Clearly, phase three called for an offensive strategy just as the circumstances of phase two had dictated a defensive strategy. The siege and surrender of Yorktown ended phase three with the decisive victory Washington sought.

Phase four lasted from the victory at Yorktown until the signing of the peace treaty recognizing American independence. Although the focus of the war shifted away from the colonies to a wider theater, Washington had to concentrate on a better state of peace. His objective was to keep his victorious army intact despite great pressures to disband the force. The Americans had everything to lose once again. Washington was successful and the favorable terms of the peace treaty were due in no small part to the fact that the Continental Army was still in being and was still a force of significant ability.

The success of the American Revolution was in large part due to Washington's accurate reading of the proper military objective at the proper time. Reckless offensive action during phase two would surely have led to decisive defeat and the probable collapse of the rebellion. Lack of aggressiveness in phase three might have left the British with a threatening position to exploit at their leisure. Disbanding the army to conform to the popular will in phase four might have had disastrous consequences for the treaty negotiations in Paris.

## Political Considerations

Throughout the Revolution purely political concerns helped to influence what happened on the battlefield. At the level of domestic politics within the colonies, there was a continual contest to nurture and sustain public support for the rebellion, and the war effort was hampered by the lack of formal legitimacy of the Continental Congress until the Articles of Confederation were ratified in 1781. Internationally, the need for outside support for the Revolution was a pressing concern until the alliance with France was completed in 1778, and significant effort was always directed at the prospect of turning British public and parliamentary opinion against the war.

As the first ideologically motivated war of the modern era, the American

Revolution had to win the hearts and minds of the American people if it were to succeed. As stated earlier, the cause was not universally embraced. A sizable portion of the population remained loyal to the Crown (the Tories), and many of these people emigrated to Canada and elsewhere after independence was achieved. At the same time, a large portion of the population was indifferent to the whole affair, especially in the South (before the war moved to the southern theater) and on the frontier.

Public support was absolutely necessary in raising and sustaining the army that stood as the principal obstacle to British reassertion for political control. As a practical matter, this created two problems for the revolutionary cause: The Revolution had to appear to have a reasonable prospect of success and Tory sentiment had to be suppressed. The conduct of hostilities can be understood only with these considerations in mind.

First, Washington faced the considerable task of projecting revolutionary forces as winners. The problem was greatest when British forces arrived in 1776 and the Continental Army was routed in the battles around New York. It has been argued that had General Howe pursued and destroyed what was left of that army—about 2,500 effectives at the low point—the British could have crushed the organized rebellion. Howe did not, apparently believing that the Continental Army would dissolve on its own and that he could mop up what was left of the rebellion in the spring. Faced with the real prospect that the army would simply vanish, Washington was motivated to attack the isolated garrisons at Trenton and Princeton, not because of their military significance but to show the American people that he could in fact win (and to gain needed military stores to survive the winter).

These same kinds of symbolic concerns forced Washington to engage in two battles that he could not win. As noted, Washington opposed the British occupation of New York and was soundly defeated (at least partially because he overestimated the fighting abilities of his troops, based on their successes around Boston). The reason for the engagement, simply put, was to show that the army was of consequence: if it would not defend the nation's major port city, what good was it? For the same reason, Washington positioned his army in front of the British force moving to occupy the colonial capital of Philadelphia in 1777, and the army only narrowly avoided envelopment and destruction at Brandywine Creek. The defense of Philadelphia was not of great military importance, but defending the seat of the Continental Congress was of great symbolic importance. In both cases, the destruction of the Continental Army, the vital force of the Revolution, nearly occurred, but political rather than military considerations forced the risk.

The second problem, the job of suppressing Tory support, fell to the revolutionary militias. These militias were irregular, locally based forces who occasionally engaged in direct combat with the British (as at Saratoga), but who served the additional purposes of maintaining revolutionary control of areas not occupied by the British and of providing a recruitment base for Washington's army.

The militias adopted classic guerrilla methods for these additional roles. When they fought, they surprised their adversaries, engaged in hit-and-run engagements, and then faded away (techniques which, at the time, were considered cowardly in the European military tradition). To suppress Tory sentiment in local communities, they harassed and intimidated the loyalists, including burning their property.

The other domestic political problem was the status of the Continental Congress which, until the Articles of Confederation were ratified in 1781, had a dubious legal status. Although the body convened regularly and made policy affecting the operation of the war, it was little more than an advisory committee since it was empowered by no legal constitutional act. Rather, its members were representatives of the various state legislatures, and any and all authority the Congress had arose from those legislatures agreeing to carry out congressional policies.

At least part of the reason the Continental Congress was given no authority was the colonial distrust of strong central government. Many in colonial legislatures feared that endowing the Congress with independent and superior authority would result in the same kind of tyranny against which they were revolting. Even when the Articles of Confederation came into force, the powers of Congress derived strictly from the state legislatures (members of Congress were representatives of the legislatures and received their instructions from those bodies), and the powers to implement policy (for example, imposing taxes) came from the state governments and not the central government.

This kind of institutional arrangement, which would later plague the Davis administration during the American Civil War, greatly impeded the war effort. The Continental Congress did not have the authority to conscript or otherwise raise troops; rather, the Congress established quotas for each colony, which the legislatures were free to meet or not. The degree of compliance is indicated by the fact that the Congress "authorized" an army of 76,000 but the fighting strength of the Continental Army never exceeded 20,000 and was generally smaller than that. Provision of such basic supplies as food, clothing, and weaponry was a perpetual problem since the Congress could not levy taxes to pay for these items, having instead to rely on the largesse of the colonies. A great deal of Washington's time was spent trying to cajole the Congress to support him more adequately, but a combination of congressional impotence and suspicion of the army itself (the fear it might be used to suppress the Congress) meant there were continuing problems.

There were international political concerns as well. The greatest concern was securing foreign support to counter obvious British advantages in military equipment (the colonies had no organized armaments industry), in control of the oceans, and in military manpower.

There were several candidates for the assistance role. The most obvious was France, seething over her defeat in the Seven Years' War, which had removed all French colonies from North America. Less likely candidates were Spain, which could always be relied on to oppose Britain's design in the new world, and such commercial rivals as the Dutch Republic and Russia. All four countries, directly or indirectly, contributed to the establishment of American independence.

None of them did so, however, out of any sense of affinity with the American cause. The Spanish, who refused throughout the war to receive American emissaries, hoped the colonials would eventually lose the struggle because they feared an independent North American state would cast a possessive eye on Spanish holdings in North America. The Dutch cast their lot with the League of Armed Neutrality in retribution for the British seizure of the islands of Saint Eustatius and Saint Martin in the Caribbean, which had been transfer points for Dutch military contraband being shipped to the colonials. The common thread in foreign motivation was, in a word, revenge against Great Britain. For these countries creation of an independent United States was at most a by-product of European power politics and not necessarily a desirable outcome at that.

The problem for the colonials was that no foreign power was about to come to the aid of the Americans unless it could be made to believe that the colonials had a chance of winning. The French were particularly interested in helping, but supporting a losing cause would not produce the desired retribution. The problem was made more difficult by the early lack of success of the Continental Army. Following the successful siege at Boston, the army had suffered a string of defeats during 1776 and 1777 that came close to breaking the back of the rebellion, and its minor military successes at Trenton and Princeton did not compensate for them.

The victory that tipped the scales was Saratoga, where Gen Sir John "Gentleman Johnny" Burgoyne surrendered his army to Gen Horatio Gates. In a matter of months a formal alliance was signed between the colonies and France. With that agreement more adequate supplies of war materiel became available to the revolutionary cause, the French navy became available, at least part of the time, to menace and harass the Royal Navy, and, in time, French forces would fight alongside the Continentals. French assistance was particularly crucial at the final colonial military victory of the war, the Siege of Yorktown, where, as noted, almost equal numbers of Continentals and

French marines formed the siege lines and the French Caribbean fleet block-aded the coast.

The other, and ultimately pivotal, international concern was the battle for British public opinion. The Americans knew from the beginning that there was considerable opposition to the war, led by William Pitt the Elder, Edmund Burke, and others. Realizing he lacked the military muscle to defeat a deter-mined British army, Washington chose a strategy of attrition aimed at in-creasing British war weariness (the fact that Britain had been involved in a series of expensive wars in the years preceding the Revolution contributed to war opposition). If the war dragged on long enough in an inconclusive way, British opinion might become a factor that would lead to independence. It was a matter of hanging on long enough to exceed Britain's "cost-tolerance," and, aided by the stunning victory at Yorktown, the strategy worked in the end.

## Military Technology and Technique

The character of battle in the late eighteenth century was largely determined by the basic infantry weapon available at the time. The standard weapon was a large smoothbore musket that was difficult to load and had a short range. The British infantry weapon, nicknamed the Brown Bess, was typical of the muskets of the various European armies. Brown Bess was over 5 feet in length, weighed 12 pounds, and had a three-quarter–inch-diameter muzzle. Although 250 yards was its maximum range, it was extremely inaccurate. Against man-sized targets, 50 yards was considered the maximum effective range, and its rate of fire was about two rounds per minute.

A key to success on the battlefield was to increase firepower, but how does one increase firepower using such weapons? The standard solution was to put more muskets on the battlefield and pack the troops tightly together. This practice, however, led to additional difficulties. The muzzle blast from the large-caliber weapons could easily rupture eardrums unless troops were placed in proper formation. The answer was rigid linear formations with the men placed shoulder to shoulder in long lines, generally three ranks deep. After one rank fired, a second stepped forward (or the first rank retired to the rear) and fired while the first rank began to reload. After the second rank fired, the third took its place and fired. If all went well, the first rank would have reloaded its muskets and be ready to fire when the third rank had dis-charged its weapons. To increase the shock effect of the weapons, each line would fire in volleys on the command of its officers. The effect was a curtain of lead, smoke, and noise, certain to terrify all but the most highly disci-plined soldiers.

As frightening as such massed volley fire was, the real terror may have been in waiting for the enemy to come within range. When attacking, a linear formation had to march with great precision to maintain its rigid alignment. (Prussian officers were known to stop their troops in order to realign them.) Slowly the distance to the enemy, also drawn up in a packed linear formation, closed. Finally, when the two sides were very close, one side or the other fired a volley that would shatter the other's line. The volley was quickly followed by a bayonet charge, which most generals believed would actually decide the battle.

Such rigid tactics, terrifying even to think about, required enormous discipline. Many European generals followed the maxim of Frederick the Great, who observed that soldiers had to fear their own officers even more than the enemy; otherwise, the ordinary soldier would break in battle very quickly. Training for such rigid tactics was long and involved. If more than one volley was to be fired, reloading had to be mastered and conducted in unison. Troops had to march with exacting cadence and pace to keep their formation properly aligned.

Both linear techniques and the available technology made eighteenth-century warfare leisurely by modern standards. It took considerable time for commanders to arrange their formations for battle, and, in effect, both opponents had to agree tacitly to fight before a battle could commence. Because the flintlock weapons of the era were extremely unreliable when wet, few battles were fought in winter when rain and snow were common. The general result was limited warfare at a leisurely pace, but warfare that was deadly once joined.

The British brought to their American colonies a professional army with a heavy concentration of mercenaries hired from other countries, a common practice in the eighteenth century. They were skilled in the exactions of linear warfare and ready to do battle with the best European armies. Doing battle with the Americans, however, led to peculiar problems for which their training provided few answers.

The Americans had the same basic weaponry as the British, except that they lacked artillery in the early stages of the war. Sufficient artillery was quickly captured and later supplied by overseas allies. At the beginning of hostilities the Americans also did not have a well-trained force, professional or otherwise. To defend the colonies, the British had relied on a small contingent of regular army troops supplemented by militias raised and trained by each colony. The quality of these militia units varied widely; for example, the Massachusetts militia required only four days of drill per year, hardly enough to engage a well-trained enemy in linear warfare.

The American solution to these disadvantages was threefold. First, Washington built a small professional army that, by the end of the war, could acquit itself favorably. Help from various European professional soldiers who fought with the Americans was invaluable in this effort.

Second, because the Continental Army was never large enough to be a decisive force by itself, relatively untrained militias were used either as skirmishers or to expand the Continental "line." As skirmishers the militia could harass the British line and inflict considerable casualties while presenting fleeting targets inappropriate for massed British volley fire. When used to expand the Continental line, untrained militia units often broke, but they could initially increase the firepower available.

Third, militias were used effectively on the defense by "going to ground" behind strong breastworks. This technique was demonstrated at Breed's Hill, where militia units behind strong breastworks inflicted grievous casualties on British regulars advancing in linear formation. In the best European tradition, the Americans held their fire "until they could see the whites of their eyes," which means the British were within effective range. Meanwhile the British were frustrated because the Americans were hiding in relative safety from British volley fire instead of standing up and fighting. The technique of going to ground would not be limited to militia armies in the future; as weapons became even more deadly, an infantryman's best method of survival was to take cover, whether he was a professional or an amateur.

Some analysts have argued that the Americans actually had a technological advantage because some of the rebels used rifles that had much longer range and far more accuracy than British smoothbore muskets. This, however, is a misconception. Relatively few rifled weapons were used, and certainly not enough were employed to make a decisive difference. Although rifles had advantages in range and accuracy, they also had two telling disadvantages. First, they had a much slower rate of fire because they were much more difficult to load. Second, rifled weapons were not equipped with a bayonet. This lack led to a disaster at the battle of Brooklyn Heights, when American riflemen were bayoneted by charging British troops before they could get their weapons reloaded. Even Daniel Morgan (whose troops used rifled weapons) admitted that the rifle was effective only when supported by muskets with bayonets.

## Military Conduct

As has been pointed out, the decisive revolutionary act occurred almost by accident. The spark that set the tinder aflame was a British expedition from Boston to seize militia arms stored at Concord. Aroused local militiamen met the British troops on Lexington Green, where someone fired the "shot heard 'round the world." Neither the gunfire at Lexington nor the running battle with the British forces during their return to Boston was the decisive revolutionary act, however. For years many of the colonists had resisted British policies and attempts to enforce those policies. The real revolutionary act came when the irate Americans sealed the British in Boston and put the city under siege. The shots fired at Lexington, Concord, and en route to Boston could be considered the acts of overwrought subjects. The "army" surrounding Boston was a clear challenge to the authority of the Crown—the makings of a true revolution.

*Army* is a charitable term. The besiegers were a motley group of militia: ill trained, poorly led, undisciplined, and with no real legal standing. But events quickly transpired to begin the process of turning this group into what would eventually become an effective fighting force. On 14 June 1775 the Continental Congress moved to take advantage of the situation by "adopting" the force surrounding Boston and appointing George Washington, a Virginian with some military experience, as the army's commander. Meanwhile, another rebel group captured the small British garrison at Fort Ticonderoga (along the river-lakes route to Canada). The booty from this victory included artillery pieces which, when hauled to Boston, would eventually convince the British to evacuate.

There was little real fighting during the siege. The only serious confrontation took place on Breed's Hill. The British sought to oust the Americans from the hill because from that position the Americans could bring the British forces under direct artillery fire. Anticipating a British countermove, American forces built a considerable redoubt on the hill where they hid waiting for the approach of the scarlet-clad British. After an unsuccessful attempt to turn the American flank, the British launched a frontal assault on the redoubt in the finest tradition of eighteenth-century warfare. The Americans waited in relative safety behind their breastworks. American volley fire took a terrible toll, but the British tried three times to break the American line. The Americans were finally forced to withdraw when their ammunition ran low. When the smoke cleared, the British held the field but had suffered a staggering 40 percent casualty rate.

Meanwhile the Americans launched a two-pronged attack toward Canada in an attempt to eliminate Canada as a base for British operations. The rebel leaders hoped the appearance of an American army would spark an uprising of French Canadians against their British overlords. One prong of the attack proceeded up the river-lakes route in good order and defeated the small British garrison at Montreal. The second column was to proceed to Maine and up the Kennebec and Chaudière rivers, then down the Saint Lawrence to Quebec. Unfortunately, poor planning caused by faulty intelligence doomed the expedition. Travel took twice as long as expected, only 30 percent of those who set out from New England actually arrived at Quebec, and those who did arrive were in deplorable physical condition. Somehow the Americans mustered an assault on the city but were repulsed. The remnants of this pitiful force remained before the city throughout the winter of 1775–76. Their hopes of sparking a revolt were dashed, however, as the French Canadians were uninterested in the entire affair.

Washington was having much greater success before Boston. In the spring of 1776, he was able to mount the heavy artillery pieces seized at Ticonderoga on Dorchester Heights and directly threaten the city and its British garrison. Sir William Howe, the British commander, saw discretion as the better part of valor, evacuated the city, and retired to Halifax to regroup and refit.

To this point the almost accidental rebellion had been a surprising success. The rebels had won a series of offensive victories. Even their setback in Canada had been on an ambitious offensive expedition. The militia had defeated the Redcoats; the British troops had been thrown out of the rebellious colonies along with the authority of the Crown. The first phase of the Revolutionary War was over. Now would come phase two of the Revolution. Independence had been declared and the rebels would have to defend their gains against an opponent who would no longer be caught unaware and unprepared.

During the first phase the advantage had been with the rebels. Only one sizable contingent of British soldiers was in the colonies (at Boston). In spite of the makeshift nature of the American army, it outnumbered the Redcoats and was nearly as well armed. Now, however, Washington faced a fundamentally different situation. He had to defend a long coastline that was highly vulnerable to attack along its entire length. Washington's victorious militia suddenly looked totally inadequate for the job. British sea power could transport troops to any of a hundred invasion points. Even with prior knowledge of a British landing point, ships could probably reach that point faster than could Washington's troops marching overland.

Clearly, the initiative had passed to the British and they seemed to have all the advantages, but the British also faced many disadvantages. First, they would be fighting at the end of a very long line of communications, supply, and reinforcement. Second, political sentiment at home was anything but united; the American colonists had many sympathizers in the home islands. Third, fighting such a war would be an expensive proposition, one not easily supported. Finally, the American colonies were but one colonial responsibility of the British. The Union Jack flew around the world and with it went responsibilities for support and protection.

Just as the British strategy had to be offensive at this point, so did Washington's strategy have to be defensive. Above all he had to prevent the destruction of his fledgling army. Decisive defeat of the Continental Army meant the death of the Revolution, for it was the only means of resistance. Washington knew he had no reasonable hope of victory against the British army in open battle. At best he could wage defensive battles, judiciously withdraw after inflicting casualties, and wait to fight again another day. With some good fortune (and poor British tactics) Washington might be able to fall upon isolated portions of the British force and inflict small defeats. Washington's objective had to be to buy time, raise the cost of the war to the British, and hope they would tire of the whole affair. The other American hope was for foreign help from France, Britain's traditional enemy and colonial rival.

The British strategy for 1776 was complex. First, a two-pronged attack was planned to isolate New England from the rest of the colonies. Sir Guy Carlton was to drive the remaining American forces from Canada, pursue them down the river-lakes route, and then turn into New England. Sir William Howe was to land at New York (clearly an important target and excellent base of operations), drive up the river-lakes route, and also turn into New England. Meanwhile Henry Clinton would lead an amphibious expedition to the southern colonies where he had been assured that thousands of Tories would rise up and subdue the rebels.

Few things went as planned for the British. Clinton's effort in the south failed because of a lack of military coordination. Tory uprisings failed to materialize as the rebel militia kept those loyal to the Crown in check. In Canada Carlton had considerable success as he chased the Americans all the way back to Ticonderoga, but he failed to press his advantage after a naval victory at Valcour Island. Carlton's lethargy and the approach of cold weather put the victorious British forces into winter quarters.

Howe's position at New York was particularly interesting. He came to wage peace as well as war. He was empowered to negotiate with the rebels and offer concessions. The rebels, still flushed with the success of their revolution, were in no mood for serious negotiations. Howe was left with no choice but to wage war. To do this he brought 32,000 professional troops and a considerable naval armada to New York. Washington was able to assemble about 20,000 men, most of them ill trained.

New York would have been difficult to defend in any case, but the task was nearly impossible since the enemy possessed control of the waterways that surrounded and divided the city. Washington was determined to offer a significant defense for political and moral reasons, if no other. If the Continental Army would not defend such an important place, what would it defend? What good is an army that defends nothing? These questions would plague Americans if Washington let New York fall without a struggle. Refusal to try to defend such an important target could be as dangerous to the Revolution as a decisive military defeat. Thus Washington had to offer resistance and then retreat to fight another day.

New York was lost, but not without a series of bloody battles. At Brooklyn Heights, Washington barely escaped total defeat. After additional defeats at Fort Washington and White Plains, Washington retreated across New Jersey as his army slowly disintegrated around him. Finally, Washington crossed into Pennsylvania as winter fell. Howe assumed the campaign was over, that Washington was beaten, and that the rebel army had disintegrated. He ordered his deputy, Cornwallis, to post detachments across New Jersey and then go into winter quarters. Howe would wait comfortably for spring. If the

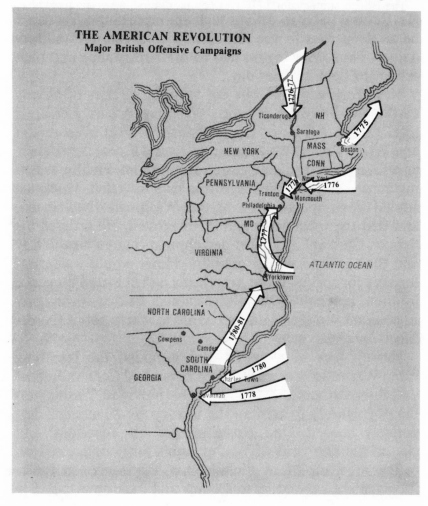

THE AMERICAN REVOLUTION
Major British Offensive Campaigns

Americans had not sued for peace by then, he could easily reestablish British sovereignty in good weather without having to worry about the defunct American army.

Howe's lack of aggressiveness provided the breathing room Washington needed. When Howe had Cornwallis post detachments across New Jersey, he provided Washington the opportunity to achieve the victory the Americans desperately needed. Had Howe pressed his advantage and chased the remnants of Washington's army or pressed on to the rebel capital at Philadelphia, the American Revolution might have come to a quick and inglorious end. But winter campaigning was no easy task in that era, particularly in the primitive conditions in the colonies.

By going into winter quarters, Howe was following the rather leisurely tradition of eighteenth-century European warfare. He seemed unaware that this would be a very different kind of war. Moreover, Howe failed to realize that the American Revolution was an ideological conflict with its attendant passions.

From Howe's perspective organized resistance seemed at an end. Any disorganized or passive resistance remaining was a job for the diplomats and politicians to resolve, with the help of the army. This task could be left safely for spring when the government in London would have its policy toward the rebels worked out, and when the weather would make implementation of that policy easier. Howe's lack of appreciation for the kind of war in which he was involved led him to miss his best opportunity to put down the Revolution.

Washington was in such a desperate situation that he was forced to seize aggressively every opportunity presented. He had been badly defeated in New York and driven in headlong retreat across New Jersey. His army was disintegrating around him as terms of enlistment expired or as the dispirited simply quit. Enlistments lagged as few were willing to risk their lives for a cause that appeared doomed. Washington needed a victory to boost the morale of his little army, keep the men in camp, and boost enlistments.

Washington could now concentrate his force against one of Cornwallis's isolated detachments rather than facing the bulk of the British army. The object of his attack would be the Hessian garrison at Trenton. On Christmas night Washington took a force of more than 2,000 Continental Army regulars across the Delaware River (the incident portrayed in the famous painting of Washington crossing the Delaware) and surprised the defenders, who, after a brief fight, surrendered. Washington then retreated back across the river. His success so shocked the British that they withdrew their detachments back from the river to Princeton. Washington was then able to recross the river into New Jersey. Cornwallis reacted by coming south from New York, gathering up British forces as he proceeded toward Washington's New

Jersey encampment. On the night of 2 January 1777, Washington slipped around Cornwallis's camp and struck Princeton. Cornwallis turned about to advance on Princeton and upon his approach Washington led his army toward Morristown in the rugged New Jersey highlands. From there Washington could easily fend off British attacks and threaten the British line of communication to their posts in southern New Jersey. Howe, recognizing the threat to his posts, withdrew them to the area immediately around New York to await spring.

In strictly military terms, the American victories at Trenton and Princeton were anything but decisive. They were hit-and-run raids, the classic method of war of a much weaker adversary hoping for little more than to wear down a stronger opponent. In the broader sense, however, these two small victories were nearly as decisive as the later victories at Saratoga and Yorktown. Washington had served notice to the British that subduing the Revolution would be no easy task and could not be accomplished quickly. More important, these victories served notice to the American people that victory was possible in spite of seemingly insurmountable difficulties. Victory was an elixir for the Continental Army that cured many of the ills brought on by the defeats in New York. As both armies licked their wounds in winter quarters, 1777 promised to be a decisive year.

The British campaign plans for 1777 were a picture of confusion. Howe, previously entrusted with the capture of New York, was again about to set off to capture a city, Philadelphia. It was unclear what Howe intended to do with Philadelphia once it was in his hands. He may have believed that the Tories would flock to him and that the seizure of the capital would dispirit the revolutionaries. He may have believed that Washington would have to defend the capital, presenting an opportunity to inflict a decisive defeat on the Americans. Perhaps Howe still believed the rebel army was of little consequence.

While Howe planned to seize Philadelphia, Gentleman Johnny Burgoyne had a London-approved plan to split the rebel colonies by moving down the river-lakes route from Canada to isolate the New England colonies. Under this plan Howe's forces in New York were to aid Burgoyne by moving north on the river-lakes route. Unfortunately for Burgoyne, Howe was on his way to Philadelphia.

Howe's campaign against Philadelphia took advantage of British sea power. His troops embarked from New York, put to sea, sailed up the Chesapeake Bay, and landed at Head of Elk in Maryland. This route was, as Washington said, a strange choice. Overland from New York the distance was less than 100 miles. By sea the journey took 33 days and the expedition landed at a point still 50 miles distant from the rebel capital. As Howe advanced on

Philadelphia, Washington rallied an army of more than 15,000 for the city's defense.

Philadelphia was not an important target in military terms. Certainly it was the seat of government, but a government can move and it eventually did. Washington needed to defend the city for the same reason he needed to defend New York. Thus Washington felt compelled to lead his army to Chadd's Ford on Brandywine Creek south of the capital. There on 11 September 1777, Washington was outmaneuvered, badly defeated, and nearly surrounded and destroyed. Again, as at New York, the head-on confrontation with major professional forces led to defeat and near disaster.

Washington retreated to Warwick while Howe advanced and seized Philadelphia. Washington resorted to the tactics of the previous winter as he led his army to Germantown, a community just north of Philadelphia, where he fell upon an isolated British garrison. Washington was narrowly defeated, but Germantown was an impressive performance for a recently defeated army that many had written off. Following the battle at Germantown on 4 October 1777, Washington again led his army into winter quarters, this time at Valley Forge, Pennsylvania. While the Americans froze and starved at Valley Forge, Howe wintered comfortably, enjoying the pleasures of the former rebel capital.

Two weeks after the battle of Germantown, the Americans achieved a victory whose impact went far beyond the confines of the battlefield. At Saratoga, New York, Burgoyne surrendered his entire command to an American militia army led by Gen Gates and Maj Gen Benedict Arnold. Burgoyne's surrender was positive proof that the British were not invincible and that the American rebels could win. The news of the American victory convinced the French to enter the conflict on the side of the Americans, and this intervention ultimately made victory possible for the rebels.

Burgoyne had begun his trek down the river-lakes route from Fort Saint John, north of Lake Champlain, with 8,000 professional troops. He had easily moved to Fort Ticonderoga, which quickly fell after a token defense. Rather than taking the water route down Lake George to Fort George, Burgoyne pursued the Americans retreating from Ticonderoga on an overland route. His men hacked a 23-mile road through rough, heavily wooded country, overcoming numerous obstacles placed in his path by the retreating rebels. The head of Burgoyne's column took three weeks to complete the trip, and his heavy artillery lagged well behind the column. Gentleman Johnny knew little about the countryside, and he had taken far too few horses, oxen, mules, and carts to supply his army at the end of an overextended supply line. His base of operations was 185 miles away in Canada. His choices were to retreat to Canada and admit defeat or to press on to Albany, where he could obtain succor.

Burgoyne tried to relieve his problem by sending a Hessian foraging party to Bennington, Vermont, where it was reported that a large number of horses were available. At Bennington the Hessians were virtually destroyed by a militia group commanded by Gen John Stark, and a British relief column arrived just in time to also be destroyed by the Americans. Burgoyne lost 900 of his best professional troops and achieved nothing except to bolster the confidence of the American militia army, which was swelling rapidly with the arrival of more militia units.

Burgoyne finally decided to move to Albany even though he knew this would be an extremely difficult task. The Americans had cut his supply lines and blocked the path to Albany by entrenching themselves along Bemis Heights. Gentleman Johnny's hungry and demoralized troops would have to attack a fortified position. On 19 September Burgoyne's attack was repulsed with heavy losses, and his situation was nearly hopeless. Surrounded by an army that outnumbered his own almost two to one, Burgoyne had nearly exhausted his food supplies. He made one last desperate effort to break the American lines on 7 October and again was repulsed. Burgoyne retired to Saratoga to consider his limited options, and ten days later surrendered his entire command. Included in the booty were 7 generals, 300 officers, and 5,600 soldiers. A considerable array of artillery plus a large stock of powder and shell also fell into American hands.

Four months after the American victory at Saratoga, France and the American government signed a military alliance. The surprising American performance at Germantown and the smashing victory at Saratoga provided the grease for the diplomatic wheels. The alliance was the pivotal political act of the war.

With the French in the war, Washington's situation was entirely different. In the past Washington had to concentrate on keeping his army intact and avoiding serious defeat. His military objective had been to survive to buy time, to tire the British, and to raise the cost of the war to a level unacceptable in London. Now the French fleet could challenge and perhaps defeat British sea power, so that the British would not have the luxury of unlimited mobility. With a strong ally Washington could afford to take risks; he had more than his own meager resources to fall back on should those risks lead to defeat. Perhaps more important in the long run, the British were seriously distracted because the war had suddenly broadened in scope, and other British possessions were threatened. Finally, the hard work of Washington and his officers, particularly such foreign advisers as Baron Friedrich Wilhelm von Steuben, produced a trained core of Continental soldiers capable of acquitting themselves well on the open battlefield. Not only could Washington take risks, he had the tools to make success possible.

The British, meanwhile, were thrown into great turmoil by the new situation. Clearly, they would have to retrench their forces in the American colonies and be prepared to embark to other destinations that might be threatened by the French. The first move was to relieve the lethargic Howe, who was still in Philadelphia, and replace him with Gen Sir Henry Clinton. After some confusion Clinton was ordered to evacuate Philadelphia and consolidate his forces in New York, where they could easily embark for other ports.

Washington struck hard at Clinton as he retreated toward New York. Deploying nearly half of his total force of Continentals against the bulk of the British army in the colonies, Washington attacked Clinton at Monmouth, New Jersey, on 27 June 1778. The two armies fought for several hours and the Continentals acquitted themselves with distinction. Clinton, however, was able to escape to New York. The British, rebuffed at every turn, virtually abandoned their hope of recapturing the northern colonies. They remained in New York, closely guarded by Washington and his Continentals.

The British still hoped to take advantage of assumed Tory sentiment in the southern colonies. To this end London dispatched Lord Cornwallis in 1780. The British won a great victory at Charleston, moved into the interior, and established a line of posts reminiscent of those in New Jersey during 1776. Meanwhile the American Congress appointed Gen Horatio Gates, the self-proclaimed "Hero of Saratoga," as commander of the southern armies over the objection of Washington. The British soundly defeated Gates at Camden, South Carolina, on 16 August 1780. Although the Continental contingent fought well, militia units broke and fled from the field along with a panicked Gates, giving the British one of their most complete victories of the war. Only about 700 of the nearly 4,000 Americans involved escaped. Following that debacle Congress bowed to Washington's wishes and appointed Nathanael Greene as army commander in the southern colonies.

Greene fought a classic guerrilla-style war against the frustrated Cornwallis. Greene led Cornwallis on a hard chase and turned and fought only when British forces were spread out, tired, and ill supplied. Along with Francis Marion, another brilliant tactician of partisan warfare, Greene harassed the British, wore them out, and occasionally defeated them. Finally, the frustrated Cornwallis broke away from the chase and retreated to the coast at Wilmington, North Carolina, to refit. Greene quickly headed back into South Carolina to attack the posts that Cornwallis had earlier established and now could not defend.

Disgusted that he could not destroy the rebel forces once and for all, Cornwallis headed north into Virginia hoping for better luck. He had little success there, again chasing elusive American forces about the countryside. Clinton, who was still in New York watching Cornwallis's campaign with great concern and a degree of disbelief, ordered Cornwallis to the coast at Yorktown to meet with the British fleet for refitting and possible embarkation. The fleet Cornwallis found at Yorktown, however, was not British.

Cornwallis's retreat into Yorktown presented Washington with a rare opportunity for a complete and politically decisive victory. Cooperating with the French, Washington quickly made his plan; speed was necessitated by knowledge that the French fleet in the area around Yorktown would soon be returning to the Caribbean at the end of hurricane season. Washington had to mass a superior army to besiege the British from the land side. Washington and the French army commander, Comte de Rochambeau, marched a mixed army from New York (where they left forces demonstrating for Clinton's benefit) to Yorktown. The movement took just over a month, a considerable feat in eighteenth-century conditions. Washington managed to mass 16,000 troops while the French fleet of 30 ships blocked a British escape by sea. Siege operations began under direction of the French engineers. Less than a month after the siege began, Cornwallis surrendered his entire army of 8,000 to Washington on 19 October 1781 after his plan to escape across the James River was foiled by a storm that destroyed his boats.

After five years of hard fighting, the British had suffered two crushing defeats at Saratoga and Yorktown and were worse off than they had been in 1776. They still held New York and Charleston (both closely watched by the Americans), which would be good bases for further operations. Also the British faced a global war against powerful enemies, and an American army that could stand and fight in the best European tradition. Worse yet, political opinion at home was badly divided.

For all practical purposes, the war was over for the Americans. Although some fighting still occurred in the south and west and the British had to be guarded at New York and Charleston, the real war was over and the Americans were victorious.

The Revolutionary War reintroduced ideological conflict, a significant step in the democratization of war. One unfortunate result was that, led by the memories of Breed's Hill and Saratoga, for the next 160 years many Americans believed that they did not need a professional army of any size and could instead rely on militia units. Although this had disastrous consequences in 1812, in the Civil War, and in the early battles of two world wars, the legend of the minutemen died hard. Only after 1945, when America entered the world of international power politics as the leader of the Western democracies, would the United States establish a sizable professional military force.

Who fared better? It is clear that in 1776 the British squandered their best opportunity to end the rebellion. Had Howe pressed his advantage after defeating Washington in New York, the war might have ended quickly. The American Revolution was, in effect, a civil war. As clearly demonstrated later in the American Civil War, rebel momentum and morale grow if they are not quickly checked. Time was clearly on the side of the Americans. Not only did American confidence grow, but British will declined at home. The Americans were aided and abetted by poor British planning (Howe going to Philadelphia instead of aiding Burgoyne in 1777) and military blunders (Burgoyne's disaster and Cornwallis's entrapment at Yorktown).

Although ultimately successful, Washington's strategy can also be questioned. Washington played for time well and did an excellent job of keeping his fledgling army together. He recognized the proper time to take the offensive and to take the necessary risks to achieve decisive victory. However, one can question his campaign in New York in 1776 and Philadelphia in 1777. On one hand, the failure to at least attempt a defense of those two vital points might have been a serious blow to American morale. On the other hand, Washington's army was nearly trapped and destroyed both in New York and at Brandywine Creek. The question remains, however, were the benefits worth the possible consequences?

Overall, Washington, the amateur soldier, must receive higher marks than his professional British opponents. Although the British had a clear political objective, none of the British commanders seemed to have a clear conception of how to reach that objective. Washington, however, seemed to have had a much clearer picture of how to achieve his objective. His immediate objectives accurately changed with the circumstances, and each one was geared toward the ultimate goal. The proof of this contention is in the outcome.

**Better State of the Peace**

The American Revolution achieved its political objective of independence with the signing of the Treaty of Paris in 1783, ending eight years of formal hostilities between Great Britain and her former colonies. Just as de facto independence was achieved in 1775 when the British evacuated Boston, so was permanent and legal independence a fact when the British sailed out of New York, Charleston, and Savannah in 1783.

Unlike most wars, and certainly the major conflicts of the twentieth century, American objectives were not truly won on the battlefield. The yardstick that suggests that the defeat of the enemy's armed forces is prefatory to imposing those peace terms by which the victor defines the better state of the peace simply did not apply in the American Revolution. The British army was certainly not destroyed as a fighting force: in fact, it won most of the battles, and with the exception of some inept generalship, it acquitted itself well. If a goal in war is to overcome hostile ability, the Revolution was at best a draw.

The reasons the war could be won in the absence of decisive military success can be boiled down to two factors. The first was the nature of warfare as practiced in the eighteenth century. Unlike modern wars, it was fought by limited means (basically because of technological limitations) and with relatively small forces (largely because of budgetary limits on raising and supporting large forces). The size and kinds of armies available might be capable of decisive action in the comparatively confined space of continental Europe, where the capture of a critical city would lead to peace. The American colonies, however, were not well suited to this kind of war; the territorial expanses were simply too great for control by 30,000 British troops, and there were no geographical points critical to the revolutionary cause. Washington could not have eluded the British had the war been fought in Belgium, but the British could not corner him in America.

The second factor that made the war militarily inconclusive was the contrast in objectives and military strategies adopted by the combatants. The European tradition called for the open, frontal confrontation of standard, stand-up fighting forces, but this was not what the British faced. The Continental Army was simply neither large enough nor good enough to take on the British in that manner. Given the military balance, a strategy of attrition, featuring generous doses of what we now call unconventional warfare, was the only available means. It was, moreover, a style of warfare that better suited the rugged, heavily wooded American topography.

This style of warfare both confused and frustrated the British, who never did devise an effective means for dealing with an enemy who hid behind trees in ambush and simply melted away into the vast countryside when confronted by a superior force.

If the rebels failed to overcome British hostile ability, they did succeed in overcoming that element of British hostile will defined as the willingness to continue to bear the costs of fighting. British cost-tolerance was, in the end, exceeded, and that was what proved conclusive. The lesson was, or should have been, instructive for future generations. The British were forced to fight an unfamiliar kind of war on unfamiliar and hostile territory. The war was fought far from home, straining supply capacities and raising economic costs (in more contemporary terms, the British had a very long logistics tail). Moreover, the war dragged on and on with apparently inconclusive results as casualties continued to mount. The longer it lasted, the stronger the protests became, and ultimately those who had opposed the war all along gained the upper hand. Finally, a lack of support forced the British to pack up and go home, undefeated militarily but with their will to continue shattered. So constructed, the parallels with Southeast Asia are stark and painful.

The question of overcoming hostile British will (defined as acceptance of American policy preferences-independence) is more difficult to assess. At one level, the British clearly did accede to the American objective by signing the peace treaty that formally created the new independent state. At the same time, the British resented deeply what had happened to them and showed disregard for American sovereignty, as evidenced by their cavalier treatment of former British sailors (impressment) who had been granted asylum by the US government. That arrogance had a great deal to do with leading the two nations to their second conflict, the War of 1812. Many observers maintain that it was not until that conflict was resolved that British hostile will toward the American state finally ended.

# 3

# Civil War

The American Civil War represents the greatest American national trauma. It was the first conflict in the American experience that clearly and unambiguously met the dual criteria of total war. The issue of union or disunion of the country was all-encompassing and could be resolved only on the field of battle, and the war became a match between totally mobilized societies. The result was the bloodiest war in American history. When the last gunpowder haze rose and Robert E. Lee and Joseph E. Johnston surrendered the remnants of their armies, more than 600,000 had died and nearly another 500,000 had been wounded. And it had all been done at our own hand.

In many ways the Civil War was warfare in transition, a junction between the classical conflicts of the eighteenth century and the massive carnage of the twentieth century. Tactically, battles were organized and fought along the lines of the Napoleonic campaigns by armies led by officers who had learned to fight that way at West Point, and both sides (especially Lee's) were obsessed with the "decisive battle" concept integral to Napoleon's success.

At the time no one really appreciated how the face of war was changing. Partly this was the case because it was a war fought and led by men who were largely inexperienced in combat when it began. The soldiers available were largely untrained militia (in the American tradition) who could neither drill nor, in many cases, fire a gun. The war's first major battle, First Manassas (Bull Run), showed both sides how poorly prepared they were for the war and how difficult the task would be. After First Manassas both sides mobilized their societies, and in the following spring when the real fighting began, war machines of unprecedented size were ready to grind against one another and produce equally unprecedented carnage.

Another reason most contemporary observers did not recognize that the Civil War presaged the new face of war was that the armies that fought never resembled the highly drilled and disciplined troops of Europe. This led to the conclusion that they and the war were aberrational. One foreign military observer, the Prussian Helmuth von Moltke, typified the war as "two armed mobs chasing each other around the country, from which nothing can be learned." Missed were such harbingers of the future as the elaborate entrenchments around Petersburg, Virginia, that foreshadowed the awful trench warfare in France a half century later.

The Civil War was our bloodiest conflict, and it is also the war we best remember and most romanticize. Certainly a large part of our obsession is deserved because the Civil War, in terms of its effect on American society, stands with the American Revolution as one of the two most important events in our history. It was a major event in the American experience in both a political and a military sense. Only the Revolution rivals this great conflict as a political event; no war before or since comes close to matching it in terms of American blood expended. It is also the great American tragedy; Americans turned the weapons of war on their fellow Americans. Why and how it all happened occupies the pages that follow.

## Issues and Events

It has been difficult to achieve anything resembling consensus about the causes of the war. Slavery, the imposition of the Northern industrial system on the South, and states' rights have all been argued as the basic issue. No attempt is made here to add to that debate or resolve the question of whether the war was inevitable based on which root cause one picks. Rather, our perspective is that there is truth in each of the ways of looking at the issues and that each contributed to the final result. Moreover, the issues leading to the war can usefully be organized as a clash between what had evolved as two distinct cultures that manifested themselves in progressively diverging political, economic, and social systems. In this view issues like slavery or states' rights are significant symptoms of the deeper incompatibility between two distinctly regional cultures and the values they represented. The American culture of 1860 was in fact two very different cultures. In the long run, those differences had to be resolved before there could be a truly *United* States of America. Whether these differences could have been reconciled differently than they were is one of history's moot points.

Northern industrialization was at the heart of the divergence between the sections. By the eve of the Civil War, Northern society was undergoing the pervasive change that attended the industrial revolution, but there was no parallel transformation in the South, which remained an agrarian society. When both sections had been agricultural, the differences between the free-holding farm pattern of the North and the slave-based plantation organization of Southern agriculture were not critical. When Northern society moved from an agrarian to an industrial base, the differences between the sections became more pronounced and vexing.

The issue of labor was at the heart of the friction. Although the majority of white Southerners owned no slaves, the plantation system that sustained the Southern economy depended upon chattel slavery. Cotton production was the core of this system, and slave labor was appealing to the culture of cotton for several reasons.

First, growing cotton was a labor-intensive enterprise, but it did not require highly trained workers or great efficiency. Unpaid labor in the form of slaves kept costs low enough to turn a profit.

Second, the planters perpetually suffered from a "cash-flow" problem. Cotton did not produce a steady flow of income; rather, it produced revenue in spurts when crops were sold. In addition there were frequently substantial lag times between harvest and payment; the unpaid slaves never knew the difference.

There were costs that made slave labor unattractive in the industrializing North. Slaves, because they were not paid, had no incentive to work harder than necessary to avoid punishment. Hence, slaves were not efficient, which was intolerable in an industrial setting. Industry, after all, has efficient production as its ultimate measure of success.

This is, of course, a very pragmatic way to look at the slavery question, but it is closer to how the average Yankee viewed the issue than can be found in abolitionist literature. The abolitionists were noisy but few in number and marginal in political clout (although many Southerners overestimated their influence). To average Northerners slavery was at worst an unfortunate institution that they could not actively support. To most Northerners who thought at all about such matters, slavery was not so much evil at it was inappropriate.

The two cultures were diverging in other ways as well. Southern plantation society had become highly stratified and stagnant. The planters were an elite who dominated the South politically, economically, and socially. In that position the planters were natural conservatives, seeking to preserve a position from which they benefited. Beneath them were merchants and artisans who benefited from the planters' largesse. Beneath the merchants and artisans, was the larger population of poor whites, who toiled on rented land at subsistence agriculture, but who, at least, had the slaves to look down on.

At the same time, the existence of the slave system effectively precluded change and development because slavery was custom-made for the cotton plantation system but was of dubious economic viability otherwise. The plantation needed slaves, and the institution of slavery needed the plantation. The consequences of breaking the circle and freeing the slaves were something few Southerners were willing to face.

The North was evolving very differently. Unfettered by slaves and nurtured by waves of European immigrants and foreign investment, the North was on its way to becoming a modern industrial state. With industrialization came the emergence of an urban working class, a merchant class, and industrial entrepreneurs, groups largely absent in the plantation South. The result was great social fluidity and social and economic leavening. The North was becoming a society of workers and shopkeepers; the South remained a society of aristocrats and farmers.

Coexistence became more difficult as the differences magnified. Northerners argued for high tariffs to protect their new industries. Southerners resisted, preferring European goods at lower prices. Northerners pushed for legislation to require Southern cotton to be sent to Europe on more expensive American (which meant New England) ships. Southerners resisted because such shipping was more expensive and made their cotton less competitive on international markets. Dual cultures were increasingly coming into conflict in practical ways; something had to give.

The issue that broke the camel's back and that, combined with the election of Abraham Lincoln, provided the proximate events leading to secession and the war was the extension of slavery to the territories. It was an issue that had been brewing for some time. The Missouri Compromise of 1820 had defused it for a short time, but it returned in the protracted fight over admitting slave-holding Texas to the Union. The Great Compromise of 1850 attempted to settle the problem, but the compromise was followed rapidly by such unsettling events as the Dred Scott decision, Bloody Kansas, and John Brown's raid at Harper's Ferry.

On the pragmatic, political level, if slavery were allowed in a territory, that territory would ultimately enter the Union as a slave state and the converse was also true. In turn, a new slave-holding state would elect proslavery representatives to Congress who would generally support Southern positions, just as free states would elect antislavery representatives of the opposite bent. In a system where there was a rough balance between slave-holding and non-slave-holding representatives (especially in the Senate), additions on either side would tip the balance.

The question of the extension of slavery also created problems at the deeper level of competing cultures. Extension was particularly vital to the South, because cotton cultivation rapidly depleted the soil. If the cotton and hence the plantation system were to prosper, it had to be able to move from depleted soil westward to fertile soil. Hemmed in, the cotton culture would die; thus, the absence of extension amounted to slow strangulation. In the North the extension of slavery was opposed because slavery was an anachronism that had no place in the kind of society that Northerners wanted and expected to build in the new lands. In this light the extension issue emerges as a lightning rod for the entire clash of cultures, and it boiled down to a zero-sum game: if one side was to win, the other had to lose.

This irresolvable, irresistible conflict came to a head with the election of Abraham Lincoln in 1860. Lincoln was not politically an abolitionist, but his candidacy had been supported by the more radical abolitionists. Lincoln's stated position (he found slavery personally offensive but protected by the Constitution) was lost in guilt by association in the minds of many Southerners.

When the calls for secession came, the issue of states' rights was the rallying cry. In the South particularly, there was great sentiment for a weak central government and primary investment of political authority in the states. This position, of course, was more than abstract and academic. The South had its "peculiar institution" and social system to protect. The closer to home political authority lay, the more compatible public policy would be with maintaining that system. In the North the development of a modern industrial state required a comparatively strong central government that could adopt national policies conducive to continued growth (protective tariffs are a good example). The South generally did not benefit from these policies and sometimes suffered from them. At the heart of Southern opposition, however, was the lingering fear that a strong central government might adopt legislation directly attacking Southern institutions. The election of a president believed to be actively sympathetic to abolitionism produced a greater strain than could be borne.

If the critical political issue was the supremacy of the rights of the states and central governance was equated with tyranny, then the new, alternative government had to reflect those beliefs. The Confederate States of America chose a confederal format, a state-dominated political system that conformed nicely to philosophical predispositions but which featured a central government with limited authority to make wartime decisions, a political problem that dogged the Davis administration and the Confederate military command throughout the war. Ironically, the very principles for which Southerners fought hampered their ability to fight.

Once the South Carolina legislature voted unanimously to dissolve the union between itself and the federal government on 20 December 1860 (an action quickly duplicated by six additional states and later by four others), the question was how the rest of the country should react to secession. The answer was not as clear then as it may appear today. There was, for instance, considerable disagreement, mostly in the North, about whether states had the right to secede, and both those who said they did and those who said they did not based their arguments on the Constitution.

The argument boiled down to the states' rights versus strong central government debate. Those advocating the legality of secession were in fact arguing states' rights, and those who maintained that the states could not secede were arguing the supremacy of the Union over its constituent parts. The latter belief formed the basis for Lincoln's famous statement that "a house divided against itself cannot stand," which clearly reflected how the president-elect felt about the matter. When South Carolina seceded, however, James J. Buchanan was a lame duck president, and he reacted officially to the secession by ignoring it. When Lincoln was sworn in as the nation's sixteenth president, some action would be necessary.

## Political Objective

Lincoln determined that the Northern political objective was to reestablish the Union, by force if necessary. As a statement of purpose, this was disarmingly simple, but there were powerful politico-military problems confronting its realization.

This first and most obvious problem was that the South did not intend to return to the Union voluntarily. The North would have to fight for reunion and that led directly to Lincoln's second problem. The objective was not popular in the North. As a political objective, in other words, reunification lacked the moral power and persuasiveness to galvanize Northern public opinion. A more morally lofty objective was necessary to gather and sustain support.

Lincoln realized his problems, and part of his answer was the Emancipation Proclamation, which added the end of slavery to reunion as the political objective. This goal was announced in September 1862 and took effect in January 1863, but emancipation had to overcome a problem of timing: throughout 1862 the Union suffered a succession of defeats in the Eastern theater. To change the objective in the midst of calamity would have appeared an act of desperation that could backfire and diminish rather than increase support. What Lincoln needed was a military victory to precede his announcement. He got his wish when Lee forayed into Maryland and was stopped by George B. McClellan at Antietam (Sharpsburg). The battle itself was a draw, but it forced Lee to retreat back into Virginia and thus looked enough like a win to serve the purpose.

The effects of adding the abolition of slavery to the political purpose of the war were mixed. In the South the reaction was mortification, reinforcing the citizenry's worst fears about Lincoln and increasing their will to resist. In the North the result was a sort of backhanded success.

The basic negative was that freeing the slaves was not an overwhelmingly popular objective to most Northerners, who were about as racist in their attitudes toward blacks as were Southerners. With the exception of the abolitionists, most Northerners shared Southern beliefs in the inherent inferiority of the Negro, and even if they found slavery repulsive in the abstract, many did not think the destruction of the institution worth dying for.

Making emancipation a major objective did, however, add moral weight to the Union cause in at least two important ways. First, opposition to the war became tantamount to being proslavery, a position that relatively few in the North held or at least were willing to admit. Second, this moral elevation of the objective effectively ended any possibility that the Confederacy would gain recognition by the European powers, notably Britain and France, which had been primary prewar markets for Southern cotton. No European state could politically align itself with human chattel slavery. The proclamation thus ended the possibility of foreign support for the Confederacy.

If the Union political objective was to restore the Union and free the slaves, the Confederate objective was just the opposite: to maintain its independence by whatever means necessary and to avoid the emancipation of the slaves. As long as the South maintained control over its territory and had a functioning government, military forces, and a loyal population, the Union could not achieve its political objective.

Unlike the situation in the North, the Southern political objective was overwhelmingly popular and sustained citizen support for the war effort until nearly the end. The Southern cause was to defend their homeland and their society from a foreign enemy who could accomplish his purpose only through physical invasion, subjugation, and occupation.

The popularity of defending home and loved ones from an invading force added greatly to Southern political support for the war, and the Confederate political objective was never seriously challenged from within. Support for the objective and its translation into military activity was one of the great advantages the South had (other primary ones being fighting on the defensive and on familiar ground and having generally superior military leaders), and this advantage was particularly obvious in contrast to the marked ambivalence about the objective in the North. In turn these political objectives translated into military objectives and strategies for waging the conflict. As we shall see, the political objectives sometimes became blurred or distorted in the process, but political concerns and considerations were never far from the field of combat.

## Military Objectives and Strategy

For the Union, that part of its political objective involving restoring the Union was simple and straightforward. It required that the Rebel government be disbanded. But how does one destroy a rival government? Clearly, the armed force that defends and supports the government must be overcome, neutralized, or destroyed. Thus, the Union military objective was also unambiguous: overcome the Confederate military so that the Rebel government could be disbanded.

An offensive strategy was certainly required, but it needed to be a strategy for a very rapid and decisive offensive. If the fighting lasted for a lengthy period, the suffering and destruction might be such that full union could be impossible to achieve for generations. Quick victory was also an imperative because of the political situation within the Union. A drawn-out struggle would breed war weariness and undermine the Union war effort. Additionally, the Union victory had to be decisive, because there could be no compromise with the supremacy of the Constitution and the illegality of voluntary secession. If either of these principles were not maintained, the concept of a United States would be in constant danger from recalcitrant states.

The Union's situation was not favorable for achieving either a quick or a decisive victory. The regular Army was pitifully small and equipped to fight frontier Indians. Many of the Army's most capable officers resigned to serve their home states in opposition to the Union. Burdened with these difficulties, Union forces had to take the offensive, but how?

Winfield Scott, veteran of the War of 1812, hero of the Mexican War, and general in chief of the United States Army, had a plan that would exploit the Union's crushing superiority in manpower, resources, and industrial power and attack the Confederacy's weaknesses in those same areas. Scott envisioned a tight naval blockade of the Confederacy's long coastline and seizure of the Mississippi River to cripple the South's economy. The blockade, combined with the limited industrial capabilities of the Southern states, would deny the Confederate army the wherewithal to wage war effectively. The Confederate army would slowly deteriorate as would the entire Rebel economic situation. The consequences of rebellion would be brought home to average Southerners in terms of empty stomachs and pocketbooks.

While the South deteriorated under the pressure of the blockade, the Union Army would expand to the proportions required. Northern factories would provide the finest equipment and most sophisticated weapons. Time would be available for proper training and the selection of capable officers. Finally, using river lines of approach, particularly from the west, the Union Army would crush the demoralized and ill-equipped Rebels. Scott's "Anaconda

Plan" aimed at a militarily efficient victory, but it would not be a speedy victory.

Lincoln, a man with no military experience, needed a quick victory. He wanted a cordon offense, that is, simultaneous offensive pressure around the periphery of the Confederacy. Such an offensive would make maximum use of vastly superior Union resources and present the Rebels with the impossible situation of trying to be militarily strong everywhere with inferior resources. The result, he believed, would be rapid Confederate disintegration. If such a plan could be executed, the Union victory would be both quick and decisive.

The actual differences between Scott and Lincoln had more to do with time than concept. However, Scott realized that the Union Army and Navy were simply not capable of such a massive undertaking and had to be greatly expanded. Proper equipment had to be provided and capable officers found. Finally, raw recruits had to be trained and disciplined if the Army was not to be a mob. Scott realized that time was needed, but Lincoln demanded immediate action.

What eventually evolved was a strategy similar in concept to Scott's plan but compressed in time to suit an impatient Lincoln. Rather than a fully coordinated cordon offensive, the Union effort was, in the beginning, two separate wars on two different fronts. West of the Appalachian Mountains, Union generals (the most successful being an obscure man by the name of Ulysses Simpson Grant) struggled to capture the length of the Mississippi River. The plan was to cut the Confederacy in two from north to south. From this base of operations, the forces in the west could then attack to the east, particularly toward the vital rail centers at Chattanooga and Atlanta.

In the Eastern theater, Lincoln and many others in the government believed that Washington was seriously threatened with a Confederate attack because the capital was, in effect, on the front lines. Such an attack would not only cause panic and destruction, but would damage Union credibility with foreign governments and perhaps add fuel to the fire fanned by the Copperhead movement. The fear that a Confederate army would march on Washington caused Lincoln to insist that significant forces guard the city at all times. As a result, inordinate attention was paid to Lt Gen Thomas J. "Stonewall" Jackson's Shenandoah Valley campaign in 1862, which was only a Confederate diversionary movement. The demand for troops to protect Washington also frustrated Maj Gen George B. McClellan as Lincoln withheld troops that McClellan had designated for the Peninsular campaign against Richmond.

The Confederate capital beguiled the Union leaders. It, too, was on the front lines, barely 100 miles from Washington. Union planners envisioned a drive toward Richmond which, they believed, would be fiercely defended. The decisive battle that would destroy the Confederate army would be fought in front of the city, and the war would quickly be over. Such a plan had much to offer as long as the purpose was to draw the Rebel army into decisive battle. However, as time wore on, Richmond itself became the objective.

The basic idea of a decisive battle fought for the Rebel capital had considerable merit when considered in light of Union political objectives. Lincoln's desire that the war be short and decisive was wholly appropriate and a campaign toward Richmond offered the opportunity for a quick and decisive victory. Execution of the plan rather than the plan itself was the problem. In this respect, some of the blame must be laid at Lincoln's feet for forcing the action before the Union Army was fully prepared. The most serious deficiency was in senior leadership. The Army suffered defeat after defeat as George McClellan, Gen John Pope, Ambrose Burnside, and Gen Joseph Hooker successively tried to lead the blue-clad troops to Richmond. Had Lincoln taken the time to ensure that the Army was well trained and well officered, the traumatic defeats at Manassas, Fredericksburg, and Chancellorsville, to name but a few, might have been avoided. The instant action Lincoln desired would have been delayed by some months, but in the long run the course of the war might have been significantly shortened.

The Confederate objective was also simple and straightforward—to defend itself from "foreign" invasion and thus protect the sovereignty of the Rebel states. Such objectives clearly dictated a defensive strategy making it possible for the Confederates to fight, in Clausewitzian terms, the strongest form of war. Despite the military advantages peculiar to a defensive strategy and the moral advantage of fighting to defend hearth and home, the Confederacy was in a disadvantageous position.

Economically the Rebel states were the poor cousins of the Union, particularly in terms of those heavy industries important to a war effort. Northern factories produced over 90 percent of the nation's firearms and railroad equipment. Perhaps most important, the North had a comprehensive rail system, while the South had a series of independent railroads built primarily to get plantation products to port cities. Only one trunk rail line connected the far-flung eastern and western Rebel states.

Manpower and political organization were also areas of Rebel weakness. Many figures have been used to estimate Northern and Southern manpower ratios. Some authorities count the slave population and others do not. Still others treat slaves as less than a full person available for combat, but count them an advantage because of the work they accomplished on the home front. All things considered, the best estimate of relative combat potential seems about five to two. Added to the South's manpower problem was its fragmented command of available manpower. The Confederacy was built on the concept of states' rights. The Rebel government never achieved the required centralized control over Confederate assets and never achieved an effective centralized command structure for its military forces.

The Confederate problem was to defend a vast territory despite the disadvantages of an inferior economic base and lesser manpower. One solution to the dilemma was to obtain foreign allies much in the manner of the rebels during the American Revolution. Cotton, needed by the factories in Europe, offered an economic bargaining chip. However, Europeans would not back a sure loser on the battlefield. Thus it was incumbent upon Southern armies to demonstrate their viability.

Robert E. Lee, first as the military adviser to Confederate President Jefferson Davis and later as commander of the Army of Northern Virginia, settled upon an offensive-defensive strategy. Although strategically on the defensive, the Rebel armies would often be tactically on the offensive. By taking the offensive, Lee hoped to dictate the time and place of battle. With tactical victories, particularly successful forays into Union territory, he hoped he could set the stage for intervention by sympathetic foreign governments.

As a result, after fending off Union attacks toward Richmond, Lee invaded the Union, first Maryland and later Pennsylvania. Both expeditions ended in disastrous losses for both sides, but losses that the Confederacy could afford less considering its manpower disadvantage. Meanwhile, in the West, the Union captured the length of the Mississippi River and began a methodical campaign to seize Chattanooga and Atlanta.

Lee has also been criticized for a Richmond or Virginia fixation. Lee was a Virginian who resigned from a senior post in the US Army to offer his services to his state, not to the Confederacy. It must be said in Lee's defense, however, that the abandonment of the Confederate capital without a spirited defense would have been looked upon unfavorably by possible foreign allies and certainly would have demoralized the home front. Virginia was the most important and prosperous of the Confederate states, and had it not been defended, its return to the Union would have been a political and military disaster of the first magnitude.

Lee's offensive-defensive strategy led to terrible and irreplaceable losses during his forays into the North. Thus the battlefield execution of these plans left much to be desired, but the basic strategy was probably correct considering the circumstances. Lee had to make some attempt to control the pace and place of the action or risk being overwhelmed and outmaneuvered by vastly superior resources.

**Political Considerations**

The line between purely military and purely political considerations was vague and shifting. The result was inevitably some level of tension between political and military leadership on both sides and a certain amount of what one might call the "low politics" of war (marked by petty bickering, political posturing, and the like). The Union side probably had the more severe problem, partly because President Lincoln was not himself a military man and did not fully comprehend the military mind (a problem so severe that he had to appoint Gen Henry Wager Halleck as his chief of staff to translate messages to and from his field commanders).

At the same time, President Lincoln had extraordinary difficulty finding military leadership willing or able to carry out the types of operations that would achieve the political objective, especially in the Virginia theater. The Union record was abysmal until Grant was transferred from the West (where, with little publicity, he had been doing quite well). Tactically, Grant made his share of mistakes; but he understood the strategic objective of the war and with the considerable assistance of William T. Sherman and Philip H. Sheridan, he was able to translate the political objective into a successful military objective where others had failed.

In the Southern case, President Davis had graduated from West Point, seen service in the Mexican War, and been secretary of war in the James Buchanan administration. As a result, he considered himself well qualified to direct the military effort and did so personally. He acted as commander of all Confederate forces until the war's waning months when that title was given to Lee.

Despite these kinds of political diversion, the war was fought with more important political considerations in mind. Domestically, a major concern throughout the war was influencing public opinion in the North. Since the war was not particularly popular and there was a sizable peace movement in the North, a prime Southern purpose in following a strategy of attrition was to drag out the war to the point that Northern cost-tolerance, always a fragile commodity, would be exceeded and the Union would simply quit the contest (a strategy closely paralleling that of Washington during the Revolution and subsequently used against the United States by North Vietnam). In other words, the South did not need to win the war to achieve its independence; rather, it needed to avoid losing only long enough for Northern public opinion to turn decisively against the war. Had it not been for the succession of Southern military reverses beginning at Gettysburg and Vicksburg and culminating with the fall of Atlanta, the strategy might well have succeeded.

Even if the political objective had not suggested a war of attrition aimed at undermining the Union's willingness to persevere, the South's physical circumstances made such an approach the most reasonable way to fight. Fighting on the defensive meant the North, which had to attack and destroy the Confederate armies to win, would be fighting away from home in hostile, unfamiliar territory, which was bound to create military and morale problems. At the same time, fighting on both the strategic and tactical defensive was likely to eventuate in low casualties for the manpower-poor South, especially given the emphasis on frontal assaults at the tactical level.

There were, of course, variant opinions about how to achieve the political objective, most notably Lee's concept of the offensive-defensive. Beyond its sheerly military aspects as already described, this strategy sought to have a political impact as well, attacking Northern morale by demonstrating Northern vulnerability to attack. The purpose of invading the North was, of course, not conquest, an objective clearly beyond the Confederacy's political aim as well as its military ability. Rather, part of the purpose was demonstration: in the 1862 invasion of Maryland to show foreign governments the Confederacy was a military force worthy of recognition; in the 1863 Pennsylvania campaign to put a major federal city (Philadelphia, Baltimore, or even Washington) in danger and hence to stir antiwar sentiment.

If the South's purpose was to exceed Union cost-tolerance, Lincoln's problem was how to avoid that fate. As suggested already, he was hampered early in the contest by the absence of a compelling political objective around which to unite his population and the inability to identify competent commanders. The ideal solution would have been a quick and decisive victory that would nominally test popular will, and it was this hope that gave rise to cries of "On to Richmond." Once thwarted, Lincoln's major need was for victories that would show progress toward the desired end, but for the first two years of combat, the only successes were in the Western theater, whereas the Army of the Potomac faced a seemingly invincible force in Lee's Army of Northern Virginia.

The differing levels of support for the war in the North and South and the delicacy of Lincoln's problem in maintaining public willingness to continue are well illustrated by the two sides' approach to conscription. In the South where the war was very popular, a universal conscription system was quickly adopted and effectively enforced, with the result that approximately 80 percent of eligible males either volunteered or were drafted into the service. By contrast the Lincoln government was reluctant to institute any kind of draft early in the war for fear of antiwar backlash. Instead it relied on appeals to governors to raise volunteer militia units to meet manpower needs. This system had serious military disadvantages. Usually the units were organized by local politicians who had no military experience, but who were elected as commanders. At the same time, since these troops arrived as units, they could not be integrated into existing veteran units, meaning the Union was constantly fighting with inexperienced units and veteran units were perpetually undermanned. When a conscription system was finally introduced, political necessity (the draft's unpopularity) required that it be easy to avoid. Thus the system featured multiple sources of exemption, and a draftee could meet his commitment by hiring someone to take his place. Only about 6 percent of Union forces in the war were conscripts, yet even this limited form of draft resulted in numerous riots.

International politics was also a concern. Recognition of the Confederacy by the European powers would create legitimacy for the Confederate government as the representative of a sovereign nation-state, meaning that, in international legal terms, reunion could only be achieved by aggression across an international border. The US government's legal justification for the war rested on refusal to recognize the right to secede, meaning that its military action was legally no more than restoration of order within territory still part of the nation. Recognition of the South by third parties would have brought that rationalization into question and strengthened the case for the Northern peace movement.

Materially, the Confederacy needed recognition to ensure continuing trading relations with Britain and France, the traditional consumers of Southern cotton. Both countries were major processors of cotton, but more important, they were potential suppliers of armaments Southern industry could not produce in adequate supply. Recognizing this weakness of the Southern economy, the Union blockaded Southern ports, both to deny the Confederacy access to outside supply and to ensure that European ships would be subject to seizure in the event they tried to trade with the South.

There were, at the outset, some temptations for the British and French to offer recognition. Both countries were heavily dependent on Southern cotton for their textile industries and the plantation system provided a good market for European goods, especially luxury items. Freedom from protective tariffs erected for the benefit of Northern industry and from having to ship cotton to market on American ships would mean lower cotton prices. Thus trade could be expected to expand. Moreover, there was growing recognition that an expanding United States would become a power to be reckoned with sometime in the future. Fragmenting that developing giant into two smaller and weaker states had its own independent appeal.

The Confederate leadership tried to push the British and French governments to grant recognition, and a lively competition between Union and Confederate diplomats in European capitals ensued. The Southern strategy for forcing positive decisions revolved around using "King Cotton" as a weapon, but the strategy proved disastrous. To create pressure in London and Paris, the Confederacy decided to withhold the 1861 cotton crop from the market, letting it pile up on Southern wharves until diplomatic recognition occurred. Although getting that crop past the Union "paper blockade" would have been relatively easy in 1861 (thus gaining needed foreign capital to buy weapons), by 1862 the blockade was real and cotton's commercial potential was greatly reduced. In effect the South squandered a year's crop and the profits it could have brought. As the blockade tightened, Britain turned to and nurtured cotton production in its colonies (especially Egypt and India) so that by war's end, dependency on Southern cotton had largely evaporated. At the same time, the Union expanded its Midwestern grain trade with Europe. King Corn replaced King Cotton.

The Confederacy also had to establish its political viability before European nations would recognize the young government. To do so required demonstrating the ability to resist reunion, which translated into appearing to be a military winner. It is generally conceded that demonstrating that capacity was a major reason that Lee decided to extend his unsuccessful 1862 campaign into the North. If Confederate armies could successfully forge their way into Union territory, it was reasoned, their prowess would be established and European qualms would be overcome. When McClellan stopped the Confederate advance at Antietam and forced the Army of Northern Virginia to retreat back across the Potomac, that hope began to fade, as did the chances of European recognition of the Confederacy. Lincoln's declaration of the Emancipation Proclamation provided the final coffin nails for those hopes.

## Military Technology and Technique

Although often called the first modern war because of the nature of the implements used, in truth the war served as bloody transition from the limited wars of the eighteenth century to the mechanized wars of the twentieth century. The contrasts between the old and the new were particularly stark. Steam power, particularly the railroads, was one of the ingredients critical to victory, but reliance on muscle power remained pervasive. Impersonal and unseen military staff work was critically important to the successful operation of mass armies and yet so were the personal leadership and bravery of frontline commanders. The "indirect approach" exemplified by deft maneuvering of troops was common and yet so were old-fashioned and bloody frontal assaults. The Civil War was warfare in transition.

The most influential technological development was the railroad. Railroads made possible the vast expansion in the scope of war. Unlike the individual small battlefields of the past, the Civil War featured separate and far-flung theaters of war, each populated by mass armies transported and supplied by rail. The addition of the telegraph meant that not only could mass armies fight across vast areas, but they could also be centrally controlled in a common coordinated effort. Railroads offered considerable advantages in mobility and speed, but with these advantages came considerable "baggage." Because of their importance to both sides, strategy began to revolve around rail lines. Armies in the field became tied to rail lifelines and thus had to protect those lifelines at all costs. Often, offensive maneuvers were aimed at seizing or cutting vital enemy rail links while defensive maneuvers were often aimed at protecting those same lifelines. Thus such relatively insignificant (at the time) settlements as Chattanooga, Atlanta, and Petersburg became vitally important because they were major railroad junctions. Although railroads may have been the most important technological advance, the industrial revolution did not overlook improvements in the tools of war themselves.

The standard infantry weapon remained the single-shot, muzzleloaded weapon. However, the Civil War weapon had a rifled barrel giving it much greater accuracy over a much longer range than smoothbore weapons used previously. The most common rifle had a .58-caliber bore and was fired using a percussion cap. Although it had a 1,500-yard range, it was most effective and quite accurate at 500 yards, a tenfold increase over Revolutionary War smoothbore weapons.

Both breech- and magazine-loaded weapons had come into use before the Civil War. The Sharps and early Winchester rifles and the Hall and Spencer carbines were all in private use. They were also used to a limited extent by the contending Blue and Gray armies. However, neither government chose to make them a standard weapon because of the extensive retooling time and expense required to convert government production facilities.

The standard artillery pieces of the Civil War were the 6-pounder bronze gun and the 12-pounder howitzer. Although really effective only at close range (less than half a mile), these smoothbore guns remained effective anti-infantry weapons using grapeshot. Rifled artillery pieces were also used but in far fewer numbers. Although they were much more accurate at longer ranges, they could not be sighted accurately against distant targets. More important, the rifled shell had a relatively small explosive charge, an important factor when the enemy is well dug in.

The Civil War saw numerous other advances in the technology of war. The first rapid-fire weapons (based on Richard Jordan Gatling's concept of revolving barrels) saw limited service during this conflict, as did a primitive submarine. Neither had a significant impact upon the war's prosecution or outcome.

However, the use of armored ships not only had considerable impact but also foreshadowed the all-steel fleets that would become standard by the end of the century. Armor more than proved its worth in combat and made unprotected wooden-hulled vessels obsolete for close combat. The design of the Northern ironclad "monitors" with their revolving gun turrets was the first attempt at a design that, in modified form, would become standard in the age of the great battleships.

The use of rifled infantry weapons with their highly accurate fire at long range meant that the linear infantry tactics of the eighteenth century and the Napoleonic era would have to change. Infantry was now under constant and accurate fire while still hundreds of yards distant from the intended goal. The close-order formations of the previous age were suicidal and quickly disappeared. Officers still attempted to align the looser formations to a certain degree in both offensive and defensive modes. On the offensive, a reasonably straight wave of attackers would increase the shock effect when the attackers struck the defender's lines and allow the defender little opportunity to reinforce points of breakthrough. On the defensive, aligned troops could increase the effectiveness of volley fire.

Infantry, whether attacking or defending, went to ground to avoid the accurate long-range fire of opponents. On the defensive, breastworks became the order of the day. On the offensive, "attack by rushes" eventually became a common practice. Infantry would charge forward and then fall to the ground after a short rush. They would regain their feet for another short rush and then again seek cover. The objective was, of course, to reduce exposure to hostile fire.

In the Civil War firepower dominated the battlefield. Casualty rates increased dramatically, with instances of 80 percent casualties in a given unit during a single engagement. Today such a casualty rate would be shocking. The impact during the Civil War was even greater considering the primitive medical treatment available. A serious wound in the trunk of the body was likely to be fatal. Serious wounds in the limbs usually resulted in amputation. To make matters worse, the causes of infection had not been discovered. Surgeons typically did not clean their instruments before or between operations, and the result was added suffering and death. The army of survivors maimed by the surgeon's knife represented an embittering postwar legacy that hindered the process of reunification.

All of these factors led to the inescapable conclusion that "modern war," as practiced during this period, depended upon a strong economic base. Mass armies required massive amounts of weapons, munitions, and other supplies. (Munitions were required in previously undreamed of quantities because of the size of armies and because longer-range weapons were fired more often both on the offensive and on the defensive.) Such massive amounts of weapons and munitions could not be provided by cottage industry. Moreover, the armor of ships and the heavy equipment required to operate railroads could be provided only by an industrialized economy.

Because of these factors, the Confederacy was in an almost untenable position. The South had almost no heavy industry (the exception being the Tredegar Iron Works in Richmond), and it did not have a first-class rail system. The South trailed even in such mundane requirements as the production of uniforms. Although blessed with an abundance of the raw material (cotton), Southern uniforms were handmade. In the North, the Howe sewing machine and the McKay shoe-stitcher manufactured uniforms in great quantity.

## Military Conduct

Tradition has it that one Edmund Ruffin, a Confederate firebrand from Virginia, fired the first shell at Fort Sumter in Charleston Harbor and thus the first shot in the Civil War. The time was 4:30 A.M. on Friday, 12 April 1861. Federal authority was physically challenged, and shot and shell were used against Union soldiers; there was no turning back. The Confederate commissioners sent to Washington by Jefferson Davis to negotiate a settlement short of war had been rebuffed, and they departed from the Union capital on the day before the guns fired upon the beleaguered fortress in Charleston Harbor.

Lincoln moved rapidly to prepare the Union for war. On 15 April he declared that an insurrection existed and called out 75,000 militiamen from the various Northern states. On the 19th he declared a naval blockade of the Confederacy. In May, Winfield Scott proposed his Anaconda Plan, and federal troops began massing in the Washington area. By July an impatient Lincoln was more than ready for his army to move south. "On to Richmond," was the cry. The Confederate legislature was due to meet in Richmond on 20 July, and Union patriots wanted to overrun the new Rebel capital before the meeting took place.

General McDowell and his Union Army departed their base on the Potomac on 16 July and proceeded toward Manassas, Virginia, to face the first obstacle on the road to Richmond, Gen P. G. T. Beauregard and his Rebel army. McDowell outnumbered Beauregard 35,000 to 20,000, but west of Manassas in the Shenandoah Valley, Gen Joseph E. Johnston had 12,000 Confederates ready. Leaving a small covering force to demonstrate and deceive the local Union commander, Johnston's forces boarded trains on the Manassas Gap Railroad and arrived at Manassas in time to tip the scales in favor of the Confederates. Among those who came with Johnston was one Thomas J. Jackson, who during this battle earned the nickname "Stonewall" for his fortitude under heavy fire as he rallied retreating Confederate units.

The battle was fought on 12 July 1861. Initially, McDowell's forces were successful and the Rebel forces fell back (it was Jackson's famous action of standing fast "like a stone wall" that helped to stop the retreat). Regrouping, Beauregard and Johnston counterattacked, and the Union forces began to fall back. Green Union troops turned an orderly retreat into a disorganized rout as they fled toward Washington amid bag, baggage, and the many spectators from the capital who had come to see the expected great victory. Had the Southern forces been able to mount an organized pursuit, it is entirely possible they could have swept into the Union capital.

McDowell's rout highlighted the need for training, discipline, and better leadership. First Manassas (there would be another battle in this same area) also indicated how costly the war would be. In this brief battle, the combined casualties numbered nearly 5,000 and both sides ended where they started. McDowell's forces licked their wounds (physical and mental) on the Potomac while the victorious Rebels remained in northern Virginia.

Few major battles were fought in the Eastern theater until the spring of 1862, as Lincoln and his generals argued over what course of action they should follow. In February 1862, however, the focus of the struggle shifted to the Western theater. There, Union Brig Gen Ulysses S. Grant moved boldly to seize Confederate Forts Henry and Donelson on the Cumberland and Tennessee rivers and thus began clearing the upper reaches of the Mississippi River and its tributaries. Grant's victories were the opening salvos in the campaign that would seal the Confederacy's doom.

Grant moved south from Fort Donelson as part of a three-pronged Union offensive. Grant moved down the Tennessee River toward the northern borders of Mississippi and Alabama, and Brig Gen Don Carlos Buell and his Army of the Ohio moved south from Kentucky to Nashville (vacated by Confederate Gen Albert Sidney Johnston after the fall of Fort Donelson). Buell was to continue his southwestward movement and join forces with Grant at Pittsburg Landing on the Tennessee River. Meanwhile Gen John Pope proceeded down the Mississippi River from Cairo, Illinois, clearing the river of Rebels as far south as Memphis by June.

Confederate General Johnston faced a serious situation. Rebel forces were scattered throughout the western portion of the Confederacy and the Union forces were concentrated in a well-coordinated offensive that threatened to divide the Confederacy from north to south. Johnston's first move was thus to begin concentrating his forces, bringing General Beauregard, erstwhile hero at First Manassas, from Mississippi and Gen Braxton Bragg from Alabama. Johnston concentrated about 40,000 men at Corinth, Mississippi, just south of the gathering Union formations encamped at Pittsburg Landing and around nearby Shiloh Church.

Johnston attacked early on the morning of 6 April and surprised Grant's ill-prepared forces. Only Grant's personal efforts on the battlefield finally established a defensive position that held the Rebels as the day drew to a close. The next morning Grant counterattacked. After hard and bloody fighting, the Rebels were forced from the field in a disorganized retreat. Shiloh was a terrible defeat for the Southerners, who suffered 11,000 casualties, including Gen A.S. Johnston, but Grant's victory was none too sweet. He had nearly been badly defeated, and had lost about 14,000 men.

For the Confederates in the West, the situation now approached desperation. In addition to the defeats in Kentucky, Mississippi, and Tennessee, Adm David Farragut forced his way up the Mississippi River in April. In May he sailed upriver and occupied both New Orleans and Baton Rouge. The Union admiral also had the audacity to sail farther up the river and bombard

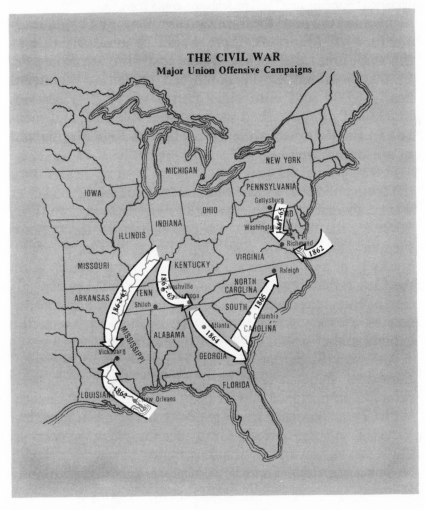

THE CIVIL WAR
Major Union Offensive Campaigns

Vicksburg, the last major Rebel river stronghold. But Vicksburg was not New Orleans (which fell without a shot). Vicksburg would require all the talent and power that Grant could muster.

While the situation in the West became ominous for the Rebels during the first six months of 1862, events in the Eastern theater were totally different. As the idle armies sat facing each other after First Manassas, George B. McClellan, the new Union commander, devised a bold plan to outflank the Rebel forces of Joseph E. Johnston that blocked the route from Washington to Richmond. McClellan planned to sail down the Potomac to Chesapeake Bay and land at Fort Monroe on the Virginia coast. From there he would quickly march up the peninsula between the York and James Rivers and take Richmond "from the rear" before Johnston could react.

Thanks to Confederate sympathizers in the Washington area, Johnston was soon aware of McClellan's plan. While McClellan waited until 17 March to move, Johnston withdrew his army from Centreville and marched toward the same area. Thus the real purpose of McClellan's giant flanking maneuver—surprise—was lost.

By early April, McClellan had landed 50,000 troops at Fort Monroe and had begun to move up the peninsula. A skillful defense by Confederate Maj Gen John B. Magruder delayed the advance and Union forces did not come into position near Richmond until 24 May, having advanced at an average rate of only two miles per day.

Johnston was outnumbered almost two to one (although faulty Union intelligence convinced McClellan that Union forces were badly outnumbered) and preparations were under way to remove the government from Richmond. Near Centreville were General McDowell and 40,000 more Union troops, who sat guarding the route to Washington. These forces were to move overland and join McClellan to add the final crushing weight to Union forces. Johnston and General Lee, then military adviser to Confederate President Davis, realized a successful Union linkage would seal the fate of Richmond. To prevent this situation they planned a large-scale diversionary action in the Shenandoah Valley by the brilliant and reclusive Gen Stonewall Jackson.

The Shenandoah Valley was a natural invasion route from western Virginia into Maryland that threatened both Washington and Baltimore. For defensive purposes, the Union had stationed Gen Nathaniel Prentiss Banks with 23,000 men near the head of the valley. Jackson's mission was to prevent any of Banks's troops from joining McDowell and to prevent McDowell from joining McClellan at Richmond. Jackson began his campaign in the valley with fewer than 4,000 effectives.

Jackson's campaign was one of brilliant rapid maneuver, in which he isolated elements of the superior Union forces in the valley and defeated them.

At one point, Jackson had totally routed Banks and chased the Union forces from the valley and across the Potomac in complete disarray. Lincoln, fearing for the safety of the capital, ordered Gen John C. Fremont into the valley from the west and McDowell into the valley from the east (and away from Richmond) in an effort to trap Jackson. Jackson escaped the trap and defeated the forces of Fremont and McDowell in separate battles.

Jackson was entirely successful in preventing McDowell from joining McClellan. After his final battle in the valley, Jackson added insult to Union injury by slipping away undetected and joining Confederate forces in front of Richmond. Lee was now in command of the forces around Richmond, and he massed his army to attack an isolated portion of McClellan's army on the north side of the Chickahominy River. Although the attack was badly handled, the Union forces were defeated and began a skillful withdrawal. Finally, McClellan yielded to fears that he was badly outnumbered and ordered a general withdrawal to Harrison's Landing, a base of operations on the peninsula. Desperately trying to turn the retreat into a rout and a decisive Rebel victory, Lee attacked the retreating Union Army again and again in a series of engagements known as the Seven Days' Battle. But the Union troops would not be routed and Lee's cherished decisive victory escaped his grasp.

Thus by July 1862, the status of the contending armies depended upon the theater considered. In the West the Confederate situation was rapidly deteriorating. Only Vicksburg remained as a major bastion on the Mississippi River, and the vital rail junction at Chattanooga would soon be threatened. Major action for the remainder of the year would continue in the Eastern theater, where the South had been more successful.

In mid-July, while McClellan and his army huddled in Harrison's Landing, Jackson was sent north toward Gordonsville to deal with the reorganized forces that had earlier opposed him in the Shenandoah Valley. The Union commander, Maj Gen John Pope, had collected 47,000 troops. This formidable force posed a serious threat to Lee's flank, particularly when combined with McClellan's force of 90,000 at Harrison's Landing.

On 6 August Jackson attacked Pope at Cedar Mountain but achieved only a tactical draw. Later, however, Jackson withdrew and moved his forces around the Bull Run Mountains to a position near Manassas, behind and directly across Pope's communication and supply line. Pope reversed course, advanced on Manassas, and on 29 August attacked Jackson. The result was another disaster for Union forces and Pope withdrew into Washington. Second Manassas was a defeat every bit as bitter as the first battle on that bloody ground. In general the Union cause in the Eastern theater was in shambles.

Lee now seized the opportunity provided by federal disarray and took the offensive. On 7 September Lee and his army crossed the Potomac River near

Leesburg and plunged into Maryland. Although strategically on the defensive, Lee had several objectives for this tactical offensive. First, he still sought a decisive Napoleonic-style victory over the Union Army that might spell permanent success for the Rebel cause. Second, the Confederates desperately needed to get both sides' armies out of northern Virginia because they had stripped the area of food and forage. Third, an invasion of Union territory might cause Maryland to secede (Maryland's status had always been questionable) and might also impress the British and French governments enough to bring recognition and badly needed help to the Confederacy.

After considerable maneuvering, Lee and McClellan (who was still in command of the Army of the Potomac in spite of losing Lincoln's confidence) met near Sharpsburg on Antietam Creek. McClellan had an opportunity to inflict a decisive defeat on Lee because he had come into possession of Lee's campaign plans, but squandered the opportunity by delaying the movement of his forces. As Lincoln would later comment, McClellan was afflicted by "the slows." Finally, on 17 September McClellan attacked. Although McClellan outnumbered his Confederate foe nearly two to one, the battle was a draw. However, in the face of a continuing influx of Union reinforcements, Lee began withdrawing to Virginia on 18 September. Antietam was the bloodiest *single* day of the war, with more than 22,000 casualties.

Lee's foray into the North had disastrous consequences for the Confederate cause. He did not transfer the fighting out of northern Virginia for long, he did not win his decisive victory, he suffered a large number of casualties, Maryland did not secede, and foreign recognition was now little more than a forlorn hope. On a personal level, however, Lee's reputation as a commander was enhanced as was the reputation of the Rebel army. Lee and his army had carried the war to the enemy and had beaten back a Union army nearly twice the size of the Confederate force.

McClellan, with a typical lack of aggressiveness, failed to follow up on his "victory" as Lee slipped back into Virginia. In fact McClellan did little but rest and resupply his army. Lee made use of the respite to do the same. Finally, on 7 November Lincoln had had enough of inaction and relieved McClellan of command in favor of one of McClellan's lieutenants, Ambrose Burnside. Burnside presented, and Lincoln approved, a complex plan to move on Fredericksburg, Virginia, and to use this important road and rail junction as a base of operations against Richmond. The plan required an assault across the Rappahannock River to seize both Fredericksburg and Marye's Heights just beyond the town.

By the time Burnside had finally forced a crossing on 12 December, Lee was well entrenched on Marye's Heights. On 13 December Burnside ordered a disastrous frontal assault on the heights. At the base of the heights, the Union troops had to attack a sunken road bordered by a stout stone wall. As the Union troops advanced, long-range rifle fire from behind the wall and artillery fire from the heights shattered their ranks. The fire was so withering that no Union soldier ever got to within 25 yards of the wall. It was not for want of effort. Union soldiers surged forward toward the wall 14 times, and the field in front of the wall became a killing ground littered with 6,000 blue-clad casualties. The battle in front of the stone wall at Marye's Heights was, perhaps, the worst example of outmoded eighteenth-century tactics applied in a more deadly era.

On the following day a truce was arranged to tend the wounded and bury the dead. That night Burnside withdrew his entire army back across the Rappahannock River. The war in the Eastern theater was over for 1862. It ended as it began, with Union blundering, Union defeat, and Union retreat. In the West, however, the Union continued to fare well in the last half of 1862.

Following his narrow victory at Shiloh, Grant proceeded west to begin his campaign against Vicksburg. Meanwhile Buell advanced east toward Chattanooga. The defeated Confederate forces under Gen Braxton Bragg regrouped and, by a circuitous route, marched north through Chattanooga, across Tennessee, and into Kentucky. Buell was obliged to follow and finally forced a fight at Perryville, Kentucky. The result was a draw, but Bragg withdrew south to Chattanooga. Buell retraced his steps back to Nashville, where he was relieved by Gen W. S. Rosecrans. Bragg and Rosecrans met at Murfreesboro, Tennessee, in a savage battle in which Bragg was forced to retreat south to Tullahoma, Tennessee. Both armies, exhausted after lengthy marching and savage fighting, spent the next six months resting and refitting.

As 1863 opened in the Eastern theater, Lee's army remained in winter quarters on Marye's Heights and Lincoln had relieved Burnside in favor of Gen Joseph "Fighting Joe" Hooker (whose nickname was more self-designated than earned). Hooker had an audacious plan to defeat Lee decisively. Hooker's plan called for small demonstrations in front of Lee's position at Fredericksburg to "fix" the Confederate army while he moved the bulk of his forces up and across the Rappahannock and Rapidan rivers to descend on Lee's rear. Trapped between this giant "right hook" and the two corps that remained in front, the Army of Northern Virginia would be destroyed. Hooker began his maneuver on 27 April 1863 and by 30 April had consolidated his forces at Chancellorsville, a crossroads in Lee's rear just nine miles from Fredericksburg. And then Hooker stopped!

Hooker's sudden timidity gave Lee a chance to react with a plan even more audacious than Hooker's. First, he divided his forces, leaving only about 10,000 men on Marye's Heights, and moved his remaining 43,000 troops toward Chancellorsville. He split his forces again by sending Jackson and 26,000 men on a flanking march across Hooker's front, while he faced Hooker with only 17,000 men. Jackson was in position by 6:00 P.M. on 2 May and attacked the Union right flank, which quickly broke and retreated toward the center of the Union position. Only darkness and exhaustion halted Jackson's drive from collapsing the entire Union line. That night, while scouting ahead, Jackson was mortally wounded by one of his men, a loss from which the Confederacy never recovered. Jackson was, perhaps, the most talented commander in either army.

The following day Lee continued to attack and Hooker continued to withdraw slowly. Meanwhile Gen John Sedgwick and his two Union corps attacked the thin Confederate forces on Marye's Heights and drove the Rebels back toward Lee's main forces. On 4 May Lee left Maj Gen J. E. B. Stuart (Jackson's successor) with 25,000 men to watch Hooker and turned the bulk of his army against Sedgwick. Hard fighting finally forced Sedgwick back across the Rappahannock, and Hooker joined him on 6 May.

Although shaken by the loss of Jackson, Lee's total confidence in his army led to his second foray into the North. Lee moved westward into the Shenandoah Valley and north across the Potomac, through Maryland and into Pennsylvania. Hooker shadowed this thrust, remaining between Lee and Washington. En route Hooker was relieved by Gen George Gordon Meade.

The two armies met at Gettysburg more by accident than by design on 1 July 1863. Minor skirmishes occurred during the first day as both armies hurried to concentrate their scattered forces. On the second day Lee attacked and a vicious battle raged, but the Union line held in hand-to-hand fighting. On 3 July Lee made his famous assault on the Union positions along Cemetery Ridge. After a lengthy Confederate artillery barrage, 12,000 infantrymen under Gen George Pickett advanced toward the distant federal lines. Pickett's charge collapsed under the weight of Union shot, shell, and bayonet, and the next evening Lee and his battered army withdrew during a driving rainstorm. The Rebels had suffered an estimated 28,000 casualties, which proved nearly impossible to replace. The tide had finally turned in the Eastern theater, and the following day disaster befell the Rebels again.

Vicksburg, Mississippi, was a natural fortress blessed with a commanding view of the great river from high atop sheer bluffs. It remained the last major impediment to opening the Mississippi to Union use and was the final link between the eastern and western portions of the Confederacy. After Grant's victory at Shiloh, Vicksburg had to be the next major objective.

Grant's task was not easy. Assault directly from the river was out of the question because of the high bluffs, and interlaced rivers, bayous, and lakes limited the dry ground upon which armies could maneuver. Finally, scattered throughout Mississippi were 35,000 Confederate troops under the command of Lt Gen John C. Pemberton, who was bent on keeping Vicksburg in Southern hands.

Grant needed to get his troops on solid ground on the Vicksburg side of the river. Attempts to establish a base of operations north of the city had failed. Solid ground was available south and west of the city, but the problem was how to move his army downriver past the guns of the fortress. After several schemes failed, Grant marched his army down the western riverbank through muddy swampland and forced a crossing south of the fortress, aided by Union gunboats and transports that had run past the city.

On 30 April 1863 Union troops began crossing to the eastern shore at Bruinsburg and embarked on one of the most brilliant, daring campaigns of the war. Grant, remembered today as the relentless "butcher" for his later northern Virginia campaigns, wielded a rapier rather than a cleaver at Vicksburg. In the 18 days that followed his crossing, Grant moved his army more than 200 miles, fought five major battles (all of which he won), and bottled up Pemberton's army in Vicksburg. After twice unsuccessfully attempting to force his way into Vicksburg, he lay siege to the city. More than a month passed before the tired and hungry Rebels finally surrendered on 4 July 1863.

Disaster had struck the Confederates in both Pennsylvania and Mississippi. Meanwhile, General Rosecrans began moving his army, idle since the battle at Murfreesboro the previous January, toward Chattanooga. Rosecrans cleverly maneuvered against Bragg and forced his withdrawal from the city without a fight on 7 September. The Confederates reinforced Bragg with Gen James Longstreet's corps, which was transferred rapidly to the area by rail from northern Virginia. After some clumsy maneuvering by both sides, Bragg narrowly defeated Rosecrans at Chickamauga Creek just southeast of Chattanooga and forced the Federals back into the city.

Now it was the Union's turn to rush in reinforcements. After securing an adequate supply line into Chattanooga, Grant assaulted Confederate positions overlooking the city on Lookout Mountain on 24 November and successfully assaulted the main Confederate forces on Missionary Ridge the next day. The broken Rebel army retreated southward into Georgia. The vital gateway into the heart of the deep South was open. In the long run, the fall of Chattanooga with its opening of the deep South was as decisive as Gettysburg or Vicksburg. The tide had turned, and the collapse of the Confederacy was only a matter of time.

Grant's reward was to be named general in chief of all Union armies. In the Eastern theater, he ordered Meade to attack Lee's army continuously, using the overwhelming resources of the Union Army and allowing Lee no time to recuperate. Additionally, he ordered Maj Gen Franz Sigel (and later Gen Sheridan) to attack in the Shenandoah Valley and to destroy Confederate war resources. Meade engaged Lee in a continuous series of bloody battles from early May through the end of June 1864. Beginning near Chancellorsville, both armies sidestepped to the south and east, fighting the major battles of the Wilderness, Spotsylvania Court House, North Anna, and Cold Harbor. Finally, they arrived at Petersburg, another vital rail center that serviced Richmond. Petersburg had been heavily fortified and there the federal campaign bogged down until March 1865.

In the west Grant placed Gen Sherman in command and directed him to destroy the forces of Joseph E. Johnston (who now commanded the forces in northern Georgia that had retreated from Chattanooga) and to destroy Confederate war resources to the maximum extent possible. Sherman set out from Chattanooga toward Atlanta. Johnston fought a skillful delaying campaign hoping to hold off Sherman until the Union presidential elections in the fall of 1864. If a major Union victory could be avoided, growing antiwar sentiment might sweep Lincoln out of office. Jefferson Davis, seeking a victory rather than a skillful retreat, replaced Johnston with Gen John B. Hood in front of Atlanta. Hood attacked Sherman unsuccessfully three times in late July and was forced to withdraw from Atlanta on 2 September. Hood retreated and then set out northward into Tennessee and reached Nashville where his army was destroyed by Gen George Henry Thomas on 15 and 16 December 1864.

On 15 November 1864 Sherman's 62,000 men departed for Savannah. Leaving the railroads in Atlanta in ruins and the city's public buildings and warehouses in flames, the Union Army systematically burned and plundered its way across Georgia on a 60-mile front. On 21 December Sherman entered Savannah and, after resting and replenishing his supplies from Union ships, turned north into the Carolinas. On 17 February he entered Columbia, South Carolina, and then pressed on toward North Carolina. Joseph E. Johnston was restored to command, but he had only ragtag forces and Sherman brushed him aside first at Averysboro and then at Bentonville.

Meanwhile Grant finally broke through Lee's defensive positions at Petersburg on 1 April 1865 at the battle of Five Forks. Lee retreated west and Grant pursued, sending Gen Sheridan's mounted forces to cut the Confederate commander's line of retreat. Within a week, all hope for the Rebel army was lost and Lee surrendered on 9 April 1865 at Appomattox Court House. On 26 April Johnston surrendered his forces near Raleigh, North Carolina. The war was effectively over.

### Better State of the Peace

The fighting ended after nearly four years of bloody conflict that produced more than a million dead and wounded. The hostilities formally ended when

Gen Kirby Smith surrendered Confederate forces west of the Mississippi River on 26 May 1865. The North had won the war on the battlefield and was hence able to impose its political objectives of reunion and emancipation of the slaves.

In the terms we developed earlier, the Union had overcome two of the three aspects of Southern hostile will and ability. Lee surrendered his army because he believed that it no longer had the ability to continue to contest successfully. By the time the Army of Northern Virginia reached Appomattox, a combination of Grant's hammer blows and desertion had reduced Lee's force to a shadow (about 15,000 effectives) of its former size. Lee faced the Army of the Potomac that had more than 100,000 effectives. Given those odds and the physical and material condition of his forces, Lee concluded further resistance could result only in needless, futile carnage. At the entreaties of such leaders as Lee and Davis, the soldiers went home in peace, rather than continuing the fight through guerrilla warfare (the outcome that Lincoln feared most). When the last Rebel army surrendered, Confederate hostile ability ceased.

By the end, Southern hostile will measured by willingness to continue the war (morale) had eroded badly as well. Until the winter of 1864–65 public support had never wavered, but the effects of bringing the war directly to the Southern people were beginning to take their toll. The chief architects were Sherman, Sigel, and Sheridan through their scorched-earth campaigns. Sherman's unopposed march through Georgia and the Carolinas and Sigel's and Sheridan's rampage through the Shenandoah Valley reduced the Confederacy's chief sources of food to ashes. The result was large-scale hunger and starvation in the Confederate armies and civilian population.

In these circumstances desertion became a major Southern problem for the first time in the war (it was a problem for the North throughout the conflict). Many Confederate soldiers, hearing of the plight of family and loved ones, simply laid down their weapons and went home to try to alleviate the suffering. This manpower drain contributed to the depletion of troop strength and the diminished ability to resist.

The question that remained was how or whether the Union would overcome hostile will defined as resistance to the policies (political objectives) the South had opposed. As is usually the case, overcoming hostile ability on the field was a necessary precursor to imposing political will. The US government then needed to bring about compliance with and acceptance of politics that had led to secession in the first place, and that had provided fuel to continued resistance for four bloody years.

The question was fundamental because the issues that led to war were fundamental. At issue, after all, was whether two distinct ways of life (societies) could continue to coexist in America, and the answer that made war inevitable was that they could not. Since the solution of separation into two sovereign nation-states had failed in combat, ultimately the peace could be won only by creating a national societal structure in which the regions would become compatible. That meant the transformation of Southern society from its plantation basis into something that resembled the rest of the country.

The direct political objectives of the war were symptoms of this basic issue. The goal of reunion had been accomplished militarily. Politically (partially through the counsel of Confederate leaders who beseeched their population to accept reunification), it ceased to be an issue shortly after the fighting ended. Emancipation, on the other hand, remained contentious because of its social effects. If, as argued earlier, slave labor was the key to the Southern economy and hence social system, then the destruction of this form of labor was the key to changing the Southern way of life. Military victory made the political emancipation of the slaves a reality. The problem was to gain the acceptance of the white population of the former Confederacy for the new status of blacks. The solution required transformation of the racial attitudes that had justified holding blacks in bondage and adjustment to the consequences of a new economy in which everyone was a wage earner. For the peace truly to be won, the citizens of the South not only had to accept the implications of emancipation, they had to embrace them as right.

For those who would direct the reintegration of a slaveless South into the Union, there were two broad options. One approach was conciliatory, a peace settlement wherein the Southern states would be readmitted into the Union with a minimum of fanfare or conditions, wherein efforts would be made to lessen the ravages of war, and wherein physical coercion would be minimized. This was the solution that Lincoln desired, but an assassin's bullet ended his ability to pursue it five days after Lee surrendered.

The alternative was a punitive peace, and with President Lincoln dead, the forces who felt the South should be punished for its attempted secession prevailed. Led by a group aptly called the Irreconcilables (the Radical Republicans), the Union imposed punitive policies on a prostrate South with little attention to convincing the former Rebels that these policies were proper. The South was not asked to accept reunion or abolition of slavery; instead, these policies were dictated by the Irreconcilables, enforced by an army of occupation, and administered by legions of "carpetbagging" Northern politicians.

How much the punitive peace contributed to a residue of hostile will toward accepting Union political objectives is, of course, conjectural. What is certain is that hostile will, particularly toward the emancipated slaves, remained, and it is at least arguable that some of it is still with us today in the vestiges of racism that continue as part of our social fabric. Certainly "reconstruction" and the harshness by which it was imposed contributed to nurturing hostile will in such visible ways as formation of the Ku Klux Klan under the leadership of the brilliant Confederate cavalry general Nathan Bedford Forrest. The North, itself largely indifferent and even hostile to the freed slaves, did little to ameliorate the conditions of the Negro beyond the formal grant of freedom. White Southerners were punished for their misdeeds, but little was done to rebuild Southern society on the Northern model or to create prosperity in which all could find substance.

Could reconciliation have occurred in another way? Was there an alternative better state of the peace that would have removed hostile will more quickly and with less resistance? Removed as we are by more than a century from the suffering of the war that gave rise to the spirit of vindictiveness, it is easier for us to see that a reconciliatory peace might have healed the national wounds far faster than was the case. Had Lincoln lived, reconstruction might have been different, or if the war had been shorter and less bloody, there might have been less cause for bitterness. For better or worse, the model of a punitive peace was imposed and would be repeated after the next major conflict in which the United States would participate, World War I.

# 4

# World War I

They called it the Great War. For many it was the "war fought to end all wars" and, for the United States, it became a war "to make the world safe for democracy." Battle after battle, campaign after campaign, and year after year passed inconclusively amid unprecedented carnage, suffering, and destruction. It was the largest, bloodiest war in human history to that time. Literally millions were mobilized to fight it, and millions died in the no man's land between the opposing trenches that scarred the Western Front in virtually unbroken lines from the Alps to the North Sea. According to demographers, France would need 66 years merely to recoup the young men who died during the war. The war's bloodiest battle claimed 650,000 lives and when it was over, the lines had scarcely moved. That outcome symbolized the futility of the fighting generally and helped create an enormous cynicism in those ordered to fight and die for no apparent reason or effect.

World War I changed the face of Europe and the face of war. The decline of Europe as the center of Western civilization began during this time and would be completed 20 years later in the second world conflagration. The once dominant countries of Europe bled themselves dry of manpower and treasure and thereby lost the physical wherewithal to control international politics after 1945. Militarily, the Great War carried the logic of total war previewed in the American Civil War forward toward its grisly fulfillment in World War II.

Although the United States was eventually drawn into the awful fray, it was not really an American war. Certainly the issues that gave birth to the war were, at most, peripheral to American concerns. Moreover, the United States entered the fighting at an extremely late date. Our contribution to pushing an exhausted Germany over the brink to defeat, while psychologically important, was minor compared to the effort of the other combatants.

90

Political scientists, historians, and others have struggled ever since to understand how and why this great human tragedy happened, and there are nearly as many explanations as there are explainers. Because our primary concern is with America at war, it is neither necessary nor fruitful to add to the mountainous literature on what ignited "the guns of August." Rather, we will look briefly at some of the common themes that run through that literature to show some of the flavor of the times that made it all possible.

As the vital center of the international system, Europe had been at relative peace with itself for the century following the Napoleonic Wars. Certainly there had been conflicts. Modern Germany and Italy had been forged on the anvil of war, and Russia had been restrained in the Crimea, but these were relatively short and isolated breakdowns in the structure of international peace. The major themes of European politics had instead been internal, adjusting both politically and economically to the impact of the industrial revolution, coping with nationalism, and witnessing the birth of the German Empire and Italy. This process itself was wrenching and consuming of energy and effort. Such foreign adventurism as occurred centered around colonialism, the subjugation of much of Africa and Asia, where colonial territory was relatively abundant and clashes between aspiring colonialists were infrequent and comparatively mild.

This tranquility between states began to break down around the turn of the twentieth century, and one of the major themes underlying the war emerged. This theme was a more contentious struggle for influence. One reason for the growing contentiousness was that the process of colonizing Africa and Asia was largely complete by the 1890s. After northern Africa fell under European control, there was essentially no place left where a European power could gain influence or control without challenging other powers. Closely related to this struggle for influence, the map of Europe was beginning to redraw itself. Two of the major empires of Europe, the Austro-Hungarian and the Ottoman, were disintegrating under the dual weights of atrophy and resurgent nationalism that had their roots earlier in the nineteenth century. As these empires crumbled, the other powers scrambled for influence in the newly emerging states. The competition focused particularly in the volatile Balkan States, and that area provided the spark that started the war when the Archduke Franz Ferdinand and his wife were assassinated by Bosnian Serb extremists at Sarajevo.

A second theme relates to the unwillingness of the major powers to prevent war once its possibility loomed on the horizon. Some Europeans actually relished the prospect, believing that war would be beneficial and that it would re-create a spirit of discipline in a generation that had not known war and that had grown soft and decadent as a result. While this purifying, martial view may not have been dominant, it was present. Despite the sentiment of those people and others, the issues that underlay the road to war were clearly inadequate to justify what followed. Yet no one acted decisively to keep it from occurring. When it began, young men rallied willingly to the banner and marched off to war. An embittered generation of widows and veterans, as well as countless analysts, would later ask why.

A large part of the answer was that no one understood the kind of war it would be. There were two visions of modern war available, and the Europeans chose to believe in the wrong one. One model was the quick, decisive, highly mobile warfare of the Franco-Prussian War. The other was the protracted and bloody American Civil War. For reasons of ethnocentrism that suggested the inherent superiority of the highly disciplined European soldier, they rejected the model of warfare based on Helmuth von Moltke's image of the "two armed mobs chasing one another across the countryside" and instead believed the 1866 and 1870 European models more appropriate. Moreover, Germany and France (the two major Western Front antagonists) believed that each could win quickly. In the process, both overestimated their own capabilities and underestimated those of their adversaries.

As the first troops left Berlin in the summer of 1914, the Kaiser promised them that they would be home amidst glory before the first leaves fell from the trees. Instead, the war quickly stalemated, the trenches were dug, and four years were spent in futile frontal assaults against heavy entrenchment, a tactic long since obsolete but all the generals could think to do. To make such tactics all the more futile, machine guns, barbed wire, and poison gas had been added to the defensive advantage. Had the leaders and people on either side possessed a premonition of these horrors, the war might have been prevented. We will, of course, never know.

A final theme that runs through the web of causation is the mediocrity of the political leadership when the war began. The institutional arrangements by which the European powers had moderated their conflicts through much of the nineteenth century, the so-called Concert of Europe, had fallen into disrepair after the Franco-Prussian War (some would argue earlier than that). Diplomatic relations had become personalized around such leaders as the German Kaiser and the Russian Tsar. As the Serbian crisis eventuated in the mobilizations and countermobilizations that greased the slide toward war, what was needed was the leadership, statecraft, and diplomacy of a Metternich, Talleyrand, Castlereagh, or Bismarck, but none was available. The war happened partly because the leaders could not figure out how to avoid it.

Americans watched these events from the sidelines. Although the United States had evolved after the Civil War into the world's largest industrial power (Germany was second), it seemed to be only peripherally involved in the

European-centered international political system. Separated from Europe by a broad ocean, the issues and problems that led to war did not appear greatly to affect American interests, nor did the Europeans have much of a sense that a totally immobilized United States could make any differences in the quick and decisive war they anticipated. Only when the war had dragged on for some time did Europeans peer across the Atlantic and ponder the contribution Americans might make to breaking the stalemate.

The initial American response to the European war was remarkably similar to our early attitudes toward the wars of the French Revolution and Napoleonic Empire a century before. That response was to declare American neutrality, a posture we maintained officially through the election of 1916 (President Woodrow Wilson campaigned vigorously and won largely on the promise of continued American noninvolvement). Also reflecting our reaction a century earlier, we adopted the policy of trading with both sides. As time went by, our trade with the Western Allies increased while trade with the Central Powers declined, but up until the eve of American entrance, the president was still calling for a negotiated settlement based on "peace without victory."

Formal American entrance into the conflict did not come until April 1917, when the hostilities were well into their third year. Other than the psychological lift it may have given the Allies, the declaration of war at that point had little practical effect on the fighting. As had been the case before, the United States entered the war totally unprepared to fight. We had essentially no standing armed forces, and it would take over a year to recruit and train the American Expeditionary Force that took part in the final push to Allied victory. America raised a 1.75 million-man army, but it was not declared fit for nor did it begin to engage in large-scale combat until the summer of 1918, about six months before the armistice.

## Issues and Events

When the war began in Europe, the initial American response was that it was none of our business. Reflecting well-entrenched attitudes and beliefs, most Americans agreed that we should remain aloof from the intramural European struggle and that sentiment prevailed during the early years of combat. This urge to neutrality in part reflected traditional American preferences that dated back to the formation of the republic. Both George Washington in his Farewell Address and Thomas Jefferson in his First Inaugural had echoed the theme that American interests were best served by remaining separate from and uninvolved in the tainted power politics of the old world. "Friendly relations with all but entangling alliances with none" had been US foreign policy for a century. At the same time, America contained sizable populations of both English and German extraction. It was therefore difficult to ascertain conclusively on which side popular sentiment lay at the outset. Neutrality was a convenient way to skirt the issue, while simultaneously providing the rationale for trading with both sides.

The American attitude was based on a myth (and it can only be described as such) that American destiny can somehow be fulfilled in isolation from the affairs of Europe. This belief was pervasive and did not really disappear until after World War II. Unfortunately, it was a myth based on a historical accident that never had much to sustain it for at least two reasons.

First, the myth was nurtured during an atypical time in European history, a period from the end of the War of 1812 until the First World War. This was a period when there were few major European upheavals. The idea took hold, however, that since the United States had remained above European power politics for nearly 100 years, this was a normal and preferable condition that was also a matter of American choice. Certainly, aloofness made a great deal of sense during the period of state-building that dominated nineteenth-century American history. Such a period lends itself to turning inward and that is what we did. What was missed, however, was that the same processes were occurring in Europe with the same effects. We did not perceive a need for Europe, and the feeling was mutual. However, at each end of the period, the United States became involved in the major European struggles that did occur. The War of 1812 was really only an extension of the Napoleonic Wars, and we eventually became involved in World War I. When the affairs of Europe have affected us and required our participation, we have not been able to avoid the call to arms. The myth could be nurtured only because Europe did not need us for a century.

The second reason was largely economic. As the United States moved to become a major industrial and commercial power during the nineteenth century, our prosperity increasingly required extensive trade with the world. The world's significant markets, of course, were in Europe and access to those markets was vital. As well, the immigrant waves that provided the manpower for industrial expansion came from Europe, and a great deal of the developmental capital that financed industrial growth came from private European banks. Without those sources, our pattern of development would have been quite different, but it has always been a curious aspect of the American worldview that economics and politics can be separated. The two in fact are cut from the same cloth.

The mythology of and desire for political aloofness while retaining commercial ties made neutrality appear attractive. Despite the illusion that the war was none of our concern, there were in fact economic and political issues that would eventually impel the United States into the war.

The economic issue had two essential aspects, one of which was the already mentioned desire to maintain normal commercial patterns with the belligerents. Such a posture was understandable from a sheerly economic viewpoint, but it was untenable politically. The reason, of course, was that both the Central Powers and the Triple Entente wanted trade with them to the exclusion of trade with the other. Although there was some US attempt to be even-handed in the flow of trade early in the war, the pattern gradually shifted to a much closer relationship with the Western Allies, especially Great Britain. Germany eventually found this pattern intolerable, which helped create the proximate events leading to the American declaration of war. In many ways, the situation was a replay of the problems that had drawn the United States into the War of 1812, except that Germany and not Great Britain would be the enemy.

The other side of the economic coin arose from the prospect of a German victory that looked increasingly probable as German troops previously committed to the Eastern Front began to move to France in 1917 after Russia withdrew from the war. America's prosperity required trade with Europe. The security of that trade, in turn, rested on guaranteed access to European markets and safe, reliable means to get American goods to those markets. A German victory threatened to alter both of those conditions.

A German victory over France would, in all likelihood, ensure that continental Europe would be dominated by Imperial Germany. Since Germany was the chief industrial rival to the United States in many important areas of trade, such an outcome offered the reasonable prospect that Germany would exclude or sharply restrict American access to continental markets.

The defeat of Great Britain would also allow German naval domination in the Atlantic Ocean, and thus posed a threat to open and secure access to the sea-lanes between North America and Europe (as well as presenting a possible future menace to the US homeland). Gradually during the nineteenth century, the United States and Great Britain had reached a condominium ensuring the freedom of the high seas for commercial purposes. By the end of the century, the informal arrangement was that Great Britain enforced that policy in the North Atlantic and the United States enforced it in the Caribbean Sea.

The policy was to the clear advantage of both countries. Both were commercial, mercantile states, and Great Britain had the additional requirement for secure access via the oceans to her far-flung colonial empire. The commonality of interest between the United States and Germany, however, was not so obvious; commercial competition could easily spill over into naval competition for control of the trading routes.

There was an underlying political issue that Americans sought to avoid but could not. After the fall of the Tsar in early 1917 (and especially after the

Bolshevik Revolution resulted in the removal of the new Soviet Union from the war), the contest did, after all, pit the world's major democracies, Britain and France, against the world's major autocracies, Imperial Germany, the Austro-Hungarian Empire, and the Ottoman Empire. In the long run, a democratic United States could scarcely avoid greater sympathy for those who shared our political form over those whose political philosophy was diametrically opposed to our own.

Each of these underlying economic and political factors manifested itself in proximate events that made neutrality progressively less tenable. The economic issue came to a head over German attempts to interrupt the lucrative flow of American war materiel to the Western Allies and specifically focused on the question of unrestricted submarine warfare. The political issue gradually emerged in the depiction of the war as a moral crusade between democracy and autocracy.

The issue of German submarine attacks on Allied shipping, especially on ships carrying American passengers (for example, the Lusitania), became the most volatile issue between the United States and Germany. It was an issue, however, not entirely lacking in irony. That irony involves both the restrictions that were supposed to be placed on submarines in war and the reasons the German navy failed to stress the submarine more in her naval competition with Great Britain.

Anticipating the introduction of this new weapon system to naval arsenals at the turn of the century, the participants at the Hague Convention had attempted to devise and include in the rules of war permissible and impermissible uses of the submarine. The provisions that came into force included requirements that virtually ruled out effective employment of the submarine; before attacking any vessel, the submarine had first to surface, announce its intention to attack, and be prepared to take aboard any and all survivors after an attack.

These were, of course, totally unrealistic requirements that, if adhered to, would destroy the usefulness of the submarine as a naval weapon. One advantage the submarine possesses is the element of surprise, which surfacing takes away. When on the surface, submarines are especially vulnerable to attack, since they carry no effective surface armament. Moreover, they are too small to take aboard more than a few survivors after an attack. Thus the only way to use them effectively was in direct violation of the Hague Convention, and that is precisely what the Germans did. When they did so, they were loudly condemned in the United States for barbaric activity in violation of the laws of war. The result for Germany was thus a classic catch-22. They could use submarines legally but ineffectively, or they could use them effectively but illegally. It was clearly a no-win situation. To make the irony deeper, the Germans were prepared to back down to American objections on the eve of our entrance into the war, in effect offering to suspend as a matter of policy (it had already been suspended in fact) unrestricted submarine warfare in return for continued American nonbelligerency.

The irony is made even greater because the U-boat was the most effective weapon (actually about the only one) Germany possessed for the naval competition with the British. Because of the influence of an American naval strategist, however, they entered the war with too few of them for decisive effect.

In 1890 the American strategist Alfred Thayer Mahan had published his seminal *The Influence of Sea Power upon History*, which argued the critical importance of control of the seas in warfare, and the book was widely read in Europe as well as America. A central tenet of Mahan's analysis was the need for a large navy with heavy capital ships as the crucial element in naval control and the consequent deprecation of naval strategies emphasizing what he called "commerce raiders," lone marauding vessels whose purpose was disrupting commercial trade routes through the capture or sinking of individual ships. The submarine, of course, perfectly fit Mahan's definition of a commerce raider, and one of Mahan's most ardent students was Kaiser Wilhelm. As a result, German naval development concentrated on the construction of heavy capital ships (in the extreme, the dreadnoughts). Germany was never able during the course of the war to get its fleet of these large ships out of the North Sea. At the same time, the Germans neglected the construction of submarines, which were able to escape the British blockade and which were quite effective against Allied shipping until the convoy became common practice.

Politically, the road to war was paved by the gradual conversion of American popular opinion away from neutrality and disdain for the entire war to a black-and-white depiction of the valiant democracies fighting desperately against evil autocracies. British propagandists were particularly influential in this effort, whereby the issues were simplified into terms of good and evil, so that, when the declaration of war occurred, the full support of the American people could be rallied behind the Allies and support for the "Huns" was equated with treason. The German submarine campaign, which enraged the American public, and devious actions like the Zimmermann note to Mexico, which proposed that Mexico declare war on the United States, simply added fuel to a growing anti-German fire.

### Political Objective

World War I was, of course, an allied operation and as is usually the case within coalitions, each of the allies had its own distinct political objective and its own vision of the better state of the peace. When the war broke out, it is fair to say that none of the original combatants had particularly clear objectives beyond a generalized belief in the need to honor alliance agreements that committed various states to one another. This lack of clarity was not entirely surprising because none of them had any clear idea what the war would be like.

In some ways similar to the way the colonial side's objectives were formed in the American Revolution, political objectives flowed from the military state of affairs rather than the other way around. The major influences of the battlefield were to produce tremendous frustration, bitterness, and hatred. The result was an increasing impulse toward vindictiveness. Total warfare produced total political objectives. One side or another had to be defeated completely and the loser would be forced to pay. No one had talked this way as the troops were rallied in the summer of 1914, but after futile years in the trenches, revenge became a common desire.

These feelings were held with varying levels of intensity by the individual Allies, depending on the amount of suffering that they had endured. Among the Western Allies, the feeling was definitely strongest in France. Most of the war was fought in France; hence French territory bore the deepest physical scars of war, and French blood had flowed freely.

In this context, French objectives came to dominate Allied political aims. In its simplest form, the objective was to create a structure of the postwar peace wherein the war could not be repeated. Stated as an aim to make the Great War "the war to end all wars," there was substantial agreement among the Allies. There was disagreement, however, about what kind of structure would best ensure a peaceful world in the future. Determining what was necessary to guarantee the peace was partly a matter of determining who was responsible for the war in the first place.

In the French view, Germany bore special and unique guilt for the war and for French suffering. From the French premise, which was debatable (as we shall see in the final section), it followed that the structure of the peace must include a Germany incapable of instigating another war, and that meant a disarmed German state and a pastoral German society. Everyone wanted peace. France wanted peace and revenge. The disagreement over whether both should be objectives would dog the Versailles peace talks at the end of the war.

American wartime political objectives are what most concern us here. The figure of President Woodrow Wilson was of overarching importance in framing American objectives and engineering the process of change from neutrality to belligerency. As a result, one cannot fully understand American objectives without some insight into the character of the American leader.

At least three characteristics of Wilson are relevant in understanding his view of the war. The first is that Wilson was an academic and an intellectual. He had gained early fame within the academic community by writing *Constitutional Government* (a study of political democracies first published in 1885, and one of the most respected works in the field we now call comparative politics). He later served as the president of Princeton University. Wilson's intellectual background predisposed him to democracies, which, the prevailing view in political science argued, were inherently superior systems. Second, Wilson was a deeply religious man and a lay Presbyterian minister. This aspect of his background predisposed him to see matters in moral terms and would assist him in framing the war's objectives in the terms of a moral crusade. Third and finally, Wilson was a Southerner. He had been born and reared in Virginia during Reconstruction and had witnessed the embitterment and suffering that the punitive peace created in a defeated Southern people. As a student of and participant in the aftermath of a particularly bloody, total war, Wilson sought consistently to avoid seeing the same mistakes made in Europe.

American objectives toward the war necessarily changed from the period of neutrality to that of military participation. When the United States was neutral, Wilson's hope was to act as a peacemaker. The operative phrase forming that objective was "peace without victory." This approach flowed naturally from Wilson's boyhood experiences and consequent conviction that a punitive peace settlement imposed by a victor would unnecessarily slow healing of the war's wounds. This theme, although later abandoned by the United States, had great appeal within Germany after American entrance into the war. Those who led the movement that overthrew the Kaiser and then sued for peace cited Wilson's statement as hope for a reasonable negotiated peace.

Fighting a war not to win, as peace without victory implied, was not the kind of cry that would rally the country to the banner, and it had to give way once the United States decided to join the hostilities. Military victory replaced military stalemate as the objective and, in a manner reflecting both Wilson's religiosity and the prevalent American worldview, had to be phrased in appropriately moral, lofty tones. Aided by the efforts of those British propagandists who had painted the issues in black and white, a rallying cry emerged to form the basis for the crusade. American purpose became an effort "to make the world safe for democracy." The moral tone is well captured in Wilson's war declaration to the Congress: "The day has come when America is privileged to spend her blood and her might for the principles that gave her birth and happiness. God helping her, she can do no other." So armed, the United States began to prepare for its entrance into the Great War.

## Military Objectives and Strategy

Each belligerent evolved specific political objectives as the war went on. Each objective required the defeat of enemy armed forces and in some cases their destruction. Events quickly showed, however, that victory would not be quick and clear-cut. Military victory could only be achieved by enemy exhaustion, and thus the war wore on endlessly. In a sense, the war itself became the objective.

No one dreamed the conflict would be so long and senseless. The general consensus at the time it began was that no country could wage a long war because of the incredible costs in blood and treasure. Modern wars, so the experts said, would be short and sharp, their brevity ensured by the perceived dominance of the offense over the defense. The side which could muster and mobilize huge modern armies first and put them on the offensive would have an overwhelming advantage. Attackers would smash into and crush ill-prepared defenders who would be unable to swiftly maneuver their own massive forces. In France, the cult of the offensive reached its zenith in the teachings of Ferdinand Foch at the Ecole Supérieure de Guerre (i.e., French War College). According to Foch, the essence of war was to attack and any improvement in firepower ultimately benefited the attacker. To attack successfully morale was critically important. No battle was lost, Foch reasoned, until the soldiers believed it was lost. With the proper *élan*, the French soldier was irresistible in the attack. And thus was born the rigid French doctrine of *offensive à outrance*—the offensive to the extreme. The birth of the French offensive doctrine brought death to a generation of Frenchmen.

Of the major combatants, the Germans faced the most difficult military problem. Situated in central Europe, Germany faced potential enemies on opposite fronts. In the east, massive Russian armies threatened to overrun East Prussia and crush the Germans. In the west, the French waited to avenge the humiliation of 1870. The only solution was to take advantage of the interior lines afforded by their central position, to mobilize more rapidly and efficiently, to eliminate one or the other of the opponents quickly, and then to concentrate on the remaining enemy.

The original plan to accomplish this complex task was devised years before the war and modified several times. Its original author, Chief of the German General Staff Count Alfred von Schlieffen, assumed that the great masses of the Russian army could not be fully mobilized for at least six weeks after the commencement of hostilities. Thus the Germans must concentrate their forces in the west and knock out France with one quick crushing blow. The blow would be a giant "right hook" of German armies marching through the low countries into France along the English Channel coast. The invasion would wheel inward, envelop Paris, roll up the French armies, and crush them back against the German border. Schlieffen expected the decisive battle to occur east of Paris within the six weeks' "grace" period while Russia mobilized. With the demise of France, the Kaiser's troops could be transferred to the east to dispose of the Russians. It was a bold plan and it was nearly successful.

When the war began, the Germans mobilized quickly in accordance with their elaborate plans and the offensive got under way. It moved through the low countries at a steady pace, pausing only to reduce the fortifications at Liège with giant siege mortars. On into France the Germans marched as the French and British forces fell back, all going according to the master plan. Unexpectedly, however, the German armies on the right flank began wheeling toward the German border before they enveloped the French capital city. Thus the German right flank was exposed to an attack from the garrison of Paris. Additionally, because of a breakdown in communications, a gap developed between two of the wheeling German armies, and this mistake presented an opportunity for the Allies. The result was a successful counterattack and the retreat of the German armies away from Paris.

Both sides dug in. Both quickly began a series of attempts to outflank the enemy's position—the so-called Race to the Sea—that resulted in the extension of defensive positions on both sides. These positions eventually stretched from the English Channel to Switzerland. The seeds of stalemate were sown. There were no longer any flanks to turn and both sides continued to improve their already formidable defensive positions. Thus the trench war that dominated the Western Front began within weeks of the outbreak of hostilities. The next four years saw a series of massive offensives, each yielding thousands of casualties but precious little progress. The war became one of physical attrition, and the loser was determined by exhaustion, not military skill.

Schlieffen's plan was boldly conceived, and its failure can be traced to many causes. First, the younger von Moltke, the chief of staff in 1914 and nephew of the victor of 1866 and 1871, weakened the right hook by shifting some troops to the east to meet a surprisingly rapid Russian thrust into East Prussia. Second, German communication and supply lines on the right flank became extremely long because of the rapid German advance. Third, German soldiers were exhausted by their long march while the Allies fell back on shorter and shorter supply lines. Fourth, the French high command did not collapse under pressure as it had done in 1870, and as the Germans suspected it might in 1914. Finally and most important, the plan assumed victory at every juncture, and that everything would go well and smoothly. There was little room for error or successful enemy counteractions. In other words, the plan was arrogant. It paid scant attention to the capabilities of Allied armies or their commanders.

By 2 April 1917, when the United States entered the war, it seemed that the Germans and their allies might finally win. They controlled a rich portion of northern France, as well as most of Belgium and Holland. At sea, German submarines threatened to starve Britain out of the war. Moreover, revolt was brewing in Russia. If the Russians dropped out of the war, the Germans could shift large formations to the Western Front. The question was whether or not fresh American troops could get to the front in time. The American Army was minuscule, with an authorized strength of only 100,000. Men had to be inducted, trained, equipped, and sent across the Atlantic. Despite the enormity of the task, more than one million American soldiers landed in France by the summer of 1918.

The United States entered the war late and pursued no innovative strategy of its own. Essentially, American troops were fresh blood with which to continue the war in the established manner. American numbers tipped the balance scale toward victory for the Allies as the exhausted Germans could not compensate for the fresh and numerous American soldiers.

The commander of the American Expeditionary Force, Gen John J. "Black Jack" Pershing, found his principal strategic battles to be with other Allied commanders who wished to use American soldiers as piecemeal replacements in their battered formations. Pershing resisted with President Wilson's support. Wilson, however, eventually bowed to Allied pressure and intervened on their behalf. Pershing recognized the authority of the civilian commander in chief and placed American units, rather than individuals, at the disposal of Allied commanders. However, after tactical training in France was complete and the American Army was fully ready to take to the field, Pershing managed to get back the units that had been amalgamated into the Allied armies.

Pershing has been praised as a leader, organizer, and manager. He has been criticized as a less than innovative strategist and technician. The praise is certainly justified as the task of building, equipping, and transporting a massive army overseas in a short period of time was formidable. The criticism also may be justified. Pershing offered little in the way of new strategic thought to the Allies and produced no novel tactical ideas. However, one must remember Pershing's circumstances. The war was four years old and the die was cast in terms of a strategy to exhaust and defeat the enemy. There was little room and no time for new strategic visions. Tactically, it is no wonder that American tactics mimicked those of our European allies. The rigors of trench warfare were new to the Americans (Petersburg being long forgotten) and, upon their arrival in Europe, the American units were often trained for combat by European veterans.

## Political Considerations

World War I was one of America's most popular wars. Public support for American intervention was high when Woodrow Wilson made his war declaration and that support never wavered. Given that neutrality had enjoyed overwhelming support only a year before, this was a remarkable turnaround. Only years after the war would the United States develop some degree of cynicism over having plucked European "chestnuts from the coals." Yet, once the fighting was over, the American urge to withdraw, to return to "normalcy," was overwhelming. It was a curious domestic situation, at least partially the result of factors in the American culture and, more specifically, the ways Americans go to war.

One reason that Americans rallied to arms and then recoiled quickly from their efforts is traceable to the American missionary zeal. The war was advertised as a moral crusade, and, as such, it appealed to that part of our national character that flows from a feeling of America as a special, morally superior place. Our goal was to "save" Europe from itself, and when that end was accomplished, we packed up and returned to the more normal state of affairs. When it became clear in the 1920s that Europe had not been cleansed as we had hoped, we turned inward once again, seeking to isolate ourselves from the vagaries of European power politics, but at the time support for the war was unquestioned.

Another reason for the high level of support was that the American part of the war was so short. As stated earlier, the United States was a formal belligerent for a year and a half, but engagement in combat was limited to the war's final six months. We began the war entirely unprepared to fight (a common theme in American military history) and set about mobilization in what our Allies found an irritatingly languid manner. The legislation to create a means to induct armed forces had passed at President Wilson's request in 1916, but our standing military was no more than a shadow in April 1917, when war was declared. Building the apparatus to induct, equip, and train a force that could be placed responsibly into combat required time. Starting from scratch with mechanisms and personnel inadequate to a task of such proportions further lengthened the process.

The effect was to romanticize the war. It was a time of parades, of soldiers coming home for leave from the training camps (most of which had had to be built for the occasion) in impressive uniforms. There was little mud and no blood and dying. The American Expeditionary Force did not arrive in Europe *en masse* until June 1918, and General Pershing was reluctant to throw it into combat even then. Instead, he maintained that the force required a period of orientation and further preparation for fighting in a new and strange environment.

The leisurely pace of American preparation and commitment created political tensions within the alliance, especially between the Allied military command and the American command. Reflecting the nature of the war and where it was being fought, the Allied general staff was dominated by France, and the supreme commander was Marshal Ferdinand Foch. The Allied command had a very different viewpoint of the American role than did its American counterpart.

From the vantage point of the Allied command, the chief contribution of the Americans should have been to provide fresh manpower to British, French, and other forces badly depleted and exhausted by the long years in the trenches. With France particularly near the brink of physical exhaustion and collapse, fresh bodies were the requirement against Central Power forces that appeared increasingly menacing after the fall of Russia. To that end, the Allies argued long and loud, if with little effect, for the Americans to speed the process of building their army and for getting that army into the field.

Pershing resisted these efforts successfully. He viewed these requests, probably correctly, as no more than an attempt to make cannon fodder of the American forces in the futile fighting, a usage that would have been unpopular at home. Moreover, he, like most observers, was less than overwhelmed with the tactical brilliance that had thus far marked the war effort on both sides. As a result, he insisted that Americans not be integrated into existing units and that, instead, there be created a distinctly American place on the lines. Foch resisted, but Pershing insisted, refusing to commit the Americans at less than the unit level until his end was achieved. Ultimately, the Allies' need for the American troops exceeded their feelings about how they should be used, and the Americans were given their own front for the final offensive.

There were, moreover, important political differences between the leaders of the principal Allied partners that simmered beneath the surface but which would become apparent when it was time to settle accounts in the peace negotiations. The major disagreements were between American President Woodrow Wilson and French Premier Georges Clemenceau. The heart of these disagreements centered on why the war was being fought and what its outcome should be.

As we have said before, the First World War was a total war. However, the war was more total for some than for others. For France and Britain, it was a total effort being fought for national survival, and both countries totally mobilized to fight it. For the United States, national survival was never a problem, and although we raised the largest army in our history to fight it, it was not a war of total mobilization for us. As an example of the contrast, the United States did not develop an armaments industry to support the effort; instead the United States relied largely on arms purchased from the British and the French.

The different levels of desperation with which the war's outcome was viewed translated into discordant views about what would constitute a satisfactory peace. While the fighting continued, these divergences were hidden behind the veil of common effort. When the guns were stilled, the discord came to the fore. The United States was disadvantaged by the combination of a lack of experience at coalition decision making (the only previous war in which we had allies was the American Revolution) and the intensity of French claims based in greater experience, sacrifice, and proximity.

The basis of disagreement was over the question of a punitive or a reconciliatory peace. Reflecting his background as a Southerner and an academic, Wilson wanted a reconciliatory peace that would feature self-determination for all countries (or at least those in Europe). He wanted a postwar world founded around the Fourteen Points, which declared these ideals and featured the League of Nations as its centerpiece to guarantee the peace. The Wilsonian vision was lofty and idealistic; Clemenceau viewed it as naive in the real world of European politics. Rather than seeking reconciliation, Clemenceau sought punishment of Germany and the reduction of the German state to impotency. During the war Clemenceau humored Wilson because he needed American help. When it came time to restructure the world, the gloves came off and the disagreements were laid on the table. The results of those interactions are discussed in the final section of this chapter.

## Military Technology and Technique

World War I has often been characterized as history's most senseless and poorly contested war. Given the objectives of the belligerents, particularly as the war progressed, the unending stalemate on the Western Front, and the incredible casualties caused by endless frontal assaults against enemy lines, it is difficult to argue against this unfavorable judgment. At the same time, however, World War I was a watershed in the evolution of modern warfare because of the technological innovations first demonstrated during the conflict. Two technological developments were of primary importance, either having a direct impact on the conduct of the war itself or foreshadowing the nature of warfare in the future.

The development that had the most immediate impact was the widespread use of rapid-fire weapons. Key to this development was the perfection of smokeless powder that did not obscure the field of fire or foul weapons to the extent previously common. Although rapid-fire weapons were used experimentally in the American Civil War (the Gatling gun, for example), it was not until 1882 that Sir Hiram Maxim designed the first machine gun widely adopted by military forces. By World War I, reliable designs permitted rates of fire from 200 to 400 rounds per minute. The weight of such a machine gun was approximately 100 pounds including its mount, which made it a defensive rather than an offensive weapon. Weapons carried by individuals also improved greatly by World War I. Modern military rifles could fire up to 20 rounds per minute and their effective range was limited primarily by the vision of the soldier.

Field artillery followed the rapid-fire trend of smaller weapons. Without question, the finest field artillery piece in the world in 1914 was the 1897 French model 75 mm. It could fire 6 to 10 rounds per minute with great accuracy. Other excellent field pieces were the US model 1902 field gun and the Austrian 88 mm developed and produced by the Skoda works. In the years leading up to World War I, heavy artillery became much heavier. Large-caliber guns were common, including huge siege mortars. For example, the Germans possessed 420 mm mortars that delivered a one-ton projectile.

The development of rapid-fire weapons and heavy artillery pieces significantly affected the way in which World War I was fought. The most obvious effect was in the number of casualties. The human toll of the war dwarfed all previous experience. The second major effect was to give the advantage to the defense, a phenomenon which thoroughly surprised most military planners. Their failure to cope with superior defense added to the human carnage. Against rapid-fire weapons and heavy artillery, the techniques of previous wars led only to failure and casualties of unprecedented proportions. Finally, rapid-fire weapons used prodigious amounts of munitions. As a result, industrial capacity on the home front became of paramount importance in determining success or failure on the battlefield.

Although the development of rapid-fire weapons had a significant impact on the war itself, a revolution in transportation would portend the nature of wars to come, even if its impact on World War I was less than decisive. The transportation revolution was caused by the invention and application of the internal combustion engine, which led to the development of not only cars and trucks but also tanks, submarines, and heavier-than-air aircraft. These weapons would eventually change the face of warfare.

Although mules and horses continued in common use, all belligerents used trucks extensively during the war to overcome the inherent weaknesses of railroads. Railroads had revolutionized military transportation, but they also brought with them some unwanted baggage. First, they were relatively inflexible, since a great deal of preparation and construction was required to establish a rail line, particularly one that would be used heavily. Second, because they were both important and inflexible, they tended to dominate strategy. During the Civil War, campaigns revolved around rail lines as opponents sought to protect their own and cut those of the enemy. Trucks, on the other hand, provided flexibility. They required no ties and rails. Troops and materials could be hauled rapidly from railheads to far-flung battlefields. Large-scale battles could now be fought wherever there were roads. Railroads did not, however, lose their military importance. In World War I (as well as in later wars) they remained critical to military success because of the quantity of men and materiel they could carry.

The tank was first introduced by the British in 1916. Its purpose was to break through enemy trench lines and clear the way for infantry to advance. Some visionaries thought that tanks could not only break through enemy lines but could also range far to the enemy rear and capture command centers, disrupt communications and supply lines, and spread panic. The World War I vintage tank did, however, have severe limitations. Although impervious to small arms fire, their slow speed, especially when used as infantry support weapons, made them tempting artillery targets. Near the end of the war, Allied planners (the Germans paid scant attention to the use of tanks) began to recognize better uses for tanks. In the last offensive thrusts of the war, the Allies massed tanks for attack rather than using them in small concentrations. In the interwar years, the relationship between tanks and infantry began to reverse, and infantry would be used for the support of armor. With this change of tactics and improved tank design, armored warfare would come of age in World War II.

The internal combustion engine was also important to the development of submarines. An undersea craft that could attack enemy warships and merchantmen had long been a dream of naval designers. The internal combustion engine provided a compact means of surface propulsion and a means to recharge the batteries used for submerged operations. Designs improved rapidly in the years preceding the war, and submarine warfare became an important part of overall German strategy as the Germans sought to starve Britain out of the war by cutting her sea-lanes.

With the development of the airplane, war entered a third dimension. Initially, the airplane was intended only for observation of enemy movements and artillery spotting. By the end of the war aerial photography of enemy trench lines was an indispensable tool of military planners. Of course, such a valuable tool had to be denied to the enemy, and as a result aerial combat began shortly after the war commenced. By the war's end, airplanes were conducting extensive air-to-air combat with sophisticated machine guns that fired directly through the propeller by the use of an ingenious interrupter gear. Airplanes also strafed enemy troops at the front and conducted bombing raids in rear areas. Finally, both sides made tentative attempts at strategic bombing. However, aircraft were not an overly important weapon in the Great War, primarily because aircraft and engine design were still primitive arts.

But aerial visionaries of the war, such as America's William "Billy" Mitchell and Britain's Hugh Trenchard, saw possibilities for a much greater role for the airplane in the future. Between the two world wars they pressed for better designs and for the development of air power doctrine that they believed would make air power a decisive factor in modern warfare.

The development of weapon systems based on the internal combustion engine represented a watershed in the evolution of modern warfare, and yet these weapons had only a limited impact on the techniques of warfare in World War I. Military tactics remained rooted in the past. The tactical problem on the Western Front, once the trench lines were firmly in place, was to achieve a breakthrough in the enemy's linear defenses and then exploit that breakthrough to bring a degree of mobility back to the war. The trench lines for both sides had no tactical flanks, and thus the only attack possible was a frontal assault.

Generals on both sides used several techniques in an attempt to achieve a decisive breakthrough. The most common method was to conduct a massive artillery barrage (some lasted for weeks) calculated to obliterate the enemy trenches. Once a gap was created, the infantry was supposed to pour through and exploit the advantage. Unfortunately, such a tactic sacrificed all surprise. Defending troops simply withdrew to deep dugouts during the barrage, waited for it to end, and emerged ready to fight. In addition, the barrage was often counterproductive for the attackers because it turned the no-man's land between the opposing trenches into a cratered, muddy moonscape through which the attackers wallowed at a snail's pace. With no surprise and slow movement, reinforcements could fill any gap in the defender's line. At that, even if an enemy trench was seized, no real breakthrough was achieved because the trench "line" generally consisted of three trenches separated by some distance. Thus the exhausted attackers, having captured the initial objective, still faced fresh troops and fresh defensive works just ahead. It is no wonder the front lines moved so little during the war.

Another innovative method was gas warfare. When first used on both the Eastern and Western fronts, it had considerable success. However, its effects often depended on the weather (especially which way the wind was blowing), and the introduction of protective equipment made gas a progressively less effective weapon.

The most innovative tactics (aside from the use of tanks discussed earlier) to achieve breakthrough were developed by the German Gen Oskar von Hutier. He employed a very short barrage combined with infiltration by specially trained assault troops who avoided strong points. Regular infantry, who reduced the bypassed strong points, followed the assault troops. The Germans used these tactics extensively during their final offensive in 1918 and had considerable success in achieving deep breakthroughs quickly. However, they could not move artillery and supplies forward fast enough to sustain the attacks. Hutier's tactics foreshadowed the blitzkrieg tactics of World War II.

For the most part, the tactics of World War I resembled the worst displayed in the American Civil War. Time after time masses of men lunged across open ground to assault well-entrenched defenders and were slaughtered at an incredible rate. It seemed the generals had learned nothing from experience. World War I tactics were not a tribute to human wisdom.

## Military Conduct

The Allies were exhausted after the hard fighting of 1917, and a revolt of the soldiers in the French army had further shaken their leaders. In these circumstances, they were content to sit on the defensive and await the arrival of the fresh American troops. The same was not true for the Germans. With the collapse of the Russians, the Germans moved massive numbers of troops to the west and, so reinforced, hoped to strike a decisive blow before the Americans turned the tide.

Gen Erich Ludendorff planned a series of German offensives all along the Allied lines in 1918. In addition to the new troops from the Eastern Front, he planned to incorporate the new tactics developed by Hutier. The first German attack came in March and was aimed at the British at the Somme River. The attack achieved astonishing success, advancing 40 miles in eight days, before it slowed. In early April the Germans struck the British again, this time at the Lys River, and again achieved some success. This was followed in late May by an attack on the French at the Chemin des Dames, an important ridge line northeast of the French capital. Once again the Germans were astonishingly successful by the standards of trench warfare. By the end of May they again threatened Paris from newly won positions on the Marne River at Château-Thierry.

At Château-Thierry the Americans were first sent into heavy combat. When the Germans attempted to cross the Marne, they were thrown back by the newly arrived American troops. Ludendorff attempted to renew his stalled offensive during the summer months, but the effort failed. The Germans had spent themselves and the Americans were now pouring into the lines. In all, ten American divisions took part in the summer operations; their presence was crucial to Allied success in stopping the German drive.

Allied counterattacks began as early as mid-July and were aimed at retaking the vast salients created by the surprising successes of the earlier German offensives. On 8 August the Allies massed several hundred tanks for an wonder the front lines moved so little during the war.

Another innovative method was gas warfare. When first used on both the Eastern and Western fronts, it had considerable success. However, its effects often depended on the weather (especially which way the wind was blowing), and the introduction of protective equipment made gas a progressively less effective weapon.

The most innovative tactics (aside from the use of tanks discussed earlier) to achieve breakthrough were developed by the German Gen Oskar von Hutier. He employed a very short barrage combined with infiltration by specially trained assault troops who avoided strong points. Regular infantry, who reduced the bypassed strong points, followed the assault troops. The Germans used these tactics extensively during their final offensive in 1918

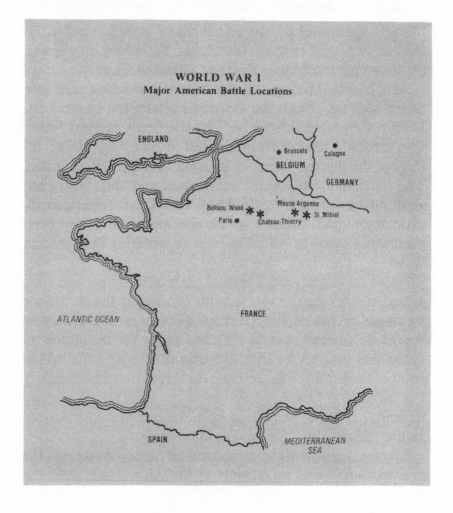

**WORLD WAR I**
Major American Battle Locations

American sector in the offensive was surrounded by the Meuse River and the difficult Argonne Forest. The fighting was bitter and extended, particularly in the Argonne, but by 10 October the Germans had been driven from the forest. By 5 November the Americans forced a crossing of the Meuse. The grand offensive rolled on, not just in the American sector but all along the front as the exhausted German defense finally disintegrated.

Germany would not be the master of Europe, at least not for two decades. But neither would the French or British, both of whom had suffered grievously. Nor would the Soviets reign supreme, as they sought to consolidate their internal position after the revolution. Austria-Hungary simply disappeared as a political unit. Europe would have to wait 22 years for a master to proclaim itself.

The United States entered the war late, but American participation was vital to the eventual Allied success. Fresh American troops stopped the final German offensive in 1918, and they broke the back of German resistance thereafter. American troops and their leaders acquitted themselves well on the battlefield, and the lessons learned about massive mobilization, training, and deployment would prove valuable in the future. The cost, in human terms, was staggering. During approximately six months of combat operations, 50,000 Americans died in battle, while 75,000 more died from non–battle-related causes. But the cost in American lives paled in comparison to the losses sustained by the other Allies. Nearly 1.5 million Frenchmen died in combat, as did nearly 1 million British and nearly 2 million Russians. The small price America paid in its short war affected the amount of influence the United States had in the peace treaty negotiations that followed the war. The United States also was spared the incredible casualties suffered by civilian populations during the war. Some estimates put the civilian death toll at over 15 million. Perhaps the price would have seemed a bargain if this war had been the war that ended all wars.

**Better State of the Peace**

The armistice that took effect on 11 November 1918 ended the formal hostilities that had raged for more than four years. When the victorious Allies gathered at Versailles, the palace of the Bourbon kings located outside Paris, their purpose was to re-create the peace that had preceded the outbreak of the Great War, to make a better state of the peace.

In essence, the Allies had three tasks facing them in their collective quest to ensure that the conflict had indeed been the war to end all wars. These were dealing with the enemy, restructuring the peace, and redrawing the political map. The first task was how to deal with the vanquished Central

Powers. German hostile ability had been finally overcome through exhaustion of German resources in its summer 1918 offensive and the Allied counteroffensive. The coup that overthrew the Kaiser and resulted in a suit for peace by the new German government demonstrated that German cost-tolerance had been exceeded as well. What remained to be decided was how to integrate Germany back into the international system. This was a question of fashioning a peace that Germany could or would accept and embrace for reordering a peaceful world. Two alternative visions were laid on the negotiating table.

As suggested earlier, the two chief protagonists in this debate were Wilson and Clemenceau. Harking back to his own childhood experience and his earlier call for a peace without victory, Wilson preferred a reconciliatory settlement toward Germany that would reintegrate the German state into the international system with a minimum of recrimination and punishment. He believed this to be the best way to overcome those vestiges of German hostile will that might resist acceptance of the policies governing the peace. Clemenceau, representing an embittered France, had other ideas. Given the suffering and privation France endured (admixed with some long-smoldering resentment arising from the settlement of the Franco–Prussian War 48 years earlier), France insisted upon a punitive peace. French insistence prevailed and Germany was punished for the war.

In essence, France had two preferred outcomes to the peace talks. The first was to recover the enormous physical and economic costs of the war (the French national treasury as well as those of virtually all the major combatants had been drained). The second objective was to destroy what France viewed as the cause of the war, which was an expansionist, militaristic Germany. The solution to the first problem was to make Germany pay for France's war expenses; the answer to the second was to transform Germany into a pastoral, permanently weakened state that could pose no future military threat to France.

The key to achieving those goals within the framework of the peace settlement was the infamous Article 231 of the Versailles Accords, the war guilt clause. That article, which the new German government was forced to accept, placed sole and complete blame for starting the war on Germany, and it served as the necessary justification and underpinning for the other punitive parts of the settlement. With German cupidity and responsibility formally established, France could justify exacting retribution, including a severe schedule of reparations aimed at compensating France for its wartime costs (a provision, one might add, in which a number of the victorious allies, notably Great Britain, rapaciously joined). Germany would pay for the war, although the effects of those payments would prove ruinous to the German

economy. At the same time, provisions were included that substantially disarmed the German state and reduced its territory to ensure against a militarily resurgent Germany.

A prostrate Germany had no choice but to accept these humiliating conditions, but the leaders who did so would later be vilified as traitors for their
actions. The conditions were so severe and humbling that the German people
could not possibly embrace these policies and hence have their hostile will
(resistance to policies) permanently overcome.

There were several factors that made acceptance impossible. The first
was the war guilt clause. That provision was, at best, questionable. As one
tries to unravel who was to blame for the war in the first place, Germany
emerges as but one candidate among several. There was too much guilt and
stupidity to lay on a single doorstep.

Another factor that ensured the survival of German hostile will was the
size of the reparations payments. These virtually ensured that Germany would
not recover fully from the war economically (as some observers such as
Lord John Maynard Keynes prophetically but futilely pointed out at the time).
The result would be enormous inflation in Germany during the 1920s with
which the democratic Weimar regime could not deal effectively and economic devastation when the Great Depression took hold. At the same time,
the demilitarization of Germany left that country at the mercy of the rest of
the international system and perpetuated German enmity. Suddenly, Germany was back where it started before unification, at the military mercy of
the system. The seeds for the emergence of a Hitler-like figure could not
have been more skillfully sown had that been the purpose of the peace treaty.

Although he objected to these aspects of the settlement, Wilson finally
acceded, because his attention was focused on the second task which confronted the conferees, the establishment of a mechanism to ensure the future
peace. The essential question was what had gone wrong with the Concert of
Europe that had allowed the war to occur.

When it had operated properly, the Concert had served as a collective
security arrangement: all the major states were members, and each agreed
that a threat to or breach of the peace threatened their own interests and must
be resisted. With that principle established, a potential aggressor knew that
the community of states, and hence overwhelming power, opposed its action, making it futile and thus deterring aggression. The Concert appeared to
work for a time, but ultimately the system failed. What had gone wrong?

The answer Wilson and others (rightly or wrongly) devised was that the
Concert system (actually a series of irregularly scheduled meetings of the
major countries called when the need arose) was inadequately institutionalized. What the system lacked, they reasoned, was a formal mechanism, an insti-

tution that would always be available whenever crises arose and which consequently could act in a timely and authoritative manner. That mechanism was to be the League of Nations, which would serve as guarantor of the peace. Unfortunately, that noble institution never had a chance to perform its role.

A collective security arrangement requires two conditions for effective operation. The first is that the mechanism must have at its disposal obviously overwhelming power to deter transgressors. Meeting that standard requires that all major powers be represented in the arrangement. This condition was never met. The United States never joined the League (to Wilson's bitter and debilitating disappointment), the Soviet Union was not permitted to join the organization until the 1930s, and it was during that decade that the countries that formed the Axis in World War II resigned. The second condition for success is the willingness of the major powers to enforce the peace, and that translates into accepting the justice of the peace system that one is upholding. For reasons embedded in the third task facing the negotiators, this condition was also unmet.

The third task was redrawing the political map of the world. The operative principle, as part of Wilson's Fourteen Points, was to be self-determination, the right of all nations freely to determine their status as states. The principle in truth applied only to Europe (nationalists in several Asian colonial states would discover this truth to their dismay). Although the principle was applied with reasonable effectiveness in central Europe, there remained another part of the agenda, which consisted of territorial rewards for the victors and penalties for the losers.

The Austro-Hungarian and Ottoman empires collapsed and disappeared as a result of the war. The European sectors of those empires were allowed to engage in self-determination, resulting in such new states in eastern and central Europe as Czechoslovakia, while the Ottoman Middle East was placed largely under the trusteeship of Britain and France. The German Empire was dismantled and apportioned among the victorious allies, and Germany's prewar boundaries were reduced through transfer of territory to France (the return of Alsace-Lorraine) and through the recreation of a Polish state. Some of these territorial adjustments placed German populations under non-Germanic rule (for example, the Sudetenland), but Germany had no choice but to accept its dismemberment—at least for the time being.

At the same time, some members of the victorious coalition, notably Italy and Japan, had territorial claims that were not honored by the dominant members of the alliance (Britain, France, and the United States). Italy had claims, for instance, in the Balkan region and Japan expected to receive the bulk of the former German dependencies in the Pacific, but most of these were placed under American stewardship instead. Germany simmered under the loss of empire and territory it considered rightfully a part of Germany, and Japan and Italy resented the rejection of "rightful" rewards for their contributions to the war effort. None of the three could be expected enthusiastically to endorse or enforce the territorial status quo, as participation in the League of Nations collective security system required. Ultimately, of course, none of them did.

All of this is to say that the better state of the peace was doomed from the beginning. The victors' policies were punitive and viewed as unjust by the vanquished and even by members of the victorious coalition. From an American vantage point, the irony was redoubled because, when Wilson returned with the peace treaty in hand, it was rejected after an acrimonious national debate by a resentful Senate. The official argument that led to the failure to ratify was the commitment to the League, which would tie the United States irrevocably to the affairs of Europe. Such a commitment, which Wilson felt was the linchpin in an enduring peace, was unacceptable to those Americans who continued to believe in the myth of American aloofness from European affairs. Underlying the failure, however, was a tactical blunder on Wilson's part; he had failed to take any senators to the Versailles conference, and hence they had no stake in the outcome (a mistake no subsequent president has made).

The outcome of the settlement of World War I is generally considered the classic case of winning the war and losing the peace. The war had been won militarily; German and other Central Powers' hostile ability and willingness to continue (cost-tolerance) had been broken on the battlefield. But that was not enough. Adversary hostile will, defined as resistance to the victor's policies, not only was not overcome, but the terms of the peace were almost guaranteed to increase that hostile will. Resistance to accepting these policies was, of course, most strongly felt in a humiliated Germany. Given the circumstances and conditions imposed upon the German state, it is hard to envision how the German people could have reacted otherwise. For policies to be embraced, they must be accepted as just, and the peace terms could hardly have been looked upon that way in Germany. In the end, short-sightedness and vindictiveness ruled the day. In the long run, the peace was lost. The manifestation of that loss was the need to fight World War II to resolve the differences that had been dealt with so abysmally in the peace ending the war to end all wars.

# 5

# World War II

The Great War had been the largest and bloodiest conflict to date in human history, but it was in many ways only a preview of what would follow. Approximately 20 years later World War II erupted and became the largest military event in history. It was a conflict that was total in all senses of that term and a *world war* in which virtually every corner of the globe served as a theater of action at one time or another. Although records are inadequate, the best guesses are that about 80 million people were in military service at a given time. Of these, between 15 and 20 million were killed and probably about the same number of noncombatants perished. There were around 10 million combatant casualties and almost that many additional civilian casualties in the Soviet Union alone. Even more than the First World War, World War II was a war between whole societies, a war of factories. The entire resources of the major combatants were dedicated to the war's conduct, and whole populations were mobilized for one aspect or another of the effort.

America's role in World War II was unique in at least two ways. World War II was almost two distinct conflicts: one in Europe, where the Western Allies (including the Soviet Union) faced Germany and her European allies, and the other in the Pacific, where Imperial Japan was the major antagonist. The US position was unique in that only the United States had major responsibilities in both theaters. In Europe the Allied effort was dominated by the triumvirate of the United States, the Soviet Union, and Great Britain, but American presence was of vital importance: the British depended heavily on the United States for the materiel and manpower necessary to open the Western Front, and the Soviets relied to some degree on American lend-lease. In the Pacific the war was essentially a conflict between the Americans and the Japanese. Certainly others were part of the Pacific campaign: the British on the peripheries (e.g., Burma) and Chiang Kai-shek's Kuomintang Chinese (who occupied a million-man Japanese army that could not be used elsewhere). The task of defeating the military might of the Japanese Empire, however, was clearly an American task. As we shall see later in the chapter, this unique position created some friction within the government and with our Allies over which enemy should receive the greatest attention and even some interservice rivalries about resource allocations (the war in Europe was basically an Army enterprise, whereas the Navy dominated the Pacific war).

The other unique aspect from an American perspective is that the United States was the only Allied power that emerged from the war stronger than it entered. When the United States entered the fray following the attack on Pearl Harbor, the vast (and, thanks to the lingering effects of the Great Depression, underutilized) American industrial base was turned into the "arsenal for democracy." The conversion and the stimulation it provided the economy ended the depression and allowed the United States to emerge in 1945 as the unquestioned economic colossus of the world. The other Allies were "winners" in the sense of being on the prevailing side, but all the other Allies were wounded seriously by the effort. Britain's expenditure in blood and national treasure accelerated its gradual decline from great power status, a circumstance with which British governments continue to grapple today. The other major ally, the Soviet Union, arguably emerged more politically unified because of the enormity of effort necessitated by the Great Patriotic War (as the war was officially known in that country), but its land was scourged by the Nazi invasion that left two-thirds of its industry destroyed, countless towns, villages, and buildings reduced to rubble, and nearly 20 million citizens dead.

The United States avoided those disasters. After the surprise attack at Pearl Harbor, American continental soil was never seriously attacked during the war, so that there was no physical reconstruction to deal with after the war's end. Our material contribution to the war had been enormous (the war cost the United States more than $500 billion in the dollars of the day), but our 300,000 casualties were comparatively light; the war did not bleed us dry in the literal sense of that phrase. Moreover, the war effort revitalized an American industrial plant gone flabby during the hard years of the depression. American industry was more productive at war's end than at the beginning.

The major effect of World War II was to critically alter the power map of the world. In the broadest sense, the roughly 150 years of European history from the onslaught of the French Revolution through World War II was a contest between France and Germany to dominate the continent and hence to dominate the international system. Ironically, World War II ensured that neither of them would. France had been defeated, humiliated, and occupied, and even though it rode to "victory" on the coattails of the victorious Allies, France clearly emerged from the war diminished in spirit and power. For Germany the outcome was even more disastrous. Its armed forces were decimated, it was occupied by its former enemies, it bore the unique moral stigma of Nazi excesses, and it was once again physically divided. Division was the cruelest blow of all, both because it returned the German people to the weakened status of a divided state and because the shadow of the Nazi past raised serious questions of when, if ever, the international system would allow a German resurgence.

The other actors were not in materially better shape. Great Britain was a member of the victorious coalition and hence technically a winner, but the British economy lay in ruins. The war would force Britain through the agony of gradual reduction from a global to a regional power. The British Empire, like that of its principal rival, France, would wither under nationalist demands for independence, setting in motion a whole new series of dynamics that are yet unfolding. Japan, like Germany, was defeated and occupied, and its reemergence would require massive assistance and nearly two decades to accomplish. The other major combatant, China, simply resumed the civil war that had raged between the Communists and Kuomintang in the 1930s.

The war ended with only two states possessing significant power, the United States and the Soviet Union. Of the two, the United States was clearly the more powerful. Although allied against the Nazi and Japanese menaces, the Soviets and the Americans moved into the postwar power vacuum with very different worldviews and motives that almost guaranteed a clash as they sought to reorder the power map.

**Issues and Events**

There are, of course, various ways to look at the question of what caused World War II, and numerous explanations have been put forward. In essence, however, there were two interactive underlying issues: Franco–German competition for dominance of the European continent that went back over a century, and the failure of the peacemakers at Versailles to create a structure for the interwar peace that could be embraced and supported by the participants in the Great War.

Competition between modern France and Germany is historical and long-standing, and treating it in its breadth and richness would only divert us from present concerns. In the modern era, however, one can usefully date it back to the Napoleonic campaigns, when Prussia, the precursor to and leader in the unification of the German state, was soundly defeated by the French *levée en masse*. From that humiliation arose the Prussian determination to unify Germany and to produce a strong, militarized state that would no longer be forced to suffer such indignities. The process of unification took nearly a half-century and was climaxed by Prussia's easy victory over Louis Napoléon in the Franco–Prussian War of 1870. A critical outcome of that conflict was the reannexation of Alsace-Lorraine to Germany, which in turn was an important element in forming the static alliance systems that contested World War I.

The Great War, round three in the competition, left Germany in essence back where it had started: politically dismembered, territorially reduced, and economically and militarily debilitated and vulnerable. Germany was once again reduced to being the "weak sister" of Europe, and the history of the German states had taught that this condition was intolerable. Moreover, the economic system that the Second Reich erected was saddled by reparations ensuring that economic recovery was virtually impossible. It was also burdened with a democratic political system that was both alien to the German political tradition and, by virtue of signing the Versailles peace treaty, held responsible for German humiliation by sizable parts of the population (a vulnerability that Hitler used to form the basis of his assault on democratic elements in Weimar Germany).

Given this unacceptable outcome of the third round of Franco–German rivalry, the Versailles peace was doomed from the beginning. Its centerpiece, the League of Nations, never had a realistic chance to organize the peace effectively: too many of its members were unwilling to defend a status quo they viewed as unjust, and others excluded themselves (the United States) or were excluded (the Soviet Union, on the premise that the way to arrest the spread of the "cancer" of bolshevism was through isolation).

Proximate events of the 1930s would transform these underlying issues into the bloodiest conflagration in human history. These events, in turn, can be traced to two related sources reflecting dissatisfaction with the peace ending World War I: economic nationalism and the effects of the Great Depression, and the rise of fascist regimes that would become increasingly aggressive and expansionist in the face of tepid responses from the Western democracies.

Economic nationalism and the depression are related events. The core of economic nationalism, which was to manifest itself in unprecedented protectionism of national industrial plants, can be found in the attempts of the drained countries of Europe to recover and recuperate from the ruinous economic effects of the First World War. National coffers had been emptied, industries had been turned to the war effort and had to be reconverted, and there were widespread scars of war (especially in France) that required rebuilding, all at considerable cost. Governments were forced to foot these bills, and one of their strategies for recovery (especially of the industrial plant) was to erect high protective tariffs against goods and services from elsewhere. Combined with the artificial flow of wealth resulting from reparations, the economic base of Europe became increasingly shaky.

The Great Depression represented the final blow to the international economic system. As businesses failed, banks defaulted, and the jobless lines increased throughout the continent, commerce between states came to a virtual standstill. The result was even more protectionism and an economic maelstrom that continued to get worse. As the times worsened, so did the political situation. In this climate, the rise of regimes that promised an end to the economic chaos, even if through escapism and adventurism, became progressively stronger. In no place was the cry louder and more inexorable than in Germany.

Fascism was not, of course, entirely a phenomenon of the 1930s. Mussolini came to power in Italy in the early 1920s, and the Japanese imperial monarchy predated the Great War. The factors that made fascism different in the 1930s and that led to war were the coming to power of fascism in its most virulent form through the National Socialist (Nazi) party in Germany and the progressively expansionistic form that the various fascist regimes exhibited as the decade progressed.

The rise of Nazism was the key factor, because only a resurgent Germany had the potential to mount a major threat to the peace; Japan and Italy could also engage in mischief, but their reaches were limited. Germany, particularly when expanded to something resembling its pre-1919 borders, could pose a threat to the whole of Europe, as had been the case in the Great War.

Hitler's Germany and its Führer have been and continue to be the source of enormous, if macabre, fascination, and there is little we can add to the voluminous literature that surrounds the Nazi era. A few points can, however, be made that are germane to our general theme.

The first is that the terms of Versailles virtually guaranteed that something like Nazism would emerge in interwar Germany. Although the monstrous directions that Hitler's policies took were not preordained by the Paris peacemakers, the combination of humiliation and degradation that Germany suffered, the artificial nature of the political system imposed on Germany, and a German political culture that associated authoritarian rule with prosperity (many Germans even today consider the Kaiser's Second Reich the golden age of German history) certainly made a militaristic, authoritarian movement seem quite appealing.

Second and significantly, the appeal of Nazism was inadequate to gain power in the relatively affluent 1920s but was inexorable in the depression-plagued 1930s. When Hitler began to organize his political movement and made his first clumsy attempt to seize power (the "Beer Hall Putsch"), he was ridiculed, rejected, and thrown in jail. A little less than a decade later, with Germany in the depths of the depression, his simplistic analyses of Germany's woes and his grandiose solutions met a more responsive audience. Granting that many of the power brokers who helped him come to power viewed him as a comic figure they could manipulate and control, nonetheless Hitler had enough popular appeal to be elected chancellor.

The pattern of unchecked aggression provided the proximate events on the road to war. Each of the three major powers in what became the Axis participated in this process, and in each case timid responses (when there was any response at all) not only did not deter future actions but almost gave them tacit approval.

Some observers maintain that World War II really began in 1931. In that year Japan made its first major expansionist move, invading the Chinese province of Manchuria (the industrial heart of the country). In fighting of enormous ferocity punctuated by numerous atrocities against the civilian population, the Japanese succeeded in establishing their domain and installing a puppet ruler on the throne of the country they called Manchukuo. The West stood idly by. The strongest condemnation came from the United States, which promulgated the so-called Stimson Doctrine of Non-Recognition. This doctrine stated that it was American policy not to recognize governments that came to power by force (a tenet that has been selectively applied ever since). The practical effect was that the United States did not recognize the government of Manchukuo but continued to deal with Japan virtually on a business-as-usual basis. So encouraged, the Japanese Sphere of Co-Equality continued to expand through the decade. By 1941 the proximity of that empire and American interests meant that something had to give.

The Fascist government of Benito Mussolini also got into the act, albeit in a more modest way. The major adventurism in which Italy engaged was the 1935 campaign against Ethiopia. Using the Italian colony of Eritrea as his base of operation, Mussolini unleashed his mechanized army against the pitifully underarmed Ethiopian tribesmen (some of them actually confronted tanks and other armored vehicles with spears). The world was shocked but not enough to act.

When the attack began, the Ethiopian Emperor Haile Selassie, the "Lion of Judah," went to the League of Nations and appealed to that organization to invoke the collective security provisions of the covenant and to come to Ethiopia's defense. After long debate, the League voted *voluntary* sanctions against the Italian regime and omitted petroleum, oil, and lubricants (on which Italy was particularly dependent) from the list of proscribed materials. Of the major powers, only the Soviet Union (which had been admitted to the League after Germany withdrew) argued strongly for effective, mandatory sanctions to reverse the situation. Britain and France, unwilling to risk war over that barren corner of the Horn of Africa, wavered. In the wake of the Ethiopian affair, League collective security was effectively a dead letter.

Center stage in the tragedy was, of course, reserved for Nazi Germany. Using the dual assertions of the "destiny and right" of all German peoples (broadly defined) to be ruled together and the need for *lebensraum* (living space) as his justifications, Hitler began his campaign of expansionism in 1935. Initially, the reaction of the major Western democracies was weak and ineffectual. When they finally determined to react, it was too late.

Hitler's first and riskiest action was the remilitarization of the Rhineland. Sharing a long common border with France, the Rhineland had been demilitarized by the Versailles accords to assuage French fears of a new German onslaught. Timing his move to coincide with one of the frequent crises in the French Third Republic (one coalition government had collapsed and a successor had not been organized), Hitler moved his forces into the area. It was a gamble because at that time the armed forces of France were clearly superior to his own (almost all his military advisers opposed the plan) and could have forced him to back down. Hitler, however, counted on the paralysis caused by the French political crisis to preclude effective action. He proved correct; neither France nor Britain reacted and he was able to present the world with a fait accompli. So emboldened, Hitler turned his attention to bigger things.

The list of Hitler's aggressions is familiar enough and need not be treated in detail here. Under the guise of the "Greater Germany," Hitler annexed the Sudetenland area of Czechoslovakia (which had a majority German population) and in the Anschluss, German troops occupied Austria as well. Confused and irresolute, the Western powers refused to respond forcefully, instead believing Hitler's assurances that each expansion would be the last or believing that domestic public opinion would not support a forceful response. The nadir of the process was British Prime Minister Neville Chamberlain's return from Munich and his announcement of "peace in our time."

Not everyone, of course, was deceived by Hitler's designs. In England Winston Churchill led the cry to prepare for a war he knew would come, but citizens still war weary from the Great War turned a largely deaf ear. Only when Hitler launched the blitzkrieg against Poland in September 1939 did the situation change. Because of treaty obligations with the Polish state, Great Britain and France were forced to make the declaration of war that marks the formal beginning of World War II. That declaration and the period that followed it, symbolically enough, were known as the "phony war": no fighting occurred because neither Britain nor France was mobilized to fight. Only when Hitler turned his war machine against France the following June did the British and French become directly involved.

America's role and reactions to this chain of events should be noted. Except in the Pacific, the chain of Axis advances did not directly involve American interests nor have much of an impact on the American people. Isolated by the Atlantic and Pacific oceans from the gathering war clouds, Americans could and did largely ignore these events, instead concentrating their energies and emotions on coping with the debilitating effects of the Great Depression. The rumblings in Europe were Europe's problem, and there was little sentiment for plucking European "chestnuts from the fire" yet another time.

This was, after all, the era of splendid isolationism in American foreign policy, a period when the lessons of the inextricable link between the destinies of Europe and North America were still not realized nor appreciated. During the rise of the fascist movements, there was even some support for the emerging regimes and particularly for the Nazis.

Because Americans generally opposed the idea that these events affected them, or ignored the situation altogether, there were adverse consequences as the "winds of war" approached. On one hand, those Americans like President Franklin D. Roosevelt who realized that our participation would eventually be necessary were greatly hampered in their efforts to prepare the country for war. Because of legislation enforcing American neutrality, aid for the Western Allies had to be supplied surreptitiously. The American armaments industry could only be developed slowly, and authorization for even a standby draft (i.e., preparing the mechanisms for a draft) passed only in 1940. In the American tradition, we entered the war almost totally unprepared to fight it. As a consequence, it was not until 1943 that the full brunt of American military power could be brought to bear.

On the other hand, the ostrich-like attitude that the war did not concern us affected our reactions when the conflict was finally forced upon us. Active and hot war had been going on in Europe for a year and a half before the attack on Pearl Harbor, and the forces of geopolitics, if closely watched, suggested that American involvement was, in the long run, inevitable. Moreover, many US leaders believed that in all likelihood Japan would be one of our opponents. Yet, the average American did not see the war coming. The "infamy" of the Japanese attack was accentuated and American outrage was all the greater for the surprise. In our reaction to the shock, our objectives were shaped by and pursued with a moral indignation that they might not have had if we had been better prepared.

## Political Objective

The American declaration of war against Japan the day after Pearl Harbor, followed by the German counterdeclaration, threw the United States into its second coalition war of the twentieth century. As had been the case in the Great War, not all who fought together shared the same political and military objectives. The Allies were united in a joint desire to defeat the Axis (especially Germany) militarily, but there were differences of opinion about what constituted that military victory. Their most serious differences were political and largely focused on the postwar map. The greatest divisions among the major Allies were between the Soviet Union and her two major English-speaking partners, but there were some items of disagreement between Great Britain and the United States.

The Americans and the British had many common objectives. Probably the clearest statement of agreed goals was articulated well before America's entrance into the hostilities, when Prime Minister Churchill and President Roosevelt met off the Canadian coast and announced the Atlantic Charter. That document, setting forth eight points, had essentially two thrusts. The first was a statement about how the postwar world should be organized. As a statement of the better state of the peace, the charter emphasized such things as abjuring territorial gains, promoting self-determination as the basis for the postwar political map, and protecting free access to trade and resources for all nations. The other thrust called for the disarmament of the aggressors and a peace that would ensure the physical security of all countries.

The first thrust was primarily political and the second military. Where the two allies disagreed was in the relative emphasis that should be placed on each, and their positions largely reflected national attitudes toward war and politics. From the American perspective, the primary purpose of the war was to rid the world of the absolute evil posed by fascism. This was a highly moralistic goal, reflecting the American tendency (so well illustrated in other conflicts) to view issues in terms of good and evil. Defining the purpose once again as a moral crusade naturally emphasized the second thrust of the Atlantic Charter rather than the underlying political purposes that made the violence necessary. Defining the better state of the peace would have to wait for the end of violence.

The British view, epitomized by Churchill, placed greater emphasis on the postwar map. Recognizing the mortal peril represented by Hitler and the consequent need to vanquish the Nazi opponent, the British view was more geopolitical, placing emphasis both on the military task at hand and on the shape of the postwar map. In Churchill's mind, the primary problem for post-war Europe would be the power vacuum created in eastern and central Europe by the defeat of Germany and how to blunt and contain Soviet aggressive, imperialistic designs on those areas. The Americans downplayed this problem, initially because Roosevelt thought he could contain Stalin's ambitions. This disagreement produced friction among the Western Allies throughout the war and became particularly evident at the time of the final offensive against Germany in 1945.

The Soviet objective was quite different and considerably more desperate. After the failure of the Soviet initiative to re-create the Triple Entente of World War I, Stalin entered into the notorious Molotov–Ribbentrop (Nazi–Soviet) Non-Aggression Treaty in 1939. The Soviet purpose, beyond the partitioning of Poland in the secret protocol, was to provide breathing space to mobilize and rebuild its military capability, which had been ravaged by the purges of the 1930s. When the Nazi onslaught (Operation Barbarossa) began on 22 June 1941, the initial Soviet objective became survival of the fatherland. This was not an easy chore as German armies spread further and further into Soviet territory. The Soviets came within a hair's breadth of losing the war (some have argued that had the invasion not been delayed for six weeks because of disturbances in the Balkans, Hitler might well have succeeded).

After the infamous Russian winter bogged down the German advance, the political objectives of the Great Patriotic War became twofold and sequential. The first objective was to ensure the territorial integrity of the Soviet homeland, and its primary imperative was the physical removal of the German army. This was, of course, an objective with which the Western Allies could scarcely disagree, although there was considerable disagreement between Stalin and his allies about the strength, location, and timing of American and British efforts to alleviate pressure on the Soviets and hence to facilitate accomplishing the task.

Disagreement was fundamental on the second Soviet objective, which was to create a physical circumstance in Europe that would preclude a repeat of Barbarossa. One aspect of this objective was to create a buffer zone between Russia and Germany to ensure that a future thrust toward Russia could be confronted in eastern Europe. A buffer zone required states in eastern Europe at least not unfriendly (preferably sympathetic) to the Soviet Union, and it was this aspect that troubled Churchill most as he contemplated the postwar European map. The second aspect was the disposition of postwar Germany. In a manner of reasoning not dissimilar to France's after World War I, Stalin wanted a permanently weakened Germany that would not be capable of again posing the menace already twice visited on the homeland during the century. This desire came to mean a permanently partitioned Germany, neither part of which would be strong enough to threaten Soviet security.

Because the Pacific theater of the war was essentially a conflict between the United States and Japan (albeit with a major theater in China and other more minor theaters elsewhere in Asia), American political objectives against Japan were neither complicated nor compromised by the problem of coalition policy-making to the degree they were in Europe. In the Pacific, Allied and American objectives were essentially the same (at least until the Soviets entered the conflict in 1945 with the apparent—now if not then—purposes of gaining a buffer zone in North Korea and a voice in the future of Japan).

The American political objective was straightforward, and was heavily influenced by the Japanese sneak attack on Pearl Harbor. The purpose was the destruction of the Japanese Empire and the abdication of the Japanese emperor, whom most Americans identified—probably erroneously—as the instigator of the Pearl Harbor raid. Roosevelt's description of that attack as a "day of infamy" set the moral tone for a crusade against the perpetrators. Nothing less than the total defeat of the enemy could create atonement; and because the emperor was, in the popular mind, the embodiment of Japan, the emperor had to go. As we shall see in a later section, this absolute requirement may well have lengthened the war in the Pacific and may even be loosely related to the later fighting in Korea.

The final consideration regarding the objective was the relative importance of attaining the political objectives of overthrowing German Nazism or Japanese imperialism: on which end should primary attention be focused? From the viewpoint of the European allies, Nazism represented the greater threat and should be dealt with first. On this point there was agreement within the alliance: Hitler should be defeated first, and then attention should be shifted to Japan. In practice military objectives and strategy only imperfectly reflected this agreement.

## Military Objectives and Strategy

The military situation upon the entrance of the United States into World War II was fundamentally different from the situation faced by Americans when they entered the Great War in 1917. In World War I the United States entered on the side of viable allies and tipped the scales toward victory. On 7 December 1941 Americans had many allies, but few were in a position to shoulder a significant portion of the burden. The United States was suddenly thrust center stage into a war for which it was ill prepared.

Most of Europe had been overrun by the Nazi war machine. France, the low countries, Norway, and the Balkans were all controlled by the Germans. The Soviet Union was reeling from the lightning-war blows of the Wehrmacht and was in the painful process of trading its vast spaces for time to recover and counterattack. Britain had survived the German air assault and prevented a Nazi invasion, but its survival was still in doubt. German submarines were taking a fearsome toll on British shipping, and the British army was heavily engaged in North Africa against a superb German general bent on seizing Egypt. Besieged as they were, the Soviet Union and Great Britain were America's only significant allies in Europe.

In the Pacific and Far East, China continued to survive despite the heavy blows of the Japanese but could offer little help to the United States other than to tie down a large portion of the Japanese army. Japan was running rampant across the Pacific. By the end of December 1941, Wake Island and Hong Kong had fallen and Japanese forces had invaded Malaya, the Philippines, and the Gilbert Islands. By mid-March 1942, Malaya, Singapore, Rabaul, and Java had all fallen; the remnants of an Allied fleet had been destroyed in the Battle of the Java Sea; and Gen MacArthur had been evacuated from the Philippines. The European colonial powers were besieged in Europe and could do little to stem the Japanese tide. Help was available from Australia and New Zealand, but it was clear the United States would have to shoulder the majority of the load.

If the world situation was bad, the condition of the American military was worse. Most of the Pacific fleet's firepower rested on the bottom of Pearl Harbor. The American Army was still building and was untested in combat. American air power was still a paper force. Although first-class heavy bombers were coming off the assembly lines, no US fighter could match those fielded by Germany or Japan. In sum the situation at the end of 1941 was dismal.

The overall Allied strategy for the war was actually mapped out well before the United States entered the war. In the winter and spring of 1941, American-British-Canadian (ABC) staff conversations produced a generalized military strategy should the United States enter the war. The plan's first priority was to stop the enemy onslaught. The first American objective was to preserve a secure operating base in the Western Hemisphere. For the British the essential task was clearly to maintain the integrity of the British Isles and, if possible, its dominions in the Far East (particularly India). The second British priority was to maintain control of its sea lines of communication, without which all else would crumble.

The most important agreement reached during the ABC talks had to do with overall Allied priorities. Germany was considered the predominant member of the enemy camp. Thus the staffs agreed that the European theater was the decisive theater and the area for the initial concentration of effort. These priorities dictated that in the Far East the military strategy would have to be defensive at the outset. Later during the war, however, this agreement would cause considerable consternation (particularly in the US Navy, which considered the naval war against Japan to be at least equally important to the war in Europe).

The offensive campaign against Germany and Italy was envisioned in stages. The first stage was to bring to bear economic pressure, including the denial of raw materials. The second stage was a sustained heavy air offensive against the German homeland. The third stage was to eliminate Italy from the war, since it was considered the most fragile of the three Axis partners. Raids and minor offensives against the enemy were envisioned at every opportunity while forces for the major offensive were built. The fourth and last stage was a major offensive against the Germans on the European continent itself.

In the European theater, the most lasting and vexing questions were where and when to invade the continent in force. The British were wary of a cross-channel invasion. The ghosts of a generation of youth lost on Flanders fields during the Great War haunted the British. They feared that they would again be bogged down in a stalemated war of attrition that they could not afford. They also feared attacking before they were finally prepared and again being thrown off the continent. The memory of Dunkirk died hard.

The Americans desired a cross-channel invasion as soon as possible and argued hard for such an undertaking as early as 1942. The situation was complicated by the need to keep the Soviet Union in the war. The Soviets badly needed a second front, and Stalin used every opportunity to press for an invasion at the earliest possible moment.

The cross-channel invasion controversy would continue throughout the war. The Americans and Soviets pressed for early invasion. The British constantly suggested such alternative (and presumably safe) invasion sites as Italy, Greece, and the Balkans.

Churchill won the first round of the controversy by posing a series of difficult questions that emphasized the enormous problems involved in mounting a cross-channel invasion in 1942. Roosevelt, however, was convinced that the Allies, particularly the Americans, must take dramatic offensive action as soon as possible. With the invasion of France put into the "too-difficult-at-present" category, he agreed to an invasion of North Africa. The object was to trap the German and Italian forces between British forces advancing from Egypt and the Anglo-American invasion forces advancing from Morocco and Algeria.

North Africa offered many advantages over a cross-channel invasion. First, and most important, the landings would not be directly opposed by seasoned German troops. Rather, the invading troops would land on shores controlled by the Vichy French. Although the French would probably oppose the landings, there was the possibility that there would be no resistance and, in any case, resistance should be far less severe than could be expected on the coast of France itself. Success in North Africa would yield several significant benefits. Victory would help to open the Mediterranean shipping lanes, facilitate the flow of supplies to the Soviet Union through the Persian Gulf, and might possibly draw German strength away from the Soviet front. Given available resources, the operation posed significant benefits at minimum risk.

The landings and the campaign as a whole were successful, and in January 1943 Roosevelt and Churchill met in Casablanca to map out the next Allied moves. Although a cross-channel invasion was discussed for the fall of 1943, Churchill won round two by convincing Roosevelt that the next step should be Operation Husky, the invasion of Sicily. Churchill argued that seizing Sicily would facilitate clearing the Mediterranean sea-lanes and would put pressure on the shaky Italians. The invasion of France was again postponed, this time until the spring of 1944. Stalin's reaction to the postponement was bitter and helped plant the seeds of disunion that would tear the Allies apart in the aftermath of the war.

The Casablanca conference is best known for two other strategic decisions. The first reaffirmed the importance of the massive bombing offensive against Germany, which was just getting under way in earnest. The air offensive had been plagued by diversions from strategic to tactical targets (support for the North African landings, for example) and controversy between British and American airmen over the advisability of the daylight, precision-bombing attacks preferred by the Americans. At Casablanca plans were laid for the combined bomber offensive in which the Americans would bomb by day using precision techniques and the British would use area-bombing techniques at night. The idea was to give German defenders and the civilian population no rest.

The other, and more famous, decision was announced at the concluding news conference, when Roosevelt stated that the Allied goal was "unconditional surrender" of the Axis powers. Ever since that news conference, the effects of that phrase have been matters of considerable debate. Critics have pointed out that such an objective probably prolonged the war because it gave the Axis powers a propaganda advantage by imbuing the enemy population with the courage of desperation. Churchill maintained that the specific retribution demanded by the Allies seemed so severe when set down on paper that unconditional surrender paled in comparison. Both Roosevelt and Churchill made significant efforts throughout the remainder of the war to explain unconditional surrender as something that the enemy population should not view with fear. Their efforts, however, had limited success.

The invasion of Sicily yielded quick success and the invasion of the Italian mainland quickly followed. By early September 1943 the Italian government surrendered, although German troops in Italy maintained strong defensive positions. Thus most of the steps in the general Allied strategy had been accomplished. The German-Italian advance had been stopped, pressure had been applied whenever possible on land and at sea, the bombing offensive against German territory was picking up momentum, and Italy had been knocked out of the war. Planning now began in earnest for the cross-channel invasion.

In early 1944 Allied air forces stepped up their strategic attacks and made their first priority the Luftwaffe itself. During the spring, the Allies seized command of the air over western Europe and began to have a serious impact on German ability to operate effectively on the ground. Control of the air was an essential ingredient in a successful invasion, and the Allies had almost total control, particularly over the channel coast.

Meanwhile the resurgent Soviet army took a terrible toll of German military power. Even though a majority of German military power was concentrated on the eastern front, the Soviet army had begun to roll toward the borders of the Reich. So great were the Soviet victories that the Anglo-American forces made plans for an "emergency" cross-channel invasion should Germany collapse and "invite" them ashore to prevent the Soviets from overrunning all of western Europe.

The successful Allied landing on the shores of Normandy and subsequent breakout from the hedgerow country sealed the fate of Nazi Germany. Unfortunately, many Germans fought on to the bitter end with fatalistic determination. Whether or not it was inspired by the prospect of unconditional surrender, the prolonged German resistance did little but cause more death, suffering, and postwar bitterness.

In the Pacific, the war against Japan progressed much faster than originally anticipated by Allied planners, thanks primarily to the incredible industrial output of the United States. The first order of business was to stop the Japanese advances. The Japanese had other ideas, including knocking the United States out of the Pacific altogether.

Thus Adm Isoroku Yamamoto sought to destroy the remnants of the American Pacific Fleet, and the Japanese appeared to have the chance for the final decisive battle when Adm Chester Nimitz offered battle at Midway in June 1942. Nimitz was in possession of Japanese war plans, thanks to important code-breaking operations (see the section on military conduct) and thus surprised and defeated the Japanese fleet. The Battle of Midway ended the eastward expansion of the Japanese. In the south, the Americans invaded the islands of Guadalcanal, Gavutu, and Tulagi in the Solomons. The objective was to blunt the Japanese offensive, which appeared to threaten Australia. After bitter fighting the US operation was successful, and the southern expansion of the Japanese was halted. With the Japanese stopped, it was time to take the offensive.

The basic offensive strategy had four steps. The first required cutting off the Japanese home islands from sources of raw materials and thus to take advantage of a major Japanese vulnerability. In the second part of the strategy, the Allies were to keep up constant military pressure to force the Japanese to use their war reserve stockpiles. The third step was to get within range of the home islands and initiate a heavy bombing offensive to pave the way for an invasion. (Originally, Allied planners envisioned the use of Chinese air bases for the air campaign. However, Chinese setbacks in 1944 made it necessary to use island bases for the final aerial onslaught.) The fourth and last step was to invade the home islands.

Controversy arose over the best route for getting within range of the home islands. General MacArthur in the southwest Pacific argued for an advance on the Philippines from the south (his command area). The Philippines could then be used as a jumping-off point against the home islands and as the place from which to interdict the flow of raw materials from the south. To some observers, MacArthur seemed obsessed with his pledge to return and liberate the Philippines, but he had an advantage: as a former Army chief of staff, he had been the superior of those officers now running the war.

Adm Nimitz favored a far different route. He recommended a naval assault across the central Pacific aimed at the Philippine–Formosa area to cut the Japanese Empire in two and separate the home island from their resource base. Naval strategists also leaned toward Formosa as the base of operations for the final assault on Japan. In a classic compromise, the Joint Chiefs of Staff authorized the "nondecision" that both approaches were the best method of placing intolerable pressure on the Japanese.

After the Americans seized island bases in the Marianas (part of the Nimitz plan), the aerial campaign against Japan began in earnest. The Japanese merchant marine had been virtually destroyed by naval action and the lines of supply from the south were cut. American airmen believed bombing would destroy remaining Japanese war production and directly attack the will of the people. In a turnabout, the daylight precision-bombing concept that the American airmen had fought so hard to preserve in the European theater was quickly abandoned in the Pacific. Bad weather, problems with the jet stream, long flight distances, the distribution of Japanese industry, and Japanese opposition convinced the airmen that night low-level attacks using incendiary munitions against highly flammable Japanese cities would be the most effective strategy.

Plans for the invasion progressed. The bitter experiences on Iwo Jima and Okinawa demonstrated that an invasion of the home islands would be a costly affair. However, the city-leveling bombing attack took its toll. The use of atomic bombs at Hiroshima and Nagasaki was the straw that broke the back of resistance and Japan sued for peace before the invasion occurred.

## Political Considerations

As in all wars, parts of World War II gain their full meaning only when viewed within a domestic and international framework where politics affects the battlefield and vice versa. From an American viewpoint, the major political concerns were international rather than domestic because the war enjoyed broad-based internal support. At the same time, the exigencies of alliance decision making created some strains that were primarily political in character.

American participation in World War II may have been the most popular of any US military excursion. Certainly it was the most strongly supported long war in US history. It was the most purely total war in the American experience, and this factor may well have contributed to America's embrace of its purposes and conduct.

Although we have described other wars as total within their contexts, the Second World War more closely meets the criteria of total war. It was a war of mass mobilization wherein the entire American population was called upon to become involved in one way or another. More than 12 million Americans were brought directly under arms for its conduct, the American industrial plant was revived and converted to become the arsenal of democracy, and an unprecedented amount of American treasure was committed to its successful conclusion. Millions, including a previously inconceivable number of women and minorities, were recruited to work in factories supporting the war (many have argued that this was the crucial underpinning of later women's and civil rights movements) and everyone was encouraged to contribute in some way, if only by growing victory gardens or making do with ration coupons. Thus for Americans (other than Southerners in the Civil War) World War II demanded a depth and breadth of involvement never seen before—or since.

Fortunately, the purposes for which the war was being fought seemed adequate for the sacrifice. The enemy was an unmitigated evil: the monster Hitler and the infamous Hirohito and Mussolini. The elimination of such evils rang a responsive chord in the traditional American moral sensibility, an emotion heightened by the way America was forced into the fray. When President Roosevelt proclaimed the unconditional surrender of the various enemies as the primary military objective to ensure the eradication of fascism, he announced a moral purpose adequate to sustain American support.

If America was firmly united behind the purposes of the war, the same cannot be said of the other Allies. The most prominent of disagreements within the alliance dealt, as suggested earlier, with how to treat the Soviet Union and what the balance should be between attaining political and military objectives when these came into conflict. These problems were interactive and were the subject of considerable discussion between the Americans and the British.

Great Britain, with its greater experience in power politics generally and its longer history of dealing with Russians, was a great deal more suspicious of the Soviets than was the United States. Churchill viewed Soviet motives within the context of the expansive tendencies of the Russian Empire by whatever name. Americans, largely naive in European politics (by choice) and painfully ignorant of the Soviet Union, were more ready to embrace the Soviets and to believe in their political reasonableness. To America, all the Allies were part of the common cause, and Soviet leader Stalin was extolled by the American propaganda network as "Uncle Joe."

This difference in attitude had practical applications regarding both elements in the disagreement. Because the British believed the ultimate Soviet purpose was to extend its domain over as much of Europe as possible, they were more content to see the Soviet and Nazi armies slug it out on the Eastern Front. The Americans wished to get onto the continent, confront the Germans in classic American style, and grind the Nazi armies between themselves and the Red Army. The British demurred from this "direct" approach to the problem, preferring the more "indirect" approach of attacking at the periphery. As discussed earlier, the British approach prevailed until June 1944 while Stalin fumed that the Western Allies' real desire was to see the Nazis and the Soviets physically destroy one another so that the Western Allies could pick up the pieces (an idea put forward early in the war by a then-obscure senator from Missouri, Harry S Truman).

One result of these disagreements was the ongoing annual debate between the British and the Americans about when and where to open the second front. Certainly part of that debate represented a philosophical disagreement between Americans, whose heritage was the direct approach inherited from Grant, and the British belief in the Anaconda-like plan that made up the indirect approach. At the same time, the question of how to deal with the Soviets, which translated into the question of how fast and where to come to their aid, had something to do with the debate.

The balance between adherence to the military and political solutions was also subject to disagreement as exemplified by the final campaigns of the war in Europe. After the final German offensive in the west was broken at the Battle of the Bulge in the winter of 1944–45, Germany lay largely prostrate. The Americans and the British were approaching from the west, and the Red Army was moving in from the east.

The American command, supported by Roosevelt, wanted to concentrate on the purely military task of engaging and destroying the German army's ability to resist. Such an approach required operating over a broad front, was time-consuming, and brought relatively small amounts of territory under control. The British preferred a blitzkrieg-style movement on a narrow front, worrying about knocking out pockets of resistance later. Their motive was simple and straightforward: Churchill maintained that a lightninglike movement could capture Berlin and thus reap considerable political and military prestige that would be important in the postwar world. The Americans, however, insisted on the broad front as militarily more effective, and because of our military predominance, we prevailed.

Another political concern was how to induce the Axis powers to capitulate once the end was in sight. The goal of unconditional surrender became a problem in much the same way that the Emancipation Proclamation undoubtedly stiffened the Southern desire to resist during the Civil War. Unconditional surrender's requirements included the physical invasion and occupation of Germany that had been avoided in the Great War, and such a prospect tended to increase the Axis will to resist. Allied armed forces were gradually grinding down hostile ability, but overcoming cost-tolerance (hostile will) was a more difficult matter in the face of Allied objectives.

The primary tool used in each theater to bring about the destruction of hostile will was strategic bombardment, followed, if necessary, as in the German case, by invasion. In the case of Japan, because of the horrible prospects of having to mount history's largest and undoubtedly bloodiest amphibious assault on those islands, the United States sought help for the final invasion. Thus the United States induced the Soviet Union to declare war on Japan in 1945 to assist in the invasion (and hence to endure some of the estimated 1 million casualties that the effort would exact). The dropping of the atomic bombs on Hiroshima and Nagasaki, however, obviated the problem.

## Military Technology and Technique

If defensive capabilities dominated World War I, the offense dominated World War II largely as the result of technological advances and new and inventive ways of using weapons first developed in earlier wars. Rather than a grinding stalemate, World War II saw sweeping, high-speed maneuver that revolutionized war on land, at sea, and in the air.

Mechanized armored formations fundamentally changed land warfare. Although the tank had some successes in the latter stages of World War I, its effectiveness was limited. Proponents of armored warfare between the two wars believed the tank's somewhat disappointing performance had been the result of transient problems, such as mechanical difficulties that could be resolved with better designs and materials. World War II tanks had heavier armor plating, much greater speed (up to 25 mph for even the heaviest tanks), heavier guns (up to 122 mm on the Soviet JS III), turret-mounted guns for greater firing flexibility, and far more reliable designs. In all, the World War II tank was a far more potent weapon than its lumbering predecessor.

The leading interwar theoreticians of mechanized warfare were two Englishmen. Gen J.F.C. Fuller had been the author of "Plan 1919," the blueprint for a massive and presumably final tank offensive against the Germans. (The plan was not put into effect because Germany surrendered in 1918.) Fuller remained a leading proponent and theoretician of armored warfare after the war and long after his retirement from active service. Basil Liddell Hart, a medically retired army captain, was the second leading proponent of armored warfare. Hart was a prolific writer, and his fame, along with that of Fuller, spread around the world. However, they were prophets with little honor in their own land. (In the mid-1930s, the British army spent far more on fodder for cavalry horses than on fuel for its armored forces.) The leading practitioner of armored warfare, building on the theories of Fuller and Liddell Hart, was Heinz Guderian, who built the German panzer divisions and trained his forces in the concepts of blitzkrieg (lightning war). Meanwhile, the French, British, Americans, and Soviets fell behind in both theory and practice.

In the Second World War, as forecast by Fuller and Liddell Hart and practiced by Guderian and his disciples, the armor–infantry relationship of World War I was reversed. Now infantry supported tank operations and tanks moved at their own pace rather than at the pace of the infantry. It was the infantry's problem to keep pace with the tanks and general land force mechanization resulted. Thus modern armored warfare emphasized rapid and sustained movement. The objective was to penetrate deep to the enemy's rear, disrupt his command, control, and communication capabilities, and surround his fighting formations. Strong defensive formations were bypassed and left for reduction by the mechanized infantry formations that followed. The flanks of armored columns slashing deep into enemy areas were long and exposed. But with enough speed and movement, the flanks would take care of themselves as befuddled enemies fell back in total disarray. Mechanized battle was not only a battle of rapid movement, but it also required the use of massive numbers of tanks and supporting vehicles.

Although modern mechanized warfare depended on the development of dependable armored vehicles, another key element in "lightning" war was the development of tactical air power. When carefully coordinated with ground operations, tactical air power provided the long-range disruptive effect provided by heavy artillery in World War I. Unlike the big guns of the first war, however, tactical air power moved easily with rapidly advancing armored columns and ranged ahead of them to disrupt enemy efforts to organize an effective defense.

Not all campaigns in World War II were lightning campaigns, but nearly all displayed the combined arms operations that, if conditions were favorable, could develop into campaigns of rapid movement and deep penetration. There were, however, numerous examples of lightning war in textbook form. The German invasion of Poland was the first example, although the battle for France in 1940 remains the classic example of blitzkrieg. The largest examples were in the German offensives against the Soviets. In the summer and fall of 1941 panzer columns slashed deep to the rear of Soviet positions and trapped huge numbers of Soviet soldiers and incredible quantities of equipment. Despite setbacks in the winter of 1941–42, the Germans again achieved significant success in the summer and early fall of 1942 against the Soviets. Late in 1942, however, the Germans became seriously overextended and got bogged down in positional "slugging matches," most notably at Stalingrad. Soviet forces linked in the German rear and trapped an entire German field army, a major turning point in the Great Patriotic War.

The foremost American practitioner of armored warfare was the colorful Gen George S. Patton. At heart Patton was a cavalryman of the old school, but he adapted well and studied the successes and failures of others. He imitated his tutors and generally improved upon their techniques. Patton's dash across France after the Allied breakout from the hedgerows of Normandy is a superb example of armored warfare at its best. Patton's use of tactical air power ahead of his columns is an excellent example of the air-to-ground coordination required in highly mobile warfare.

The value of air power was primitively demonstrated in World War I. Air-to-ground cooperation and coordination was improved in the second war, thanks to the development of reliable radio equipment. As a result of improved coordination and the inherent speed and mobility of air power, it became critically important to successful ground operations, particularly, highly mobile ground operations. But in World War II, air power also played a much different role: to attack the ability of an enemy society to wage war.

The concept of strategic bombing flowed from the ideas of the Italian airman Giulio Douliet and the American soldier-airman Billy Mitchell. Both of these iconoclasts believed that bombing the enemy's "vital centers" could destroy the enemy's will and ability to wage war. In the United States the ideas of Mitchell, who was forced out of service, were carried to fruition by his disciples at the Air Corps Tactical School. They promulgated a doctrine of strategic bombing to destroy the enemy's industrial centers and thus destroy his ability to support warfare. The "true believers" at the school thought that strategic bombing alone could be decisive and that surface forces would become passé. The initial American plan for the air war in Europe even indicated that, if correctly executed, a strategic-bombing campaign could make an invasion of the continent unnecessary.

Two key elements were required for a successful strategic bombing campaign. The first was equipment capable of striking the enemy's vital centers. After several unsuccessful attempts to produce a heavy bomber, success was finally achieved with the development of the B-10 in 1932. However, it was the famous B-17 and later the B-24 that formed the backbone of the American bombing effort during the European campaign in the second war. In the Pacific theater, the much larger, heavier, and longer-range B-29 was the aircraft that ranged across vast distances and struck at the Japanese home islands.

The second key element was the identification of the vital centers or the key elements of the industrial web, the destruction of which would bring down the enemy. During the bombing campaign in the European theater, campaign plans were continually revised in a search for these key elements. Electric power plants, ball bearings factories, and other "vital" industrial elements were attacked with significant success, and yet the German war machine fought on. Finally, the American airmen struck at German synthetic oil production and found the key. The destruction of these facilities significantly degraded the capabilities of German ground and air forces by causing acute shortages of petroleum products essential for mechanized warfare.

The effectiveness of strategic bombing is still a subject of considerable controversy. Clearly, the idea of strategic bombing was oversold by zealous airmen before World War II. Armies and navies did not become obsolete as some had predicted. Europe had to be invaded and many bloody battles fought before the Nazis surrendered. In the Pacific, however, the destructiveness of firebombing raids on Japanese cities and the devastation caused by two atomic bombs convinced the Japanese to surrender without an invasion. The Japanese navy had been destroyed, but much of the Japanese army remained in the field undefeated. The airmen believed they had been vindicated, but the land and naval battles required to get the airmen within range of the Japanese home islands cast at least some doubt on their claims.

Naval warfare was also drastically altered by the advent of air power. The age of the battleship as queen of the fleet ended decisively at Pearl Harbor. The aircraft carrier quickly became the centerpiece of the naval battle force. Often during the Pacific campaigns, fleets fought at ranges so great that opposing ships were never in sight of one another. Aircraft ranged out from their carriers hundreds of miles to attack enemy fleets and island strongholds. Although surface engagements did occasionally occur, for the most part naval war in the Pacific was an air war. Naval guns were used to protect vulnerable aircraft carriers or to support amphibious landing and ground operations.

Other technological developments before and during World War II were less dramatic but equally important in changing the face of warfare. Of particular importance was the use of electronic warfare. Radar was an indispensable warning device against attacking aircraft, as was well demonstrated in the Battle of Britain. Counter-radar devices thus became important as did radio direction finding and guidance techniques. Radar was also important at sea both for air defense and for surface operations. Electronic eavesdropping, the gathering of intelligence by electronic message interception, became a fine art that led directly to success on the battlefield. Perhaps the best example of this was the electronic intelligence gathered prior to the Japanese assault on Midway in 1942. Not only were radio transmissions intercepted, but the Japanese code was broken, revealing Adm Yamamoto's plan. As a result, a ragged force built around the three surviving US aircraft carriers was able to ambush the Japanese invasion fleet and turn the tide in the Pacific. Equally important was the electronic intelligence gathered from the Germans. The ability to read German codes provided a singular advantage to the Allies.

Many would argue that the most significant technological development of World War II was the atomic bomb. However significant its development may have been, its primary influence lies in the postwar world, and thus is discussed in a later chapter. In World War II the development and use of atomic bombs were little more than the crowning blow that convinced the Japanese that they must surrender or face total destruction.

World War II saw the mechanization of war begun in the Civil War and advanced through World War I come to fruition. Although mechanization changed the face of war on the battlefield, the most significant change it wrought was to change the very nature of war. War, which had been a battle of masses since the time of Napoléon, became a battle of factories. The industrial base of the antagonists was increasingly important as were lines of communication, sources of raw materials, and complex logistical networks. As a result, the home front became a target of critical importance, and a target that could be struck directly because of the mechanization of war. The home front was now on the front lines.

**Military Conduct**

Both Germany and Japan achieved stunning successes before the United States entered the war. The Italians achieved some limited success in Ethiopia but were for the most part embarrassed by the results of their military ventures. Japan invaded China proper in 1937, and on 1 September 1939 Germany invaded Poland. By the end of December 1941, these three unlikely partners had overrun most of Europe, much of North Africa, most of European Russia, the richest portions of China, and many of the island complexes in the East, Central, and South Pacific. Their setbacks had been few in number and minor in nature. And yet, by the end of 1942, just one year after the entry of the United States into the war, the tide of conquest was reversed and the Axis powers began long and painful retreats.

Although the Allies agreed that attention would be focused on the European war first, the tide first turned in the Pacific. Adm Yamamato, the architect of Japanese naval victories in the Pacific, attempted to lure the remainder of the American Pacific Fleet—primarily the aircraft carriers not caught in the Pearl Harbor attack—into a final climactic battle. Yamamoto planned to seize Midway Island in early June 1942 to bait the trap. When the American carriers arrived to counterattack, he would overwhelm them with an incredible assemblage of ships and planes. Unfortunately for the Japanese, the Americans were reading the most secret Japanese naval codes and knew Yamamoto's plan. As a result, the aircraft from three American carriers were able to ambush Yamamoto's carrier force north of Midway. The island base remained in American hands, but more important, US aviators sank four Japanese fleet carriers and Japan lost the best of its naval aviators. The cost to the Americans was many good aviators, one destroyer, and one carrier. The tide had turned in the Pacific only six months after the United States entered the war.

In North Africa, the seesaw war that raged back and forth across the desert finally turned for good against the German-Italian forces on 23 October 1942, when British Gen Bernard L. Montgomery launched the second battle of El Alamein. In a well-prepared set-piece battle, Montgomery sent the Axis forces under the command of Gen (later Field Marshal) Erwin Rommel reeling back out of Egypt and across Libya. On 8 November, with the Germans and Italians in headlong retreat, Anglo-American landings took place near Casablanca in Morocco, as well as near Oran and Algiers in Algeria. Vichy French forces controlling these areas offered some resistance but were quickly overcome, and the Allied troops began moving east to trap the Axis forces retreating in front of Montgomery. After much hard fighting and the evacuation of Rommel, nearly a quarter million German and Italian soldiers trapped in Tunisia surrendered on 12 May 1943.

The tide turned in the European war on 19 November 1942, north and south of the shattered city of Stalingrad on the Volga River. In August of that year, the German Sixth Army had reached the outskirts of Stalingrad. This

advance was the high water mark of the German offensive in southern Russia. The city that bore Stalin's name held a special fascination for Hitler, and
Soviet troops defended the city with great tenacity for perhaps the same reason. The Germans abandoned the mobile, armored warfare that had given
them great success and became bogged down in house-to-house fighting in
which their superior armored forces offered no advantage. Meanwhile the
Soviets massed forces north and south of the city to strike the exposed Axis
flanks. On 19 November the Red Army attacked and by 22 November had
trapped Gen (later Field Marshal) Friedrich von Paulus and the German Sixth
Army. Despite attempts to relieve the army and to supply it by air, the shattered German army surrendered at the end of January 1943.

The Allied counterattack continued in 1943. In the Mediterranean the Allies invaded Sicily on 10 July and liberated the island by 17 August. In September Anglo-American forces leaped the Strait of Messina and invaded
Italy. Although the Italian government and forces surrendered, the Germans
under the command of Field Marshal Albert Kesselring waged a tenacious
defense of the peninsula that lasted until nearly the end of the war.

In the Pacific limited Allied offensive action began. Operations on

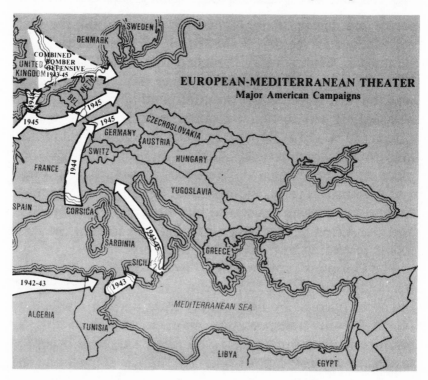

Guadalcanal were completed in early February. New Georgia, New Britain, Makin, and Tarawa all fell; Bougainville was invaded and counterattacks liberated much of New Guinea. Of particular importance was the death of Adm Yamamoto, whose plane was shot down by American pilots flying from Guadalcanal. American signal intelligence code breakers discovered that the admiral would be visiting forward bases in the Solomons and the timing of his itinerary. American P-38 twin-engine fighters ambushed the admiral's aircraft and the chief strategist of the Japanese navy was lost.

Meanwhile the long-awaited Allied heavy bombing offensive against Germany began in earnest. British bombers had raided deep into Europe under the cover of darkness almost since the beginning of hostilities. The Americans entered the war with excellent heavy bombers (B-17s and B-24s), an accurate bombsight (the Norden), and a different bombardment theory. While the British bombed large areas at night to avoid heavy losses to enemy air defenses, the Americans advocated precision bombing during daylight hours.

During 1942 and early 1943, the American bomber force slowly increased in Europe. Equipment arrived with green crews, and training was intense.

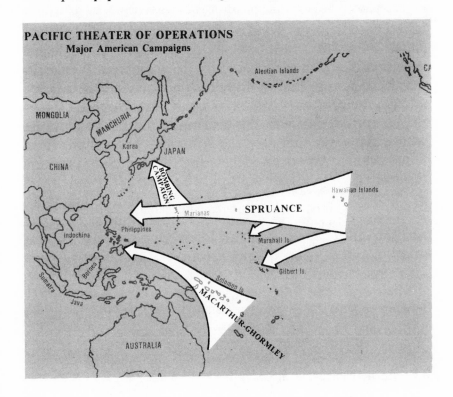

**PACIFIC THEATER OF OPERATIONS**
Major American Campaigns

Short missions over the continent began on 17 August 1942. The long-range American bombing effort began in earnest late in the summer of 1943, first against the Romanian oil refineries at Ploesti and then against Germany itself.

The strategic bombing campaign reached a thundering climax during 1944. During "Big Week," which began on 20 February, armadas of Allied aircraft bombed German aircraft plants and challenged the Luftwaffe to fight. Although the bombing raids did significant damage, the telling blow was in air-to-air combat, as Allied escort fighters directly battled hard-pressed German fighters. In mid-May some bomber missions were allocated to attacks on German synthetic oil production, the source of much aviation fuel for the Luftwaffe. Although the results were not apparent for several months, synthetic oil was the key to total air supremacy for the Allies. Without fuel, the Luftwaffe could not defend against the Allied air offensive, and the destructiveness of the bombing raids mounted rapidly. The vital center had been found, the air battle was won, and the stage was set for the invasion of the continent.

The Germans believed the invasion would be launched directly across the Channel at the Pas de Calais. The Allies nurtured this notion through elaborate deception schemes while preparing to invade across the beaches of Normandy. Although some difficulties were encountered, particularly on Omaha Beach, the invasion went well and a lodgement was quickly achieved. However, it soon became obvious that the planners had worried more about securing a beachhead than they had worried about subsequent operations. It is difficult to imagine fighting territory more unsuited to mobile warfare than the Normandy hedgerow country. The Allies could not take advantage of their superior mobility and quickly became involved in a heavy slugging match that yielded slow progress.

Finally, after a climactic battle in July near Saint-Lô, the Americans breached the German line and poured through the gap into more open country. General Patton's newly created Third Army led the charge across the breadth of France in an armored dash reminiscent of the German blitzkriegs of earlier years. Suddenly, the front was far more fluid and a general Allied advance quickly began. By 19 August American elements were across the River Seine, and Paris was liberated on 25 August. Meanwhile on 15 August, the Allies launched a second invasion, this time on the southern French coast near Saint-Tropez. The troops were quickly ashore and moved north. German resistance in France was in shambles.

In March 1945 the Allies were across the Rhine in force, and the victorious armies fanned out across Germany. Resistance to the Soviet advance continued to the bitter end while resistance in the west rapidly disintegrated. The Germans capitulated on 7 May 1945.

In the Pacific 1944 was a year of relentless Allied advance. American troops seized Kwajalein, Eniwetok, and Saipan by midyear. Allied operations continued successfully on New Guinea, and a Japanese thrust from Burma into India was defeated. By year's end, American bombers were within range of the Japanese home islands, and the stage was set for the destruction of the Japanese will and ability to continue the war.

After midyear Guam and Tinian quickly fell. Finally, on 20 October, Gen MacArthur fulfilled his promise and returned to the Philippines. The US Sixth Army landed on the island of Leyte and began a long struggle to liberate the islands. The landings provoked the remnants of the Japanese navy to an almost suicidal mission to destroy the American fleet supporting the landing and thus to isolate the troops ashore. The Japanese attack surprised the American forces in Leyte Gulf and caused considerable damage and confusion. However, the Battle of Leyte Gulf was the gasp of a dying fleet and a disaster for the Japanese. In widely separated actions, the Japanese lost four carriers, three battleships, six cruisers, and 14 destroyers. For all practical purposes, the Japanese fleet ceased to exist.

While the campaign for the Philippines continued, another facet of the war began. On 24 November 1944 the first B-29 raid against the Japanese home islands was launched. Using bases in the Marianas, the pace of attack began to build but with mixed results. The new aircraft caused some problems as did the long flight times. Additionally, finding good weather over Japan was difficult. Precision bombing was made difficult because of the jet stream encountered over Japan and because much of the Japanese industrial base resembled a cottage industry—dispersed and difficult to find. As a result, on 9 March 1945 Gen Curtis LeMay stripped down his B-29s, loaded them with incendiary bombs, and ordered them on a low-level night bombing mission over Tokyo. The raid destroyed nearly 16 square miles of the city, killed 84,000, and injured 40,000 others. Nearly 1 million people were made homeless. American losses were negligible. The die was cast; low-level firebombing would be the principal aerial tactic. By war's end 178 square miles of Japanese cities had been completely destroyed in firebombing raids.

As the B-29s bombed the heart out of Japan, the ground and naval offensives continued, culminating in the campaigns for Iwo Jima and Okinawa. In spite of suicide attacks by Japanese planes, the islands were secured. The jumping-off points for the invasion of Japan were in American hands. Meanwhile the campaign against Japanese shipping, the naval blockade of the islands, and the firebombing had taken their toll. Finally, atomic bombs were dropped on Hiroshima (6 August 1945) and Nagasaki (9 August 1945). On 8 August the Soviets declared war on the Japanese and invaded Japanese-held Manchuria the following day. Even the most die-hard Japanese saw that continued resistance might mean the death of Japanese civilization. On 14 August 1945 Japan surrendered. The only invasion required was peaceful as occupation forces entered the Land of the Rising Sun.

## Better State of the Peace

When the war finally came to an end with the formal capitulation of Germany and Japan, the victorious Allies were faced with the task of re-creating the peace. Mindful of the failure of the Versailles conferees to reach a solution guaranteeing an enduring peace, the three major victorious Allies faced the same essential tasks that had confronted the preceding generation. What to do with the losers? How to build an international structure that would allow peace to last? How to restructure a political map torn asunder in the world's greatest bloodletting?

The prerequisites to forming a better state of the peace had been achieved. German and Japanese hostile ability and willingness to continue had been overcome, although in different ways. In the case of Germany, her armies had been effectively destroyed and her industrial web lay in ruins; hostile ability had been decisively overcome. As the Allied armies marched inexorably toward one another in central Germany, hostile willingness (cost-tolerance) evaporated as well. In the end, Germany lay prostrate, more physically defeated and vulnerable than had been the case in 1918.

Japan was a somewhat different proposition. Because of the way the island-hopping campaign against the Japanese Empire was conducted, Japan still retained significant military power even at the end of the war. Certainly Japan's navy lay mostly at the bottom of the ocean and its air force had been reduced to nonexistence; but the Japanese army remained, though scattered at garrisons throughout eastern Asia. Japan's hostile ability was tottering, dispersed, and incapable of being linked together because of the destruction of her naval and air assets, but the Japanese armed forces were not decimated in the way that Germany's were.

What broke decisively for the Japanese was the willingness to continue to resist. Air power, so widely acclaimed as the solution to the European problem, proved the key element in convincing the Japanese leadership that going on was futile. With its navy and air force destroyed, Japan's home islands had been subjected to a merciless pounding, particularly through the use of incendiary bombs. The dropping of atomic devices on Nagasaki and Hiroshima was the coup de grace of the strategic bomber's art that finally brought about capitulation.

Two comments need to be made about this process of overcoming hostile will and ability. The first has to do with the Allies' stated policy (at least the

American policy) of unconditional surrender. Although it can never be proved conclusively, that goal and its likely concomitant of physical invasion and occupation undoubtedly stiffened hostile will and prolonged the war against both adversaries. In Germany the major fear was the advancing Red Army and the likely retribution the Soviets would exact. In Japan unconditional surrender resulted in the nonnegotiable US demand that the emperor abdicate. The evidence now suggests that had the United States recanted on that one demand, agreeing in effect to leave the emperor as a figurehead like the British monarch, Japan might have surrendered earlier. Once unconditional surrender became the goal, however, it was politically impossible to reverse gears without appearing to change the goals that had activated sacrifice in the first place.

The second comment has to do with the unique contributions of strategic bombing to overcoming Axis hostile will and ability. World War II was, after all, the test case for the strategic bombardment theories that had been developed in the interwar period, and it was also the only instance when those theories have been tested against developed societies possessing the "vital centers" and industrial web for which the ideas were formed.

In some ways the air power enthusiasts' hopes and claims were clearly excessive. As pointed out, strategic bombardment did not make naval and ground operations obsolete or ancillary. Instead air, land, and sea power were interactive. Naval and ground operations in the Pacific provided staging grounds for the bombers that could not have been secured otherwise, for instance. That the most extreme prior claims for strategic bombardment were overdrawn does not, however, necessarily belittle air power's overall contribution.

The important role that strategic bombardment played in the war emboldened its proponents and probably caused them to over-extrapolate from the experience: because bombardment had worked against Germany and Japan, it would work elsewhere. What was lost in the process was an appreciation of the unique characteristics of the two countries: both were highly industrialized countries with peculiar vulnerabilities and dependencies. When faced by opponents that have not shared these characteristics, strategic bombardment has not been so clearly applicable, and the controversy over strategic air power continues to swirl partly as a result.

If hostile ability and cost-tolerance had been overcome, the crucial remaining task was how to structure the peace. That task in turn meant having to deal with the three questions posed at the beginning of this section. The Allies' answers would determine if the failures of Versailles would be revisited in the wake of World War II.

The first question to be answered was how the vanquished powers would be treated. The answer in 1919 had been to impose a vindictive peace, and it had been a failure. In 1945 the Allies' ability to impose was even greater, since both Germany and Japan were occupied. Fortunately, lessons had been at least partially learned.

In both Japan and Germany, democratic political systems were installed (except in the Soviet occupation zone in Germany), a reminder of post–World War I Germany. The difference was that in 1919 the new political system was burdened with a settlement that virtually ensured economic chaos. That chaos was blamed on the fledgling republic and undermined any likelihood that the people would embrace the system. The installation of democracy after 1945 was accompanied by generous programs of economic rehabilitation and development. These programs nurtured recovery and generated support for the imposed political regimes, thereby removing the vestiges of resistance to victor policies.

The Soviet Union did not share in this process. In the Soviet's occupation zone, an essentially vindictive peace was imposed through a harsh military occupation, the imposition of a Communist regime, transformation of the East German economy into a feeder for the Soviet Union, and punitive reparations (even to the extent of literally transporting German industries to the USSR to replace destroyed Soviet factories). This spirit of vengeance was not unlike that of France after the Great War. Given its parallel suffering, the Soviet Union's urge to vindictiveness should not be entirely surprising (although there were additional Soviet motivations as well).

The second question was how to fashion a postwar order that would prevent a recurrence of war. This task largely fell to a working group in the US State Department that began its work before formal American entrance into the war. The State Department personnel began their job by examining what there was about the mechanism erected in 1919 that had caused its failure. Their answer was that the League of Nations had inadequately institutionalized the process of responding to threats to or actual breaches of the peace, a deficiency they sought to remedy in the new United Nations Charter. Under the League of Nations Covenant, no nation had a specific obligation to respond to any crisis, and the League had no permanent armed forces assigned to its jurisdiction. As a result, the League could only issue a call to its membership to respond to a crisis and hope the members would rise to the occasion. If, as happened during the 1930s, the membership did not heed the call, the League was powerless to stop aggression.

The framers of the UN Charter sought to overcome this problem. In drafting the collective security provisions of the charter, they proposed a radical solution. The permanent members of the new Security Council—the major Allies (the United States, Soviet Union, United Kingdom, France, and China)—would jointly take on the role of policemen of the world. Only they would retain significant military force, while all other nations would be disarmed to the level required for maintaining internal order. These disarmed states would simply act as bases for UN troops from the major powers. Thus overwhelming military force would always be available to confront a potential aggressor.

The victorious Allies had limited success in dealing with the second question, but it was the third that ultimately proved most vexing: the shape of the postwar political map. At this point Anglo-American visions (slightly altered) embodied in the Atlantic Charter clashed directly with Soviet security and hegemonic interests. The inability to resolve these differences satisfactorily has provided much of the basis of conflict in the international system during the cold war.

The operative American, and to a lesser extent British, idea was self-determination for all peoples, although this ideal was occasionally compromised in practice in the third world—for example, as in acquiescence in French reimposition of colonial rule in Indochina. The Soviets, obsessed with physical security and the spread of their ideology, insisted on forming a *cordon sanitaire* (buffer zone) of friendly (Communist) governments in the east European countries they occupied. The Soviet position flew in the face of Anglo-American desires but, given the Soviet occupation of the affected countries, the Western Allies were in a position to do little about Soviet actions.

Where there was joint occupation, matters were even worse. Germany was divided originally among the three combatants (France was later given its own zone carved out of the American and British sectors) and cooperation quickly broke down. Western policy was to push for normalization and economic revitalization as quickly as possible, a preference best served by reintegration of the zones in a united Germany. The Soviets, however, desired (as the French had before them) a permanently weakened Germany, and their best bet in this regard was a divided Germany. Ultimately, division became effectively permanent over the issue of currency reforms in the western zones that precipitated a Soviet response in the form of the Berlin blockade. The Berlin Wall and the miles upon miles of no man's land separating West and East Germany were grim reminders of the inability to resolve the issue.

Korea was the other divided country. In return for the Soviet pledge to assist in the invasion of the Japanese home islands in 1945, the Soviet Union received an occupation zone in the formerly Japanese-controlled nation. According to agreements reached during the war, the purpose of the occupation was to disarm remaining Japanese troops, to establish civil order, and to prepare both sections for free, unifying elections in 1948. Instead a

Communist regime was installed in the north and an anti-Communist regime in the south.

Was a better state of the peace achieved? If one uses the Versailles yardstick for comparison, the answer is that this peace has certainly been overwhelmingly more successful than that following 1919. There has been no military resurgence of the defeated powers and a third worldwide conflagration has been avoided. In Europe, the center of international violence for the centuries preceding, bloodshed has been limited to Soviet actions in east Europe for more than 40 years. In that sense the peace has been a notable success.

It was not, however, a perfect peace (if such is possible). The formal mechanism for regulating the peace was ineffective as a collective security instrument when the wartime Allies fell out, and the inability of East and West to redraw the political map in a mutually satisfactory manner sowed the seeds for future conflict. The series of controversies over Berlin was a direct legacy of World War II's better state of the peace, and so are the histories of Korea and Vietnam, to which the discussion now moves.

# 6

# Korean War

If World War II had been the ultimate example of total war, the Korean conflict began the trend back to limited engagement. Begun a mere five years after the conclusion of the Second World War, Korea started a process of adjustment for American military and political leaders. It is a process of understanding and interaction that still continues.

The Korean War was a new experience for the United States and for the international order that emerged from the ashes of World War II. For the United States, the experience was unique in at least three ways. First, it was our first limited war in modern (twentieth-century) times. As such, it represented a discontinuity in experience that required painful learning and adjustment. Second, it was the first significant cold war confrontation and represented a novel challenge to the emerging American role in the world. Third, it was the first major American military engagement not preceded by a formal declaration of military intent by the Congress of the United States, and it began a constitutional and political process that culminated in the War Powers Act of 1973. For the international system, Korea was the first instance of the application of the collective security provisions of the United Nations Charter, although not an application as envisaged by its framers. Each of these points is of sufficient importance to merit elaboration.

Although the United States had fought wars that were limited in terms of the severity with which they were fought (e.g., the War of 1812) or the ease of their accomplishment (e.g., the Spanish-American War), the Korean conflict was the first time the modern US military, developed and prepared for total war and led by an officer corps steeped in the total wars of the twentieth century, was thrust into a situation in which the political objectives were limited. The result was to create friction between the military and political leaderships. It was a disagreement for which neither group was especially well prepared, and the result was probably unnecessary ill will and inefficiency in the conduct of the hostilities.

A large part of the conflict came straight from the pages of Clausewitz. The Prussian had warned over a century earlier that there is a natural tension between military and political leaders. To the military leader, the military goal is to prevail over the enemy in combat, and the result is a tendency to intensify the level of combat. The military naturally concentrates on a concerted effort to destroy the enemy's armed forces in order to overcome hostile ability. Such was the appropriate military objective in the total war environments of the world wars, and it was a military purpose that a leadership trained in the traditional American military style and blooded in total wars could embrace.

The problem was whether such an approach was appropriate to the politico-military task at hand in Korea. Clausewitz had warned that when the military tendency to expand a war overruns the war's political objectives, political leaders must be especially vigilant to ensure that the political objectives remain supreme. To make matters somewhat more perverse, the tendency to intensify seems to operate regardless of whether one is winning or losing; raising the ante appears the universal reaction. The United States had not, at least in living memory, encountered a situation where military and political objectives clashed, but it did in Korea.

An example may help to clarify this point, because it represents a particularly bedeviling phenomenon. The best example surrounds that tragic figure of the Korean conflict, Gen Douglas MacArthur, and the politico-military role that ultimately led to his dismissal from command.

MacArthur was very much a product of the American military tradition (it can be argued that he was its epitome). He came from the West Point tradition that taught warfare Ulysses S. Grant style (he was even superintendent of West Point between the world wars), and his most significant service had been in the total-war milieu of World War II.

When he came to command the United Nations forces in Korea, he brought that experience with him. His consistent position and predilection throughout his tenure was to expand the action. When he routed the North Koreans following the Inchon landing and chased them back across the 38th parallel (thus fulfilling the original mandate to rid the south of its foreign invaders), his counsel was to continue onward and to destroy what was left of the Korean People's Army (KPA). When he was allowed to do so and was met by the Chinese intervention that sent his forces reeling south, his advice was to up the ante significantly, taking the war directly to the People's Republic of

China (PRC). That such an act, discussed more fully later in the chapter, would have altered substantially the nature of the war did not seem troublesome to someone so thoroughly imbued in the American military tradition of apoliticism. The "American Caesar" exemplified how to violate most of Clausewitz's maxims.

In Korea, the United States encountered another aspect of limited war that it did not recognize at the time and that it would also have difficulty spotting when that aspect reappeared in Vietnam. That phenomenon was an asymmetry in the political purposes of the adversaries that translated into different military approaches as well.

For the United States, the original purposes in Korea were strictly limited: remove North Korean forces from South Korea and ensure they could not return. Accomplishing the goal of liberating South Korea required neither the destruction of the enemy's armed forces (although doing so might aid in ensuring they did not come back) nor the surrender of the enemy and occupation of his territory.

The situation was quite different for the North Koreans. Within their more limited physical resource base, their purpose was total: the occupation of South Korea, the overthrow of the South Korean government, and the forceful uniting of the country. Thus, a form of contrast arose that made the war seem all the more perverse. The United States had the physical wherewithal to wage a total war, but the nature of our political objectives made the use of all those resources undesirable. Had our purposes been total, we might, for instance, have used the atomic bomb. In this circumstance such action was deemed inappropriate for a variety of reasons, including the nature of the objective (Korea was not important enough to warrant the expenditure of part of a scarce resource). On the other hand, the North Koreans had total purposes in mind, but they lacked the manpower and physical resources to achieve those goals after the United States and other United Nations members entered the fray.

Korea was also the first major military confrontation in the developing cold war competition between the Communist and non-Communist worlds. Certainly the two sides had confronted one another earlier, as in the Berlin blockade and airlift, but Korea was the first instance of actual, bloody conflict. It represented the first real test of the American policy of containment that had been articulated by the Truman administration during the second half of the 1940s.

The Korean War was viewed initially as the first opportunity to confront and arrest the spread of communism beyond the Sino-Soviet periphery. In the light of the "fall" of China to Mao Tse-tung and the Communists in 1949 and a rising anticommunism in the United States that was moving toward the excesses of McCarthyism, the idea of stopping communism through the resort to force was initially quite popular, both within the United States and elsewhere in the non-Communist world. There would be no Munichs for the masters in the Kremlin.

Korea was important because of its own geopolitical importance (especially in regard to Japanese security) and as a test of wills. For Americans the real enemy in Korea was not the North Koreans, even if it were they and the Chinese whom one was fighting. The real enemy was the Soviet Union, since Americans assumed that the North Koreans were acting as surrogates for the leaders in the Kremlin, who directed and orchestrated Communist activity everywhere as part of a closely coordinated international conspiracy.

We may never know for sure exactly what the Soviet role in the North Korean attack was, although the gradual opening of Soviet archives by the Russian government has improved the chances. Many assume that the decision process goes back to Secretary of State Dean Acheson's speech in early 1950 in which he outlined the containment line in East Asia and omitted all mention of South Korea (some allege that the omission emboldened the Soviets to authorize the attack on the assumption the United States would not react). Evidence for this position is adduced from the absence of the Soviets from the UN Security Council when the vote was taken to make intervention in Korea a UN enterprise. (The Soviets were boycotting the United Nations because of Western refusal to seat Communist China in place of Chiang Kai-shek's Chinese Nationalists. As a member of the Security Council, the Soviet Union had the right to veto the intervention motion had it been present at the meeting.)

It is likely that the Soviets did at a minimum authorize the North Koreans, possibly at North Korean initiation, to make the invasion. Such a minimal interpretation is justified by the heavy dependence of North Korea on the Soviets for war supplies. The North Koreans simply could not have sustained much of an effort without resupply from their benefactors.

Whatever the nature of the relationship, the North Korean invasion was clearly viewed in the United States as part of the East–West, cold war confrontation. At one level, such a challenge could not go unheeded lest the Soviet Union be emboldened to believe American commitments were meaningless; in that sense Korea was a symbol of the whole evolving shape of postwar international politics. At the same time, many in this country and in Europe firmly believed that the Korean action was a feint to divert American attention away from an impending invasion of western Europe. Such was the prevailing military view during the early months of the conflict, and this belief dissipated only slowly as the Soviet invasion failed to occur.

As noted earlier, Korea was the first major commitment of American forces to combat that was not preceded by a formal declaration of war by the US Congress. Certainly there were precedents for sending Americans into combat without such authorization. These included most of the western Indian wars and the campaign against the Barbary pirates, but all the previous actions had been minor and peripheral. When President Truman went before the American people on 27 June 1950 to announce that American assistance would flow to Korea (as well as to Indochina), there was little concern about the constitutional impact of the action. Only as the war dragged on did such concern arise.

The debate that developed is by now familiar. The Constitution, of course, provides that the Congress has the prerogative to raise and maintain armed forces and to declare war, whereas the president is designated as commander in chief of the armed forces. The problem that arose in the heat of Korea was how much control the Congress exercised in how those forces were used. The framers of the Constitution clearly envisaged that all wars would be declared, thereby giving Congress veto power over the commitment of forces. The Korean War was not formally declared, and, therefore, there was no constitutional (as opposed to practical political) need to get congressional approval. The debate as to whether Congress should have a voice in committing troops to such actions was joined only as public support for the war soured. In the aftermath of Korea, the debate continued inconclusively and was not raised again until another American president used the precedent in Vietnam.

Korea was also the first real test of the fledgling United Nations and the collective security system by which it was supposed to ensure the peace. By virtue of the Soviet boycott mentioned earlier, the US government was able to go before the world body and have the action it would have taken anyway sanctioned as a UN operation. Although the vast majority of the fighting in the war was waged by the United States and the Republic of Korea (ROK), technically the forces combating the North Koreans and the Chinese were those of the United Nations.

The Korean War was as close to a real collective security application as the United Nations ever mounted before the Persian Gulf War over Kuwait in 1990–91, but it was a far cry from the action envisaged in the UN Charter. The charter, attempting to overcome weaknesses in the peacekeeping provisions of the League of Nations Covenant, called for a permanent United Nations force composed of the armed forces of the permanent members of the Security Council (the United States, Soviet Union, Britain, France, and China—the victorious Allies in World War II). In this scheme, all other nations were to be substantially disarmed, providing only basing for the forces of the permanent members, who collectively would police the world and put down threats to or actual breaches of the peace. United States–Soviet enmity had, of course, torpedoed the scheme by 1950.

Clearly, the UN force that fought in Korea did not meet the criteria set forth in the charter. A number of countries did respond to the call of the United Nations and did commit troops, but in most cases the contribution was more symbolic than significant. Gen Douglas MacArthur and his successor, Gen Matthew B. Ridgway, were technically UN commanders first and American commanders second, but it was always clearly understood that their orders and authority came from the White House and not the "glass house" on Manhattan's East Side (UN headquarters). Certainly the charter never contemplated a UN action in which a permanent member of the Security Council would be the major supplier and supporter of the force opposing the United Nations.

**Issues and Events**

From an American perspective, the North Korean invasion of South Korea came as an almost total surprise, making it somewhat difficult to track underlying causes for the action. Certainly the gradual deterioration of US–USSR relations in Europe had produced a strain in the international system and had led many to expect overt conflict between the two giants; that such a confrontation would occur on the Korean peninsula, where the United States had no clearly defined interests, was a nearly complete surprise.

If there was a basic, underlying issue that defined the American position in and interest about Korea, it was embodied in the nature of cold war competition and the question of implementing the new American national strategy of containment. The Korean invasion was the first overt test of the new strategy, the first time that the communist world stepped across the containment line and threw down the gauntlet.

Seen in that light, the situation in Korea took on a symbolic importance well beyond its objective, discrete value to the United States. When the invasion occurred, the majority of Americans had probably never heard of Korea and most of those who had could not have explained why it was in the American interest to defend that harsh land. After American leaders explained the Korean intervention in the context of the crusade against godless communism and as a symbol of American will to compete, the US action had considerable initial popularity (the effort was actually quite popular until the middle of 1951 when the lines stagnated at the 38th parallel).

Korea was both the first test of containment and the opening event in a debate about the nature of American commitment arising from that doctrine that continued throughout the cold war. As the KPA poured south across the border and routed an ROK force pitifully underequipped to meet the onslaught, the question of what containment meant had to be answered. The failure to respond effectively could mean the policy was a hollow shell and invite further Soviet-inspired actions. A direct response would mean the expenditure of American blood and treasure less than five years after the end of the Second World War.

The United States determined that it had no choice but to respond militarily, and despite the rapidity with which it did so, the response came barely in time to turn the situation around. At the same time, the debate was begun about how the United States should respond to probings of the containment line in the future. One side to that debate (generally associated with Democratic presidents) has argued our commitment is encompassing and the United States must be prepared to assist the beleaguered with armed force whenever there is an attempt to breach the line. The other side (historically associated with Republican presidents) has maintained such a commitment is too expensive and that we should be prepared militarily to defend only those strategic places clearly vital to our interests (e.g., western Europe and Japan). In this view the United States should grant material aid but leave the defense of other areas to indigenous hands.

The proximate events leading to the crisis can be traced back to the latter stages of World War II. As mentioned in the previous chapter, the United States induced the Soviet Union to declare war on Japan in 1945 so that Soviet forces would be available to participate in the anticipated invasion of the Japanese home islands. A significant measure of the cost that the United States was willing to pay for that commitment was the agreement that the Soviet Union would be given an occupation zone in a liberated Korea.

Under the formal terms of agreement, the Americans occupied the territory south of the 38th parallel and the Soviets occupied the area north of that line. The stated purposes of the occupation were to disarm Japanese troops, to restore domestic order, and to prepare each zone for unifying elections scheduled for 1948. Clearly, things did not go according to plan. Instead the Soviets installed Kim Il Sung and the Korean Communist Party in the north and trained and equipped the formidable KPA to a size and equipment level far in excess of agreed upon standards. The United States, meanwhile, helped bring to power the pro-American Dr. Syngman Rhee in the south and established a military force at a constabulary level as the wartime agreements called for.

When 1948 arrived, the United States pulled out of Korea as agreed, but the Soviet Union did not. The elections to unify the country (to be supervised by the United Nations) similarly did not come about, as both sides refused to allow UN observers in their zones and each accused the other (both probably quite correctly) of trying to rig the returns. Korea was a de facto divided state. The only way it could be returned to its historical unified status (there is no strong historical or cultural basis for a division) was through an act of violence.

The North Korean invasion was the major precipitant, of course, of US action. The invasion caught the Americans and the South Koreans by surprise. Because of deficiencies in intelligence collection, both were unaware of a massing of the KPA until the day before the invasion began. When the North Korean forces streamed across the border on 25 June 1950, they quickly routed the unprepared and ill-equipped South Korean forces. (The KPA attack was, for instance, spearheaded by Russian T-34 tanks; ROK forces did not have a single antitank weapon.) As the KPA threatened to overrun the south completely and thus present a fait accompli that would be extremely difficult to counteract, the United States was forced to act quickly if it was to react at all.

President Harry S Truman's reaction was indeed swift and decisive. With information on the nature of the attack still pouring in, the president requested UN action and on 27 June 1950 announced the American intention to come to South Korea's aid. The first American combat troops arrived in South Korea from Japan on 1 July. Unfortunately, these initial forces were garrison troops accustomed to the relative tranquility of occupation duty rather than the rigors of combat, and they fared little better than the ROK troops they had been sent to assist. By the time frontline American troops arrived on the scene, the forces opposing the KPA were cornered with their backs to the sea at Pusan.

### Political Objective

As the first modern limited war in the American experience, Korea was the first instance in living American memory of war fought for less than total purposes. From the Civil War forward, Americans had come to regard war as an enterprise whose purpose was to excise some overwhelming evil. Thus war required the enemy's total defeat and capitulation, and Americans were comfortable with that concept. Korea, however, was not that kind of war and because it was not, Americans ultimately became uncomfortable with it and turned against the experience.

A large part of the problem from the American vantage point was that not only was our purpose limited, but it kept changing. The changes that occurred related directly to the state of the battlefield, recalling Clausewitz's useful admonition mentioned earlier. Had there been constancy in the objective being pursued, much of the American bitterness associated with the Korean experience might not exist. In fact, had the United Nations not strayed from its original statement of purpose, the Korean War would have been a brief and successful enterprise that we might well remember today with a sense of considerable pride.

The assertion runs counter to prevailing wisdom about our three-year campaign on the Korean peninsula, and thus requires some explanation and justification. To provide such a rationale requires looking at the question from two angles. The first vantage point is exactly what the objective was, or rather what alternative objectives were available. The second vantage point is examining how and when the objective changed and how those changes affected popular perceptions of the war.

The major source for determining the political objective is the UN mandate given to the forces that went to Korea. Unfortunately, from the original statement and subsequent debate, two not entirely compatible objectives emerge. The first and most basic was to repel the North Korean invasion, to rid South Korea of those invaders, and to allow reinstitution of South Korean control of its territory. The second objective that can be discerned is tied to the earlier UN role in Korea, supervision of the unifying elections. The first objective translated militarily into the need to simply push the invaders out of the country and to establish some reasonable assurance they would not return. Realizing the second objective required pursuing the KPA into North Korea, destroying it as a fighting force, and occupying the north as prerequisites for holding the elections. Clearly, one objective was much more ambitious than the other. (One might add that Gen MacArthur, after the Chinese "volunteers" intervened, suggested attacking Chinese territory, which would at least implicitly have expanded the political objective even more.)

When United Nations forces were first committed to combat, the situation in Korea was desperate. The South Koreans and their American allies were pinned down within the Pusan perimeter, and the question was whether sufficient force could be brought to bear quickly enough to keep them from being pushed into the sea. In that circumstance, initial objectives were modest: the goal was to relieve the situation and to rid the Republic of Korea of its invaders (the first objective).

The battlefield situation, however, soon provided the impetus for change. MacArthur's brilliant and unanticipated landing at the port of Inchon, combined with a breakout from the Pusan perimeter, caught the KPA in a classic hammer and anvil maneuver, crushed its ability to resist, and sent it reeling in disarray back across the border. United Nations forces followed the KPA to the border, paused, and weighed their options.

The major question was whether to pursue the North Koreans into their country and totally destroy them. From a military point of view, as MacArthur continuously argued, the task appeared a mere mopping-up exercise, and the original UN mandate on unification provided the justification for the counterinvasion. Moreover, MacArthur dismissed as idle bombast repeated warnings by Chinese Foreign Minister Chou En-lai that the new People's Republic would not stand idly by should the Americans press toward Chinese territory. MacArthur reasoned that China was still too weak from its recently concluded civil war to field an army of any size or capability.

In the end President Truman agreed to broaden the objective, and he authorized the invasion of the north. With the perfect vision of hindsight, the decision was a monumental mistake that doomed the war effort to historical ignominy in the popular mind. The reason for this, of course, was MacArthur's miscalculation about the Chinese and their impact on the military situation. When the Chinese "snuck" more than 300,000 troops across the border, ambushed the UN troops, and sent them reeling back south of Seoul, the situation changed radically. In January 1951 a regrouped UN force counterattacked, broke the combined KPA and Chinese force, and sent it fleeing back into the north. This time, however, the UN stopped at the 38th parallel, and appeals to go north again (which was militarily possible) fell on the deaf ears of political leaders who had become deeply suspicious of the military advice they were receiving. (Some observers have argued that, given the disarray of the enemy, the decision not to invade in 1951 was as disastrous as the decision to invade in 1950.) With the decision made not to go north, the KPA and Chinese were able to regroup and the war became a static engagement along the 38th parallel that dragged on for two more years until President Eisenhower's threat to use nuclear weapons brought the enemy seriously to the negotiating table.

In the end the result exactly met the original objective. North Korea's political goal of uniting the country by force had been thwarted, and the UN political objective of freeing the Republic of Korea had been achieved. The irony was that the goal had been achieved before, in September 1950, when the KPA had been routed and sent fleeing home. At that point the United Nations had considerable leverage, in the form of the threat to invade, to force the Kim Il Sung regime to negotiate the same settlement. The war could have been over rapidly, Americans would have won quickly and decisively, and the bulk of the forces might have been home by Christmas to be greeted by a hero's welcome. The Korean conflict then might have been remembered as one of America's finer hours, perhaps equatable with the Spanish-American War in terms of length and success.

The decision to expand the purpose destroyed that possibility. When the liberation of the North and unification became the goal, then the act of liberating the South no longer constituted victory in a military or a political sense. When circumstances forced the United Nations to readopt the original goal as the objective, the American public no longer accepted accomplishment of this objective as the definition of winning. Moreover, when negotiations began in 1951, with the KPA and China safe and regrouped behind the 38th parallel, the United Nations no longer had the leverage to force a favorable peace settlement. China and North Korea were able to stall coming to terms for two years while casualties continued and American frustration heightened. The tragedy is that it was all unnecessary; Korea is the story of opportunity lost because of inconstancy in pursuing the objective.

## Military Objectives and Strategy

The Korean War is a nearly perfect case study in the relationship of military objectives to the fortunes of battle. The war also illustrates the difficulty of trying to set obtainable and supportable military objectives in a limited conflict, difficulties not found when prosecuting unlimited war. The nature of total war makes the military objective obvious; the enemy's ability to resist must be destroyed. Hence the Allied objective in World War II was total military defeat resulting in unconditional Axis surrender. America's first limited war in the nuclear age presented a far more complex and frustrating situation.

United Nations military objectives in Korea fluctuated directly with the fortunes of the war itself. In the early days of the conflict as the disorganized and surprised South Korean and American forces reeled back under heavy pressure from the invading North Korean army, the immediate military objective was simple survival. The invaders had to be slowed to buy time for the buildup of American forces. Had the defenders not been able to maintain a foothold on the peninsula, an invasion to liberate the overrun territory would have been much more difficult. Without the Allied foothold at Pusan, the North Koreans might have consolidated their conquest, regrouped and resupplied their army, and prepared effective defensive positions. The psychological blow to the South Koreans might also have had an immense impact.

Fortunately, the defensive perimeter at Pusan held, and the UN command could move on to the first real military objective, a counteroffensive to drive the invading forces from South Korea. This UN military objective was limited, circumspect, geographic, and aimed at the political objective of liberating South Korean territory. No mention was made by the United Nations of punishing North Korea, destroying the North Korean army, or forcing North Korean surrender. At the time the United Nations established this objective, no one was sure that enemy troops could be driven out of South Korea. The picture was bleak. Clearly, this limited objective was meant to be nonthreatening to the Chinese and Soviet mentors of the North Koreans. The specter of a wider war and the fear of escalation formed the background for decisions about military objectives.

Success, however, tends to increase expectations and open new possibilities. After MacArthur's master stroke at Inchon and the breakout from the Pusan pocket, the North Koreans fled north in total disarray. The time seemed ripe to clear Communist forces from the entire peninsula. After some deliberation this mission was ordered, encouraged by MacArthur's assurances that the Chinese would not dare enter the war, and that if they dared, he would destroy their intervening forces. Thus the ease and speed with which UN forces achieved their original military objective gave rise to new and expanded military objectives in support of expanded political objectives. In the game of international military poker, the holder of the high hand had just raised the bet.

It seemed to be a good bet. The North Korean army quickly ceased to be an effective fighting force as it fled north in confusion toward China. MacArthur's troops followed, advancing so rapidly that their own organizational and logistic structure began to deteriorate. When the Chinese called the US/UN bet by striking in surprising force, these factors contributed to the subsequent UN retreat.

As UN forces streamed back south in reasonably good order, the immediate objective changed again to survival. Some wondered whether any positions could be held on the peninsula because of the overwhelming numerical superiority of the Chinese forces. The Chinese were, of course, stopped, but not before they had invaded South Korea, captured Seoul, and inflicted severe losses on UN forces.

In this new situation it appeared that UN forces would find it very difficult to clear the peninsula of the numerically superior enemy without significantly widening and escalating the war. As a result, the military objective again changed. The objective reverted to the original purpose of driving the invaders out of the south, and then holding on to the status quo ante bellum. To some this was merely a return to the original objective that, given the original conditions, constituted a significant (if limited) military victory. To many, however, such a limited objective seemed an unconscionable compromise. The rallying cry of the discontented was Gen MacArthur's statement that "There is no substitute for victory."

UN forces regrouped, fought their way north, reliberated Seoul, and inflicted murderous losses on the Communist forces. Communist forces were in disarray, but because the limited objective of restoring South Korean territorial integrity was met by driving the Communists north of the 38th parallel, the UN advance halted along that line. There both sides dug in and the war settled into a bloody stalemate. The combatants were either unwilling or unable to escalate the war in an attempt to achieve complete military victory.

The strategy to achieve the objectives sought was very familiar. Military strategy mimicked World War II. Tactics on the ground were very similar to those of that war, particularly those used in fighting in the "narrow places" of World War II. A military strategist in the Italian campaign would have found himself at home with the military strategy used in Korea. For example, MacArthur staged his version of the Anzio landing at Inchon, only with much greater success.

American airmen attempted to conduct strategic bombing against North Korea as they had in World War II. However, since North Korea had only a limited industrial base, strategic targets were quickly exhausted, and air assets turned to more profitable tactical targets. Rather than being a producer of war materiel and thus vulnerable to strategic bombing, North Korea was a funnel for war materiel produced elsewhere. Such a situation led to enormous frustration because the sources of enemy war supplies and manpower were in China and the Soviet Union, both of which were off-limits to US bombers. American pilots attacking the bridges spanning the Yalu River (the boundary between North Korea and China across which Chinese troops and supplies flowed) were instructed to attack only the southern (North Korean) halves of the spans. If there was any danger of hitting the northern (Chinese) halves, they were told to abort their missions. And thus was born the idea that "we fought with one hand tied behind our back."

The limitations placed on UN military activities caused significant rancor. To one degree or another, the issue and its debate led to the downfall of Gen MacArthur and to the downfall of the man who fired him, President Truman. But the crux of the matter was that the United States and the United Nations wanted to risk no wider war. MacArthur's counterinvasion of the north (with US/UN approval, of course) had widened the war significantly and led to the Chinese intervention. Further widening the war to attack targets in China could have led to a Soviet-American confrontation and the possibility of nuclear war. Such a circumstance had to be avoided, much to the frustration of those who sought traditional military victory.

## Political Considerations

There were two major sets of political concerns that affected the conduct of the Korean conflict. The first was American and centered around continuing public support for the effort. The second had to do with the international scene and specifically focused on the Soviet Union and its role in the Korean adventure.

Domestically there were two distinct phases of public opinion toward the action. The initial phase, which roughly equates with the period when the war was mobile and fluid, was marked by a high level of public support. Motivated by the high level of domestic anticommunism and a crusader's zeal for freeing a beleaguered people from the yoke of "godless communism," Americans endorsed the decision to enter the Korean fray. Their support remained constant throughout the early phases of the war as the armies chased one another up and down the peninsula, and whether the United Nations appeared to be winning or losing at any given point did not seem to influence that support much.

The beginnings of erosion more or less coincided with the 1951 decision not to pursue the enemy back across the 38th parallel, and that erosion was progressive during the remainder of the conflict. In large measure the war lost support because it appeared to lose meaning. Overshadowed by the notion of uniting the country, the original objective no longer seemed like winning; the United States had apparently abandoned winning as its purpose. At the same time, there was the specter of the intransigent North Koreans and Chinese engaging in seemingly endless and pointless negotiations while some of the heaviest fighting of the war raged over barren hills that had numbers rather than names. Casualties continued to mount with no end in sight and for no visible effect. As part of American anti-Communist xenophobia, which was moving toward its crescendo in the Army-McCarthy hearings, the failure to liberate the north became ignominious and equatable with the "sellout" of Nationalist China in 1949.

Since the war's continuation appeared pointless, it took its domestic political toll. MacArthur, rightfully relieved of command for disobeying his commander in chief, was lionized as a hero and became a serious, if unsuccessful, contender for the 1952 Republican presidential nomination. President Truman, who had planned to run for reelection, concluded that the war had made him too unpopular to stand a reasonable chance of winning and withdrew from consideration. The military hero of World War II, Dwight D. Eisenhower, meanwhile swept into the White House in a landslide, with much of his popularity based on his promise that "I will go to Korea" and end American involvement.

The adverse public reaction to the Korean War was, or should have been, a harbinger regarding public attitudes toward American engagement in limited wars. If such was the case, however, it was not evident in public assessments after the fact. Rather, postmortems tended to focus on the failure of American arms and on the inadvisability of becoming involved in future land wars on the Asian continent. With the debate so directed, the problem of whether the American public could or would support a long military engagement for limited political purpose was avoided. Even the admonition to avoid Asian land wars was forgotten a little over a decade later.

The major international political consideration during the Korean War was the Soviet Union. This concern took two forms. On the one hand, there was the question of what the Soviet role had been in authorizing or ordering the invasion, to which allusion has earlier been made. Gathering anti-Communist hysteria tended to place the most sinister interpretation on that question.

If one started from the assumption, as most Westerners did, that the Soviets directed the operation, the second question was what they were up to, and there were two possible interpretations. One was that the Korean invasion was simply a probing action intended to test Western, and more specifically American, resolve. In that case reaction was warranted to avoid setting the wrong precedent, but the situation was not otherwise terribly ominous.

The other interpretation of Soviet motivation was indeed ominous. In this view, shared widely on both sides of the Atlantic Ocean, the invasion was the first move toward general war, a diversionary tactic to draw American attention and forces away from Europe in preparation for a Soviet thrust westward. Throughout the early months of the conflict, this interpretation was widely believed, and it receded only grudgingly in the obvious absence of a Soviet aggression. The sway of the argument, however, is evident in the American reluctance to use nuclear weapons against the North Koreans and Chinese; it was assumed that the arsenal, limited as it was to around 300 bombs, needed to be reserved for use against the Soviets.

## Military Technology and Technique

At the time of the North Korean invasion, the American military establishment was in considerable disarray induced partially by postwar demobilization and partially by reorganization of our military establishment under the Department of Defense. But the major cause for confusion was the advent of nuclear weapons. No one knew exactly what to do with them or what their impact would be. To the air power enthusiasts, somewhat perplexed by the mixed results of strategic bombing in World War II, nuclear weapons seemed to bring the bombing theories of Douliet and Mitchell to maturity. At last the decisive destruction of enemy sources of power could be accomplished in a swift and short air campaign.

Air power theorists quickly gained the upper hand in the American military establishment, for few could dispute the decisiveness of the nuclear destruction rained down on the Japanese in World War II. As a result, in the reduced military budgets of the postwar years, the scarce developmental monies available went to the fledgling Air Force. The general American consensus at that time was that air power using nuclear weapons would prevent aggression or, failing in that, would end the aggression through destruction of the offender. As a result, when the North Korean army crossed the 38th parallel, American ground and sea forces were equipped with World War II vintage weapons. And although nuclear weapons were never used in the struggle, the war was fought in the shadow of the mushroom-shaped cloud.

The fear of starting World War III and letting the nuclear genie out of the bottle influenced nearly every decision concerning the conduct of the war. Thus the full potential of American military power was never unleashed, to the anguish of those who saw no substitute for total military victory. The enemy was granted sanctuaries well within range of American air power. Although military commanders pleaded for permission to attack these sanctuaries beyond the Yalu River, permission never came because of the fear of escalation to nuclear confrontation with the Soviets.

The threat to use nuclear weapons may have had a significant impact on bringing the conflict to an end. After his election to the presidency, Eisenhower let it be known through several channels that if the armistice negotiations did not quickly reach fruition, he would seriously consider unleashing America's nuclear might. Such a threat seemed credible because of Eisenhower's military background and because the American Air Force had the means to deliver the weapons. Whether due to Eisenhower's nuclear threats or not (some observers maintain the Chinese never received the threats), the truce negotiators reached agreement six months after the new president took office.

The monies spent on the improvement of American air power changed the nature of the air war in Korea. The Korean conflict saw the first use of large numbers of jet-powered aircraft in battle. American fliers, using the swept-wing F-86 Sabre jet, quickly won air superiority over Korea although the threat of Chinese air power, operating from sanctuaries, was ever present. UN air superiority was so complete that UN ground forces were never seriously hampered from the air, and UN air power attacked enemy ground targets on the peninsula almost at will.

The Korean War also saw the first large-scale use of helicopters. Under development for years, their principal use was in medical evacuation (with a significantly improved survival rate for wounded soldiers), but they also saw duty in a variety of transport roles. Such use only vaguely foreshadowed their eventual use in a variety of important roles in the Vietnam conflict.

The fear of escalating a relatively small war was not the only factor that affected the military techniques used in Korea. Perhaps the dominant factor controlling the conduct of the war was geography. The rugged, mountainous terrain and narrow coastal plains prevented the large-scale armored-maneuver warfare often seen during World War II. Korea was an infantryman's war, a slogging, slugging match up and down the ridges of the Korean peninsula.

On the other hand, the fact that Korea was a peninsula presented several military opportunities. Naval power could be brought to bear, particularly naval air power and amphibious assault techniques. MacArthur saw this clearly and used the amphibious approach to deal the North Koreans their terrible setback at Inchon when they appeared to be on the verge of complete victory.

The peninsular shape of Korea also brought air power into great play, particularly in terms of interdicting the enemy's logistical lifeline. The most concentrated effort to cut the enemy supply lines was entitled Operation Strangle, the same name applied to a similar effort in the Italian campaign in World War II. Strangle was sufficiently effective to seriously affect the enemy's ability to conduct offensive actions. Time after time enemy offensives could not be sustained for lack of materiel. But air power could not completely cut the flow of supplies to the front. When the enemy controlled the tempo of conflict, as he often did when the fighting became a stalemate along the 38th parallel in late 1951, supplies could be slowly stockpiled from those that successfully ran the gauntlet of American air power. Thus the enemy could launch serious offensive actions even though they could not be sustained for long periods.

**Military Conduct**

Although two-thirds of the population of Korea lived south of the 38th parallel, by 1950 North Korea had a larger, better-equipped, and better trained military establishment than South Korea, thanks to the considerable aid furnished by China and the Soviet Union. The North Korean army numbered nearly 130,000 (augmented by a politically reliable border constabulary of nearly 20,000) and was reasonably well equipped with World War II vintage Soviet equipment, including some 150 T-34 medium tanks and a considerable amount of light artillery. The South Korean army numbered just under 100,000 and possessed no armored forces and a small amount of artillery. Neither North nor South Korea possessed naval forces other than a few patrol boats. The North Koreans boasted a small air force that included just over 100 combat aircraft of various types, while the South Korean Air Force was virtually nonexistent. Thus when the war began, neither side could boast a large, modern military establishment, but the north had a considerable advantage in both numbers and equipment.

When the invasion began in the early morning hours of 25 June 1950, the North Korean plan was to make a quick thrust south through the Uijongbu Gap to seize Seoul (a communications and transportation hub as well as the capital city) and then quickly overrun the remainder of the south. The plan was nearly successful. The ill-prepared and ill-equipped South Koreans fell back in total disarray. Seoul fell in just three days. To meet the emergency, Gen MacArthur, the American theater commander, sent the American 24th Division directly into the fighting from its relatively sedate garrison duty in Japan. After arriving on the peninsula, units of the division fought a series of desperate delaying actions as they attempted to slow the enemy advance south from Osan to Taejon. (It was during the confusion and desperation that the apparent slaughter of several hundred South Koreans by American soldiers occurred at No Gun Ri.)

By 5 August UN forces had been forced back into a rectangular pocket, its front roughly following the line of the Naktong River. Although UN forces had their backs to the sea, the pocket included the major port of Pusan through

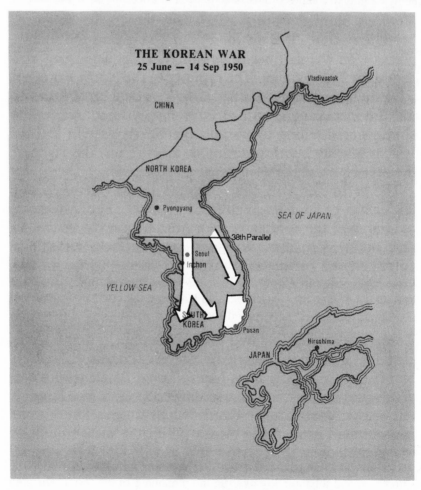

THE KOREAN WAR
25 June — 14 Sep 1950

which reinforcements could be landed or, if the need arose, through which UN forces could be evacuated. However, as the North Koreans began their assaults on the pocket (the Pusan perimeter), actions elsewhere were beginning to take their toll on the invading forces.

The UN air forces (almost exclusively American forces) quickly seized control of the sky over Korea and by 10 July had destroyed the North Korean Air Force. With total air superiority, UN air forces turned to the aid of the beleaguered troops within the Pusan perimeter. Close air support missions blunted enemy attacks on the fragile defenses. More important, UN air forces put severe and continuous pressure on enemy lines of communication beginning well above the 38th parallel. The rapidity of the North Koreans' advance had severely strained their logistical capabilities, as did the increasing length of their supply lines. Air power administered telling blows and the North Korean logistic system quickly began to crumble. As a result, the vigor of the attacks around Pusan began to dissipate.

The perimeter held, thanks largely to the often brilliant leadership of Lt Gen Walton H. Walker. The American general used the shorter interior lines within the pocket to shift his meager forces to meet enemy attacks at various points on the perimeter. Meanwhile as the battle for the Pusan perimeter raged, MacArthur gathered his forces in Japan and planned the UN counteroffensive.

Several factors influenced MacArthur's thinking. First, Korea was a peninsula and thus vulnerable to amphibious assault at many points along its extensive coastline. Second, North Korean supply lines had followed the general route of advance to the south, converging at Seoul before fanning out across South Korea. Third, North Korean forces were concentrated around the Pusan perimeter with only light forces protecting their flanks and rear. If UN forces could stage an amphibious landing and quickly seize Seoul, North Korean supply lines would be severed and the bulk of the enemy army would be trapped. If this action was combined with a major push from the Pusan perimeter, the North Koreans would be trapped between the "hammer" of the Eighth Army advancing out of the Pusan perimeter and the "anvil" of the UN amphibious invaders. From these considerations, the plan for the Inchon landing was bom.

Inchon was far from an ideal invasion point. Treacherous tides and confined approaches made the area particularly inhospitable to a seaborne invasion. On the other hand, these same factors increased the probability of surprise. On 15 September 1950 MacArthur successfully put ashore the newly activated X Corps commanded by Maj Gen Edward M. Almond. The landing and subsequent rapid advance were models of military efficiency and testified to the complete surprise fostered by MacArthur's choice of a landing point. On 16 September the Eighth Army began its offensive from the Pusan perimeter. By that time, the North Korean forces around the perimeter were a hollow shell that cracked quickly. On 26 September the first elements of the hammer and the anvil joined forces near Osan and MacArthur announced the liberation of Seoul. By then the North Koreans were fleeing north. South Korea was quickly cleared of enemy forces except for those who took to the mountains to wage guerrilla warfare.

UN military success raised the possibility of complete military victory and the accomplishment of much more significant political objectives than those originally sought. On 6 October the UN General Assembly approved MacArthur's proposed advance into North Korea to destroy the remnants of the North Korean army and reunite the two Koreas. On 9 October UN forces crossed the 38th parallel. Although it met some stout resistance, the UN advance was extremely rapid as the North Korean army continued to disintegrate. On 20 October Pyongyang, the North Korean capital, fell, and on 26 October some elements of the South Korean army reached the Yalu River.

The Communist Chinese had given several warnings through back channel diplomatic sources that they would intervene in Korea if United Nations troops entered North Korea. Apparently the Chinese decision to intervene was based on whether or not UN (rather than South Korean) troops crossed the 38th parallel. MacArthur was convinced that the Chinese were bluffing, because he believed China remained in considerable turmoil in the wake of its civil war. Moreover, MacArthur had complete command of the air over Korea, total control of the surrounding seas, and a victorious army that had just smashed the North Koreans in a matter of weeks. These factors seemed to make Chinese intervention both difficult and foolhardy. Yet when UN troops advanced into the north, Chinese troops began moving into North Korea.

The Chinese move into North Korea was undetected by UN forces. This remains one of the great feats of military security in modern warfare and one of the most prominent failures of American intelligence. By 15 October 1950, while MacArthur was assuring President Truman that the Chinese would not intervene, 150,000 Chinese troops were already in Korea. By November 300,000 Chinese troops had crossed the Yalu River and were ready to fight. Still, UN forces did not expect a Chinese attack.

To say that the Chinese were totally undetected actually overstates the case. Chinese prisoners were captured. Reports of prisoner interrogations were forwarded to MacArthur but were dismissed as isolated instances not indicating a general Chinese offensive. MacArthur had convinced himself that the Chinese were bluffing.

The Chinese remained in the rugged central mountains, away from the bulk of UN forces. Moving only by night and employing superb camouflage techniques, the Chinese covered signs of their presence and remained hidden from aerial reconnaissance. It is difficult to fathom how nearly one-third of a million Chinese soldiers could go almost undetected and ignored for a considerable period of time. Part of the answer is found in the clever Chinese strategy and in their movement and camouflage discipline; another part is that UN forces were not really looking for the Chinese (when examining aerial photography, one tends to see only what one expects to find). Moreover, aerial reconnaissance technology was relatively primitive at the time, and the UN forces had limited reconnaissance equipment available. Finally,

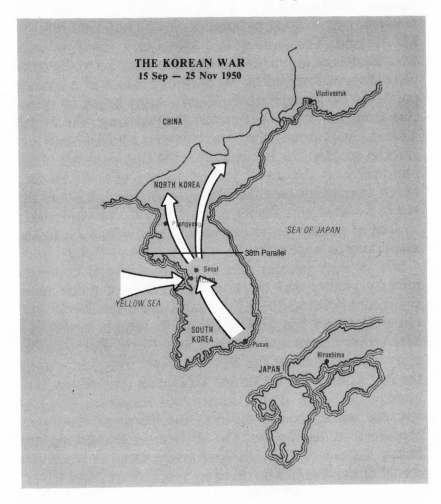

one suspects that no one, particularly at MacArthur's headquarters, wanted to find any Chinese forces. Whatever the reasons, the American and UN intelligence failure was complete and led to nearly catastrophic results.

The Chinese counteroffensive began on 25 November 1950. The Chinese planned to turn the interior flanks of UN forces (which were split into eastern and western forces by the mountainous terrain) and then trap each of the isolated forces in pockets against the seacoast. With this accomplished, the Chinese forces could quickly sweep south and clear the remainder of the peninsula.

In the east some Marine Corps elements of X Corps were quickly surrounded near the Choshin Reservoir, while other elements were simply overrun. MacArthur realized that the scattered units of X Corps were in danger of defeat in detail and ordered the evacuation of the corps by sea, a feat accomplished with great skill by 24 December. The remainder of UN forces fought a delaying retreat and by year's end occupied stable defensive positions along the 38th parallel. The Chinese offensive slowed and finally ground to a halt because of logistic difficulties exacerbated by concentrated UN air attacks.

By New Year's Day 1951 Chinese forces were resupplied and reinforced to a strength of about one-half million men, and they resumed their offensive all along the front. General Ridgway was now in command of all forces in Korea under the overall theater command of MacArthur in Japan. Ridgeway's tired forces slowly retreated south. Seoul fell again to the Communists on 4 January. The Chinese advance continued, but growing logistic difficulties quickly slowed its momentum as UN resistance increased. Finally, the Chinese attack stalled along a line running roughly from Pyongtaek in the west to Smachok in the east.

To this point the war had been characterized by rapid movement. In just seven months the contending armies had covered the length of Korea nearly three times. First, the North Koreans streamed south, then UN forces advanced north to the Chinese border, and then the Chinese advanced south past Seoul. In each case the rapid advances had stretched the attacker's supply lines and logistic systems to the limit. In each case the defenders had fallen back on shorter supply lines and waited for the opportune moment to counterattack. The first seven months of the Korean War markedly resembled the ebb and flow of battle in North Africa during the early years of World War II.

On 25 January 1951 Ridgway began a methodical counteroffensive that met with considerable success. In spite of occasional savage counterattacks, Ridgway pushed the Chinese north and by 19 April had established a strong defensive line slightly north of the 38th parallel. In the meantime, MacArthur had clashed with President Truman over the conduct of the war and the limitations placed on UN military operations. The result was the sacking of MacArthur and his replacement by Ridgway. In turn, Ridgway's vacant position of commander in Korea was filled by Lt Gen James A. Van Fleet.

For the remainder of 1951, the contending forces fought a series of bitter struggles with limited success. The front lines moved back and forth a few miles on either side of the 38th parallel with neither side gaining decisive advantage. Both sides had dug in across the peninsula and the war took on the stalemate characteristics of the Western Front in World War I. In a sense, there were no flanks to turn and both sides could only resort to bloody frontal assaults. Although the seacoast provided inviting open flanks, the Chi-

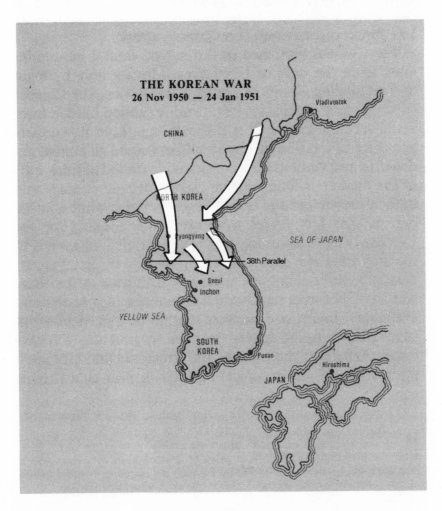

THE KOREAN WAR
26 Nov 1950 — 24 Jan 1951

nese were not capable of major amphibious operations. On the UN side, the return to the limited political objective of restoring the original status quo obviated the possibility of amphibious operations in the north.

By late October truce negotiations (under way since early July but used primarily as a propaganda forum) were moved to Panmunjom and resumed with more seriousness. In light of the negotiations and the fact that UN forces occupied positions satisfactory both in terms of the political and military situation, Ridgway ordered Van Fleet to cease all offensive operations and assume an active defensive.

While the negotiators argued, blood continued to flow in constant but minor fighting. The war was a stalemate, punctuated by patrol actions, outpost skirmishes, and occasional large-scale, but largely unsuccessful, Communist attacks. Finally, after 18 months of fruitless and bloody stalemate, the negotiators at Panmunjom reached bitter agreement. The fighting officially ended on 27 July 1953.

## Better State of the Peace

In the popular mind, the Korean War is generally considered either a failure or, more charitably, the absence of a "victory." In Korea the United States did not bring its adversaries to their knees and force their capitulation, an outcome that Americans had come to expect. Rather than an imposed peace, the conflict ended at the negotiating table between unvanquished opponents. The outcome was not like the Japanese surrender aboard the USS *Missouri*, and it was nowhere nearly as satisfying.

Judging whether a better state of the peace was achieved is a matter of deciding whether the political objectives of the United States were realized. The difficulty of making that assessment in the case of Korea is that, as noted earlier, the objectives changed. In turn, the contrasting political objectives translated into different military objectives in terms of enemy hostile ability and will. By one set of objectives, we won. By the other, we did not. However, we can say the North Koreans lost. They failed to unite South Korea under their leadership, and they paid a terrible price for their attempt to do so.

Although UN forces twice came close to overcoming North Korean (and the second time Chinese) hostile ability, in the end that ability was not destroyed. The main reason for this, of course, arises from the fact that the United Nations did not pursue the adversary back across the 38th parallel the second time, when the enemy probably could have been broken. This failure has been widely criticized, but its effect was to allow the KPA and Chinese to regroup and replenish their forces, which were intact at the war's end.

Adversary hostile will was largely overcome in the end. President Eisenhower's threat to use nuclear weapons if the opponent did not agree to an armistice effectively overcame hostile will defined as the willingness to continue (cost-tolerance). The prospect of nuclear devastation was a larger price than either China or North Korea was willing to pay. Similarly, the terms of the peace, which included a divided Korea, forced the North Koreans, however grudgingly, to relinquish the political purpose for which they had initiated violence in the first place, the forceful uniting of the Korean peninsula under Communist rule.

Whether this outcome represents fulfillment of American political purpose or not depends on what that purpose was. If the purpose was the original aim simply of reestablishing the status quo wherein South Korea remained a sovereign and independent state, then the political objective was clearly met. To achieve that goal did not require overcoming hostile ability, although doing so might help ensure the long-term viability of the Republic of Korea. All that was truly required was to force the KPA out of South Korea and to get the North Koreans to agree not to come back, and that was done.

The political objective was not achieved if that purpose was the goal set during the invasion of North Korea: uniting the country and holding elections under UN auspices. To accomplish that end did in fact require the overcoming of enemy hostile ability, since an extant KPA could be expected to oppose such elections on the grounds that they would eventuate in an anti-Communist Korean peninsula. Such a goal was symmetrical with the North Korean aim, and if that was the objective, it can be said that both sides lost.

One can, quite obviously, disagree about whether a better state of the peace was accomplished depending on what the objective was. In the process, however, one must also raise a question about what kind of political objective is satisfying to the American people. Americans do not generally look back upon the outcome of that clash with pride, even though it is possible to argue that it was a success. A reason for this attitude may be that although the goal was achieved, it was not an adequate goal in American eyes. It was not the kind of political objective for which the American public is willing to make a sustained sacrifice. One can debate the proposition put forward earlier that Americans would remember Korea positively, in much the same way we are likely to remember Desert Storm, if the goal of liberating the South had been accomplished in a few months with minimal sacrifice in terms of blood or treasure. It may also be that Americans are willing to support a sustained conflict only if the ends appear grand enough, something like the second objective.

# 7

# Vietnam War

The Vietnam War is one of America's greatest military traumas. It was a bewildering affair from start to finish, and we are still trying to understand what happened to us in that corner of the world. Analysis has evolved; while the war was going on and shortly after our involvement ended, commentary was highly subjective and mostly vituperative, seeking to lay blame for blunders made. That tone has changed somewhat as a second generation of analyses, more removed from the passion of the occasion, attempts to present a more balanced, less emotional treatment of the events. The twenty-fifth anniversary of the war's end has stimulated another surge of remembrance and questions.

The beginning of American involvement in the Southeast Asian conflict is difficult to establish. Our first formal commitment to the fighting there came on 27 June 1950, when President Harry S Truman included assistance to the French in Southeast Asia as part of his message dispatching American fighting forces to Korea. The beginnings of our involvement could be dated earlier. We could choose 1945 when Ho Chi Minh declared the independence of Vietnam, and members of the American military delegation in Hanoi saluted the new republic. We could go back even further to the actual conduct of World War II, when the American Office of Strategic Services (OSS), the predecessor of the Central Intelligence Agency (CIA), collaborated with Ho and his embryonic forces to subvert the Japanese occupation. Thus, there are many possible choices for the date of the start of American involvement.

The choice for an ending date is far more limited. Regardless of when one says our involvement began, it came to a halt with two events. In March 1973 the last American combat troops left the country, leaving behind only a skeletal military advisory presence. Even that presence ended when the last Americans scrambled aboard helicopters at the embassy in Saigon on 30 April 1975, as the capital fell to the advancing North Vietnamese army (NVA) amidst panic and confusion. In total, involvement spanned a quarter of a century (1950–75) or 30 years (1945–75), depending on one's perspective.

American commitment of combat troops to the war's prosecution was also the longest in our experience. Military advisers entered the country officially in 1961 (nonuniformed personnel preceded them in the late 1950s), and by 1963 the number of advisers had climbed to more than 17,000. Officially they were noncombatants, but many performed combat roles. In terms of formal fighting commitment by American soldiers, our part of the war spanned eight years, from the introduction of the first Marine brigade in early 1965 to protect the American air base at Danang, from which combat flights were being conducted, until the final withdrawal of the last combat units in 1973. This length of engagement compares to our second longest war, the American Revolution, which lasted in terms of real warfare for about six years (not counting the military standstill from the Siege of Yorktown until the peace treaty was signed).

The state of American public opinion about Vietnam can be divided into two phases punctuated by the Tet offensive of 1968. Between the introduction of combat forces in 1965 and that event, opinion was divided, with no clear-cut majority in either support or opposition (except for such specific demographic groups as 18- to 24-year-olds, a majority of whom opposed). During this period, however, the United States appeared to be making military progress in the war, as measured by the "body counts" reported on the evening network news and optimistic statements from government officials and even newsmen. As noted, organized opposition tended to be limited to large universities and to center around activities such as the Vietnam teach-ins.

Tet dramatically changed opinion. The reason was simple enough: The Vietcong and the North Vietnamese army launched a major offensive throughout the country (including action within eyesight of the hotels in Saigon where most of the American press corps resided) that belied the optimistic reports and supposed enemy losses. The initial American reaction was shock and was probably best depicted by television news anchorman Walter Cronkite's purported response to the first film of the attack: "Just what the hell is going on here?" Shock quickly gave way to disillusionment and cynicism. The media in particular believed they had been deceived and came to suspect most of the favorable information.

The result of Tet was politically and militarily ruinous to continued public support for the war effort. Gen William C. Westmoreland was replaced as commander of American forces by Gen Creighton W. Abrams. By the end of

March, President Johnson had announced his intention not to run for a second term, ostensibly so that he could devote his total attention to resolving the war.

Realistically, the only political goal that could be espoused in that presidential year was to get the United States out, and all candidates jumped on the bandwagon of disengagement in one form or another. The tragedies that occurred at the 1968 Democratic national convention and later at Kent State and Jackson State universities only punctuated the pathos.

Another unique aspect of Vietnam was more strictly military in nature: the war was the first major conflict in which the United States confronted a highly dedicated, nationalistic force employing unconventional, guerrilla warfare strategies and tactics. That the United States was basically unprepared to fight the kind of war we encountered was ironic, and it speaks poorly of our collective memory. Certainly Vietnam was not the first guerrilla war in which we engaged. As argued earlier, American adoption of unconventional warfare techniques, especially by the revolutionary militia, helped lead to our independence. In the nineteenth century, the US military was confronted on several occasions with these kinds of operations, notably the Seminole War, several of the western Indian wars (e.g., the campaigns against the Apaches), and the Filipino Insurgency. In the twentieth century, Gen John J. Pershing encountered the same kind of foes in Pancho Villa and his supporters. The lessons that these experiences might have suggested were largely ignored as our European-style armed forces hit the beaches of Vietnam.

## Issues and Events

Vietnam's strong tradition of nationalism is both ancient and finely tempered in the flames of centuries of combat against foreign invaders. The history of Vietnam's struggles can be tracked back to the Trung sisters' insurrection against the Chinese, the ancient enemies of Vietnamese nationalism, in A.D. 40. The modern history of the struggle for Vietnam begins in the 1860s, when the French colonized the region. By 1883 the French controlled all of Vietnam and in 1887 established the Indochinese Union, which included both Vietnam (divided into three parts) and Cambodia (Laos was incorporated into the Indochinese Union in 1893). Vietnamese efforts to cast the French out began almost immediately after the French arrived and continued to greater or lesser degrees throughout the remainder of the nineteenth century and into the twentieth.

French rule spread the seeds of its own downfall. In many respects French rule in Vietnam was colonialism at its worst. However, one change the French brought about stands above all others as the major reason for unrest among the Vietnamese. When the French came on the scene, they found a society dominated by small landowning peasants. When they were forced to depart less than a century later, they left behind a society of landless peasants dominated by an absentee landlord oligarchy.

Ho Chi Minh, who would become the leader of the Vietnamese independence movement, departed Vietnam as a young man in 1911 and did not return until World War II was under way. In the meantime, he gained fame as a leader, in exile, of the nationalist movement. Ho first appeared on the political scene when he attempted to petition the Versailles Peace Conference for Vietnamese independence in 1919. Later Ho joined the French Communist Party, became a party functionary in Moscow, and in 1930 formed the Indochinese Communist Party.

When Ho returned in 1941, Vietnam had been occupied by the victorious Japanese who had, for convenience, left the Vichy French colonial administration in power. Ho's task was to fight both the Japanese and the French. As the war drew to a close, the political situation quickly became even more muddled. In March of 1945 the Japanese attempted to gain public support in Vietnam by ousting the French administration and having Bao Dai (the figurehead emperor of Vietnam who had served under French and Japanese supervision since 1932) declare the independence of Vietnam under the auspices of the Japanese. However, the war was quickly ending and on 18 August 1945, the Japanese turned over governmental power to their principal adversaries in Vietnam, Ho's Vietminh forces. Bao Dai abdicated shortly thereafter and Ho declared his version of Vietnamese independence on 2 September 1945.

In the meantime, Allied leaders at the Potsdam Conference (July 1945) had agreed that the Japanese in Vietnam should be disarmed by the British (in the south) and the Nationalist Chinese (in the north). Ho feared the presence of Chinese troops might lead to permanent Chinese control, yet he had insufficient power to oust them. Thus, he was forced to reach an accommodation with the French to replace Chinese troops with French forces, a most difficult choice between the lesser of two evils in Ho's eyes. In return, the French were to recognize Vietnam as a free state within the French Union and to negotiate about Vietnam's future.

The Chinese left Vietnam and the French returned in accordance with the agreement. However, the Paris negotiations over Vietnam's future quickly broke down because once the French regained control, they had no intention of granting Vietnamese independence. The United States, to whom Ho turned for support on the basis of President Franklin D. Roosevelt's commitment to the Atlantic Charter, stood by ambivalently; we deplored the French return as a violation of self-determination, but recognized that Ho was a Communist as well as a Vietnamese patriot.

After French warships bombarded Ho's supporters in Haiphong, Ho withdrew his forces to the countryside in December 1946 and established a rural guerrilla resistance base. The French controlled the major cities and some of their environs while the Vietminh expanded and consolidated their control of the countryside. On the Vietminh side it was a war of ambush and avoidance of decisive defeat. For the French, punitive expeditions to search for and destroy the enemy in the countryside seemed either to hit only thin air or to be ambushed with tragic results.

During this period (1946–50), the war did not attract much attention in the United States. That changed with the fall of China, the North Korean invasion of South Korea, and the appearance along the Vietnamese border of

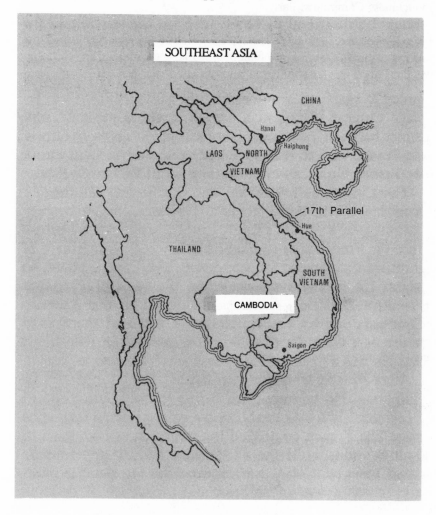

Mao's Communist Chinese forces. Ho's logistical problems were simplified by a steady supply of modern weapons and munitions from the victorious Communist Chinese. The French, still desperately weak after World War II and suffering from considerable political disarray at home, were in real difficulty.

Suddenly, Indochina appeared to Americans to be part of a coordinated worldwide Communist effort that had to be opposed. President Truman thus included aid to the French in his message committing US troops to Korea. The French then attempted to fight a modern mobile war on an American shoestring. The shoestring grew (by 1954, the United States was footing three-quarters of the tab for the war), and US leadership increasingly viewed Ho as no more than a front for the worldwide Communist effort. American recognition that the war in Vietnam was at least partially an anticolonialist struggle to create a unified Vietnamese nation was lost in the tumultuous aftermath of Mao's victory in China, the Korean War, and the strident anticommunism of the McCarthy era.

French military and economic exhaustion coupled with political instability led eventually to the 1954 Geneva Accords that halted hostilities, divided Vietnam at the 17th parallel, and called for elections within two years to determine the form of government for a reunited Vietnam. Ho was in control of the north while the ever available and compliant Bao Dai, who had been returned as a figurehead by the French as an alternative to Ho in 1949, became chief of state in the south. With American assistance, Bao Dai chose as his prime minister an anti-Communist Catholic nationalist, Ngo Dinh Diem.

Both Ho and Diem began consolidating their power bases as refugees flowed north and south to their government of choice. Two de facto states were emerging in Vietnam, and for Americans it was difficult not to draw an analogy with Korea. Both new states turned to their natural allies for aid and received it. Ho negotiated aid agreements with both China and the Soviet Union in 1955. In the south the United States added Vietnam as a protocol state to the new Southeast Asia Treaty Organization (SEATO). America moved quickly to supplant France and became the chief supporter of South Vietnam. Thus, the United States almost immediately began supplying aid to Diem and agreed to train the South Vietnamese army while Diem moved quickly to suppress various dissident sects that threatened his control. In July 1955 Diem (with full US support) rejected the notion of a national referendum because he feared that Ho, as a national hero, would surely triumph. In October Diem defeated Bao Dai in a popular referendum in the south and thus became chief of state of the newly declared Republic of Vietnam. Diem continued to consolidate his power by cracking down on dissident groups, particularly former Vietminh and their supporters.

By 1957, with the encouragement of Hanoi, Vietminh-led insurgent activity against the Diem regime had begun in the south. As the years passed, the guerrilla activity increased, as Hanoi supplied arms and equipment. Many of the southern Vietminh who had resettled in the north infiltrated back into the south to assist the insurrection.

American involvement expanded gradually. President Dwight D. Eisenhower authorized the first military assistance programs, including the sending of military advisers to the country, and President John F. Kennedy expanded that commitment, including the dispatch of the American Special Forces (Green Berets) to the country. The military situation was not going well. Increasingly, the reason attributed for the deteriorating military situation was President Diem, and he certainly deserved much of the blame.

Although Diem had done a remarkable job in consolidating his power, he still did not enjoy a broad popular base of support. Aloof and distant, he had difficulty forming strong bonds with the people. Effective land reform was not accomplished (it was often thwarted by corrupt officials in Diem's regime), which tended to alienate the landless peasants. Diem's Catholic faith alienated the majority Buddhist population. Diem's government, centered on his family and close Catholic associates, was riddled with corruption. He was petitioned for reform but either ignored the requests or responded with further repression. As a result, the insurrection gained support and momentum, particularly in the countryside.

American aid continued to flow and military advisers continued to arrive. In February 1962 the United States formed the Military Assistance Command, Vietnam, to command and coordinate US military efforts. Meanwhile, in the central highlands, the Vietcong (a derisive name applied to the insurgents by the Saigon government) were forming into battalion-size units as the insurgent momentum accelerated. By the end of 1962, the American commitment had deepened and more than 11,000 advisers were "in country" and were often participating in combat operations.

In spite of US aid, training, and advisers, the military situation continued to deteriorate. Diem's army was led by an officer corps often promoted on the basis of loyalty to Diem rather than military ability. Senior officers often suffered from a warlord mentality—using their troops for personal gain and avoiding too much success in the field for fear that such success would cast them as threats to Diem. As the army became more politicized, it was often more interested in Saigon political intrigues than in combating the enemy. When the army did take to the field, it was often beaten by numerically inferior enemy forces.

By the middle of 1963, the situation was becoming desperate. Buddhist demonstrations against the Catholic-dominated government grew in size, frequency, and intensity. Diem countered with more repression and bloody attacks on the Buddhist temples. In the face of the deteriorating situation both in the field and in Saigon, a group of South Vietnamese army generals staged a coup and killed Diem. However, rather than relieving the situation, the assassination brought on a period of political instability lasting until mid-1965. In 1964 alone, seven different governments were in power in Saigon.

The United States and South Vietnam began small-scale operations against North Vietnam in 1964 to bring the war home to the North Vietnamese and to convince them to cease and desist. South Vietnamese commando teams harassed enemy coastal installations, and American ships cruised in the Gulf of Tonkin (but outside North Vietnamese territorial waters). On 2 August 1964 North Vietnamese patrol boats attacked the USS *Maddox*, a destroyer on an intelligence-gathering mission, and two days later a second attack allegedly occurred against the USS *C. Turner Joy* (whether that attack actually occurred is hotly contested). In response, President Johnson ordered retaliatory air raids against North Vietnamese naval bases on 5 August. On 7 August Congress approved the so-called Gulf of Tonkin Resolution giving the president broad powers to act in Vietnam. The resolution set the stage for direct US combat involvement, the retaliation was the first overt American military act in the war, and the precedent was set for the future.

If there was an underlying, pervasive issue common to the entire sweep of US involvement in Vietnam, it was the containment of communism: the determination not to allow the expansion of another Communist regime. Different presidents expressed this commitment in different ways. Eisenhower, for instance, believed that the failure of the United States to stop Communist expansion in Vietnam would lead to the fall of all Southeast Asia to communism (the domino theory). Truman and Johnson placed more emphasis on the consequences of not stopping an aggressor early, for fear that the failure to do so would encourage further aggression (the analogy with Britain and France at Munich in 1938). Richard Nixon and his vocal national security adviser, Henry Kissinger, later emphasized the importance of honoring commitments so that future as well as current victims of aggression would accept American constancy.

To be sure, the emphasis on containment as a basic issue changed over time, as American foreign policy changed toward the world generally and especially toward our adversaries. In the early period of involvement when anticommunism was at its zenith in this country, containment was a strong, broadly supported policy. When Truman included support for the French in Indochina (a part of the world about which most Americans had heard only vaguely) in his speech on Korea, it was accepted without a raised eyebrow. But times change and so does policy. By the middle 1960s (and certainly by the end of the decade), American policy toward the Soviet Union had shifted in rhetoric (if less in substance) away from the confrontational tenor of containment to the more cooperative language of détente.

Unlike other American military experiences, there simply was no single, dramatic event that drew us into the war, no grand casus belli (the closest candidate is the Gulf of Tonkin incident, which is hardly equivalent, for example, to the North Korean invasion of South Korea). Rather, the theme of events in Southeast Asia is one of gradualism and incrementalism, which trapped decision makers in a maelstrom of ever-widening and deepening involvement by bits and pieces. It is a story not of duplicity or stupidity (as is sometimes portrayed), but of individuals caught in circumstances in which the individual decisions they reached, each of which seemed the best alternative at the time, had the unintended cumulative effect of slowly and gradually dragging the United States deeper and deeper into the fray.

The entire situation is not without irony. Five presidents and their advisers wrestled with the problem of Vietnam, and each was baffled by it. In each case, there were alternative approaches that could be taken, but none seemed attractive. In most instances, there were three things that could be done when crisis emerged (as it regularly did). One alternative was to cut our losses and get out. The universally recognized consequence of this approach was the quick demise of the Republic of Vietnam, an outcome that each president deemed to be ideologically and politically unacceptable. At the other extreme, each crisis could be met with direct insertion of American combat forces, an alternative deemed equally unacceptable until Johnson finally succumbed to it (although in a gradual, incremental way). The third alternative, and the one deemed the lesser evil most of the time, was the incremental way, doing just a little bit more. The irony is that most of the time, those who made the incremental decisions had very little hope that their choices would prove effective or decisive; the other alternatives just seemed worse.

The irony of incremental decision making worked in another way as well. After the initial decision to support the French, the decisions that each president made would have been impossible or unnecessary had it not been for those of his predecessors. In turn, each president's choice of the incremental alternative meant that subsequent presidents were likely to be placed in the same position. The effect of each decision was cumulative, with two results. Since each decision enlarged the American investment in the Vietnam outcome, it became increasingly difficult to cut losses. Our South Vietnamese "clients" recognized this American self-entrapment and realized the great difficulty we would have extricating ourselves (which we periodically threatened to do). As a result, US leverage over the South Vietnamese did not expand and in some cases contracted as our efforts grew.

With these general comments in mind, we can turn briefly to the critical but incremental decision path. The first decisions, of course, were made by Truman: the promise to grant and the gradual enlargement of economic and military assistance to the French fighting the Vietminh. Eisenhower, building on this initial investment, came next. His official rejection of the Geneva Accords laid the groundwork for American military and economic support for the Diem government. Kennedy followed the lead by increasing the volume of aid to the beleaguered Diem regime and by introducing the first uniformed combat advisers into the country. Johnson made the big plunge by introducing combat units into the country and, with the agreement of the military, gradually increasing their numbers. Nixon brought the process full circle through Vietnamization, which allowed the United States slowly to extricate itself, but at the cost of geographic expansion of the conflict into Cambodia (Kampuchea) and the intensification of the conflict in Laos.

**Political Objective**

Making sense of Vietnam is difficult because the war was at a minimum a three-actor event (if one does not ascribe an independent purpose to the Vietcong, which one can do certainly after the early 1960s), wherein each player had different purposes. For the United States, the war was limited in terms of US purposes, if not always in firepower. For the North Vietnamese, the war was one of total political purpose that commanded the complete resources of the people, and the purpose was hardly less desperate for the leadership (if not necessarily the total population) of South Vietnam. Vietnam was, in other words, a war of asymmetrical purpose: the outcome was clearly more important to America's adversaries than it was to Americans.

The political objective of the Democratic Republic of Vietnam (DRV), embodied in Ho Chi Minh, was the unification of Vietnam under its rule, by force if necessary. As such, it was a total and indivisible goal, just as American independence had been in the eighteenth century. Moreover, it was an objective that was maintained constantly from 1945 until its final achievement in 1975.

The goal of the various governments of South Vietnam was to avoid being absorbed by the North. Because overarching Vietnamese nationalism (where it existed) was identified with Ho Chi Minh, the leaders in the South could not embrace the idea of unification under their own control; the support base was not there. Instead, their objective was defensive. Unfortunately, the objective was not overwhelmingly popular nor compelling among the South Vietnamese. Partly this was because the war was more than a simple invasion; it was also an internal insurgency (that part of the war, especially in its early going, conducted by the Vietcong). There were at least four other reasons why the South Vietnamese objective was never accepted.

The first reason was that maintaining the freedom of South Vietnam was a defense of artificiality. The agreement that divided the country at the 17th parallel was an arbitrary matter of convenience, not a reflection of prior political reality. Certainly, there was historical rivalry and even animosity between the primarily rural, agricultural southerners and the more urbanized and industrialized northerners. However, nationalism was not North or South Vietnamese; it was Vietnamese.

Second, the government whose enslavement the RVN sought to avoid was headed by the one Vietnamese politician who had widespread support throughout the country. Ho was the embodiment of Vietnamese independence, the George Washington of his country, because of his role in ridding the land of the French colonialists. No one in South Vietnam had that kind of reputation or popularity.

Third and related, those who ruled the government of the South were less than inspiring. The corruption and repression of the Diem regime had a great deal to do with the original formation of the National Liberation Front, and Diem tenaciously resisted attempts by Americans to institute reforms that might have brought support to his regime. The string of incompetent generals who followed Diem into the presidential palace were no more inspiring.

Fourth and finally, South Vietnam's association with the Americans was a problem. To the average Vietnamese, northerner or southerner, the Americans were not a particularly welcome sight, especially when they began arriving in large numbers. Rather, they were viewed by many as just another group of foreign invaders taking the place of the French and thus to be resisted in the same manner.

The exact nature of the American political objective was considerably more complex than the objectives of the indigenous combatants. As noted, the common thread linking American purpose over time was the extension of the containment idea to Vietnam and, by further extension, to the rest of Southeast Asia. In translation from the central tenet of American foreign policy to specific actions, containment meant the United States had the political objective of ensuring that the South Vietnamese political system not be overthrown by force (at least after 1956). Over time, the underlying purpose (containment) was used in different ways to explain why the objective was worth pursuing. The problem with each of the various containment rationales was that each had a counterargument either in factual content or interpretation.

A further thread running throughout these justifications was the question of who was really being contained in Vietnam. There were always four possibilities, and their plausibility was inversely related to the importance of containing them. The most plausible enemy was North Vietnam and its National Liberation Front collaborators; they were all Vietnamese, they were proximate, and unification was their goal. The second candidate was China (a particular fixation with Secretary of State Dean Rusk). China aspired to superpower status, certainly wanted to be recognized as a primary power in Asia, and hence was worth containing. Third, some argued that the United States was really containing Soviet expansion in Indochina. The Soviets were the most worth containing, but their lack of proximity or obvious interests in the area made them the least plausible. Finally, monolithic communism that must be opposed everywhere was a candidate. This basis is countered by the Sino–Soviet split that began in the 1950s.

The American political purpose in Vietnam was never entirely clear to sizable portions of the American population. Until American involvement in the country became overt in terms of an American military presence, the lack of understanding was tolerable. As first advisers and then combat personnel entered the country, the lack of knowledge of the situation (and even the country; a survey in 1966 demonstrated that more than half the American population did not know where Vietnam was) began to be felt. The American people began to ask exactly what the purpose was.

A second problem was whether Vietnam was important enough to justify an American commitment. In the early days, when involvement was limited to economic and military assistance, the question was relatively unimportant because the sacrifice was minimal and unnoticed by most Americans anyway. When the war began to consume larger portions of American treasure and blood, then it became important to determine whether the objective matched the sacrifice.

The worthiness of the objective could be justified only in geopolitical terms since there was no plausible historical or economic basis for the commitment. Thus, the debate centered on containment but in a different context than the Korean War. In 1950 there was no question about whether halting monolithic communism was worthwhile, but by 1964 perceptions had changed. Communism was no longer viewed as monolithic because the Sino–Soviet split had demonstrated it was not. Moreover, a newer, probably more permissive and less sacrifice-oriented group was entering the American adult population, and its response to calls based purely on patriotism was not so certain as that of a previous age. An objective of arguable vitality was inadequate to appeal to all the population, and especially to that portion which would be forced to fight for it.

As time went by, the question increasingly framed by segments of the American public was whether the United States had any substantial interests in Southeast Asia that could be translated into political objectives that demanded protection. As time went by and casualties increased, the public progressively answered the question negatively, and the political leadership in Washington seemed unable to devise a compelling argument that vital American interests were at stake.

South Vietnamese leadership did not make matters any easier. The succession of leaders who paraded across the television screen lacked the broad-based support of their people, and instances of corruption and inefficiency were rampant. The image created was one wherein the side we were supporting did not appear to be much, if any, better than those we opposed, and many of our memories of Vietnam are of those demeaning characteristics.

In these murky circumstances, devising a political objective that would galvanize the American people to the task at hand proved impossible in the long run. Those characteristics of a "good" political objective discussed earlier (e.g., simplicity and moral loftiness) were never successfully attained. More to the point, the objective never translated clearly into a military objective to guide strategy.

## Military Objectives and Strategy

American understanding of the nature of the war posed the first major obstacle in formulating an effective military strategy. The United States viewed the Vietnam conflict as a limited war, a conflict fought with limited means for limited political objectives. Although viewed as part of the larger struggle against an aggressive Communist threat to the free world, Vietnam was at the outer periphery of US national interests. The United States could not allow itself to become overly involved because the important struggle would come in western Europe. Like Korea, Vietnam was a sideshow that could easily divert attention and weaken America's ability to resist at the critical points. No matter what other issues were involved, US policymakers viewed the conflict in Vietnam as one more confrontation with the Communists.

Such a view was at best overly simplistic and at worst so far from the truth that our efforts could not help but fail in the long run. The important enemy motivation was nationalism rather than communism. This is perhaps best illustrated by the events that took place after the North Vietnamese had seized control of all Vietnam. Rather than a great victory for monolithic communism, fragile Communist alliances quickly disintegrated as Vietnam invaded Cambodia (ruled by the Communist Khmer Rouge) in December 1978, which in turn led to the Chinese invasion of northern Vietnam in February 1979. Even the Asian Communist "monolith" proved to be little more than a figment of American imagination.

Spurred on by nationalist fervor, the Viet Cong and North Vietnamese waged an unlimited rather than a limited struggle. Their objective, to overthrow the government of South Vietnam and to impose their own control, was unlimited. Although compromise might be accepted in the short term, it would be only a pause in the ultimate struggle. There could be no compromise with the long-term nationalist goal. Populations were mobilized for the effort and every means of battle at the enemy's disposal was used. Only the limitations on the resources available to the enemy preserved the American illusion that this was a limited war.

American understanding of the war was further confused by the complexity of the struggle. In essence, the war was fought at three levels. The first level, on which the American military focused its efforts, was the war against enemy main force units—both Vietcong units and units of the regular North Vietnamese army. The second level was the shadow war against the enemy guerrilla fighters. The third level was the war for the loyalty of the population, perhaps the most important part of the entire struggle.

All three levels were intertwined. Although enemy main force units were somewhat dependent on supplies from North Vietnam, they also depended on the cooperation, or at least the neutrality, of the South Vietnamese population for succor, recruits, and intelligence. This was particularly true of Vietcong main force units. Guerrilla units were almost totally dependent upon the cooperation or neutrality of the population. Without the aid of the people, the guerrillas would have been exposed, resisted, and starved of supplies, and thus could not have operated. All of this points out the importance of the struggle for the loyalty of the population. But to win over the population, it had to be protected from enemy main force units and guerrillas. Thus, US forces faced somewhat of a "chicken-or-egg" problem. If efforts were concentrated on the main forces, the enemy's infrastructure within the population would be left alone to spread, gain support, and supply troops and materials to the main force and guerrilla units. If efforts were concentrated against the infrastructure, enemy forces in the field might be able to consolidate their positions and further intimidate the people and embarrass the government.

The American position and perception of the war were further complicated and confused by three other factors. First, US forces could not be a decisive factor in the struggle for the loyalty of the population. Actions to win the hearts and minds of the people had to be performed by South Vietnamese to be fully effective. The United States could help with organizational skills, expertise (if there was any real expertise in such a task), and money. A second complication was the difficulty American forces had combating guerrilla fighters on their own terms. The average US soldier was trained and equipped to move and fight in large units and to make use of overwhelming firepower. Few were trained to operate alone or in small groups, to operate with great stealth, and to fight effectively at very close quarters. A third problem was that the American style of war made it difficult to fight enemy main force units and achieve decisive victories. The enemy stood and fought only on its own terms. Seemingly trapped enemy forces were often able to melt away into the mountains and jungles, avoiding decisive defeat because their mobility was based on the foot power of the individual soldier rather than the mechanization typical of large American units.

US strategy was also dominated by what the country, as represented by our political leadership, was willing and able to do in Vietnam, a factor that varied over time. From 1954 until 1964, the United States was willing to send large amounts of aid to bolster the South Vietnamese government and growing numbers of military advisers to train its army.

From 1965 through 1968, American political leadership was willing not only to engage in large-scale combat operations but also to carry the major portion of the war-making burden. But the United States did not leap precipitously into large-scale combat. The American response to the challenge in South Vietnam was gradual and graduated. Rather than being bent on a full-scale war, American political leadership continually sought compromise solutions and attempted to use the gradual escalation of its efforts as a bargaining tool, with very limited success.

From the latter part of 1968 through the end of 1972, US leadership was unwilling to continue its large-scale prosecution of the war. Disillusioned with a long war without apparent progress, Americans wanted out. The most the United States was willing to do was to scale down its participation gradually, to withdraw its troops, and through provision of training and equipment to attempt to leave South Vietnam in such a position that it could defend itself. However, the United States was willing to fight at arm's length through the use of air power. The final chapter, 1972 through 1975, witnessed the total collapse of American will to aid a faltering ally under heavy attack.

It did not become clear to Americans until well after the war that North Vietnam was constantly willing to increase its efforts in the South because the North was fighting an unlimited war. While American willingness to fight rose and fell over time, North Vietnamese willingness never wavered. During the period from 1965 through 1968, the United States believed it was escalating the war, hopefully to a point at which the North Vietnamese would realize that their objective was not worth the cost. From the North Vietnamese viewpoint, the war was already escalated because North Vietnam was engaged in a total war for an invaluable objective.

Finally, American strategy was influenced by the willingness and ability of the South Vietnamese to prosecute the war. In the struggle for the loyalty of the peasants, the pacification efforts of the South Vietnamese were often poorly conceived, badly organized, and haphazardly executed. The government resisted the sweeping political reforms required for success (particularly land reform) until late in the war. In the military struggle, the South Vietnamese displayed varying capabilities. In the early years, a warlord mentality sapped the leadership of the army. Later, as political upheavals shook the South, the coups and countercoups of the highly politicized army diverted attention from the military struggle in the field. By 1965 the South Vietnamese army was on the ropes and ripe for defeat. The American entrance into the war saved the day and gave the South Vietnamese army time to regroup and reorganize. By 1968 the South Vietnamese army had developed a number of first-class fighting units that conducted themselves well during the Tet offensive. Improvement continued through the departure of the American troops.

In the long run, however, the American training and equipment that turned the South Vietnamese army into a credible force contributed to its final undoing. US advisers trained the South Vietnamese to fight in the American style, relying on heavy firepower, unlimited air support, and the logistical system to make it all work. When the Americans left and the logistical pipeline dried up, the South Vietnamese found themselves at a fatal disadvantage.

With all of the foregoing as background, what were the strategies used by US forces? As one would suspect, the strategies changed over time and must be dealt with by time periods. The period from 1954 through 1964, the advisory years, can be dealt with quickly. The objective was to help the South Vietnamese help themselves by equipping and training their forces. It was also a time for testing the various theories of counterinsurgency being touted in the United States. Army Special Forces units were sent to Vietnam and operated extensively in areas far from the political intrigues of Saigon. Other members of the ever-expanding advisory force trained South Vietnamese forces and accompanied them on operations in the field. American airmen trained their South Vietnamese counterparts and often flew with them on combat missions. In 1962 American planes and crews also began spraying herbicides to defoliate the jungle hiding places of the insurgents and, within certain areas, to destroy the crops the insurgents used.

The arrival of large numbers of American ground combat troops in 1965 led to a considerable debate over the appropriate strategy for their use. The original rationale for the insertion of American troops was to protect American air bases in the wake of several inordinately destructive raids by enemy troops. Some officials argued that the American role should be limited to protecting these enclaves rather than becoming deeply involved in a war on the Asian mainland. Others argued that limiting the American role to guard duty was a waste of superior military capability and went against the "aggressive nature" of the American soldier. By mid-1965 the enclave strategy had been discarded and America became fully involved in a ground war in Asia, thus ignoring a long-held Western military phobia. And, as had been predicted by some, the Americans began to take over the ground war, a role quickly and easily relinquished by the South Vietnamese.

A major factor in the decision to widen the American involvement in the war was the military situation in South Vietnam in 1965. The Vietcong were massing in large units, and an increasing number of regular North Vietnamese units were operating in the south. Both enemy forces were on the offensive and the South Vietnamese army was rapidly disintegrating as it lost nearly a battalion per week through battle and desertion. As the enemy offensive gained momentum, district capitals fell at the rate of one per week. In the language of protracted war, the guerrilla war had advanced to the third or large-unit maneuver phase.

Without direct American intervention, an American enclave strategy might have been pointless as South Vietnam collapsed under the enemy onslaught. Thus, as more American troops poured into South Vietnam with a fighting mission, Gen Westmoreland, commander, US Military Assistance Command, Vietnam (COMUSMACV), mapped out his master plan. The first step was to halt the losing trend and to stop the enemy initiative. Once the crisis had passed, Westmoreland would move on to step two, which envisioned aggressive offensive action to seize the military initiative and destroy enemy forces. Once enemy main force units had been defeated, US forces would enter phase three, in which they would mop up the remaining guerrilla force structure and clean out any enemy units in remote base areas. Meanwhile the American air campaign against the North, named Rolling Thunder, would continue in an effort to persuade the North that it should end its support of the battle in the South. Air power would also play a significant role in the South by providing interdiction and close air support for ground troops.

By the end of 1965 the crisis had passed. The major enemy thrust, aimed at cutting the South in half from the mountains to the sea, had been defeated. Two major American operations (Starlight and Silver Bayonet) had tested American troops, blunted the enemy offensive, and demonstrated the concept of air cavalry in the Ia Drang Valley. It was now time to move on to the second step of Westmoreland's plan and aggressively seize the offensive.

The enemy, its ambitious large-unit offensive blunted, became less aggressive and operated in smaller tactical units. American troops initiated a series of spoiling attacks and "search-and-destroy" sweeps through the countryside, but they occupied no land for any length of time. In the purely military sense there were no strategic points to occupy, yet every point was strategic because a significant portion of the war was waged for the loyalty of the people. Although the Americans could "sweep" an area clear of enemy forces, when they moved on, the enemy returned, forcing the peasants into some kind of accommodation. Although South Vietnamese pacification personnel often followed in the wake of American sweeps, their mission was made doubly difficult when US forces moved on to other operations, leaving the Vietnamese to defend themselves against enemy forces that might return.

Westmoreland's strategy was to keep the enemy off balance with spoiling attacks and to inflict the maximum number of casualties. In other words, Westmoreland's was a strategy of attrition as he attempted to exhaust the enemy's manpower and will to fight through superior American firepower. If overwhelming US firepower could kill the enemy fast enough, North Vietnam would not be able to sustain its support of the war in the south, or so the idea went.

Ironically, the enemy strategy for defeating the American forces was also based on attrition. The Vietcong and North Vietnamese had been on the verge of administering the coup de grace to the hapless South Vietnamese forces before the American forces arrived on the scene. However, they could not hope to inflict decisive battlefield defeats on the well-trained and superbly equipped US forces. They fell back on the concepts of protracted warfare, a kind of warfare unsuited to democracies in general and anathema to impatient Americans. Their strategy was to avoid defeat, harass the Americans (and their allies, of course), prolong the war, and cause as many American casualties as possible. Combined with a well-orchestrated propaganda campaign, the bodies of dead American soldiers returning home would have a devastating effect on the American will to continue the struggle (cost-tolerance).

Thus both sides pursued an attrition strategy, but there were differences. US attrition was aimed at killing a maximum number of enemy soldiers on the battlefield, which became an end in itself. The enemy strategy of attrition was aimed at the morale of the American people. The enemy considered the war a struggle between entire societies while American strategic interests concentrated on the narrower confines of the battlefield.

In early 1968 the enemy attempted to speed up the process of American and allied defeat by fomenting a national uprising among the people of South Vietnam. The tool to accomplish this end was a major offensive against South Vietnam's cities beginning during the Tet holidays. After some initial setbacks under the massive onslaught, US and South Vietnamese forces soundly defeated the enemy. The Tet offensive failed to start an uprising and resulted in a crushing military defeat for the enemy, but it provided the straw that broke the back of American will to continue the struggle.

In the wake of Tet, the American objective in the war clearly changed.

Rather than a military solution, the United States sought a way out of the war with minimum damage to its prestige. Strategy quickly changed to accommodate this new goal. The United States started the process of Vietnamization—turning the war back over to the South Vietnamese—and reducing US troop levels (although for a while troop numbers increased, reaching their zenith in early 1969). As American troops departed, efforts were made to bolster the South Vietnamese army's ability to stand on its own by providing both training and equipment. American forces continued combat operations on the ground but at a reduced level. Many of these operations, including an incursion into enemy sanctuaries in Cambodia, were aimed at protecting the withdrawal of US forces.

The defeat of the enemy in its Tet offensive also offered a great opportunity for the United States and South Vietnam. The offensive was led by Vietcong forces, and their destruction left a power void in the countryside. In effect, the Vietcong, who had avoided defeat against superior American forces for years, had been destroyed by the enemy's decision to make them the shock troops for Tet. The Saigon government quickly moved to fill the void with massive new pacification programs. In essence, the guerrilla war was won (or more accurately, lost by the Vietcong when they abandoned guerrilla tactics during Tet) and the war for peasant loyalty was being won. But the Americans continued to withdraw.

After a conventional invasion by North Vietnamese forces in the spring of 1972 and its defeat by the South Vietnamese with the assistance of American air power, the North Vietnamese and remnants of the Vietcong signed a cease-fire in early 1973, but only after a final massive US bombing offensive in North Vietnam centered on Hanoi and Haiphong. The cease-fire allowed the United States to leave with some arguable degree of honor. In 1975 the North Vietnamese again invaded and the South Vietnamese army, without the massive ground firepower, air power, and logistical support of the United States, quickly crumbled.

Having discussed the factors that influenced US strategy in Vietnam and traced the changes in strategy over time, it is appropriate to evaluate the strategic choices made by the United States. Had the United States not taken to the field in 1965 to battle directly with the enemy, any subsequent strategic decisions would have been academic as the enemy would have overrun the South. The situation in 1965 was desperate. The strategic choices made after the crisis passed are more legitimately questionable.

Perhaps the biggest error made by American strategists was not realizing that the enemy was fighting an unlimited war. In a sense, the enemy turned President John F. Kennedy's famous inauguration speech on its head. It was the enemy who would "pay any price, bear any burden, meet any hardship" to gain its objective of a united Vietnamese nation. Given such total commitment, a policy of gradualism—slowly increasing the pressure—had little effect except to strengthen enemy resolve and slow their progress to the ultimate goal.

Gradual escalation of the American effort severely reduced Gen Westmoreland's strategic choices. As the American buildup slowly progressed, he did not believe he had enough combat forces or the political backing to launch an overwhelming attack against the enemy (either in the south or the north), or to seize and hold an ever-expanding area that could be effectively and permanently pacified. Short of withdrawing, an attrition strategy seemed to be one of his few choices. And from the standpoint of superior American firepower and mobility, it seemed to be a logical choice.

Unfortunately for the Americans, the choice of an attrition strategy ignored several critical factors. First, it ignored the commitment of the enemy to the cause. Attrition would have had to be of incredible proportions to dent the enemy's resolve. Second, adopting an attrition strategy assumed that we could inflict the appropriate casualties upon the enemy. Time and again, the enemy slipped from the grasp of elaborate operations and eluded the overwhelming American firepower. Although enemy forces suffered enormous casualties, they never approached the attrition level required to bring American victory. Third, by its very nature, a war of attrition is a long and drawn-out affair. This factor played against the American penchant for quick and decisive results. America's characteristic impatience had a great deal to do with its ultimate undoing in Vietnam.

**Political Considerations**

If the United States had a difficult time translating the political objective in Vietnam into a working military strategy that could achieve American purposes, our government had an even more difficult time devising a translation of those ends into terms the American people could support and sustain. The central reality of the Vietnam experience politically was its growing unpopularity, and both the Johnson and Nixon administrations labored diligently if unsuccessfully to develop a positive consensus around the war effort.

As we have already noted, it was not the clarity of the political objective that was the problem, as some earlier observers have maintained. The principle of containment rather precisely defined American involvement, and this objective remained the rationale at least until the Tet offensive and counteroffensive. The real problem was that for segments of the population, this purpose was not an adequate reason for sustained sacrifice. Partly this may have been because the containment policy was not obviously applicable to the kind of struggle going on in Vietnam. Containment was, after all, devised to blunt aggressive, presumably Soviet-inspired expansion, and although the North Vietnamese and Vietcong were Communists, they were also nationalists. At the same time, overt national support for containment, which had been high in the anti-Communist atmosphere of the 1940s and 1950s, had flagged by the latter 1960s. This was, after all, the period of dawning détente with the Soviet Union, and the fact that we conducted business as usual with the Soviets throughout the war certainly did not contribute to containment-based fervor (all of SALT I, for instance, was negotiated while American soldiers were fighting and dying in Vietnam).

In this atmosphere, the government labored hard and long to produce adequate justifications for our sacrifice, and a series of explanations was "run up the flagpole" to see if they would prove convincing. At one point, it was the Munich analogy that underpinned our commitment, while at another it was the threat of falling dominos in Southeast Asia. If the worth of containing a minor power like North Vietnam was questioned, American leadership argued that it was really the Soviet Union or the People's Republic of China that we were combating. The longer and harder that government officials tried, the more their efforts fanned an increasingly large and cynical antiwar movement.

The Tet offensive in 1968 was the straw that broke the camel's back in terms of popular support. Before the television extravaganza that the Tet offensive provided, opposition was significant but limited. When Tet appeared to reveal that the progress reported in the war was illusion, overall public opinion turned decisively against the war and forced the objective to change to extrication from the war. Vietnamization was directly attributable to public pressures surrounding the 1968 presidential election.

There were international political considerations as well. One major category of those concerns, similar to the same phenomenon in the Korean War, was Soviet and Chinese commitments to the DRV. Both countries were openly supporting and supplying our adversary, and both had mutual defense arrangements with North Vietnam. The problem from an American vantage point was to keep the hostilities at such a level that those commitments would not force a direct confrontation between the United States and China, or even worse, the Soviet Union. These worries caused the United States to impose limits on the levels of violence, especially in the air war over North Vietnam and particularly on target restrictions for American bombers. The result was detailed instruction and control of military operations by civilian authorities, motivated by political rather than military considerations.

At the same time, the United States had to be concerned with international opinion about the war. Because we were fighting against another third world country, much of the Afro-Asian world opposed our participation and voiced its objections loudly in such forums as the United Nations. While these were relatively minor irritations, there was also fairly widespread opposition to our participation among our major allies. Whether motivated by basic opposition to the enterprise, a belief in the futility of the entire effort, or the debilitating effects Vietnam was having on the level and quality of our participation in NATO, America's principal allies showed considerable disgruntlement with our efforts. American diplomats were forced to expend a fair level of energy attempting to justify our case.

## Military Technology and Technique

Because of the extraordinary length of the Vietnam conflict, the military technology available changed significantly over its course. As weapons and equipment changed on the battlefield, military techniques also changed as the antagonists struggled either to take full advantage of new technology or to avoid its lethal impact.

During the 1950s and early 1960s, the American military focused most of its attention on the Soviet threat to western Europe. Even the vaunted Special Forces were originally designed and trained to foment insurgent activities behind Soviet lines in eastern Europe. The Special Forces' eventual use came in the very different terrain of Southeast Asia with the very different mission of *countering* an insurgency. As to the rest of the world, the American military assumed that being prepared for the worst case in Europe was sufficient to counter a least case in another part of the world. But in Vietnam, the American military found that many of its techniques and weapons were of limited value against a very different kind of enemy in a very different kind of war in a very different part of the world.

During the Vietnam War, the vast technological capabilities of the United States were harnessed to develop and produce an array of highly sophisticated equipment and weapon systems to find and target the elusive enemy, and then to deliver large amounts of firepower on the target with great accuracy. But it was a more mundane piece of equipment—the helicopter—that shaped the character of the American ground war effort. The helicopter became nearly as ubiquitous and certainly as versatile in Vietnam as the jeep had been during World War II.

When American advisory personnel first introduced large numbers of combat helicopters into the conflict during the early 1960s, they proved to be highly effective. In many instances during these early encounters, enemy guerrilla troops broke and ran at the approach of helicopter borne forces. Before long the panic faded, cooler heads prevailed, and the enemy developed tactics to counter the helicopter. Although helicopters offered tremendous mobility and flexibility, they were noisy, relatively fragile, and quite slow. The enemy could hear their approach at a considerable distance and either take evasive action or prepare active defenses. Thin-skinned helicopters moving slowly or hovering at low altitudes were vulnerable to ground fire and even small-caliber weapons had considerable effect. During the course of the war, the United States lost nearly 5,000 helicopters.

In spite of their vulnerabilities, helicopters offered advantages to ground troops that simply could not be ignored. And so it was that the United States brought to the war a totally new kind of fighting organization, the air cavalry. Such units were designed and structured from the ground up for rapid movement by their own helicopters. Troop transport, artillery transport, supply, medical evacuation, close air support, and reconnaissance were all accomplished by organic assets. The effectiveness of the air cavalry concept was first demonstrated in October 1965 against North Vietnamese regular army units in the Ia Drang Valley. Moving in coordinated "packages" of infantry supported by mobile fire bases (each emplaced and then displaced by helicopter as the battle moved on), the air cavalry successfully countered the foot mobility of the enemy and soundly defeated the NVA forces.

The American infantry forces that the helicopters delivered to the battlefield were the most potent in the history of warfare thanks to their new standard weapon, the M-16 automatic rifle. In the early months of its use, the M-16 was the subject of considerable controversy concerning its reliability in difficult combat situations. Overall, however, the M-16 gave the individual infantryman much more firepower than had previously been available. It was lightweight (8.4 pounds loaded), which meant that the individual soldier could carry more ammunition than ever before without increasing the overall weight of his pack. Because of the very high muzzle velocity of its 5.56-mm (approximately .22-caliber) bullet, the weapon had superior "killing power," particularly at ranges of 100 yards or less. Finally, if needed, the M-16 could spew out fire at the rate of 700 rounds per minute in automatic operation.

As significant as it was in terms of infantry fighting power, the change in standard infantry armament was minor compared with other sophisticated equipment used during the war. Light amplification devices and other detection devices tracked enemy movement through the seismic shocks of their steps as they walked down jungle paths. Once the enemy was found, he could be struck with numerous new weapons including cluster bombs (small bomblets dispensed from a larger bomb to give larger-area coverage) or smart bombs that could be guided to their target with pinpoint precision. Defoliants dispensed from aircraft destroyed jungle foliage and thus robbed guerrillas of their hiding place. Guerrilla areas were saturated with bullets from transport aircraft modified to carry electrically driven Gatling guns that fired over 6,000 rounds per minute as the gunship relentlessly circled the target.

In the air war, the United States used its most sophisticated aircraft, and the enemy countered with sophisticated antiaircraft artillery and thousands of antiaircraft missiles imported from Communist-bloc countries. In turn, US forces countered the antiaircraft threats with electronic jamming devices to foil enemy aiming and guidance systems and with air-to-ground anti-radiation missiles that homed in on the transmissions of enemy radar sights. Success in the electronic war often spelled the difference between victory and defeat in the air.

Vietnam was also the first war to incorporate the large-scale use of computers. Computers were particularly important to the American logistical effort. The massive planning and control problems of moving mountains of supplies and munitions for both American and allied troops 10,000 miles across the Pacific were ready-made for solution by computers. The fact that US troops were lavishly supplied with both combat essentials and creature comforts speaks well for the logisticians and their computers.

The traditional weapons of the guerrillas stood in sharp contrast to the wizardry of smart bombs, light amplification devices, and computers. Although many guerrillas used modern weapons (infiltrated into the country or captured from their enemy), they continued to rely on more primitive but no less effective weapons. Punji stakes (sharpened bamboo shafts dipped in excrement or other infectious substances) hidden along jungle trails penetrated many a soldier's boot with particularly nasty consequences. Guerrillas commonly remanufactured captured or unexploded munitions into ingenious booby traps that killed or wounded the unwary and unlucky. The guerrilla aspect of the war remained a technologically primitive affair.

As in every war, the military technology available affected the way the war was fought. The American position was simple. American lives should be spared by the effective exploitation of modern technology. This very reasonable outlook translated into substitution of American firepower for American bloodshed. US forces relied on overwhelming firepower to aid and save the infantryman on the battlefield. Whether it came from artillery or air power, whether it was used directly on the battlefield or behind the lines to interdict the flow of enemy forces and materiel, Americans became incredible spendthrifts with firepower. US artillery fired an average of 10,000 rounds every day. American aircraft dropped 8 million tons of bombs (four times the total tonnage dropped in World War II). Never had firepower been so one-sided and so lavishly used to save American lives.

Such great firepower requires targets or it is wasted. The objective of American tactics on the ground was to find targets for firepower and then to destroy those targets, if possible at "arm's length." Large-scale sweeps through the countryside, called search-and-destroy missions, had as their object finding the enemy, fixing the enemy in place by cutting off escape routes, and then bringing overwhelming firepower to bear from the air and from supporting artillery fire bases.

The problem was finding the enemy. It was difficult and often impossible to tell friend from foe unless the enemy was ready to fight. Thus, in spite of the offensive nature of the American search-and-destroy tactics, Pentagon analysts estimated that in 90 percent of the ground combat with the enemy, the enemy opened fire first. In other words, the enemy forces initiated the combat and fought only when they wanted to fight. Thus, a major difficulty for the American military was in finding the enemy so that overwhelming firepower could be brought to bear.

Air power was used to destroy and harass enemy logistics in South Vietnam, in North Vietnam, and along the enemy lines of communication through Laos and Cambodia (the Ho Chi Minh Trail). The effectiveness of these interdiction efforts remains a matter of conjecture. On one hand, there is no question that air power made the North Vietnamese logistical efforts extremely difficult and vastly increased the cost of supporting enemy troops in the field. On the other hand, some supplies always got through, and this was the crux of the American problem. An enemy that was difficult and often impossible to find and who would stand and fight only on his own terms controlled the tempo of the fighting. As a result, interdiction efforts had minimal effects because, when short of supplies, the enemy lowered the tempo of combat and built stockpiles from the trickle of supplies that survived the air power gauntlet.

The interdiction effort was also hindered by supplies transshipped from Sihanoukville (Kompong Som), a port in "neutral" Cambodia, to Vietcong and North Vietnamese forces in the southern portion of South Vietnam. Weather also played a role as the monsoons limited air operations during long portions of each year. The relatively primitive North Vietnamese logistic system in itself helped to lessen the impact of American air power. Tons of supplies were transported on the backs of porters or pushed on bicycles along narrow footpaths through the jungle. Such transportation methods were largely immune to the application of air power.

Perhaps the greatest hindrance to the interdiction effort was the inability to strike at the sources of the supplies. Strategic targets, those parts of the industrial web of a nation that produce the wherewithal of modern warfare, simply did not exist to any significant extent in North Vietnam. The "reservoir" of strategic targets lay outside North Vietnam and were off-limits to American bombers. Since the reservoir was out-of-bounds, the next most effective way to interdict the flow would have been to turn off the "spigot";

that is, to mine the North Vietnamese harbors through which the supplies were imported. Such action was politically unacceptable (for fear of sinking Soviet or Chinese ships and escalating the war) until 1972. Thus, massive American air power could only poke holes in the enemy's logistic "hose," and the enemy was largely able to compensate for such losses by increasing the flow of supplies through the spigot.

The American substitution of technology for bloodshed was natural. When one possesses overwhelming technological and materiel superiority, one should use it, particularly if it saves the lives of one's soldiers. This is the rich man's technique. Conversely, the Vietcong and the North Vietnamese fought a poor man's war. Guerrilla techniques, used throughout the war but most in evidence before the slaughter of the Vietcong during the Tet offensive in 1968, were the classic techniques of the weak. Guerrillas strike by surprise at isolated elements of the enemy and then melt away into the jungle or mix with the noncombatant population. As a result, guerrillas are difficult to find and target, and must remain so if they are to survive. The purpose of guerrilla techniques is to negate the superiority of the enemy by not giving the enemy a lucrative target. The political infrastructure that recruits and supports the guerrillas is virtually immune to firepower because it lives among the "friendly" population. A Vietcong cell in Saigon, for example, was not subject to destruction by overwhelming American or South Vietnamese firepower.

North Vietnamese regular army units at times stood and fought against American forces, and each time they did they were soundly defeated. For the most part, however, the North Vietnamese satisfied themselves with protracted-war techniques. Operating from sanctuaries in Cambodia and Laos, they struck at US forces with the purpose of inflicting casualties rather than gaining decisive victories and then melted away into their sanctuaries to prevent their own defeat. The North Vietnamese technique changed to a considerably bolder approach as US combat troops withdrew from the war. In 1972 the North Vietnamese launched a conventional invasion across the demilitarized zone that the South Vietnamese army defeated only with the massive use of the still available American air power. In 1975 American air power was no longer available, and another massive invasion from the north quickly resulted in the fall of South Vietnam. With the Americans and their superior firepower no longer on the scene, the North Vietnamese no longer had to fight a poor man's war.

## Military Conduct

As discussed earlier in this chapter, enemy military activity had grown larger and bolder over a number of years, as had the size of the American commitment to South Vietnam. American actions had not reached the point of overt combat intervention by 1964, but it was clear a military crisis was fast approaching. The 2 August 1964 attack on the destroyer *Maddox* (and the disputed attack on the destroyer *C.Turner Joy*) resulted in the near unanimous passage of the so-called Gulf of Tonkin Resolution, which gave the president nearly carte blanche authority to employ American military forces. The United States clearly had unsheathed its sword, and it was obvious that American patience was in short supply.

However, the enemy forces were not deterred by the threat of American responses to their attacks. On 30 October 1964 the Vietcong attacked the Bien Hoa Air Base, killing five Americans and destroying six American aircraft. On 24 December the Vietcong planted a bomb in the Brinks Hotel, an American military billet in Saigon. The explosion killed two and injured nearly 60 others. On 6 February 1965 the Vietcong attacked the American base at Pleiku, killing eight and wounding more than 100. Fed up with enemy actions and armed with the Gulf of Tonkin Resolution, President Johnson ordered a reprisal air raid into North Vietnam, an operation called Flaming Dart. As the enemy attacks continued, so did the Flaming Dart reprisals. Finally, on 2 March 1965, reprisal raids ceased and a continuous bombing campaign (Rolling Thunder) began. Closely controlled by the president, Rolling Thunder was designed to display American determination, to persuade the North Vietnamese to stop their support of the war in the South, and to disrupt North Vietnamese military capabilities. Rolling Thunder continued for three years, the longest and largest (in terms of bomb tonnage) aerial bombing campaign in history.

The fact that Lyndon Johnson thought Rolling Thunder could cause the North to stop its efforts probably displays more vividly than any other event how little we understood the nationalist resolve underlying the North Vietnamese war effort. At the same time, this step up in American involvement meant US air facilities became important targets for the enemy and would henceforth require greatly heightened security that we did not trust the ARVN to provide. To that end, on 8 March 1965 Marine Corps Battalion Landing Team 3/9 set foot on the sandy beaches north of Da Nang and became the first US ground combat unit committed to the war. Its mission was to protect the American installation at Da Nang, the most important base in northern South Vietnam. More Marine combat troops followed as well as logistical support troops.

Although a considerable debate ensued about the use of US troops, the president sided with Gen Westmoreland, the MACV commander, who stressed that the best defense was found in offensive actions. Once the precedent of putting Americans in the field was established, it became easier to add more in the same incremental manner. As the South Vietnamese position continued to deteriorate, the deployment of American troops increased. By the end of 1965, there were nearly 200,000 American troops in Vietnam; at the war's zenith in early 1969 that number was well over a half million.

The military problem for the United States was how to fight this kind of war. The immediate problem as Americans entered the country in large numbers was how to turn the military tide, which had been running consistently in favor of the enemy. By mid-1965 the crisis point had been reached. The Vietcong large-unit offensive was in full swing and regular North Vietnamese army units were in evidence on the offensive in the south. To alleviate the crisis, American troops began large-scale offensive operations. In mid-August the Marines launched Operation Starlight to destroy a Vietcong stronghold on the Van Tuong Peninsula south of Da Nang; after seven days of bitter fighting among fortified villages with extensive protective tunnel complexes, the Marines reported nearly 700 enemy dead.

In late October Gen Westmoreland sent units of the First Air Cavalry Division to search out and destroy regular North Vietnamese units in the highlands of Pleiku province. The North Vietnamese objective was to cut South Vietnam in half from the Cambodian border to the sea. Using their helicopters for total mobility of troops, artillery, and logistics, the Air Cavalry searched for the elusive enemy. Heavy contact was made in the Ia Drang Valley in mid-November, and fierce close-quarter fighting lasted from 14 to 18 November. For the first time, Strategic Air Command B-52 heavy bombers loaded with conventional iron bombs were called upon to provide tactical support to the ground troops. The North Vietnamese units were badly mauled and limped back across the Cambodian border, leaving more than 1,300 dead comrades behind.

American troops had been blooded successfully. By the end of 1965, the immediate crisis had passed. American offensive actions had blunted enemy momentum. The Rolling Thunder bombing campaign continued until 25 December, when President Johnson temporarily halted the campaign as a conciliatory gesture to induce the North Vietnamese to sit down at the negotiating table. The effort was unsuccessful and Rolling Thunder resumed on 31 January 1966.

The problem was what to do next. If the enemy had lost the initiative, he had not quit the field. The question was how to bring about the defeat of the North Vietnamese, which meant bringing enough pressure to bear to convince them to abandon their objective of forcefully uniting the country. This effort was hampered, of course, by our lack of understanding of the North Vietnamese objective (from their perspective the war was a civil war) and the tenacity with which it was held. The US effort would be two pronged. On the ground, the method (one is reluctant to call it a strategy) was search and destroy. In the air, the solution was the continuation and intensification of the Rolling Thunder bombing campaign in the North.

With enemy momentum stopped, Gen Westmoreland's search-and-destroy method was an attempt to seize the military initiative by going out aggressively after the enemy, locating him, and destroying him. Westmoreland planned to inflict such enormous casualties on the enemy that he would not be able to sustain the war effort in the south. During 1966 and 1967 the Americans mounted a multitude of large-scale search-and-destroy operations with such names as Masher, White Wing, Thayer, Irving, Double Eagle, Lanikai, Fairfax, Cedar Falls, Attleboro, Junction City, Malheur, and Pershing. Many of these were massive and complex operations. Operation Junction City, for example, involved 26 battalions (22 American and 4 South Vietnamese) in a complex mission using armor, parachute drops, and helicopters.

The missions were largely unsuccessful for a number of reasons. First, when the enemy was confronted with such an operation (about which his intelligence organs had usually given him advance knowledge), he reverted to guerrilla tactics, breaking up his units and disappearing. Westmoreland's strategy forced him to send his troops where the enemy was (or where he thought the enemy was). All too often, many if not most of the enemy escaped, only to return to the area after the Americans moved on. As a result, other operations at later dates took place over the same ground in pursuit of the same enemy.

Second, this method did not translate into a military pattern that was easy for politicians or the public to follow. American battle maps (and newspaper maps for the home front) portrayed a series of separate and seemingly unconnected operations rather than cohesive campaigns. In a sense, the large-scale operations were not part of a strategy. The objective was attrition, and the operations themselves became the strategy.

Third, it was difficult to measure real success. Throughout this phase, progress in terms of the body count was reported at the "Five O'Clock Follies" and on American television, but where was the end? Body counts became the standard measure of success (since careers were made and broken on the body count, inflation was almost inevitable), and taking and holding territory had no meaning. It is unclear how many of the enemy were killed by American large-unit operations, but the enemy casualty rate was significantly higher than the rate of American casualties. By our standards, it was hard to imagine that the North Vietnamese would or could continue to accept the casualties we were inflicting. They, however, placed a different importance on the objective, making their cost-tolerance much higher than we realized. The ground strategy of attrition, in other words, was not going to work as long as there were able-bodied North Vietnamese who could be put in the field.

The other part of the strategy was Rolling Thunder. As originally proposed by the military, Rolling Thunder was to be a short, intensive bombardment campaign to cripple the North Vietnamese lines of communication to the south and virtually seal off North Vietnam from outside aid. Instead, Rolling Thunder was implemented gradually in an attempt to limit its violence. Thus, although Rolling Thunder was originally designed to achieve specific military objectives, it was implemented in a fashion designed to persuade the North Vietnamese to negotiate rather than to destroy their capabilities. In the final analysis, Rolling Thunder had only limited success in achieving either objective.

Rolling Thunder was at first concentrated in the area immediately north of the demilitarized zone at the 17th parallel and limited to a small number of the targets proposed in the original campaign plan. Between its inception in 1965 and its termination in 1968, the attacks gradually expanded northward, and the target list grew longer. Airmen took great pains to avoid unnecessary civilian casualties and to avoid provoking a strong reaction from the Chinese. The campaign was also halted several times in attempts to get the North Vietnamese to the negotiating table.

Rolling Thunder unquestionably inflicted terrible damage upon the North Vietnamese war effort. The bombing destroyed numerous ammunition depots, oil storage facilities, power plants, and railroad shops. Road and rail rolling stock were decimated. The small North Vietnamese industrial base was virtually destroyed, and over 500,000 North Vietnamese had to be mobilized for repair, dispersal, and transportation duties. Many more were mobilized for air defense efforts.

Although the Rolling Thunder campaign undoubtedly hampered the North Vietnamese war effort, ultimately it was of limited effect. Certainly it never had the decisive results that were hoped for. At least four reasons underlie this failure. First, the manner of implementation almost guaranteed minimal results. Piecemeal attacks on important targets allowed the enemy to make repairs or find alternate means to accomplish ends. Second, North Vietnam was a developing nation with no particular industrial base and thus no significant "industrial web" that could be attacked and destroyed. Third, the only way to attack the basis of enemy supply was to go to its sources, which were the Soviet Union and Red China, or at least to interdict the supply of materiel coming from those sources. For fear of widening the war, targets near the Chinese border were off limits, as were the ports of Haiphong in North Vietnam and Sihanoukville in Cambodia through which supplies flowed. Finally, the North Vietnamese effort was nowhere near as dependent on outside supply as the American effort anyway, so that it was questionable how much effect any aerial bombardment campaign could have. North Vietnam was not World War II Germany.

As the Americans pursued North Vietnamese and Vietcong main force units on the ground and bombed the North Vietnamese at home and on the infiltration routes into South Vietnam, the war in the villages to win the support of the people continued but with little success. South Vietnamese troops and officials were supposed to follow the victorious American troops on their massive sweeps of the countryside, and "pacify" the population. These efforts were hampered by insufficient forces, inefficient management, poor leadership, corruption, and a host of other factors.

The temporary nature of American successes in the big-unit war, the limited success of bombing in the north and on the infiltration routes, and the failure of the pacification campaign were all revealed in the enemy's 1968 Tet offensive. The tone of Americans reporting on the war through the end of 1967 had generally been one of progress and success. For that reason the Tet offensive of January 1968 was a tremendous shock to the American public. During these Buddhist holidays, an estimated 80,000 Vietcong troops launched an all-out offensive against South Vietnamese population centers, Hue was virtually overrun and even the American embassy grounds in Saigon were penetrated. Three dozen provincial capitals, several autonomous cities, and more than 60 district capitals came under heavy attack. The official object of the attack was to foment a massive uprising (a peculiar Vietnamese twist to traditional protracted-war theory) by the South Vietnamese people to throw out both the Saigon government and the Americans.

Militarily, the attack was a disaster for the Vietcong. After some striking initial successes, the attacks were driven back with heavy losses. By the end of February, Gen Westmoreland claimed that his forces had killed 45,000 of the enemy. The Vietcong, who had spearheaded the attack, were destroyed as a fighting force and were never again a major military factor in the war. Enemy hostile ability was crippled, but American cost-tolerance was broken.

The Tet offensive had a devastating effect domestically in the United States. The scenes of fighting in the streets of Saigon and the virtual devastation of Hue as Americans and ARVN fought door-to-door to dislodge the enemy contradicted the reports about American success and about victory being in sight. An enemy who had been attrited systematically for three years was not supposed to be capable of such an action, and commentators in the print and electronic media were left to speculate about the futility of three years of combat and (to that point) 20,000 American battle deaths. When MACV requested an additional 206,000 troops for the final, climactic push against the enemy, internal debate revealed that such an action was no longer possible. The antiwar movement, long isolated on college campuses, spread throughout the land. On 31 March Lyndon Johnson appeared on national television to announce that he would not seek reelection.

Ironically, the Tet offensive also presented the Americans and the South Vietnamese with an unparalleled opportunity. In essence, the Vietcong had destroyed themselves, and a power vacuum existed in the countryside. In the months and years following Tet, the allies took quick advantage with a well-coordinated pacification program developed and organized in 1967. Civil Operations and Revolutionary Development Support (CORDS) made all parts of the pacification program integral parts of the military command. Combined with the controversial Phoenix program (which sought to destroy the enemy's rural political infrastructure), CORDS largely pacified the countryside by 1972.

For the Americans, the die had already been cast. From the 1968 Tet offensive onward, the American objective was withdrawal with honor while still attempting to preserve an independent. South Vietnam. In mid-1968 Gen Westmoreland was promoted to chief of staff of the Army and replaced in Vietnam by Gen Creighton Abrams. Abrams was less sanguine about big-unit actions, although they often still occurred. Vietnamization, the gradual process of turning the war over to the South Vietnamese, became the American strategy. Given the tide of American public opinion, Vietnamization seemed the only possible option for the United States.

From 1969 through 1972 the war continued but with a different tone. The enemy, badly weakened by Tet, reverted to the tactics of protracted war, launching operations out of sanctuaries in Cambodia to inflict casualties but avoiding decisive battles. The allies launched operations against the enemy, but now Vietnamese code names reflected the steady withdrawal of American troops. Training the South Vietnamese army became a top priority, as did providing the new equipment and supplies needed to let the South Vietnamese stand alone. At the end of April 1970, allied forces launched a short campaign against enemy sanctuaries in Cambodia, which touched off additional antiwar demonstrations in the United States. By the end of 1970, American troop strength had been virtually cut in half from its peak in early 1969. In February 1971 South Vietnamese troops struck into Laos to cut the Ho Chi Minh Trail. After some initial success, however, the North Vietnamese counterattacked and routed the South Vietnamese. Training and equipping the South Vietnamese continued, and by the end of 1971, American strength was down to only 140,000, half the level of a year earlier.

The first real test of the newly trained and equipped South Vietnamese occurred in the spring of 1972, when the North launched a major conventional offensive across the demilitarized zone. Although the northerners achieved some initial success, the South Vietnamese forces performed relatively well and, with the help of massive American air power, drove the invaders back. Included in the bombing effort was a massive campaign against North Vietnam code-named Linebacker during which many of the bombing restrictions were lifted. Targets close to Hanoi and Haiphong were attacked and North Vietnamese harbors were closed by mining. New smart bombs made short work of important railroad bridges that had survived many Rolling Thunder attacks.

Meanwhile negotiations that had been continuing since 1968 in Paris took a favorable turn. Secret negotiations between the North Vietnamese and the Americans finally yielded results in the late fall of 1972. However, the Saigon government opposed the agreement since it provided for an in-place cease-fire that did not require the withdrawal of enemy troops. Negotiations broke down over changes proposed by the South Vietnamese.

On 18 December 1972 President Nixon ordered a new bombing campaign against the North, Linebacker II, to convince the North Vietnamese to sign the cease-fire agreement. In a campaign featuring massive B-52 bombing raids, remaining military targets around Hanoi and Haiphong were systematically destroyed. Although enemy air defenses were initially very robust, the North Vietnamese quickly ran out of sophisticated ground-to-air missiles and were, by the end of the campaign, essentially helpless. Finally, after 11 days of pounding, the North agreed to resume talks. The final cease-fire agreement was initialed on 23 January 1973. The American war in Vietnam was over. On 29 March the last American combat troops left the country, and on 1 April the final American prisoner of war was returned.

In early 1975 the North launched another invasion of the South. After some early setbacks, southern military leaders attempted to consolidate their positions by withdrawing troops from the northern provinces of South Vietnam. The withdrawal turned into a panic and the South Vietnamese army fled south in total disarray. Meanwhile Americans debated whether to aid the South Vietnamese. Although promises had been made at the highest executive level, Congress prohibited all support, and the rout in Vietnam continued. Finally on 30 April 1975, Saigon fell to North Vietnamese troops.

**Better State of the Peace**

As has been mentioned, the main distinguishing feature about Vietnam was that it was the first and only occasion when the use of US military force did not accomplish any of America's purposes. Enemy hostile ability was not overcome; nor was enemy willingness to continue. Rather, for the first time an adversary accomplished its political goals against us; and if North Vietnam did not defeat the United States on the battlefield, it most certainly overcame our cost-tolerance and thus our willingness to continue. By so doing, North Vietnam was able to impose its will on the Republic of Vietnam and force us to accept its policies.

The agony of Vietnam is that we "lost," although it has been the burden of much of our analysis to try to frame what is meant by losing. Vietnam was not a military defeat for the armed forces of the United States, but it was certainly not a military victory either. At the tactical level of individual engagements, superior American firepower consistently carried the day against an enemy willing to endure staggering losses. At the strategic level of overcoming hostile ability, the United States was unable to prevail. In retrospect, a major reason for this was that the North Vietnamese clearly found their cause to be more important than we found ours. For the Democratic Republic of Vietnam, the war was a total contest with unlimited objectives (at least within its means), and it was willing to pursue those objectives with all its energies. For the United States the purposes of the war, to the extent they can clearly be stated, were limited and bounded, and that limitation was eventually reflected in the vigor and resolve with which Americans pursued those ends. This asymmetry of purpose certainly had something to do with our ultimate failure.

There were at least two major political failings in our handling of the Southeast Asian situation. The first and possibly most basic was our failure to adequately comprehend the situation. As several recent accounts of Vietnam have shown, American presidents from Truman forward had Indochina as a constant concern, but most of the series of incremental decisions they reached were made in ignorance of the situation in the country or because other influences, generally domestic in nature, were more important.

Early policy toward the area well illustrates the point. In 1945, when Ho Chi Minh declared the independence of the country, the American attitude was generally supportive. Ho had, after all, collaborated with the United States during the war, and President Roosevelt had been explicit in his determination that the area would be allowed to determine its own future.

Ho Chi Minh did not change between 1945 and the beginnings of American aid to the French in 1950. He had been both a patriot and a Communist in 1945 and he still was in 1950. What was different, of course, was the international situation and the way the United States viewed itself in its changed environment. Wartime cooperation between the United States and the Soviet Union had been transformed into an all-encompassing confrontation, and this altered environment was dramatically demonstrated by the North Korean invasion of South Korea in June 1950. In that light, Americans could not countenance dealing positively with a Communist of any ilk. Thus, if Ho was viewed as more patriot than Communist in 1945, in 1950 the perception was just the opposite and that meant he was the enemy. That he also represented the nationalist sentiment of a large portion of the Vietnamese population was almost beside the point. Moreover, the situation in Europe had also changed. In 1945 the United States was not overly concerned about alienating a prostrate France (especially given President Roosevelt's well-known animosity toward Charles de Gaulle). By 1950, however, France was an important NATO ally, faced a difficult internal political dilemma in the form of a popular Communist party, and appeared both in need of and worthy of American assistance in the worldwide fight against communism.

The important point to note about all this is how little any of these circumstances had to do with the situation in Vietnam itself. This lack of correspondence between the objective situation and the bases on which American decisions were made haunted the United States throughout its Vietnam involvement. Certainly there were those both within and outside the government who had expertise and understanding, and many within the government recognized that the prospects for decisive success were remote. Nonetheless, those who saw the situation as either hopeless or not amenable to a military solution and who early on counseled disengagement were not heeded. One wonders and can only speculate what the nature of American involvement in Vietnam might have been had the sole criterion for decision making been an accurate assessment of the politico-military situation.

The second political element in our failure, which contains a military component as well, was in deciding what parts of the problem were amenable to political as opposed to military solutions. A war fought on the model of Mao Tse-tung's war of national liberation strategy is as much, if not more, a contest for the hearts and minds of men as it is a military struggle. A war for the hearts and minds of men is a contest over loyalty, and it is primarily a political contest in which the adversaries, through deed or promise, seek to gain those loyalties.

While this seems obvious enough, it is not at all clear that American policy recognized or appreciated this distinction and translated it into action. The task of winning hearts and minds is not something for which military force is especially well suited. Military force may provide the necessary shield behind which political conversion occurs, but the military itself has no unique capabilities to perform this role. And yet, that is exactly the way the military was used repeatedly during the war, while the South Vietnamese governmental officials who were the only ones who possibly could engage in civic action too often remained on the sidelines. The failure of the South Vietnamese to win the hearts and minds of the population may have made any American success impossible.

In understanding this failure, the military cannot be totally exempted from blame. If the war did not result in a conventional military defeat, it certainly did not result in a military victory (even if we came close to such an outcome during the Tet counteroffensive). Moreover, the professional military did not exactly distinguish itself in its ability to recognize its lack of progress and to innovate appropriately in the face of this quagmire. Why was this so?

The most obvious answer is that our military as an institution simply did not understand the nature of the war or how to fight it. At one level, this may have been the result of our enemy's successful mixture of guerrilla insurgency and conventional war tactics as prescribed by Maoist doctrine. At another level, however, it may have been that the military did not comprehend how to fight against the kind of mixed guerrilla and mobile warfare with which we were faced.

The latter point should come as no great surprise to anyone familiar with American military history. Despite the use of guerrilla tactics by the revolutionary militias during the American Revolution, the US Army has never shown particular talent or enthusiasm for unconventional forces. Our history of combating irregular, unconventional forces has never been particularly distinguished. Moreover, the military has always resisted preparing for this kind of conflict. Possibly the greatest failure of the United States military in Vietnam was in not recognizing and admitting this frailty to political authorities. Had the services said "we're not sure" rather than "can do," different decisions might well have been made.

The United States failed miserably in Vietnam. There was a better state of the peace after the North Vietnamese captured Saigon in May 1975, but it was their better state and not ours. That is the unique and bitter legacy of Vietnam. What lessons may be learned from that tragic outcome and how those lessons can be applied to the future are discussed and assessed in the final chapter.

# 8

## America's Minor Wars

In addition to its major military conflicts, the United States has fought a number of smaller wars. Some, like subduing the Barbary pirates, many of the Indian campaigns, and more recently the action in Grenada, were of such minor extent as not to warrant individual attention here. Post–cold war minor engagements are covered in Chapter 10. Three historical cases, however, stand out as being of sufficient significance to merit some detailed discussion: the War of 1812, the Mexican War, and the Spanish-American War.

Although each was a unique event, these wars shared some common characteristics. The first and most overarching commonality was that they lacked the polarity of moral crusades, and this made them limited, both in terms of the political purposes for which they were fought and the means available and/or necessary to prosecute them. Because they were not moral crusades, each had within it the seeds of potential unpopularity, and the War of 1812 and the Mexican War were, at best, limited in their popularity. The apparent exception was the Spanish-American War. The public was solidly behind the war when it began and that support never wavered because it was over too quickly and successfully for opinion to turn against it.

The second and third commonalities, which are related, represent common themes in American military history through World War II. These threads are that the United States was unprepared to fight any of these conflicts and, as a result, had to raise and put in the field amateur armies that succeeded almost despite themselves. The militia tradition was alive and, if not well, at least prominent in each case. Of all of America's wars, the country was least prepared for that theater of the Napoleonic Wars we call the War of 1812. The period between the end of the American Revolution and the outbreak of war in 1812 was marked by an almost immediate dismantling of the Continental Army (total active duty strength in 1784 was 80 soldiers protecting military stores). A national security debate dominated by Jeffersonians suspicious of the military had resulted in virtually no expenditure for military preparedness. Similarly, an army had to be raised almost from scratch to fight the Mexican War, although the young West Point system had at least provided the country with a professional officer corps. To fight Spain, an armed force of 275,000 was mustered into service, but the war was over so quickly that only about 35,000 ever saw combat.

Because the United States had no real standing force with which to prosecute any of these conflicts, it had to rely on the traditional recruitment methods of appealing to the state militias and making exhortations to individuals to volunteer (conscription was unthinkable in any of these wars). Because at least some of the political purposes for which the United States entered combat were served in each case, the myth persisted that this was an effective and efficient way to field an armed force capable of prosecuting the full range of military operations. The myth is just that and does not hold up under scrutiny. In fact, the military forces raised in this manner, although competent at some defensive tasks, were generally ineffective and succeeded, when they did, thanks to overwhelming odds or the incompetence of the adversary. Since Americans did not critically scrutinize this myth, it persisted well into the twentieth century, guaranteeing the United States would enter the world wars unprepared as well.

The fourth and final source of commonality was that American territorial expansion was an underlying cause of each. In the War of 1812, a major issue that united the "War Hawks" was the annexation of Canada. The Mexican War was fought for and succeeded in fulfilling America's "manifest destiny" to control the continent from ocean to ocean. The Spanish-American War had as part of its motivation and as a large part of its outcome the creation of an American Empire.

If there were common themes in these three wars, there were unique aspects to each as well. The War of 1812 has the distinction, if that is the proper term, of being the closest thing to a decisive military defeat the United States has ever suffered. In that conflict, the most notable American victory in a land battle (and one of very few victories), the Battle of New Orleans, was fought three weeks after the peace treaty ending hostilities had been signed and was the only occasion when the British attacked strong fortifications. As the result of unpreparedness and an amateur military leadership, the conduct of the land portion of the war was almost a national disgrace. The reason the United States avoided a decisive military defeat and achieved at least part of its objectives was that the British were too tied down and war weary from their campaigns against Napoléon to administer the whipping that was physically theirs to give.

The Mexican War has the distinction of being the first US war that was overtly political in the sense that purely political considerations intruded into the way military operations were conducted. President James K. Polk intruded into military action to an extent previously unheard of. The reason was that the two major commanders in the field, Generals Winfield Scott and Zachary Taylor, were considered the leading contenders for the Whig presidential nomination in 1848 and were hence potential opponents of the incumbent president. Polk is said to have directed his generals so as to minimize their headlines rather than maximize military advantage.

The war with Spain had at least two distinguishing aspects. First, it was the shortest and least bloody of America's historical wars. The invasion of Cuba was a walkover hardly more difficult than the 1983 assault on Grenada, and the major naval engagement at Manila Bay resulted in one American death, a coaler who died of natural causes. Second and more important, the war was the most openly imperialistic American military adventure. Many American citizens were moved to support the war out of humanitarian concern for the plight of the citizens of Cuba, but there was more. That additional motivation was imperialistic and manifested itself in the belief that American manifest destiny could be fully served only through the acquisition of empire. To some, empire was the symbol of great power status. To others, such as Alfred Thayer Mahan, the United States needed an island empire in the Pacific Ocean to secure American access to Asian markets. In the end, of course, America acquired its island empire by stripping Spain of its possessions.

## War of 1812

In many ways, the largely unnecessary War of 1812 was the final episode of America's fight for independence and recognition within the family of nations. At the same time, the fact that the United States found reason to declare war on Great Britain provided evidence, if unrecognized at the time, of the de facto bond between the fate of the United States and the affairs of Europe. The two themes came together because it was British harassment of American attempts to trade with both sides in the Napoleonic Wars that created the passions that resulted in an American theater of that conflict.

### Issues and Events

Although the United States had won formal independence from England in 1783, it was a freedom that did not carry with it much British respect. Apparent British disrespect took two major forms. The first and most important was British treatment of a burgeoning American maritime enterprise. The

United States, after independence had been won, rapidly blossomed as a major trading power with a large merchant marine but without a navy of any note. The decision not to build a "blue-water" navy reflected traditional American distrust of military force in peacetime, but also was based on an assessment that we could not compete with the Royal Navy under any circumstances. As a result, American trade was reliant on the goodwill of the Royal Navy. When the Napoleonic Wars broke out and the United States attempted to engage in trade with both sides (a phenomenon that would be repeated a century later), the British understandably were much more enthusiastic about promoting and protecting trade with themselves than with their enemies, a sentiment the French reciprocated in regard to American trade with Britain. Lacking the means for self-protection, the United States was in a position of intolerable vulnerability.

The other form of disrespect was supposed British activities along the American Frontier. From its territories in Canada, the British dispatched traders and agents along the western boundaries of the United States. Their purported purpose was to engage in trade with Indian tribes who lived along those western reaches, but Americans believed they did more than that, notably fomenting harassment and attacks by the Indians against the settlers as a way to retard American westward expansion.

The issue that provided the proximate cause of war was the British policy and practice of impressment of sailors from American ships into the Royal Navy. This practice was part of the general British harassment of American shipping. It took the form of halting and boarding American merchant vessels and impressing deserters from the Royal Navy who had been granted protection by the United States. Although the problem of desertion was vexatious for the British, impressment was clearly in violation of international law. Having been granted protection and, in some cases, citizenship, these sailors were Americans. Their forcible removal was thus an act of war, and British defense of the action based in the idea of "indefeasible nationality" (that the sailors could not renounce their British nationality as a way to avoid service) was at best a shaky argument. What the practice really demonstrated was the disdain with which the British regarded American independence and sovereignty. Between 1809 and 1812, the annual rate of impressment ran between 750 and 1,000, and nearly 6,000 sailors had been impressed by the time war was declared.

### Political Objective

At heart, the war came about because of US frustration over its inability to resolve satisfactorily those matters that irritated British-American relations.

From the point at which commercial desires had come into conflict over trade with France, the United States had tried a number of political methods to deal with the problem, but none of them worked. Of all those measures, the Embargo Act of 1807 probably best demonstrated American frustration. This act forbade any American ship to sail from any American port to any foreign port, and thereby guaranteed that the price for American security would be the loss of trade on which much of American prosperity rested.

Growing frustration created a mood in at least part of the American public that led to the election in 1810 of a group in Congress whom the Federalists dubbed the "War Hawks" because of their determination to build up and possibly to employ military force. By 1812 parts of the United States were simply itching for a fight.

That fight had to have a political purpose, and the stated objective was the ending of impressment as a symbol of the British practice of naval harassment. As an objective, ending impressment could hardly have been more ironic: crop failures during the winter of 1811–12 had forced the British government to move to reinstate trade with the United States, and on 16 June 1812 the orders allowing impressment were formally rescinded. The US declaration of war passed Congress two days later. Because of the slow speed of contemporary communications, Congress was unaware of the rescission when it voted, but Congress did not reverse the declaration when it learned that stated objective was no longer at issue.

There was a secondary goal as well. That goal was the conquest of Canada, although there was disagreement on why that purpose was to be undertaken. In the view of the more radical elements within the country, the purpose of conquest was annexation. The North American continent was to be rid of the British once and for all, removing a major barrier to American expansion. To less ambitious individuals, the purpose of the invasion and occupation was to create leverage with the British, a "bargaining chip" to gain concessions from Great Britain on the more fundamental issue of naval harassment.

### Military Objectives and Strategy

Put in the simplest terms, the American military objective was to seize Canada. How the seizure of Canada would protect neutral rights, guarantee freedom of the seas, or secure the other objectives for which the United States went to war was never clearly established. Canada was the nearest British target that the Americans could strike, and its capture became the rallying cry for the War Hawks.

The fundamental problem was to determine how to defeat the British forces and drive them from Canada. The seat of British power north of the border was the city of Quebec, which was the most obvious American target. However, as long as the British navy controlled the Saint Lawrence River, the city was virtually impregnable.

The second choice was Montreal, a city that could easily be reached by the river-lakes invasion route used by both sides during the Revolution. In retrospect, it appears that a strong, concentrated thrust against Montreal by the small American Army might well have succeeded. However, American planners cast their eyes on several other targets as well.

On the northern shore of Lake Ontario, Kingston and York presented tempting targets as did the British forts between Lake Ontario and Lake Erie in the area known as the Niagara Frontier. Finally, Fort Malden opposite Detroit seemed to be a fine target. Attacking these places could have provided excellent diversions to complicate British defense problems. Unfortunately, as planning progressed, these targets became less diversionary and were transformed into major military objectives that seriously diluted the American effort. Given the poor state of American forces, a concentrated thrust against Montreal was a reasonable strategy, although far from a guaranteed success. Dividing the small American forces over several objectives virtually guaranteed failure on all fronts.

The final campaign plan called for three simultaneous thrusts into Canada. The first, composed of the main regular Army, was to advance from Plattsburg, New York, by the river-lakes route against Montreal. The other two thrusts, composed mostly of militia, were to cross the Niagara River to attack British forts on the other side and to advance from Detroit on Fort Malden. The limited American skill in military planning and staff work was revealed in the lack of a coordinated start time for the three offensives.

The British plan was simply to hold on. The difficulties with the United States were a minor affair compared with the struggle with Europe. The British gave almost complete discretion to their generals on the scene, even though they did not represent the cream of the British army. By 1814 all of this would change as the British were able to concentrate far greater forces in North America and undertake an offensive strategy.

At sea the American Navy wrestled with the problem of confronting the mighty British fleet. Commodore John Rodgers experimented with battle squadrons formed around the few heavy American frigates, but had little success. American captains preferred single-ship sorties to prey on English commerce and engage single English warships. They achieved some success with this tactic, but their impact was of little consequence to the outcome of the war. The Navy was unable to lift the British blockade of American ports and could not prevent the destructive and embarrassing British raids in Chesapeake Bay.

## Political Considerations

The War of 1812 was, until the Vietnam experience, America's least popular war, and the major political consideration during its conduct was how to gain enough support to continue it. Lack of popular support was largely sectional, but grew because of the incompetent manner in which the war was conducted and the debilitating economic consequences of its dragging on.

Such support as the war had at its onset was regional. The War Hawks, by and large, came from the South and the Western Frontier, and these were the areas where support was greatest. Their interests were in subduing the Indian "allies" of the British and opening up the continent for expansion. Sentiment for invading Canada was, consequently, greatest in these regions as well. Ironically, the part of the country that would have benefited most from ending naval harassment was commercial, maritime New England, where opposition was greatest. In New England, there was widespread belief that the United States had no real military chance against Great Britain and that the only possible outcome was a military defeat that would destroy what little was left of American commerce with Europe.

If public opinion was a problem at the beginning of the war, it increased as the war continued. Part of the growing opposition was fueled by the incompetence of the military effort and the obvious fact that no military progress was being made. The dreary outcome of the Canadian campaigns reinforced New Englanders' skepticism of the enterprise, and the fact that the United States had few victories in land battles until New Orleans meant the government had few glories with which to rally support. Moreover, paying for the war threatened to bankrupt the treasury by 1814, American overseas trade was reduced to a trickle by the Royal Navy's blockade, and the combination of these economic factors produced a runaway inflation. Lack of public support was a bad problem that got worse, and only the American victory at New Orleans served to assuage the bitter memories and allow some positive reconstruction of support for the government after the war ended.

Internationally, the war has to be considered within the context of the overall struggle in Europe. European issues created the conditions that brought the war about, and the conclusion of the titanic struggle against Napoleon set the stage for its conclusion. As a part of that great struggle, the North American theater was militarily little more than a minor irritant to Great Britain that warranted a minimum military holding action (fortunately for the Americans). In the end, Britain agreed to a cessation of hostilities not because of any negative assessment of the military situation, but because the British people were war weary at the end of the Napoleonic Wars and wanted peace.

## Military Technology and Technique

The War of 1812 was fought only three decades after the final battles of the American Revolution. The military technology available to the antagonists was nearly identical to that available in the Revolution. The standard infantry weapon remained the smoothbore flintlock musket. Its slow rate of fire and its limited range and accuracy put a premium on linear formations using massed volley fire. Such tactics, as discussed in the chapter on the Revolution, put a premium on continuous drill and training. Iron discipline was required if opposing lines of infantry were to march toward one another properly aligned for volley fire and to get within effective range of the smoothbore muskets.

Discipline and training were the weak points of the American Army. Virtually disbanded after the Revolution, the regular Army had a total strength of only about 11,000 men by 1812, and nearly half of them were recent recruits brought into service for the conflict. These forces were augmented by militiamen, many of whom served only short tours of duty lasting from one to six months. Although their intentions were good, these forces appeared as rabble compared to their well-trained and disciplined British opponents. The saving grace was that there were few British professionals available to defend Canada because the British were occupied in Europe with the Napoleonic Wars. Only 6,000 British regulars were stationed in Canada in 1812, augmented by several thousand militia and Indians.

American troops were inexperienced and so were the officers who led them. Nearly 30 years had passed since the Revolution, and only the most senior American officers had any experience fighting a modern European army. At lower levels, officers were almost wholly deficient in the technical skills of warfare. Few realized the benefits of constant drill, and those who did had to rely on copies of European drill manuals. The only bright spot in this otherwise dismal picture was the presence of some graduates of the United States Military Academy at West Point, which had been founded in 1802. However, only 89 officers had graduated by 1812 and all were junior in grade.

At sea the Americans faced the world's greatest naval power with a fleet of between 15 and 20 vessels. (Fortunately, the British fleet had considerable obligations throughout the world in opposing Napoléon's forces.) At the heart of the American naval forces were seven frigates, three of which were classified as heavy frigates. These three ships, each of which mounted 44 guns, were the most powerful of their type in the world. Larger and more heavily gunned than comparable British frigates, the American ships were constructed of fir rather than oak. Unlike the Army, the navy provided excellent training, with particular emphasis on gunnery. American naval gunners were among the most proficient anywhere.

One major change from the days of the Revolution was in the availability of arms. The American government had encouraged a significant arms industry and had established two government arsenals, one at Harper's Ferry, Virginia, and the other at Springfield, Massachusetts. Although arms were available in plentiful numbers, getting them to the troops in the field along with the other wherewithal of war was a difficult task. The logistical capabilities of the American military had been all but ignored in the period since the Revolution.

### Military Conduct

The ill-conceived American offensive into Canada got off to a poor start when the three prongs of the planned offensive failed to begin at or near the same time. The first prong to start was led by William Hull, governor of the Michigan Territory, who sought to capture Fort Malden across the Detroit River from Fort Detroit. Hull marched from Dayton and had to cut 200 miles of road through the wilderness over which to haul supplies. He crossed the Detroit River on 12 July 1812 with a force of roughly 2,000 (about 1,500 of whom were Ohio militiamen). Meanwhile, Fort Malden had been reinforced by a small British force led by Gen Isaac Brock. The elderly Hull suddenly became worried about his supply lines, which were vulnerable to raiding parties that could be landed across British-controlled Lake Erie or to attacks by Britain's Indian allies. Giving in to his fears, Hull retreated across the river into Fort Detroit on 7 August. Brock quickly followed, and bluffed Hull into surrendering his entire command on 16 August. Brock's victorious forces numbered only 730 Canadians and about 600 Indians. Thus, the first American offensive ended in total disgrace with hardly a shot fired in anger.

The second prong was on the Niagara Frontier, where Stephen Van Rensselaer, a major general in the New York militia, led a force of more than 3,000 (including 900 regulars) across the Niagara River against Queenston. On 13 October 1812 the regulars crossed the river and quickly captured the heights above Queenston. However, the militia refused to follow the regulars and would not leave American territory. They stood idly by while forces led again by Isaac Brock, who had rushed to Queenston after his victory at Detroit, destroyed the American forces on the heights. Thus, the second American offensive also ended in disgrace and defeat.

The third prong had Montreal as its target and was originally planned as the main thrust into Canada. In mid-November, Maj Gen Henry Dearborn led his 5,000 troops from Plattsburg to within two miles of the Canadian border, but again the militia portion of his force refused to cross into Canada. As a result, Dearborn returned to Plattsburg and went into winter quarters.

Thus, the third American offensive aborted, and the American ground strategy was in total disarray.

At sea the Navy had considerably greater success. Facing overwhelming odds, American ships engaged in several brilliant single-ship actions. However, the British blockade was beginning to strangle commerce along the Eastern Seaboard. By the end of 1812, nearly 100 British naval vessels were participating in the blockade, including 11 ships of the line that the American Navy could not match.

Early in 1813 Brig Gen William Henry Harrison was given command of a large, mostly militia, force with orders to recapture Detroit. Moving forward toward the mouth of the Maumee River in January, an advanced unit of his force was destroyed while attempting to relieve the beleaguered residents of Frenchtown. Harrison was subsequently ordered to bide his time until the Americans could seize naval control of Lakes Erie and Ontario. While Harrison waited, Oliver Hazard Perry was building ships at Presque Isle on Lake Erie. By the fall Perry was ready and totally defeated the British squadron at Put-in-Bay. Harrison then pressed his advance; the British evacuated both Detroit and Malden, and were decisively defeated at Moravian Town on the Thames River.

Meanwhile on Lake Ontario, Gen Dearborn attacked and burned York in April, sailed to Fort Niagara, and in May attacked and captured Fort George. However, the British contingent was allowed to escape, and Dearborn was replaced by Maj Gen James Wilkinson. By October Wilkinson had stripped most of the troops from the Niagara area to launch a campaign down the Saint Lawrence River against Montreal. The campaign aborted after a defeat en route at Christler's Farm. Worse, the British quickly captured the almost defenseless Forts George and Niagara. In all, 1813 was not a sterling year for American arms.

Action was renewed in March 1814, when Wilkinson took to the offensive but was defeated by a smaller British force at La Colle Mill on 30 March. Wilkinson fell back on Plattsburg and was replaced by Maj Gen Jacob Brown. On 2 July Brown crossed the Niagara River and quickly seized Fort Erie. Pressing on to the north, the Americans defeated the British at Chippawa on 5 July. At Lundy's Lane on 25 July, the Americans fought to a draw with the advance units of British reinforcements from Europe. Brown retired to Fort Erie and the British followed and laid siege to the Americans. On 17 September Brown's successful sortie from the fort broke the siege.

Meanwhile more British reinforcements arrived from Europe after the fall of Napoléon in April 1814. Sir George Prevost led a veteran army of 11,000 south along the river-lakes route to confront a much smaller force of Americans entrenched at Plattsburg. However, a brilliant naval victory by Commodore Thomas Macdonough at Plattsburg Bay defeated the supporting English fleet on the lake and Prevost quickly returned to Canada.

Along the Eastern Seaboard, the British planned raids against both Washington and Baltimore. In August Maj Gen Robert Ross's British troops arrived on the Patuxent River supported by a fleet commanded by Adm Sir Alexander Cochrane. After defeating the Americans at Bladensburg, the British burned most of official Washington. When the British moved on Baltimore, they were heavily engaged at Godly Wood, and then determined that Fort McHenry and the hastily erected defenses around Baltimore presented too difficult a challenge. The entire British force subsequently sailed away.

In the South, the British launched a campaign to capture New Orleans. Maj Gen Andrew Jackson rushed to the scene, mobilized all available forces, which were mostly militia, and established a defensive line along the Rodriguez Canal. On 8 January 1815 Sir Edward Pakenham launched an infantry attack against Jackson's well-fortified position. The attack was re-

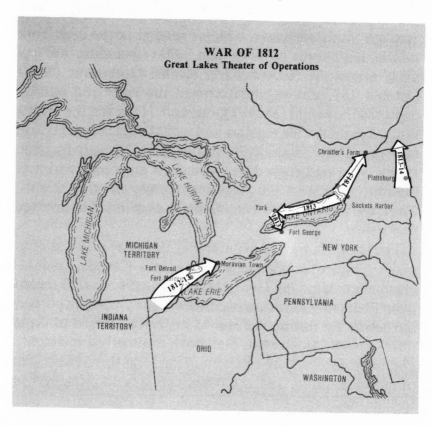

pulsed and the British suffered 2,100 casualties plus an additional 500 captured. Jackson lost 7 killed and 6 wounded. On 18 January the British withdrew. Neither side realized that the Peace of Ghent, which officially ended the war, had been signed on 24 December 1814.

## Better State of the Peace

In the end, something resembling the attainment of American basic political interests occurred, although in small measure as the result of American military activity. The War of 1812 is a war that the United States lost by most military measures one might apply. Unlike Vietnam, however, a better state of the peace for both Great Britain and the United States did come to pass.

If the basic issue was an end to British naval harassment, the objective was achieved before the war began, and the American war effort had nothing to do with a British decision based in domestic considerations. As it worked out, freedom of the high seas and British–American trade served the interest of both countries. Once the Napoleonic Wars were finally concluded in 1815 and the conflict between the two Anglo-Saxon states was resolved, that mutual advantage came to be recognized. The best statement of British recognition is that through the rest of the nineteenth century the same navy that had been the prime tormentor of American commercial maritime activity acted as its primary shield and protector.

The other political objective, the conquest of Canada, quite obviously was not attained, and was in fact abandoned after 1813. Given the resources available to the United States and the sheer size of Canada, it was probably an unattainable objective anyway (as a military matter the objective created problems not unlike those facing the British in the Revolution). Moreover, had the United States pursued that objective with greater rigor and especially if we had had any success, the British might well have been forced to turn full force against the United States after Napoléon was defeated rather than agreeing to the Peace of Ghent.

The primary American objective (the end of impressment) was achieved by indirection, but it was achieved. The question that must be asked is whether anything was learned from the experience. The answer, especially from a military standpoint, is mixed. On one hand, Americans quickly forgot about the ignominy of the war, and thus the method of recruiting armies to fight for America, the militia tradition, was not amended. On the other hand, the extreme deficiencies in military leadership evident throughout the war did lead to the invigoration of the US Military Academy at West Point to train a professional officer corps to fight in America's next war. The fruit of that lesson would first be demonstrated in the Mexican War.

## Mexican War

The war between the United States and its neighbor to the south was a clash between expansionist American nationalism and a protective Mexican nationalism that sought to preserve control over a vast stretch of the western portion of the North American continent. From the American perspective, the war was a struggle to fulfill the sense of what Americans had come to view as their "manifest destiny" to control the continent from the Atlantic to the Pacific. Equally virulent Mexican nationalists sought continued control of lands that were part of Mexican independence from Spain.

### Issues and Events

The issue of manifest destiny had grown in the years after the War of 1812 as Americans forged westward. In that period, the territories of the Louisiana Purchase received their first large-scale settlement, Florida was wrested from Spain, and the location of the northern border of the Oregon Territory was fixed after we had nearly gone to war with Great Britain over the issue ("54–40 or fight"). When that latter dispute was resolved with the border along the Washington-British Columbian boundary, the United States spanned the continent. All that was left were the territories of the Southwest, especially after Texas was annexed in 1845.

These territories were, of course, parts of Mexico that had been colonized originally by the Spanish and that became part of sovereign Mexican land after Mexican independence. The Mexicans had not, however, done much to settle any of the affected lands, which were largely populated by Indians and a few missionaries before the Americans began to arrive in numbers. The largest number of Americans came to California, and the American claim to the land rested largely in the fact that the majority of the population was American and desired to be part of the United States rather than Mexico.

Complicating the entire situation was growing American sectionalism and the resultant tendency to view any attempt at expansion in the context of the balance between slave and non-slave states. The desire to annex southern territories as diverse as Cuba and the Yucatan had been squelched because either would have tilted the balance of power in Congress toward the slave-holding states, and the same issue had been the major factor in delaying the entrance of the Texas Republic into the Union. Ironically, there was also opposition to the war in the southern United States because the lands of the Southwest were poorly suited for the plantation culture.

The proximate event that made war between the two countries inevitable was the admission of Texas into the United States, and it did so in two ways.

First, although Mexican authority over Texas had been ended by the military defeat of Mexican forces in 1837, Mexico did not accept the independence of the Texas Republic. Rather, the government of Mexico maintained that it retained sovereign authority and that the Texas Republic was a rump state with no legitimate authority. The recognition of Texas by the United States and the consequent decision to admit Texas into the Union was, in the Mexican view, a simple act of imperialism.

Regardless of the international legal niceties involved, American authority in fact was being exercised in Texas, which raised the second problem. That problem, which ultimately led to the start of the war, was in determining exactly where the boundary between Texas and Mexico was. In the American view, the border was the Rio Grande River. Mexico maintained that the Nueces River formed the boundary. Although the disputed territory was largely unpopulated, American accession to the Mexican claim would have ceded most of west Texas to Mexico. When Gen Zachary Taylor endeavored to settle the matter by occupation and encountered Mexican forces, war was the result.

*Political Objective*

The political purposes for which the two nations fought the Mexican War were clear, concise, and symmetrical, as well as limited. For the United States, the objective was the annexation of the territories of New Mexico, Arizona, and California to the United States and the accession of Texas south of the Nueces River. For Mexico, the objective was to keep those same territories as part of Mexico. The objectives were limited in that neither required the physical conquest and overthrow of the opposing government (although that was the ultimate means the United States used to accomplish the task).

The major question was how to go about resolving the issue. Both Mexican and US nationalisms were too strong to allow a diplomatic compromise, and Mexican realization that a majority of the population in the pivotal territory, California, was American meant Mexico could not accede to decision by majority will. At the same time, the lands under question were vast and mostly unpopulated except for indigenous Indian tribes. Hence de facto control in the form of occupation was impractical. The only way left for settling the issue was the sword.

*Military Objectives and Strategy*

The Mexican War was a new experience for Americans in two major respects. First, it was the first American war in which the United States was the more powerful antagonist. Although the regular Mexican army was larger than the American Army, the United States could mobilize and field a far larger force. The American industrial economy was vastly superior to the primitive Mexican economy and far more self-sufficient. In every measurable respect, Mexico was the weaker of the two powers.

The Mexican War was also a new experience because it was America's first offensive war. Although the War Hawks had attempted to turn the War of 1812 into an aggressive seizure of Canada, the Mexican adventure was the first truly offensive war. Offensive wars require offensive military objectives, which caused President James Polk a certain amount of concern.

The problem was how to make the Mexican government give up its claims to the disputed territories. Polk was determined to act as the commander in chief, and he played a significant role in the determination of offensive plans, in the supervision of the military staff, and in the selection of key personnel to lead the war effort. Polk was also concerned that the war be over quickly. He was particularly concerned that a long war might become so unpopular that the Democratic party would suffer at the ballot box in the next election. However, he also believed that the Mexicans could be easily and quickly beaten if attacked with enough vigor.

The Americans' general plan was for an expedition into the northern Mexican provinces to seize and hold them until the Mexican government came to terms. In addition, the Navy's Gulf Squadron was ordered to blockade the eastern coast of Mexico and to seize Tampico as a logistics base. The blockade was particularly significant because the Mexicans had no arms industry and imported nearly all of their armaments. The blockade meant that the Mexicans could rely only on the stock they had on hand. At the same time, the Pacific Squadron was to seize San Francisco and blockade the California coast.

Zachary Taylor was given command of the main effort in northern Mexico (after command had been offered to and refused by Winfield Scott). Taylor achieved considerable success in northern Mexico as he captured Monterrey and Victoria and then soundly defeated the Mexicans at Buena Vista. But despite these American victories and the tightening American blockade, the Mexicans refused to give in. Finally, Polk approved of Scott's plan for landing a major force at Vera Cruz, followed by a direct march on the capital at Mexico City. This campaign, conducted brilliantly under adverse conditions, finally broke the back of the Mexican resistance 16 months after the outbreak of hostilities.

### Political Considerations

"Mr Polk's War," as its opponents labeled it, was not a terribly popular event. As in the War of 1812, its popularity varied considerably by section of the country. At the same time, domestic, partisan politics affected the war's conduct in a way previously unknown in American military affairs.

Because the war's successful completion meant that the extension-of-slavery issue could not be avoided, the war had significant opposition in those parts of the country where the issue produced the most passion. In New England, a large part of the population viewed the whole endeavor, coming as it did on the heels of the admission of slave-holding Texas to the Union, as little more than a Southern plot to add more slave territories to the Union. Southerners, on the other hand, believed the land and climate of the Southwest were inhospitable to the cotton agriculture that underlay plantation society, and they were equally suspicious of Northern intentions. Beyond those Americans in the Southwest, support for the enterprise came from people in the Mississippi Valley and the Northwest who, as pioneers themselves, were most infected by the notion of manifest destiny.

As stated earlier, the Mexican War was, to that time, the most blatantly political war (in terms of its conduct) in American history, and Polk's role in directing the military effort was the most active that a president had ever undertaken. Partly, this phenomenon resulted from the fact that Polk was an activist president. At the same time, the partisan issue of who would be his opponent in an expected reelection bid in 1848 always loomed in the background and influenced military decisions. Had the war been a more difficult military undertaking and had the outcome been in substantial doubt, this intrusion might have created the kinds of howls about political interference that plagued later American military endeavors. As it was, controversy over the conflict was a large factor in Polk's subsequent decision to retire at the end of his first term in office.

### Military Technology and Technique

Several improvements in military technology took place between the War of 1812 and the Mexican War. However, most military tactical techniques remained almost unchanged because most of the basic limitations of the principal weapons remained unchanged. The standard infantry weapon was still the smoothbore musket with its limited range and poor accuracy. The standard artillery piece was still the smoothbore muzzle-loading cannon. Both of these weapons, however, had undergone significant improvements that increased their reliability.

The standard flintlock musket was being replaced both in the United States and in Europe by the percussion musket. The development of the percussion cap, although it did not appreciably change infantry tactics, did have a significant impact on war itself. Unlike flintlock weapons, percussion weapons operated reliably regardless of rain or snow. Thus, one of the reasons for seasonal campaigning and standing down in "winter quarters" in past wars was eliminated.

The stand artillery piece had also undergone a significant change. Field artillery had become far more mobile and now could be dragged into battle by horses at a rapid pace and swung into action quickly. In this particular war, American "flying artillery" was superior in both speed of maneuver and in numbers to its Mexican counterpart.

The distances to the Mexican battlefields presented significant logistical problems. Much of the logistic load was carried by sea, and although steamships were available, few were used in the oceangoing transportation effort. However, steam-powered riverboats were used extensively to transport men and supplies to ports of embarkation. River transport was particularly important because few rail lines had extended far enough west and south to be of significant assistance in the logistics effort. Within the theater of operations, supply still depended on horses and wagons, and the American effort was so large that a shortage of wagons hindered some of the early operations.

The Mexican War also witnessed significant American amphibious operations. Gen Scott's landing at Vera Cruz was exceptionally well done and was the result of considerable planning. Much was learned about amphibious combat techniques that would prove useful during the Civil War. As will be seen later in this chapter, these lessons were, for the most part, long forgotten by 1898.

Although several American general officers acquitted themselves well, Scott came away with a reputation as a great military tactician that remains untarnished today. He won and won consistently, with limited casualties to both sides. He preferred to defeat the enemy by superior maneuver, thus forcing the enemy to retreat. His campaign from Vera Cruz to Mexico City was a model of eighteenth-century maneuver warfare.

West Point-educated officers also built their initial reputation during this war. None of the American generals had any formal military education. As a group, however, they made good use of the skills of the West Point graduates on their staffs. Scott, in particular, was impressed and claimed that the war might have lasted far longer had it not been for the skilled work of the West Point officers, including many future Union and Confederate generals in the Civil War.

### Military Conduct

The Mexican War was not declared until 13 May 1846, but several important battles were fought before that date. Following orders from President Polk,

Gen Taylor with most of the regular American Army (about 3,500 men) advanced south from Corpus Christi to the Rio Grande and established a camp opposite Matamoros on 24 March 1846. Additionally, he established a supply depot at Point Isabel some 45 miles to the northeast on the Gulf Coast. The Mexicans reacted by concentrating nearly 6,000 troops at Matamoros.

Both sides glared at each other for a month. Finally on 25 April, the Mexicans mounted a strong cavalry sweep north of the river and overwhelmed a small American reconnaissance force. Taylor reported to the president that hostilities had begun and took part of his command to Point Isabel to protect the depot from the marauding Mexican cavalry. Meanwhile, Mexican Gen Mariano Arista led his 6,000 troops across the river against Taylor's base camp, which was under the command of Maj Jacob Brown. Arista laid siege to the camp from 3 to 8 May, but Brown's defense was successful, although he died in the action.

Arista then moved to place his force between the camp and Taylor's force, which was returning from Point Isabel. The two forces met at Palo Alto on 8 May and the Mexicans were forced to retire primarily because of superior American artillery. The following day, 9 May 1846, Taylor attacked a strong Mexican position a few miles to the south at Resaca de la Palma. The Mexican forces broke after a brief but fierce fight, and Arista withdrew across the Rio Grande, retreating nearly 100 miles to Linares. Four days later, the United States declared war on Mexico.

Taylor crossed the Rio Grande and entered Matamoros on 18 May, but was forced to delay further operations while he awaited the transportation (wagons) and reinforcements needed for offensive operations. By August, Taylor had the wagons and men he needed and moved south on Monterrey with a force of 6,000. The city was well fortified and defended by Gen Pedro de Ampudia with a force of about 10,000. On 24 September, after a fierce three-day fight, Ampudia offered surrender of the city and an eight-week armistice, which Taylor accepted. Polk repudiated the agreement, but the news did not reach Taylor until seven weeks had elapsed. In the meantime, the Mexicans had fallen back to San Luis Potosí where the new Mexican president, Antonio López de Santa Anna, was reorganizing his forces. Taylor, in the meantime, moved slightly south of Monterrey and occupied Saltillo.

To this point, the Mexicans had met with consistent failure. Taylor had marched into northern Mexico and defeated two different Mexican generals, each of whom commanded a larger force than Taylor's. Elsewhere, Brig Gen Stephen Kearny had seized New Mexico and advanced into California. Monterey, had been occupied by American naval forces in July, and it was clear that Kearny and the naval forces would force a climactic battle with the Mexicans in California.

Despite these grim circumstances, the Mexicans would not accede to American demands. Polk was left with little choice but to follow Scott's plan to attack the seat of Mexican political power, Mexico City. Scott left Washington on 24 November, and after gathering many of Taylor's troops at Point Isabel, sailed to Tampico and established his headquarters.

Meanwhile Santa Anna learned of Scott's plan and resolved to crush the weakened forces of Taylor before Scott could strike. Moving north from San Luis Potosí, Santa Anna arrived at Buena Vista, having lost nearly 20 percent of his force on the grueling march. On 23 February 1847 Santa Anna launched his attack. In a wild and confused battle, he was repulsed, with 500 dead and about 1,000 wounded, and fell back across the desert to San Luis Potosí.

On 9 March Scott arrived with 10,000 troops near Vera Cruz, landed unopposed, and laid siege to the city. After a five-day artillery bombardment, the city's garrison surrendered with little bloodshed on either side. Scott moved inland quickly to get away from the disease-infested coastal plain. On 18 April Scott found Santa Anna with 12,000 men at Cerro Gordo. Thanks to his West Point–trained engineers (including then Capt Robert E. Lee), Scott was able to flank Santa Anna's position and rout the Mexicans after a sharp fight. The Mexican's lost 1,000 killed and wounded with 3,000 captured while Scott suffered about 400 total casualties.

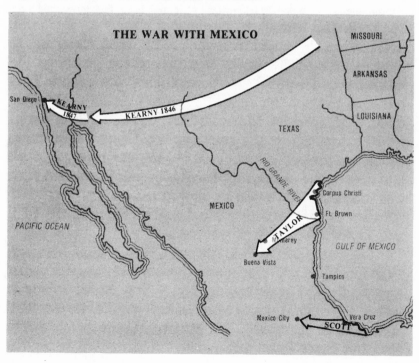

In May Scott was forced to pause in his advance until those volunteers whose 12-month enlistments had expired were replaced with new enlistees. Finally on 7 August, Scott set out for Mexico City, severing his lines of communication with the coast since he did not have sufficient troops to defend them. Circling south of Lake Chalco and Xochimilco, Scott met Santa Anna's defenders on 20 August in the Battles of Contreras and Churubusco, in which the Mexicans were defeated and forced to retreat within Mexico City's walls.

Peace negotiations ensued as Santa Anna attempted to reorganize his battered forces. Finally, negotiations broke down and on 8 September 1847, Scott attacked and defeated the Mexicans at Molino del Rey. Five days later, on 13 September, the Americans stormed the last bastion outside the city itself in the Battle of Chapultepec. It was here that 100 cadets from the Mexican Military College made a gallant but hopeless stand. The next morning, the remaining garrison in Mexico City surrendered, Santa Anna having left during the night.

Following the capture of Mexico City, peace negotiations began in earnest at Guadalupe Hidalgo and an agreement was reached on 2 February 1848. The last American troops left Mexico City in June and evacuated Vera Cruz in August.

### Better State of the Peace

After the US Army had compelled the toppling of a hostile Mexican government and seen it replaced by a regime more amenable to negotiating a settlement on the basis of American objectives, the war ended. The terms of the peace were negotiated in the form of the Treaty of Guadalupe Hidalgo in February 1848. The United States acquired the territories it had desired in the beginning (the disputed areas of Texas, California, New Mexico, and Arizona territories) in return for a $15-million payment to the government of Mexico. After the Gadsden Purchase of 1853 added remaining sections of New Mexico and Arizona to the Union, the territorial boundaries of the 48 contiguous states took on their final shape; manifest destiny was served.

The settlement was certainly imposed. Militarily, the forces of the United States had all but destroyed Mexico's ability to resist the imposition of our policies, and the occupation of Mexico City exceeded Mexico's cost-tolerance, the factor that proved pivotal in the end. At the same time, Mexican hostile will (defined as acceptance and embracing of our policy) was not overcome, and no serious efforts were made to convince the Mexicans of the virtues of manifest destiny. Instead, we sought to buy the Mexicans off in the peace treaty and the Gadsden Purchase. Much of the anti-Americanism that still exists in Mexico surely has its roots in our failure to overcome that aspect of hostile will.

The war had its consequences and its lessons. It provided, among other things, a training ground for the officer corps that would lead the forces (especially Southern) in the Civil War a little over a decade later; virtually all of the major military leaders of the fratricidal conflict received their first major blooding in Mexico. Moreover, the performance of that portion of the officer corps who had attended the academy proved to be a vindication for the West Point system. At the same time, the soldiers who fought under those leaders were, by and large, the same sort of citizen-soldiers who had fought all of America's wars, apparently supporting once again the virtues of the militia system. Manifest destiny was served and, for the time, sated. It would return again a half-century later, and the result would be the Spanish-American War.

## Spanish-American War

The conflict between the United States and Spain in 1898 was labeled by its most prominent war hero, Theodore Roosevelt, "the splendid little war" and in many ways it was. The war lasted only a little more than three months, and all of America's objectives were achieved at the cost of less than 300 combatants killed in action. In the process, the United States established itself among the world's powers, a force that would have to be reckoned with in the future.

### Issues and Events

The underlying, pervasive issue that gave rise to war with Spain was the question of manifest destiny, and it was an issue that had both humanitarian and imperialistic aspects. As a humanitarian concern, there was a rising missionary zeal in the country that reviled repression and sought to share the American political and social experiment. This concern was focused most explicitly on the island of Cuba and the fate of its citizens under Spanish rule. In addition, there had grown in the 1890s the first strong imperialist sentiment in US history (if one does not consider the settlement of the continent an act of imperialism). This sentiment argued that for the United States to achieve the status of a major power, it must have colonies (colonies bestowed great power status in a way not unlike nuclear weapons do today). Since the Afro-Asian world had been thoroughly carved up into European empires, the only way to acquire an empire was to take one away from someone else.

The resurgence of manifest destiny followed the lapse of that concept

after the Mexican War. During the interim, of course, the country was con-
vulsed by the Civil War and the process of bitter reconstruction that followed, and national energies not trained on that trauma were focused on the
settlement of the American West. It was a time for introspection and not
external expansion. By the 1890s, the worst of reconstruction was past, the
West was largely settled, and the country had emerged as a commercial and
industrial giant. It was time to assert America's place in the community of
states and to protect its position in the international economic system. The
average citizen might be more moved by America's mission to "save a savage world," but its leaders marched increasingly to the drum of geopolitics.

The proximate events that led Americans into war focused on Cuba. That
island so close to the Florida coast had held a special place in the American
conscience for half a century. At one time many Americans had considered
colonizing Cuba, and its fate was seen as intertwined with ours. Americans had
watched with compassion during the "Ten Years' War" Cubans had waged unsuccessfully against Spanish colonial rule between 1868 and 1878, and had
watched the Cubans revolt again in 1895. Cuba held a special fascination.

Adding fuel to this fascination and concern was the "yellow journalism"
of the New York press. The two giants of the newspaper world, Joseph Pulitzer
of the New York *World* and William Randolph Hearst of the rival New York
*Journal*, were locked in a titanic circulation war, and coverage of the situation in Cuba became the primary weapon for selling newspapers. To increase
circulation, events in Cuba were pictured in especially lurid and sensational
terms that undoubtedly magnified and distorted Spanish suppression and acts
of terror. Americans who had these sources as their primary basis of knowledge, however, looked on with increasing horror that led to a growing sentiment for war.

The situation in Cuba was also bad for business, and the American business community had a special concern with evolving events. Before the 1895
revolt, Americans had invested more than $50 million in Cuban plantations,
transportation projects, and business establishments, and all those investments were threatened by the revolution. Moreover, trade between the island
country and the United States was severely hampered.

The movement toward intervention in Cuba grew steadily and inexorably. When William McKinley was elected president in 1896, he sought to
avoid war, telling outgoing President Grover Cleveland that he hoped he
could avoid American involvement in "this terrible calamity." Events would,
however, not allow this to happen. The event that led directly to war was the
sinking of the USS *Maine* in Havana Harbor.

The sinking of the *Maine* is shrouded in controversy. The battleship had
been summoned to Cuba by American Consul Fitzhugh Lee (who had been

given that authority by President McKinley) on a purported courtesy call that was in fact a response to the storming of Havana newspaper offices by Spanish officers in retaliation for negative articles written about the military. The vessel sat at anchor for three weeks under heavy security, but on the night of 15 February 1898 a massive explosion ripped the ship, causing the death of 260 crewmen out of a total crew of 350.

No one knows for sure who sank the *Maine* or why. We will never know because the ship was raised from the bottom of Havana Harbor in 1911, towed to deep sea in the Atlantic, and sunk without detailed inspection, leaving the mystery intact. If the facts were in dispute, however, the apportionment of blame at the time was not. Americans learned of the tragedy in the New York *Journal* on 17 February. The paper's banner proclaimed that "The War Ship *Maine* Was Split in Two by an Enemy's Infernal Machine." That enemy, of course, was Spain, and the incident fanned the flames lit by the revelation of the famous de Lome letter earlier that year (a missive written by the Spanish ambassador in Washington describing the president in especially derisive terms).

The combination of events greatly increased pressure on McKinley to declare the war he sought to avoid. He demanded and received an apology over the de Lome incident. He also received Spanish assurances that the violence in Cuba would end and that they would institute economic reforms. These assurances were too little too late. American war fever could be sated only by fire, and on 11 April 1898, a reluctant President McKinley issued his war message. After 33 years of peace, America was once more at war.

### Political Objective

As framed in President McKinley's war message to the Congress, the American political objective in the war with Spain dealt exclusively with alleviating the situation in Cuba. In the process of the war's conduct, however, the United States came into possession of other Spanish territory, creating the empire that was an objective of many Americans but which had not been a stated goal of the administration.

Exactly what was to become of Cuba was not stated in the message. Rather, McKinley said American military intervention was rooted in four concerns: a humanitarian concern over the devastation occurring on the island, protection of American citizens and rights on the island, an end to threats to Cuban-American commerce, and a guarantee that American strategic interests in the area would be honored. In time, this objective translated into Cuban political independence coupled with heavy American economic penetration and control.

The acquisition of empire occurred almost by accident. On 1 May 1898, Commodore George Dewey engaged the Spanish fleet in the "battle" of Manila Bay, sank it in its entirety, and thereby ended Spanish political dominion over the Philippines. The American flag flew over Manila, and it was only after some considerable debate that we decided it should stay there. Likewise, a force was sent to Puerto Rico after the fall of Cuba to overcome the Spanish garrison there, and once that was accomplished, McKinley simply decided to keep the island as a war indemnity.

### Military Objectives and Strategy

American military strategy was controlled by President McKinley. Rather than having a well-thought-out plan, strategy and objectives unfolded with events, threats, and opportunities. The essential military problem was that no one knew exactly what McKinley sought as political objectives when the war began. Was it to aid the Cuban rebels or to seize Cuba? Questions remained concerning other such Spanish colonies as Puerto Rico and the Philippine Islands.

The Navy had the fewest problems making its plans. As early as 1896, officers at the Naval War College had developed a plan for fighting Spain. The plan called for a blockade of Cuba to starve the Spanish troops followed by the occupation of the island by a small American force aided by the Cuban rebels. Simultaneously, the Americans would attack the Spanish Pacific Squadron at Manila Bay to safeguard American commerce in the Pacific. This general plan was quickly approved.

The commanding general of the Army, Nelson A. Miles, proposed a full-scale invasion of Cuba by an 80,000-man regular Army to take place in the fall after the rainy reason had passed. McKinley thought such a delay would be intolerable. Miles then suggested that Puerto Rico should be the main focus of American operations.

The first approved and coordinated plan relied on naval action to bring the Spanish to heel. In addition to the Cuban blockade and the attack on the Spanish Pacific Squadron, the plan called for a small Army force of 5,000 to land on the Cuban coast and to funnel supplies to the rebels. This plan changed quickly for two reasons. First, on 29 April 1898, news arrived that a Spanish fleet had set sail under the command of Adm Pascual Cervera. American ships were quickly detached from the blockade to form a "flying squadron" to protect the Atlantic Seaboard and to find the Spanish fleet. Second, a cable confirmed that Commodore Dewey's Asiatic Squadron had smashed the Spanish Pacific Squadron at Manila Bay and asked for 5,000 troops to seize Manila.

McKinley became much more aggressive with the good news from the Pacific. Additionally, the blockade seemed to be having only a limited effect on the Spanish, but it was taking its toll on American ships and men. The plan changed and the target became Havana. Army troops would land near the city and then march on the seat of Spanish power. However, it was soon learned that Cervera's small fleet had arrived and entered Santiago Harbor. The target of the ground attack was quickly changed to Santiago. A force of 17,000 men sailed for Cuba with more to follow as training was completed and shipping became available.

The American force seemed small for the job, as the Spanish army had 150,000 troops in Cuba. However, tropical disease had taken its toll of the Spanish and perhaps only half that number were effective. Worse, the soldiers were scattered throughout the island in an attempt to withhold ground from the rebels. The Spanish army could not quickly concentrate because of the primitive transportation system on the island.

### Political Considerations

In some senses, the Spanish-American War was a model event, a prototype for America's wars of the second half of the twentieth century. This may seem an odd statement, since the resemblance between the war with Spain and say, Vietnam or Korea is, to say the least, tenuous. The Spanish conflict is not a model for how the United States has fought wars in the contemporary period, but the analogy has meaning when the conflict is seen as a model for the kinds of limited wars the United States can successfully sustain. The measure of sustenance in America, as in any democracy, is continuing popular support for military action to its conclusion.

Public support for the campaign against Spain not only nurtured the endeavor, it virtually forced it. The war with Spain was the first instance in American history wherein the news media played a crucial initiating role and, as pointed out earlier, the New York circulation war was a critical element in forcing President McKinley to declare war. America's desire for war was strong, and it was sustained throughout the campaign.

The critical question is why this was the case. At least three factors come to mind that distinguish the war with Spain from Vietnam and Korea, but which bear similarity to more recent adventures such as the US invasion of Grenada and the British war with Argentina over the Falkland (Malvinas) Islands. First, the war's stated aim of relieving Cuba was clear, unambiguous, and popular. The liberation of Cuba as the major goal was well known, had overwhelming popular support, and translated readily into military requirements the accomplishment of which were clear and easily measurable. Only when the war spread to empire did the objective become muddy. Second, the war was short and relatively bloodless. The military campaign took only three months and caused modest casualties. Such criticism of the war as did occur was raised after its end and centered on the abysmal medical support conditions that resulted in many needless noncombat deaths among American servicemen. Third, the war was an easily achieved military victory. San Juan Hill and the Battle of Manila Bay were the crowning blows, and they were both walkovers against an overmatched foe. There was plenty of glory and little bloodshed.

## Military Technology and Technique

The "splendid little war" was a joint Army-Navy operation, and both services bore little resemblance to their forebears from the Civil War. In many respects, the Spanish-American War was a modern conflict in that most of the weapons and techniques used were much more like those of the twentieth century than those of the Civil War.

The standard American infantry weapon was the .30-caliber Krag-Jorgensen rifle. Unlike its immediate predecessor, the so-called Trap-Door Springfield, the Krag-Jorgensen was a five-shot repeater that used smokeless cartridges. Unfortunately, by 1898, only the regular Army had been equipped with the Krag-Jorgensens, and national guardsmen mobilized for the war were forced to use the obsolete single-shot Springfields.

American artillery was plentiful, but technical development had lagged, and the quality of the artillery had fallen far behind that of most European armies. Many pieces still required slow and dangerous muzzle loading, and all fired black powder. The smoke from the black powder instantly gave away artillery positions and made the gunners' situation dangerous against a first-class adversary. Perhaps more important, American gunners still had no method of sighting for indirect fire, which meant that they could engage the enemy only at ranges not much longer than those of the Civil War.

The American Navy had made significant technological strides since the Civil War. Spurred on by Mahan and others who argued for a first-class navy and overseas possessions, the Navy had embarked on a large building program that had produced, by 1898, the sixth-largest navy in the world. The Navy had five battleships, four of which were of the most modern types and listed as "First Class." For example, the USS *Oregon*, which fought in both the Pacific and Atlantic, displaced 10,000 tons, mounted a total of four 13-inch guns on turrets fore and aft as well as eight 8-inch guns, and had a top steaming speed of nearly 17 knots. The Navy also had 30 cruisers such as the USS *Olympia*, Dewey's flagship, which displaced 6,000 tons, mounted four 8-inch guns as well as ten 5-inch guns, and could steam at nearly 22 knots.

Although well armed, American forces were not well prepared for a war of any size. The regular Army of just over 28,000 was well trained and experienced in the frontier Indian wars. However, it was skilled only in small-unit actions. The largest regular formation was the regiment and few officers had ever seen larger formations. Likewise, the Navy was inexperienced in fleet operations.

Perhaps the greatest shortcomings were in joint operations and in amphibious operations. Coordination between the services during the conflict was appalling. The embarkation at Tampa of Army forces bound for Cuba was a scene of mass confusion, including the last-minute discovery that there were not enough ships to carry the troops. At the end of the voyage, the landing operations were also chaotic: there were not enough small boats to get the troops and supplies ashore quickly. The landing took four days, in sharp contrast to Scott's landing at Vera Cruz a half-century earlier. That operation, which involved an equally large force, was accomplished in one day.

The Spanish-American War also exhibited the continued growth of modern centralized command and control. President McKinley established a "war room" in the White House complete with detailed maps and markers, and equipped with 25 telegraph lines. These lines connected him with the various military departments and with officers occupying important posts in other cities. McKinley did not hesitate to use his communications capability in directing the efforts of the military staffs.

## Military Conduct

The first military action of the war was not an engagement, but the destruction of the American battleship *Maine*, which was officially on a goodwill visit to Havana. As noted, the circumstances of the explosion that sank the ship on 15 February 1898 are a matter of some debate. Regardless of how it happened and who was responsible, the sinking led more or less directly to the American declaration of war on 25 April. At the same time, the regular establishment of the Army was increased from 28,000 to 60,000, and President McKinley called for 125,000 volunteers. A month later McKinley called for an additional 75,000 volunteers.

The Navy was ready for immediate action and quickly clamped a blockade on Cuba. On 25 April Commodore Dewey sailed his Asiatic Squadron to Manila Bay. He entered Manila Bay on the night of 30 April, and on 1 May engaged the Spanish squadron commanded by Adm Patricio Montojo. The engagement was less a battle than an execution. Montojo's fleet was outclassed and outgunned. Dewey's force totally destroyed the Spanish force while losing only one dead (via heatstroke) and eight wounded. Dewey then waited for the arrival of sufficient troops to seize Manila.

In the Atlantic, the Americans learned on 29 April that Admiral Cervera had sailed with the main Spanish fleet from the Cape Verde Islands. A small flying squadron was detached from the blockading force to protect the Eastern Seaboard and intercept the Spanish fleet. Surprisingly, Cervera avoided the American forces and slipped into Santiago Harbor on 19 May. Rear Adm William T. Sampson, who commanded US naval forces in Cuban waters, immediately blockaded the harbor.

By mid-June, despite tremendous logistical snarls and a lack of planning for almost everything needed by a large modern army, Maj Gen William R. Shafter was ready to sail to Cuba with 17,000 men. Shafter's forces arrived off the Cuban coast on 22 June and commenced landing at Daiquiri. The landing was unopposed, but confusion reigned, and it was not until 25 June that the full force was ashore. Had the Spanish been able to oppose the landing, the story of the war might have had a far different ending.

After some minor skirmishes, and great difficulties in unloading supplies from the poorly loaded ships, Shafter moved on Santiago. On 1 July he assaulted the San Juan Heights that protected the eastern approaches to Santiago. By nightfall, after confused maneuvering, several sharp setbacks from the Spanish, and the Rough Riders' "charge up San Juan Hill" led by Lt Col Theodore Roosevelt, the positions were in American hands. The Spanish fell back to their inner defense line.

On 3 July Cervera led his trapped fleet out of Santiago Harbor in a valiant but doomed attempt to escape the American blockade. As was Dewey's triumph at Manila Bay, the Battle of Santiago Bay was one-sided. Running along the coast, the Spanish ships were overwhelmed with heavy fire and forced aground as burning hulks. All six of the Spanish ships were lost. Incredibly, total American losses were one killed and one wounded.

Faced with insurmountable odds, the Spanish commander in Santiago, Gen José Toral, surrendered the city on 17 July. The surrender included all Spanish forces in eastern Cuba. Toral was unaware that tropical diseases were taking their first toll of American forces and that Shafter's supply problem remained difficult.

On 25 July Gen Miles landed on Puerto Rico and after being reinforced, pushed inland. He met almost no opposition as Spanish forces fell back into San Juan. Before Miles attacked San Juan, word arrived that Spain had asked for peace.

Meanwhile, on 25 May 1898, Gen Wesley Merritt departed San Francisco with the vanguard of troops bound for Manila. He arrived at Manila on 30 June with a force that would eventually total 15,000. The situation was delicate because the Philippine rebel leader, Emilio Aguinaldo, had Manila under siege and had declared a Philippine Republic. While the American political leadership pondered what to do with the Philippines, Merritt and Dewey wanted to take the city as soon as possible. Squadrons from some of the great powers were beginning to appear in Manila Bay, and Merritt and Dewey feared serious problems if American control was not quickly established.

The Spanish commander in Manila, Fermin Juadenes, was willing to surrender but not to the rebels, whom he feared would seek retribution against the Spanish. After secret negotiations, a sham battle was staged on 13 August, and the Americans entered the city. The Spanish were therefore able to surrender to the Americans, and Merritt took control of the city. Neither Juadenes nor Merritt was aware that the war had ended two days earlier.

### Better State of the Peace

Because the war was such a military mismatch, achieving the stated political goals forced upon McKinley was relatively easy. Spanish hostile ability was minimal to begin with, and once the United States had sunk the Spanish fleets and thus left the island garrisons isolated, overcoming the vestiges of hostile ability was simple and straightforward. Moreover, the Spanish, fully aware that they stood no reasonable military chance against the Americans, possessed little hostile will, so that both their cost-tolerance and unwillingness to accept our policies were quickly overcome as well.

American objectives were achieved, at least in the short run. Cuba was relieved of the Spanish yoke, but the full independence they expected was only questionably theirs. McKinley's war message had not guaranteed independent status, and although political independence was granted, economic penetration by the Americans left the island in a position of dependency that many Cubans believe was broken only by Fidel Castro's revolution 60 years later. At the same time, the United States acquired an empire in the form of Guam, Puerto Rico, and the Philippines. Those imperialist ambitions were not clearly defined when we entered the war but evolved. Filipino insurgents, for example, first viewed us as liberators and made common cause with us in helping remove the hated Spanish. They began to oppose us when they recognized that the Yankees had no intention of leaving, either. The result was a bloody counterinsurgent campaign and, once that was concluded, an exposed empire that stuck out like a sore thumb in the way of Japanese expansion in the western Pacific.

# 9

## Desert Storm and the Post-Vietnam Experience

The American people and the American military staggered away from the calamity of Vietnam. Combined with the impending Watergate scandal, Vietnam helped undercut the faith and trust of Americans in their government. The professional military retreated, shunned by a population reluctant to be subjected to military service and deeply suspicious of the government and the media. All three links in the Clausewitzian trinity (the bond between the people, the military, and the government) lay fractured.

The period since Vietnam can be seen as a process of healing those fractures, as both the citizenry and professional military that serve it have reassessed and adjusted the role of military force in American society. That adjustment, in turn, has been influenced by three different factors: the Vietnam experience and adjusting to its meaning, the changing attitudes of the American public toward the military and the use of military force, and the end of the cold war.

The primary, immediate legacy of Vietnam was a turning inward of both the American people and the military. The American people wanted nothing of foreign military involvements: "no more Vietnams" meant, at least temporarily, no more military engagements. The people let the military know their disdain by avoiding service in the new All-Volunteer Force (AVF), at least initially. They let the politicians know in 1976, the first presidential election year since the fall of Saigon, by electing a president who promised an absolute reduction in military spending.

The military became introverted as well. Many of the best and brightest left military service; those who remained asked, Why had the catastrophe occurred? Most felt betrayed. On reflection, however, two things happened. First, the armed forces dedicated themselves to professionalism to overcome the general perception of their incompetence. Second, their analysis brought them back to Clausewitz and the trinity; in the future, support from the American people would be sought, even demanded, in advance of committing American forces into harm's way.

The revival of the American military paralleled changing attitudes in the American electorate. As Vietnam faded in the public mind, so did the overt animosity toward the military fade in most minds. The change, a renaissance in support for an active military role, was symbolized—even energized—by the presidential career of Ronald Reagan. In 1976, Reagan sought the presidency on the conservative, promilitary platform that propelled him into the White House in 1980. In 1976, he could not wrest the Republican Party nomination from Gerald Ford. In 1980, the same combination of patriotic values and a pledge to reverse the "unilateral disarmament" of the Carter years produced a landslide victory. Reagan had not changed; the people's attitudes had.

The result was a decade of prosperity and prestige for the American military unprecedented in peacetime. Money was available, high quality recruits streamed into the recruiters' offices, and morale soared. The military was back.

Initially, the diet was too rich. Resources alone could not instantly produce the quality of military we associate with adventures such as Desert Storm. Quality took time to rebuild; in the interim the military floundered in places like Beirut and Grenada.

Support for the military, especially as it translates into monetary backing, runs in cycles. The good times of the early 1980s leveled off as the decade drew toward a close, and the door slammed closed as it ended. The precipitating events were the revolutions of 1989 in Eastern Europe and the gradual breakup of the Soviet Union, which cumulatively ended the cold war that had provided the *raison d'être* for the size, composition, missions, strategies, and doctrines of the armed forces since 1945.

The result has been traumatic. With threats on the wane, an interest–threat mismatch has occurred in which the traditional vital interests of the United States are challenged in no other place than in the Persian Gulf (and arguably the Korean peninsula) and where all the other threats are located in places peripheral to the traditional calculus of where America should use force. The military establishment became vulnerable to severe cutbacks (what is there to protect against?) and forced to define new missions to justify itself; the crucial question is how and when to use force.

In the final 15 years of the cold war, the US was called upon to use force only in modest ways: attempting to rescue the hostages held in the American

Embassy in Teheran and saving American medical students at risk in Grenada. Since the end of the cold war, however, things have changed, and not in entirely positive ways.

The end of the cold war, and the greater democratization that has accompanied it, has had two largely unanticipated consequences. First, many of the restraints that the cold war overlay produced have been removed. In the formerly Communist countries, the suppression of ethnic minorities that was part of authoritarian rule has been stripped away, resulting in large-scale ethnic and communal violence that would have been crushed in the past. In the third world, the constraints that the superpowers placed upon their clients have also dissipated; violent outbreaks can no longer be controlled. Second, democratization has produced some very unanticipated instability and violence as artificially conceived states held together by coercion fall apart, accompanied by bloodshed.

These dynamics provide the context within which the United States has used military force between the end of the Vietnam War and the end of the cold war and give some indication as to where the opportunities will appear in the future. For this purpose, the ensuing discussion will be divided into two major sections. The first will deal with the Persian Gulf War, the most conspicuous military success and the only major military adventure of the post-Vietnam period. We will also view it in its geopolitical context and raise the question of whether it was the first major challenge of the "new world order" or the last of the old order. The second section will look at the minor operations in which the American military was employed prior to Desert Storm. These include the Beirut and Grenada missions of 1983 and the invasion of Panama in 1989.

## Operation Desert Storm

### Issues and Events

The underlying issues and events leading to the American involvement in the effort to evict Saddam Hussein's Iraqi army from Kuwait are both simple and complex, depending upon the level at which one investigates them. In one sense, the precipitating event—the lightning conquest of the tiny, oil-rich state of Kuwait by the Iraqi armed forces—is straightforward. Moreover, with the conquest complete, there was no physical barrier to the Iraqis continuing to plunge farther south and grabbing the Saudi oilfields on the Persian Gulf as well.

A deeper understanding requires looking at two different items. The first is the period leading to Iraq's invasion, including both Iraqi attempts to gain financial assistance from Saudi Arabia and Kuwait, and American attempts to woo the Iraqi government and hence bring it into the international mainstream. The second is the reason Saddam acted militarily as he did, rather than pursuing alternative objectives.

Iraq had a set of grievances with Saudi Arabia and Kuwait that arose from Iraq's "protection" of Arab interests in the Iran–Iraq War. The eight-year struggle ended in 1988 and left Iraq exhausted militarily, politically, and economically. Iraq had borrowed over $30 billion during the war, mostly from the Saudis and Kuwaitis, and could not repay it. Saddam requested cancellation of the loans; he was refused. Next, he requested additional credits to help rebuild the shattered economy. This request also had political bases: Saddam's popularity and stability required a return to normality. His requests were not honored.

Finally, Saddam requested that the price of oil be raised and production reduced as a way to maximize Iraqi oil revenue. Not only was the request denied, but Kuwait engaged in "slant drilling" from Kuwaiti soil into the Rumalia oil fields claimed by Iraq, in effect stealing Iraqi oil. In the months preceding the invasion, Iraq threatened consequences if Saddam's requests were not honored; no one paid any attention.

Iraq had a new suitor during this period—the United States. The US had reopened relations with Iraq in 1985 (Iraq broke relations with the US in 1958), in effect tilting the Americans against Iran in their war. When the war ended, relations continued to warm and expand; ultimately Iraq diverted US grain credits to military purchases—a scandal that has become known as "Iraqgate." The purpose was to try to curry influence that could steer Iraq into the mainstream of international life.

In the process, the United States averted its gaze from Saddam's more atrocious behavior, such as gassing Iraq's own Kurdish population in 1987. Prior to the fall of the Shah of Iran, Saddam Hussein had been the pariah of the region; he looked better compared to the Ayatollah Ruhollah Khomeini, but it was not because he had changed. Had he bullied Kuwait in 1978, we would have believed him; we chose not to in 1990. Two weeks before the invasion, April Glaspie, US ambassador to Iraq, assured Saddam that the US had no interest in oil negotiations among the Arabs or in boundary disputes. When asked after the war why we did not foresee the impending invasion, she replied, "We didn't believe he was that stupid."

When he contemplated military action, Saddam had three options: simply occupy the Rumalia oil fields and annex those fields; invade, conquer, and annex Kuwait; or invade Kuwait and move onto the Saudi fields. Had he simply seized Rumalia, he probably would have succeeded: the slant drilling gave him a case, and no one in the region would have felt very sorry for the arrogant al-Sabah Kuwaiti ruling family. Similarly, had he seized the Saudi oil fields, the Saudi royal family probably would have negotiated a cash settlement to ensure withdrawal.

Saddam chose, instead, the one option certain to elicit a military response. The UN had no choice but to act: this was the first and only time a member state had conquered and annexed another UN member state. If the UN did not reply, why have a UN? At the same time, Saddam violated the unwritten law of the region, which said that Arab states do not alter the 1919 boundaries of the Arab world by force. Saddam broke both rules; both the UN and the Arab world had to react.

### Political Objective

Although Operation Desert Storm was overwhelmingly an American enterprise, it was authorized as a United Nations action, and its objective, clear throughout the duration, was defined by UN Security Council Resolution 678. That resolution authorized the liberation of Kuwait and the restoration of Kuwaiti sovereignty. As UN action, *that was the only political objective that could have been authorized*, and that was the objective accepted by the US. To have authorized any broader objective (such as overthrowing the Iraqi government) would have exceeded the mandate stated in the UN Charter.

This question of the objective has been the subject of some unnecessary confusion, for three reasons that we have seen previously. First, as Desert Shield (the preparatory aspect of the Desert Storm military campaign) was forming in fall 1990, President Bush began referring to Saddam as a Hitler figure. This was meaningless, loose rhetoric, the implications of which were probably not well thought out, but which was intended to rally support for the enterprise. Since Hitlers are to be removed, however, some felt the objective included getting rid of Saddam. This was never the case.

Second, the ease of the 100-hour ground war made it seem easy to "finish" the job by rolling on to Baghdad, grabbing Saddam, and destroying his supply of nuclear, biological, and chemical (NBC) weapons in the process. This might have been militarily possible, but it would have transformed the purpose of the war in much the same way as occurred in Korea the first time the allies got to the 38th parallel. Third, subsequent UN efforts (authorized by Security Council Resolution 687, which also created the cease-fire that ended the war) to disarm Iraqi NBC capabilities met with some frustration. Thus, some have thought that if we had "done the job right" in the first place, there would have been no problem. To repeat, however, the UN could not order such an invasion; Resolution 687 was directed at Iraqi violation of international treaty obligations (the Non-Proliferation Treaty), not the invasion of Kuwait.

The confusion had two Korea-like aspects. In Korea, the original and eventual objective was to restore the status quo; the UN mandated the same end in Kuwait. In Korea, the objective expanded when the North Korean Army was broken in the initial counteroffensive; the alternate objective of freeing the peninsula to hold unifying elections was made possible by military success. In the Persian Gulf War, military success made the removal of Saddam seem possible; fortunately, this time restraint held. However, in both cases flirtation with broader objectives left the attainment of the original objective seem a bit hollow and unfulfilling.

## Military Objectives and Strategy

Changing military objectives and strategies divided the Persian Gulf conflict into two distinct but closely related phases, Desert Shield and Desert Storm. Desert Shield, as the name implies, was almost entirely defensive in nature. The only exceptions were the United Nations economic sanctions, enforced by Coalition naval forces, which were intended to force Iraqi withdrawal from Kuwait. Desert Storm was purely offensive, designed to drive the Iraqis from Kuwait by force of arms, to destroy Iraq's offensive military capability, and thus to create a better state of peace in the war's wake.

### Desert Shield

Following the invasion of Kuwait on 2 August 1990, hurried conferences involving the president, Secretary of Defense Richard Cheney, commander of Central Command Gen H. Norman Schwarzkopf, and other key officials reviewed military options. They quickly decided to deploy US forces to Saudi Arabia, if invited by the Saudi government. The objectives of the deployment, quickly dubbed Desert Shield, were fourfold. The first was to deter the Iraqis from further aggression beyond the Kuwaiti-Saudi border where their advance had stopped, perhaps only temporarily. Second, if the Iraqis were not deterred, it would defend Saudi Arabia, and by inference, the United Arab Emirates. Third, the forces would enforce the economic sanctions dictated by the United Nations Security Council Resolutions 661 and 665. Fourth, the Central Command commander would put together an effective military force among the Coalition members. It would not be easy to attain any of these objectives.

The crux of the problem was to get sufficient forces to Saudi Arabia quickly enough to defend the kingdom. If the Iraqis attacked quickly, before adequate forces were in place, Schwarzkopf had to have a defensive strategy that would both effectively defend and still retain the air and seaport facilities to continue the buildup. This "window of vulnerability," the amount of time it would take to get sufficient forces in place, could be as long as 17 weeks, according to Central Command Operating Plan 1002-90.

Schwarzkopf based his initial concept of operations on an enclave strategy that would trade space for time. The enclaves would be the ports and airfields on the Gulf coast, principally Al-Jubayl and Dhahran. Holding these areas would be essential to continuing the buildup. Saudi land forces would provide a screening force along the Kuwaiti border to slow an Iraqi advance, but the major combat power available to the Coalition in the early stages of the buildup would be Coalition air power.

Without adequate ground forces on the scene, heavy reliance on air power was an obvious choice. The terrain in the region was ideal for rapid armored movements—an Iraqi strength—but it was also the most ideal possible terrain for air operations—a US, and hence Coalition, strength. The relatively flat desert terrain meant that there was no place for Iraqi ground forces to hide from Coalition air power. Further, the nature of armored warfare placed great reliance on mobile resupply of munitions, fuel, and other expendables—ideal targets for air power ranging deep behind advancing Iraqi armor. Schwarzkopf understood that air power would be an advantage of the Coalition even after sufficient ground forces were in place.

While the Saudi ground forces and Coalition air power slowed an Iraqi advance, trading space for time, US ground forces would defend the enclaves and the buildup would continue. The Saudis expressed some reservations about this strategy. Their natural instinct was to defend all of Saudi Arabia, fighting for every inch of Saudi soil. Fortunately, the Iraqis did not attack and the differing approaches to the problem were not put to the test in battle.

## Desert Storm

Although Desert Shield was defensive, plans began to take shape almost immediately for offensive operations should the Iraqis fail to withdraw from Kuwait under the economic pressure of the United Nations sanctions. The earliest effort was a broad conceptual plan called Instant Thunder, an obvious play on the name of the Rolling Thunder air operations in the Vietnam War. The contrast between the two operations was stark. Twenty-five years earlier, the Rolling Thunder campaign had emphasized slow, graduated pressure on the enemy. Instant Thunder visualized an aerial blitzkrieg designed to destroy 84 strategic targets in Iraq during the first week alone. The entire concept plan included four phases, the first three using air power (land and sea based) almost exclusively. Phase I consisted of the aforementioned strategic air campaign designed to isolate the Iraqi leadership from their fielded forces, to destroy their ability to command and control their forces effectively, and to destroy Iraqi nuclear, biological, and chemical warfare research, production, and storage facilities. Phase II sought air supremacy over Kuwait and its immediate environs, the Kuwaiti theater of operations (KTO). Phase III shifted attention to the Iraqi ground forces in Kuwait, particularly the elite Republican Guard units, and to an interdiction campaign to isolate the Kuwaiti battlefield from effective reinforcement and resupply from Iraq. Phase IV was a combined air and ground offensive to drive the Iraqis out of Kuwait.

Over the months of Desert Shield operations, this concept plan was expanded and refined but still retained its basic thrust and flavor. The final plan had five objectives: (1) to neutralize the Iraqi command capabilities, (2) to eject the Iraqis from Kuwait, (3) to destroy the Republican Guard, (4) to destroy the Iraqi missile, nuclear, chemical, and biological warfare capabilities, and in the aftermath, (5) to assist in restoring the Kuwaiti government.

The four-phase strategy of Instant Thunder continued, but with some adjustments in priorities and nomenclature. The Phase I strategic attacks now also included attacks on the Republican Guard and high-value interdiction targets. Phase II remained relatively unchanged while Phase III became "Battlefield Preparation," but otherwise remained relatively unchanged. Phase IV, the ground war, changed significantly over time, as discussed below.

In reality, the military objectives looked almost as much toward the aftermath of the struggle as they did toward the current conflict. Destroying the Iraqi nuclear, biological, and chemical warfare capability had at least as much to do with possible future conflicts in the region as it had to do with Desert Storm. The destruction of other military production facilities also looked more toward the future than the present. Once Desert Storm actually began, it would almost certainly be over before any factory production could have an impact on the war. Clearly, a better state of peace was on the minds of the planners.

The first three phases of the aerial campaign were those initially to be put in final form, although target sets and tactics were continually updated and expanded as additional forces became available during the buildup. Ground operations posed a more complex planning problem. Although Coalition air power quickly moved to Saudi Arabia and its nearby waters, heavy armored forces took considerably longer to arrive. In the meantime, there was great pressure for Gen Schwarzkopf to devise the fourth phase—the ground offensive portion of the strategy. Unfortunately, when the planning began, sufficient forces were not available to wage the kind of quick, decisive ground campaign that would limit Coalition casualties. Nor were projected deployments scheduled to result in the numbers of ground forces Gen Schwarzkopf believed he needed.

Bowing to pressure, Schwarzkopf and his staff devised a high-risk offensive plan that called, essentially, for a frontal assault on the extensive fortifications the Iraqis were building along the Kuwaiti-Saudi border. In early October, Gen Schwarzkopf reluctantly allowed a member of his staff to present the high-risk ground plan (along with the now expanded air plan) to the president. But he insisted that the briefing include the caveat that an additional heavy corps was required to guarantee success in the ground offensive.

The weaknesses in the high-risk plan were clear to the president and his advisers. By 31 October, chairman of the Joint Chiefs of Staff, Gen Colin Powell, notified Schwarzkopf that his forces would be increased significantly—well beyond the heavy corps he had asked for—and that Gen Schwarzkopf should begin planning seriously for offensive operations including an expanded ground campaign to liberate Kuwait.

Iraqi dispositions dictated the final ground offensive plan. To nearly everyone's amazement, the Iraqis were building formidable defensive barriers only along the Kuwaiti-Saudi border. The Iraqi-Saudi border remained unfortified and almost unmanned. The classic strategy would be to strike at the Iraqi weakness (i.e., across the undefended Iraqi-Saudi border), outflanking the Iraqi forces and rapidly advancing to the Euphrates River to trap the Iraqi forces in Kuwait.

The problem, of course, was that the Coalition had concentrated its forces in a defensive posture in front of the Iraqi forces in Kuwait. To strike across the undefended Iraqi-Saudi border would require a giant "left hook" to the west. However, positioning the forces to the west would undoubtedly warn the Iraqis, who would also move their forces and build defensive barriers. Gen Schwarzkopf's solution to this dilemma was unique and daring.

The solution required total air supremacy and a complete pin-down from the air of all Iraqi ground and air forces. This strategy would essentially blind the Iraqis to any Coalition movements, and even if discovered, would make it next to impossible for the Iraqis to respond effectively. Only after the air campaign had begun would Gen Schwarzkopf move his powerful armored striking force to the west for the left hook into Iraq. The logistical task, however, would be enormous and tightly constrained by time.

Once the ground attack began on the left flank, other Coalition forces would attack into the teeth of Iraqi defenses now seriously weakened by air power and artillery-battlefield preparation. The effect would be to keep the Iraqi forces in place while the flanking action moved forward in the west. This pinning action would be complemented and reinforced by a potential amphibious assault from the Gulf, an operation very publicly rehearsed (for Iraqi benefit) during Desert Shield.

One of the military problems facing the diverse Coalition was the reluctance of one Arab state to attack another—even in the face of Iraq's naked aggression against Kuwait. Schwarzkopf soothed Arab sensitivities by assigning them to attack into Kuwait (thus liberating, rather than attacking, an Arab neighbor) and designating the Arab forces as those who would actually liberate Kuwait City.

As Gen Schwarzkopf planned the ground war, he emphasized to his commanders the importance of trapping and destroying the Republican Guard units. It was not enough for the great left hook to trap the elite Iraqi force. His commanders were to turn to the east and crush it. Conventional wisdom held that the Republican Guards were both the central prop of the Iraqi regime and the potential nucleus of possible postwar Iraqi military power. In this sense, Gen Schwarzkopf s plans for the ground war addressed both the present conflict and the state of the peace that would follow.

## Political Considerations

Within the complex of actions taken to reverse Iraq's military action were purely political concerns. From a domestic viewpoint, the main concern was how to gain congressional acquiescence to a military action. Internationally, the problem was how to form a coalition of states that would make the liberation of Kuwait seem more like an international than an American action. The two were related because the success of the Coalition required American participation (425,000 of the Coalition total of 675,000 were American), which in turn politically required congressional approval.

The campaign to gain congressional acquiescence to military action hinged on how long the economic sanctions that were the first UN action against Iraq (Security Council Resolution 660) should be allowed to work before military force was employed. Those who wanted a maximum application of economic sanctions also believed that when war came, it would involve many—some estimated thousands—American casualties. The debate was heavily partisan; most of the opponents of early use of force were Democrats, led by Senator Sam Nunn, chair of the Senate Armed Services Committee.

Ultimately, proponents of the war prevailed, although not by much. Congress voted to authorize the use of force on 12 January 1991, four days before the air campaign began. The vote was close in the Senate: 42 Republicans and 10 Democrats voted in favor; two Republicans and 45 Democrats voted against, a slim margin of 52–47. In the House of Representatives, 164 Republicans and 86 Democrats voted for the measure; 179 Democrats, three Republicans, and one independent voted against, a margin of 250–183. The authorization took the form of a resolution in support rather than a formal declaration of war.

Internationally, the formation of the Coalition that eventually numbered 25 countries ranging from those in the Arab world to the first and third worlds was the major imperative. Led by Secretary of State James Baker, who darted between national capitals, an impressive array was assembled.

Not taking away from Baker's accomplishments, the Coalition is less amazing in retrospect than it seemed at the time. Those who supported the UN came because not to have done so would have gutted what little credibility the organization had at that time; instead the action energized the world body. At the same time, Saddam's violation of basic tenets of the Arab world reasonably guaranteed Arab participation as well.

What should be noted, however, was that the Coalition existed for the purpose of restoring Kuwaiti sovereignty and nothing more. To have invaded more of Iraq would have forced the UN to withdraw support. Similarly, the Arab members could justify punishing Saddam for his transgression; the occupation and conquest of Iraq by Westerners (principally the Americans) would have been viewed as an unacceptable Arab humiliation. To have upped the ante would have made the action almost exclusively American. Gen Schwarzkopf stated publicly after the war that had we gone further, it would have been us and "maybe" Great Britain alone.

*Military Technology and Technique*

In the nearly two decades between the inglorious departure from Vietnam and the stunning victory in Desert Storm, the US military establishment journeyed from agonizing catharsis through robust rejuvenation. Both parts of the journey affected military technology and technique.

The humiliating withdrawal from Vietnam led to an almost immediate search for scapegoats, with fingers pointing in all directions. A spate of books written by former senior military commanders blamed the political leadership, while others accused the military leadership of incompetence. It was not until near the end of the 1970s that more objective and balanced analyses concluded that there was plenty of blame to go around.

A crisis in confidence shook the US military for a decade following the withdrawal from Vietnam. At least three factors fueled this crisis. The first was the aforementioned search for scapegoats and the accusations of military incompetence. Second, the end of conscription changed the US military to a smaller professional force. Third, US superiority in military technology had seriously eroded. While the US was heavily engaged in the jungles of Southeast Asia, many weapons system modernization programs were delayed or canceled. Meanwhile, the Soviet Union, still perceived as the paramount threat, continued to modernize its forces rapidly.

The perception of incompetence was a mixture of both fact and myth. While it was true that the US military was poorly prepared for the kind of war it faced in Southeast Asia, it did not necessarily follow that the US was poorly prepared for or incapable of prosecuting a modern, high-tech conventional or nuclear conflict. On the contrary, the tactics, technology, and techniques used in Vietnam were ultimately unsuccessful because they were better suited for conventional warfare. This fact was lost in further accusations of incompetence that followed the military disaster in Beirut and the less than sterling military performance in Grenada (see part two of this chapter).

Considerable skepticism greeted the end of conscription and the birth of the first professional army since before World War II. Analysts of every persuasion wondered if the military services could attract enough men and women. Beyond worries about sufficient numbers were worries about the quality of those attracted to service. Would they be capable of handling the sophisticated technology of modern warfare? Would they be capable of effectively leading and managing the military in peace and war?

Ultimately, the answers to these questions were in the affirmative. In retrospect, the key to recruiting sufficient numbers of high-quality personnel seems to have been a sense of exclusivity. The services set higher standards for personnel quality than had been the case during the years of conscription, and flaunted these standards. Typical was the Marine Corps recruiting slogan noting that they were looking for a "few good men," with emphasis on the "few." Combined with clever promotion of traditional service values and the lure of high-tech "adventure," the services were consistently meeting their personnel quantity and quality requirements as the 1980s began.

The military technology problem was both disturbing and real, particularly in the area of conventional weaponry. Analysts refer to the 1970s as the era of the "hollow force" both because of the general reduction in force following the withdrawal from Southeast Asia and because of the outdated equipment used by that smaller force. In the early 1970s there was serious need in the ground forces for a new main battle tank, a new armored personnel carrier, and many other types of equipment. In the air, where technology is king, both the Air Force and the sea services were using fighter aircraft originally designed in the mid to late 1950s, and the principal Air Force long-range bomber was even older.

The technological rebuilding of the American military began in the early 1970s (for example the Navy's F-14 and the Air Force's F-15 fighters became operational in 1974), but shifted into high gear as the 1980s began. The results of the massive rebuilding program were spectacular, and produced the remarkable technology used in Desert Storm.

The technological revolution of the American military was so vast and reached into so many areas of military operations that it cannot be discussed comprehensively in this survey history. However, at least four areas of development were so important that they merit discussion because of their impact on Desert Storm: precision-guided munitions, night vision devices, space systems, and low-observable (stealth) technology.

Precision-guided munitions had the most visible impact on Desert Storm. During the month-long air campaign that preceded the ground war, television news organizations broadcast hundreds of pictures showing guided munitions striking their targets with almost unbelievable accuracy. Taken from aircraft targeting systems and distributed at military news conferences, these grainy, black-and-white video pictures were the only images available of a war that ranged hundreds of miles into Iraq.

Precision-guided munitions had their modern introduction during the latter stages of the war in Vietnam. They were used successfully to attack high-value targets (bridges being the most notable example) that were both difficult to hit and heavily defended. In the intervening years, these systems were steadily improved and became much more commonplace in the US arsenal. Although their best-known use is from aircraft dropping "smart" bombs, other systems also used precision targeting and guidance techniques. Cruise missiles used variations of the precision technologies that allowed attacks on heavily defended targets without putting air crews at risk. In Desert Storm, the Navy used the Tomahawk cruise missile successfully in this role. These systems accounted for about 7 percent of the bombs used in Desert Storm.

Precision munitions guidance technologies were not limited to aircraft and missiles. Among ground forces, other variations on the precision theme became commonplace for US forces. For example, the US MIA1 "Abrams" main battle tank was equipped with a sophisticated fire control system that included a laser range finder, a ballistic computer, and a gun stabilizer. Its accuracy approached the "one shot, one kill" ideal, even while firing on the move.

The effect of precision munitions was extremely significant in Desert Storm. In the air, they redefined the meaning of "mass." During World War II, hundreds of heavy bombers were sent to strike targets that a few well-placed bombs would have destroyed. Unfortunately, well-placed bombs were not the norm even with the best bombsights then available. Thus thousands of bombs were dropped in the hope that some would strike the target at the critical points. "Mass" required hundreds of bombers and thousands of bombs. In Desert Storm, "mass" often meant one aircraft or one cruise missile with one bomb or warhead striking the target at exactly the right point to destroy it.

The impact was to allow the Coalition air forces to destroy more targets faster—and the results staggered the Iraqis. Saddam quickly lost his ability to control and supply his forces, and Coalition air power then turned its attention to destroying deployed Iraqi ground forces, while continuing to pound strategic and interdiction targets. Historically, air forces conducted such operations sequentially. In Desert Storm they were essentially conducted as parallel operations, thanks to the effectiveness of precision-guided munitions. The shock effect on Iraqi forces was overwhelming, as evidenced by their lack of resistance and desire to surrender when the ground war began.

On the ground, the impact of precision munitions and sophisticated firing systems was also significant. Fast-moving armored forces gutted what was left of the Iraqi armored forces, often at great distances, often with one-shot, one-kill efficiency. The advantage of those who have such systems over those who do not is almost incalculable.

Night vision devices also had their debut in Vietnam. By the time of Operation Desert Storm, they had—in one form or another—become commonplace for US forces. No longer would the dark of night become a time of relative calm in combat, nor would the dark offer a place to hide. Night vision devices made combat a round-the-clock proposition. Further, they offered enormous advantages if the enemy did not have the same capabilities. If you can see in the dark and the enemy cannot, you prefer to engage in the dark; the dark offers you safety but none to the enemy.

Combat aircraft contained some of the most sophisticated night vision systems. For example, FLIR (forward-looking infrared radar) and LANTIRN (low-altitude navigation and targeting infrared for night) systems allowed Coalition aircraft to use the cover of darkness for protection, to find precise targets on the ground, and then to attack them with precision munitions. For many pilots, night was the preferred time to fly combat missions during Desert Storm.

Although secrecy veils many of the military capabilities of space systems, it is clear from published accounts that space systems played a major role in Desert Storm. Among other things, spaced-based systems provided both warning of Iraqi Scud missile launches and vital weather data; they were essential for communications both within the theater of operations and between the Gulf region and other parts of the world.

Of particular interest concerning space systems was the success of the Global Positioning System constellation of satellites. The terrain in Saudi Arabia and much of Kuwait and Iraq is featureless desert. Finding one's way is difficult at best, yet crucially important in a war of rapid movement. At night, the situation was just that much worse. The Global Positioning satellites, combined with a small hand-held receiver, allowed personnel to find their position within a matter of a few feet.

Low-observable technology, generally referred to as stealth, was exemplified by the Air Force F-117 aircraft. The F-117 was first used in Panama (see below) with limited success. In the Gulf War, it had outstanding success. It flew primarily at night to maximize its stealthy characteristics—it could not be seen in the dark with the naked eye and was very difficult to detect on radar. The aircraft's success in delivering precision munitions in heavily defended areas was notable both for its precision and because none of the stealth aircraft received any battle damage.

Stealth aircraft did not significantly affect the general outcome of Desert Storm. They did, however, make the attacks on heavily defended areas more effective and far less costly to the Coalition. The importance of stealth technology lies in its foretaste of things to come. The general trend in aircraft design will be to make them less and less vulnerable to radar detection. Perfection of such techniques could cause major changes in the nature of aerial warfare in the future.

The general impact of technology upon the technique of modern warfare, as demonstrated in Desert Storm, was at least threefold. First, it increased the intensity of combat. Modern combat has become a round-the-clock proposition with no respite. Second, technology has made combat much more efficient. Precision munitions make it possible to do much more much faster, with fewer assets. The side benefit is less collateral damage—fewer unnecessary casualties and less unnecessary destruction. Third, the gap in capabilities between those who can exploit modern military technology and those who cannot is growing ever more significant. Precision munitions, 24-hour capability, space systems, stealth technology, and many other technologies provide the possessor with much more than marginal improvements in military capabilities. Properly used, they provide an overwhelming advantage.

One other factor deserves mention. Dismayed at perceived interservice bickering, rivalry, and lack of cooperation, the US Congress passed landmark legislation in 1986. The Goldwater–Nichols Defense Reorganization Act forced greater cooperation between the armed services on a number of fronts. Perhaps most important for Desert Storm, the legislation gave much more power to the chairman of the Joint Chiefs of Staff and to the commanders in chief of the various unified commands. One of those unified commands, US Central Command, had overall responsibility for Desert Storm.

Central Command's commander, Gen H. Norman Schwarzkopf, was able to command and control his disparate forces with far greater authority than had been the case previously. The result was vastly improved coordination between land, sea, and air forces that further compounded the problems faced by the Iraqis. For example, with Schwarzkopf's new authority, his air commander, Air Force Lt Gen Charles Homer, could centrally control all US air power (and in practice, all Coalition air power) using a single daily Air Tasking Order. Unlike Vietnam, where there were as many as six different air wars in progress at any one time, in Desert Storm there was one highly coordinated air campaign. The results were devastating to the Iraqis.

## Military Conduct

The initial order to deploy US combat forces to the Gulf was issued on 6 August 1990. By 9 August, Air Force F-15 fighters from the continental United States were flying combat air patrols along the Saudi northern border, and the first 82nd Airborne Division ready brigade from Fort Bragg, North Carolina, was establishing a defensive perimeter around the airport at Dhahran.

The overriding fear was that the Iraqis would quickly move south from Kuwait after pausing to regroup. Early arrivals among the ground troops feared they might be little more than "speed bumps" in the path of the Iraqi advance. But the Iraqis continued their pause and the Coalition buildup quickly gathered momentum, closing the "window of vulnerability" without incident.

The rapid deployment of massive air, land, and sea forces to the Gulf region was a logistical feat without parallel. Airlift forces transported the most urgently needed personnel, equipment, and supplies on what came to be called an "aluminum bridge" from the United States and some European locations to Saudi Arabia. Other heavier equipment stored aboard prepositioned ships at the Indian Ocean island of Diego Garcia quickly arrived at Saudi ports. The bulk of the heavy armored equipment arrived later via a massive sealift from the United States and Europe.

At sea, Coalition naval forces clamped a tight blockade on Iraqi shipping to enforce the UN-imposed economic sanctions. While politicians and diplomats argued over how long the sanctions should be given to force an Iraqi withdrawal, Gen Schwarzkopf made good use of the time by training his forces in the harsh desert environment, designing the complex command and control arrangements, planning for an offensive campaign, and addressing problems caused by the clash of Western and Middle Eastern cultures.

Command and control of such a diverse coalition presented exceptional challenges. Political and cultural differences became of extreme importance in holding the fragile Coalition together. Eventually a dual chain of command evolved with Gen Schwarzkopf controlling the non-Arab forces, and the Saudi commander, Gen Khaled bin-Sultan, controlling the forces from the Arab states. Although Gen Schwarzkopf and his Saudi counterpart sat as technically equal partners in command, the US commander was clearly the senior partner. Fortunately, the war went well and the strains of conflict never put this delicately devised structure to a severe test.

In many respects, Gen Schwarzkopf played a role similar to that of Gen

Eisenhower during World War II. As supreme allied commander in the European theater, Eisenhower became a de facto diplomat, holding the Allies together, at times with considerable difficulty. In some ways, Gen Schwarzkopf's job was more difficult because of the clash of Western and Arab cultures.

The culture clash manifested itself in many ways. Western female military personnel essentially offended Muslim traditions by their very presence. Christian religious services had to be downplayed or concealed. Alcohol was forbidden. In spite of these problems, compromise, coordination, and understanding minimized difficulties and the Coalition endured.

Israel posed the most serious potential threat to the Coalition. If for whatever reason the Israelis joined the attack on Iraq, the Coalition might quickly disintegrate. To many Arab states in the Coalition, Israel remained the supernumerary enemy even in the face of Iraqi aggression. The Coalition expected the Iraqis to provoke the Israelis, particularly if the war went badly. The tool of provocation would likely be Iraqi Scud missiles, which had sufficient range to strike Israel. Too inaccurate to be an effective military weapon, the Scud could still cause significant casualties when launched against population centers. It was a terror weapon, but useful for Saddam's purposes.

Iraq ignored the UN ultimatum to withdraw from Kuwait by 15 January 1991. Live television announced the commencement of Desert Storm to the world from Baghdad at 3 A.M. (Baghdad local) on 17 January. A CNN news team, broadcasting via satellite, displayed fantastic pictures of the night sky over the Iraqi capital filled with antiaircraft fire. Impressive as the antiaircraft appeared to be, it was almost random—no central direction, no good targets. The Iraqi air defense radars and control centers had already been destroyed and the aircraft overhead were F-117 stealth fighter-bombers— virtually invisible to any remaining Iraqi detection systems. Iraq had lost the air war in the first minutes of the struggle. CNN and the other electronic media were broadcasting the beginning of the most successful air campaign in history.

Spectacular as the television pictures were, they did not reveal the crushing results achieved by Coalition land and naval air forces during the first three phases of Desert Storm. Strategic targets were destroyed quickly. It rapidly became very difficult for Saddam to communicate with and effectively control his deployed forces. Known military production facilities, particularly those associated with nuclear, biological, and chemical weapons, were hit hard. Air superiority was achieved within hours and total air supremacy within days.

The Coalition achieved the objectives of the air campaign so rapidly that the second and third phases of the campaign began quickly. Rather than a sequential execution of the campaign, Coalition airmen were able to execute the phases almost in parallel, magnifying the shock effect on the Iraqi war machine. Overwhelming amounts of Coalition air power enhanced by the efficiency of precision-guided munitions made parallel execution possible. Careful planning, superior technology, and clever tactics kept Coalition losses far below what many military pundits had projected. During all four phases of the war, Coalition air forces lost only 39 fixed-wing aircraft in combat plus eight in non-combat operations while flying well over 100,000 sorties.

As expected, the Iraqis quickly began launching Scud ballistic missiles toward Israel in the hope of provoking an Israeli reaction that would strain and perhaps divide the Coalition. The Israelis refrained from entering the conflict, and the Coalition diverted considerable air resources to "Scud hunting" in an effort to end the threat. Although mobile Scud launchers proved to be elusive targets, the Iraqi missile offensive proved to be of no significant consequence.

As the air campaign continued during January and February, the full weight of the air offensive came crashing down on the heads of the deployed Iraqi forces. The aerial onslaught pinned the Iraqi forces down, isolated them, and cut them off from food, water, munitions, and fuel. As the date set for Phase IV drew closer, these troops came under more severe and nearly constant attack. For the Iraqis, if there was an aircraft overhead, it belonged to the enemy. And there were enemy aircraft overhead around the clock. Gen Schwarzkopf estimated that the air campaign reduced most of the Iraqi forces near the Saudi border to 50 percent effectiveness or less. Further, it had significantly damaged the Iraqi fortifications and mine fields behind the Kuwaiti-Saudi border. The battlefield was well prepared.

Meanwhile, as the air campaign blinded and pinned down the Iraqis, Gen Schwarzkopf moved his heavy striking forces far to the west, away from the fortified Kuwaiti border area and to the nearly undefended Iraqi border. By 24 February all was ready. The air war had stunned, isolated, and devastated the Iraqi forces. Coalition ground forces moved into position for the great "left hook" without being detected.

At 4 A.M. on 24 February, the ground war began. Massive Coalition armored forces swept over the Iraqi border toward the Euphrates River and Basra. The advance was spectacularly rapid. Coalition forces brushed aside limited resistance as they raced to close the trap. To the east, Coalition forces slashed into the teeth of the Iraqi defenses on the Kuwaiti border and breached them with remarkable ease. They raced toward Kuwait City.

The air campaign and the shocking tactics of the fast-moving ground forces had done their job. The Iraqi forces, particularly those deployed far forward, were far more interested in surrendering than in fighting. Dazed, hungry, thirsty, and often deserted by their leaders, they surrendered in such numbers that they were difficult to handle and get to the rear efficiently.

In 100 hours, it was all over. At least one Republican Guard formation, still willing to fight, attempted to slug it out with the Coalition forces, but was manhandled by the better-equipped, -led, and -trained Coalition armored forces. As other Iraqi forces attempted to flee Kuwait, they were under continual assault. Reports of carnage on what was dubbed the "highway of death" leading away from Kuwait City brought pressure in Washington to end what appeared to be a wholesale slaughter of the Iraqis. The result was a cease-fire at the 100-hour mark of the ground offensive. Significant Iraqi forces escaped complete destruction, but they were insufficient to maintain Iraq as any sort of regional threat for the foreseeable future.

In the war's aftermath, some criticized the termination of the conflict before the Iraqi armed forces were totally crushed. The Iraqi forces that remained effective were no threat to Iraq's neighbors, but were sufficient to quell both Shiite and Kurdish rebellions in Iraq and keep Saddam in power. Although the president seems to have chosen the 100-hour mark for a cease-fire because it had a "ring" to it, the decision was far from frivolous. The UN objective had been accomplished. Kuwait was liberated. The remaining Iraqi forces were no longer a regional threat, and continuing the war would have risked the lives of more Americans for what appeared to be only marginal advantages.

### Better State of the Peace

Whether the better state of the peace was achieved in the Persian Gulf War depends on what that better state was defined to have been before the war began. Here again, the answer seems to be that the initial objective—freeing Kuwait and reinstalling the al-Sabah regime—was clearly achieved, meaning the better state of the peace was clearly and overwhelmingly achieved.

Unfortunately, the Gulf War in retrospect seems less than triumphant to many in the American public for two reasons. The first and most obvious is the continuation in power of a notably unrepentant Saddam Hussein in Baghdad. Although removing Saddam was not an objective as the war effort was being mounted, that limitation was never publicly stated at the time. Moreover, George Bush's demonization of the Iraqi leader left the implication that his removal was indeed desirable, a point reinforced by Bush's call to the Iraqi people to rise and overthrow Saddam on 15 February 1991.

This latter declaration created the second, and ultimately most sour, failure of the war effort. When Bush called on the Iraqis to rise, he presumably was exhorting internal Sunni Baathist elements within Saddam's cohort base to rise against him. They did not and realistically could not have been expected to do so; any dissidents had either been exiled or executed by Saddam. Instead, the Kurds in the north and the Shiites in the south rose to arms.

The Bush administration wanted neither to succeed, because it feared an Iraq fractured into three countries as the result would not provide a counterweight to Iran. Neither revolt succceeded, and because some of the Iraqi military was left intact at the end of hostilities, it could be employed to crush the rebels.

The US responded with Operations Provide Comfort (renamed Northern Watch in 1997) for the Kurds and Southern Watch for the Shiites. By the terms of these operations, the Iraqi government is prohibited from exercising authority over enclaves of these groups in sovereign Iraqi territory. The agent of enforcement is the American military, augmented by the British and French.

This part of the better state of the peace was apparently not anticipated when the war began, but it is important for two reasons, each of which tarnishes the success of Desert Storm. First, it created the precedent that infringement on territorial sovereignty in a good cause is justified, a direct repudiation of the organization of the international system since the Peace of Westphalia in 1648. There is no public evidence that the Bush administration even considered this when it organized the operations. Second, it created a perpetual obligation for the United States. Put simply, the Kurds and Shiites are safe from Saddam's revenge for as long, and only as long, as the Americans are willing to enforce the violation of Iraqi sovereignty. The minute we leave, it is open season on both groups.

## Minor Operations

The United States was also involved in a number of smaller, more minor military operations after Vietnam and before or in conjunction with Operation Desert Storm. Individually and collectively, these are not of an importance commensurate even with the minor wars described in Chapter 8. We have not, the reader may note, devoted space to the Whiskey Rebellion of 1793. Why, then, are these more recent minor cases included here?

Their inclusion is justified on two grounds. First, these incidents demonstrate the transition of the US military from Vietnam to Desert Storm and appear to be the kind of military adventures that lie ahead in a post–cold war world (the topic of Chapter 10). All occurred in the third world in areas on the margins of important American interests, and all elicited ad hoc American responses. Second, and most unfortunately, each represented actions for which there were not clear and attainable goals enunciated in advance, meaning assessment of reaching the better state of the peace was either impossible or negative (mostly the latter).

Five such incidents occurred. Two, the *Mayagüez* incident of 1975 and the Desert One incident intended to free the diplomatic hostages held in the American embassy in Teheran in 1980, are not treated here beyond saying that they were hostage rescue attempts and abysmal failures. Those that are included are the Beirut mission and Grenada invasion of 1983, and the invasion of Panama of 1989 (Operation Provide Comfort in 1991 and Operation Southern Watch are mentioned in passing).

### Issues and Events

Although each of these actions was a discrete response to a unique set of circumstances, there were certain commonalities that suggest precedents, mainly unfortunate, for the future. Two commonalities stand out.

The first is that all these operations were at the margins of American interests. If, as we have argued, vital interests are those worth going to war over, then it is hard to understand why American forces were involved in any of them. Only an extension of the notion of vital interests to include the idea of something like humanitarian vital interests can justify any of them. What, for instance, was important enough to send the Marines on their ill-fated adventure in Beirut? To send the armed forces onto the tiny island of Grenada, other than vague fear the Cubans might build an airstrip there and to protect some American medical students? To mount a naked aggression against Panama? To flout international convention and establish "security zones" (secure from administration by the government under whose sovereign jurisdiction they exist) in Iraq?

The second commonality arises from the first: each operation appeared to be a reaction to a horror widely publicized by the encompassing eye of the global media, and especially global television. Ronald Reagan sent the Marines into Beirut because of reports of massacre in the refugee camps after the expulsion of the PLO from Lebanon. American medical students were reportedly the hostages of a leftist government in Grenada with reported links to Cuba. Americans had been attacked in Panama by forces loyal to the Noriega regime. Kurds were starving in the Turkish mountains, driven from their homes by Iraq's military. Shiite resisters were being strafed by Iraqi warplanes.

### Political Objective

The military assessment of these operations varies, depending on one's assessments of what the military was being asked to do and whether that task was achievable by the application of military force. The closer one goes back toward Vietnam, the worse the military performance, in general. The Marines, who were the least suited form of military force for the garrison duty in Beirut (they were used because they were nearby and hence cheaper to get to the theater than more appropriate Army units), failed there, and the Grenada operation, while ultimately a success, was hardly a picture book of military efficiency. Panama seemed more successful, but the military operation did not face serious, sustained opposition.

An assessment of the articulation and attainment of political objectives cannot be so positive. Each of the actions was an intrusion into the domestic politics of the country where it occurred. Each was an attempt to right some visible wrong that was a manifestation of some underlying malaise of the object polity. None addressed the underlying political cause of conflict and hence violated the Clausewitzian dictum. Each appeared to succeed while the troops were there; each situation unraveled when the troops were withdrawn. Each represented a very limited action for very limited purposes.

Beyond this, it is difficult to cull from the various situations any commonality of purpose that would allow one to predict when force might be used in the future, unless one argues that a precedent is being set justifying the right of forced entry into the sovereign affairs of states when states abuse the rights of some or all of their people.

Two points should be made here. First, there is nothing particularly new about American intervention into the domestic politics of other countries to serve American interests: American gunboats and Marines have long played a prominent role in Central American politics, for instance. Second, none of these actions has been taken explicitly under the moral or legal banner of promoting the rights of individuals and groups over the rights of state sovereignty. Each appeared to be a tactical response to a specific problem—the Kurds dying on the Turkish hillsides, the massacre in a Beirut refugee camp—rather than a part of some grand and principled approach to international politics.

Two things distinguish this pattern and raise questions about the future. On one hand, they all involve using force in situations where the traditional calculation of interests would not suggest that force be used. This raises the question of whether, implicitly or explicitly, the definition of vital interest is being widened to encompass abuses of human rights (humanitarian vital interests), a proposition explored in the next chapter.

On the other hand, whether justified as altering the traditional rules of international conduct grounded in the sovereign sanctity of national territory or not, that is exactly the position that is being supported, even normalized, by these efforts. Practice is a recognized source of international law, and the more often force is used in this manner, the greater the claim to legitimacy such action gains. Moreover, there are champions of just such change; former United Nations Secretary-General Boutros Boutros-Ghali is among the most vocal.

## Military Objectives and Strategy

The cases under consideration illustrate at least three important points about military objectives and strategy. Just Cause, the invasion of Panama, marked a post-Vietnam turning point in US military strategy—the implementation of the Powell corollary to the Weinberger doctrine. In the early 1980s, Defense Secretary Caspar Weinberger outlined six criteria for the commitment of US troops to combat. Included in this so-called Weinberger doctrine were such items as clear objectives, a commitment to victory, public support, and the like. When Gen Colin Powell became chairman of the Joint Chiefs of Staff, he made it abundantly clear that unlike the incrementalism of the Vietnam strategy, the employment of overwhelming force to achieve quick and decisive results should be a corollary to Weinberger's six points. Operation Just Cause illustrated the point as the US deployed over 20,000 troops equipped with tanks, massive air power, and the latest military technology—including the first combat use of the F-117 stealth fighter-bomber—to achieve quick success with minimal US casualties.

The Powell corollary was much less a new idea than it was an old idea whose time had come again. Military strategists have always preferred overwhelming force. But during the cold war, when most US military combat was somehow connected to the containment of communism, the use of overwhelming force and the total defeat of perceived Soviet and Chinese surrogates raised the specter of Soviet or Chinese intervention, escalation, and nuclear confrontation. The Chinese intervention in Korea was a grim reality that lingers as an ever-present and overwhelming memory. Thus limited forces, limited military objectives, gradualism, and incrementalism became the hallmarks of US military objectives and strategy during the cold war.

Just Cause, however, had nothing to do with the containment of communism. The Berlin Wall had come down and the Soviet empire was breaking up. The old fears were gone. There was no reason not to use overwhelming force—and it resulted in quick success. Desert Storm drove the point home again just one year later. There is no reason to believe that the Powell corollary will not continue in effect well into the future.

The second point concerns the importance of clear military objectives. Previous segments of this chapter have alluded to the murky political objectives that plagued some of the cases under consideration. Confused or confusing military objectives can also lead to disastrous consequences, as evidenced by the Marine peacekeeping adventure in Beirut.

The Marines were to be peacekeepers, but there was no peace to keep in Lebanon. They were supposed to prop up the Lebanese government, but they were confined to an enclave, supporting no one and propping up nothing. Their main concern became avoiding actions that would make a bad situation worse, and thus restrictive rules of engagement ensued. The result was disaster for the Marines, a clear defeat for US policy, and Lebanese agony that would get worse rather than better.

The third point illustrated by these cases is that effective and efficient military strategies require time to develop. Urgent Fury (Grenada) and Just Cause (Panama) are cases in point. Urgent Fury was thrown together on extremely short notice. The little intelligence information that existed was old and faulty. Even military maps of the island were not available. Supporting forces were patched together on an ad hoc basis with almost no warning. For example, 1,900 of the Marines involved had been aboard ship bound for duty in Lebanon. The operation that resulted, although successful, was far from a classic display of military efficiency.

The contrasting case is Operation Just Cause. It was a far larger and more complex operation and thus had more "opportunities" for things to go wrong. However, the entire operation went well, better than many had come to expect in the wake of Beirut and Grenada. But an invasion of Panama had been under serious study for several years. The original operations plan was named "Blue Spoon," and had been thoroughly reworked and updated to become Operation Just Cause, and it worked well.

### Political Considerations

Political concerns did not disappear with the end of the cold war. Rather, as the post-Vietnam period lurched toward the collapse of the communist menace, those concerns simply changed, both domestically and internationally.

Two domestic considerations stand out. The first is economic—a question of the American taxpayer's willingness to support differing levels of military activity. This support has been cyclical (as always in American history). Coming out of Vietnam, defense spending plummeted. The end of the Vietnam War and its attendant expenses explain part of the fall; the revulsion of the public with things military explains most of the rest. The cycle reversed itself under the Reagan buildup, which, unfortunately, produced the enormous federal deficits and accumulated debt to which military spending was a contributor. With debt and the burden of its service rising, defense spending began to fall in the late 1980s and early 1990s. It likely would have fallen much faster had there not been the realization that further steep cuts in military spending would have added measurably to the ongoing recession.

The other domestic factor that emerged in the latter 1980s was global television and its publicizing of global situations that have tempted us to intervene—to "do something." We saw this first in the Chinese government's repression of students in Tiananmen Square in 1989, and it has been a major element ever since. We lack a clear understanding about how the televised image of misery affects governmental decision making, at least partly because it is such a recent phenomenon. What can safely be said, however, is that the relentless glare of television makes it much more difficult to ignore atrocity than was the case before global television. Moreover, global television's publicizing of horrible events is now a permanent part of the context in which policy must be made. If it has an impact, we had better figure out what that impact is and how to deal with it. Clearly, those interested in getting us involved will try to use television to their advantage.

Internationally, the obvious political consideration is the end of the cold war and its impact on the national security problem. The cold war was a marvelous organizing construct; we knew who the enemy was, we knew the military problem he presented for us, and his apparent permanence gave shape and meaning to the entire national security enterprise, including the justification for force size, structure, strategy, and claim on national resources.

And then Soviet communism collapsed. In the words of Georgi Arbatov, a prominent Soviet academic, "We have done a terrible thing to you. We have deprived you of an enemy." Much of the scrambling that has gone on since has been an attempt to adjust to that new reality. Who is the adversary? What threats exist for which American force remains necessary? How do we size and configure American forces for a radically changed environment? None of the answers are intuitively obvious. We inhabit a period when our interests are hardly threatened and the threats that exist are barely interesting.

Domestic and international concerns collide at this point. On one side, federal budgetary difficulties cry for a pruning of the budget, and defense spending is a highly vulnerable target. That vulnerability is enhanced by the lack of obvious enemies and apparent contingencies where large-scale force might be needed. On the other side, the horrors of the evolving international system, where ancient hatreds are being unleashed on our television screens, tempt us toward far-off lands and unfamiliar situations. The result is a high level of fluidity, uncertainty, and conceptual ambiguity.

### Military Technology and Technique

Looking for common threads concerning military technology and technique among such dissimilar operations as the Marine mission to Beirut, the invasion of Grenada (Urgent Fury), the invasion of Panama (Just Cause), the sustenance of the Iraqi Kurdish population (Provide Comfort), and the protection of the Iraqi Shiite Muslims (Southern Watch) is difficult at best. A peacekeeping operation, three more or less standard combat engagements, and a humanitarian relief operation spread over more than a decade would seem to have little in common, even at the conceptual level. However, there are at least two broad threads of continuity concerning military technology and technique that warrant discussion.

The first is that modern military technology and superior military techniques are of little avail if improperly applied. The Marines in Beirut had all the technology required to secure their position and were aware of the techniques to thwart terrorist attacks. Neither was employed effectively, and over 200 Marines were killed in their barracks by a terrorist driving an explosives-laden truck. Security barriers were either inadequate or not in place, guard posts were unmanned, a lone sentry's weapon was not loaded, and the Marine barracks arrangement, which massed the sleeping Marines together to form a particularly lucrative target, invited terrorist attention.

Urgent Fury demonstrated that superior technology, technique, and overwhelming numbers do not necessarily lead to quick and easy success. Inadequate planning and preparation, an almost total lack of up-to-date intelligence, communications problems, and less than aggressive leadership made the operation in Grenada far more difficult than it should have been.

The second thread concerns the broad utility of military technology and technique. The cases under study illustrate both the traditional uses of military capabilities (deterrence and combat operations in the cases of Urgent Fury, Just Cause, and Southern Watch) and nontraditional uses such as peacekeeping and humanitarian relief. The nontraditional uses of military capabilities are certainly nothing new, but the examples cited may signal a shift in US military emphasis in the post–cold war world order. Peacekeeping, peacemaking, humanitarian relief, drug interdiction, and other such missions can make excellent use of military technology and techniques and they may well play a far more significant role in the future of the US military than they have in the past.

Two questions arise from this possibility. First, although military technology and techniques may be useful in situations other than combat and deterrent operations, will they be properly and effectively applied? The Beirut experience raises significant doubts. How are military technologies and techniques best used in peacemaking and peacekeeping operations? The US military establishment has not addressed this question in depth.

The second question concerns the costs of nontraditional applications of military power in terms of traditional combat capabilities. Every day spent engaged in nontraditional roles is a day lost preparing for the ultimate role of military forces—armed combat. Training suffers and equipment is expended. How does one balance the requirements of non-combat operations with readiness for combat, often on short notice, in some distant corner of the planet? Clearly, these are questions that the US military must address as it looks toward the uncertainties of the post–cold war world.

## Military Conduct

The conduct of military operations in the cases under consideration ranged from a lack of conduct—inactive confinement to an enclave in Beirut—to complex joint offensive deployment and combat in Just Cause. It also ranged from total disaster to nearly unqualified success.

The peacekeeping operation in Lebanon was doomed from the start. Plagued by murky objectives and restrictive rules of engagement, failure was almost inevitable. Furthermore, although the disaster that overtook the Marines when a terrorist crashed his explosive-laden truck into their barracks was not inevitable, placing the Marines in such an ambiguous and vulnerable position certainly invited trouble. The conduct of Urgent Fury was less than exemplary but nevertheless successful. Here the problem was inadequate preparation time, poor intelligence, and difficulties in command, control, and communications among the service elements that had been quickly patched together for the operation.

The US military carried off the Just Cause, Provide Comfort, and Southern Watch operations with considerable efficiency and effectiveness. In most cases, they had what was lacking in the Lebanon and Grenada cases: sufficient planning time and clear, realistic military objectives. Moreover, they were all situations where American forces encountered minimal military opposition.

The latter and more successful cases also had two other advantages that added to the skill with which operations were conducted. First, they had the benefit of learning from the problems encountered in Lebanon and Grenada. Both of these incidents underwent extensive "post-mortems" within the Department of Defense and within the Congress. Analysts identified and spelled out shortcomings in strategy, planning, leadership, training, communications, interservice cooperation, and equipment. Further, between Urgent Fury and Just Cause, the services had nearly a decade to attack and correct the problems.

The second advantage possessed by the more successful cases was that they occurred well after the passage of the landmark Goldwater–Nichols legislation mentioned earlier. This legislation, among other things, clarified command arrangements, giving far greater powers to the chairman of the Joint Chiefs of Staff and to the theater commanders. Theater commanders could now demand and receive the total cooperation and support of all the services within their theaters of operations. The result, as also demonstrated in Desert Storm, was effective and efficient joint operations, with Army, Navy, Marine, and Air Force forces working in concert with one another.

## Better States of the Peace

Assessing the ultimate success of the kinds of small involvements in which the United States is likely to become engaged is made very difficult for at least four reasons that collectively bedevil achieving the better state of the peace. These reasons reflect the military and political problems that need addressing in these kinds of situations.

The first and foremost difficulty is in assessing the basic underlying problem in a target country and hence what change must occur for long-term success. In this regard, short-term actions and objectives may either ignore or exacerbate long-term solutions. Take the Panama (Operation Just Cause) case. The pretensive purposes of that operation, in addition to protecting American lives (the official purpose) were dual: the capture of Manuel Noriega and interruption of the drug trade through the country. Noriega was the key: He blocked the installation of the elected government and ran the drug trade. He was captured; mission accomplished? Years after the invasion, the drug trade flourishes and democracy remains a chimera. Is that the better state of the peace? The other adventures are similar. Operation Provide Comfort/Southern Watch, for instance, is dedicated to protecting Kurds and Shiites; in the longer term, it is about the balance of political power in Iraq.

There is a pattern here. American military force is useful in achieving short-term goals but essentially irrelevant to treating underlying malaise, which is an internal matter. The US military cannot create or reconstitute internal political systems. We tried in Panama and failed; we will fail again if we try again. If the political objective is short term, then better states of the peace are possible; if it is the longer term that counts, then the objectives are likely to be frustrated.

A second problem is the vagueness of the objective in the first place. What became Provide Comfort, for instance, was initially no more than a tactical decision to get the Kurds out of the Turkish mountains: the Turks wanted them out, but they feared going home, so we said we would protect them. In Grenada, there was little more of an objective than protecting a handful of medical students. What we might call the "do-something syndrome" provides little concrete guidance for conducting an operation or assessing its success.

A third problem relates to the military manner in which operations occur.

The current preference of the US military is captured in the Powell corollary to the Weinberger doctrine: the fast, overwhelming, and decisive application of maximum force in the minimum time. Such an approach may produce effective short-term results, as discussed. It is irrelevant, probably even counterproductive, when matched against the very difficult internal problems that form the underlying problems in target countries.

The fourth point follows from the third: in most of the second and third world countries where interventions have been and will continue to be tempting in the future, the issues that must ultimately be decided are extremely complex and intractable. Quick-fix solutions will provide no more than Band-Aids when internal processes must address the underlying problems. Inserting American—or United Nations—forces can do no more than stop the shooting *for as long as forces are there* unless the will of the indigenous population indicates that the prospects of peace outweigh the benefits of continuing war. In many of these situations, one side—or both—has not clearly shown a preference for peace.

What this all suggests is that the United States, as it has become involved in this new kind of military activity, has embarked into uncharted, and possibly hostile, territory. Better states of the peace that are truly satisfying to Americans and to those whom we attempt to assist may prove elusive and the results potentially frustrating. If we wish to avoid being dragged into quagmires, we need to proceed very deliberately. This problem is addressed more fully in the next chapter.

# 10

# The Post–Cold War Experience: Somalia to Kosovo

The Persian Gulf War (Operation Desert Storm) provided a transition from the cold war military experience of the United States to the present. Whether the war with Iraq over Kuwait was the last episode of the cold war era or the first instance of the post–cold war use of force remains a matter of conjecture. In some ways, it was very much an "old-fashioned" war. It was an interstate war where one country invaded and conquered another and where another group of countries coalesced to reverse that situation. It was a military campaign that pitted two conventional armies configured and fighting tactically in ways familiar to students of twentieth-century European warfare. Moreover, the vital interests of the United States, as articulated in the Carter Doctrine, were clearly applicable and provided justification for the American effort.

Although Desert Storm resembled cold war engagements in important ways, it was also different. The major differences were political, in the sense that this was not a battle between ideological adversaries (communism versus anticommunism, in the cold war mold). Rather, it pitted a rogue state (Iraq) with regional grievances and aspirations against a coalition that had the support of the cold war's traditional adversaries. The Iraqi side of the ledger included an internal struggle between Saddam Hussein's primarily Sunni Arab support base and the Kurdish and Shiite minorities within Iraq. Such internal struggles are a primary feature of the contemporary environment.

The Persian Gulf War provides both a transition to the present and is a part of the current landscape. One of the major outgrowths of the conflict was a campaign by Hussein to suppress the Kurds and Shiites, who had arisen to oppose him. When this campaign caused the Kurds to flee into Turkey and this act caught the global eye, an ongoing mission to protect the Kurds was launched in 1991 under the rubric Operation Provide Comfort (changed to Northern Watch in 1997) and expanded to include the Shiites in southern Iraq in 1992 (Operation Southern Watch). Both missions involve military reconnaissance and punitive military action to assure the Iraqi government does not move to crush either group. Northern Watch is headquartered in Turkey and Southern Watch in Saudi Arabia. As military exercises, they primarily involve aerial overflight and air strikes against Iraqi targets to ensure the integrity of these "exclusion zones"; both are ongoing and open ended.

The situation in Iraq mirrors in important ways the changed international political environment in the post–cold war world and the military requirements that accompany those changes. With the utter collapse of the central military confrontation of the cold war, the potential for violence and conflict have moved away from the Eurasian center to the peripheries, especially those parts of the old third world that have remained outside the economically globalizing international system that has spread about the world. Most of the contemporary conflicts are in the marginal regions, particularly in Africa, but also important parts of central, southern, and southeastern Asia. Possibly most important, almost all of them are internal wars largely, if not entirely, confined to the territory of a single state and having internal groups or factions as the primary "combatants." In fact, most of these conflicts are hard to portray in traditional military terms, as the primary "combat" involves armed assemblages of so-called fighters attacking unarmed civilians (casualty rates where upwards of 95 percent of the victims are unarmed civilians are not unusual).

Internal wars in the developing world were the major form of violence during the cold war. While most were fought for traditional political purposes, this new kind of violence was not unknown during the period leading to Desert Storm. There were clear prototypes such as the Khmer Rouge rampage against the population of Cambodia between 1975 and 1979, the ongoing Tamil Tiger separatist campaign against the government of Sri Lanka, and Azad Kashmir's campaign to separate Kashmir from India. What is different is the prevalence of particularly vicious internal war not clearly fought for the political objective of gaining political power and governing in accord with some set of principles, the sheer savagery and level of suffering these wars have produced, and the inability of the international community to intervene or their indifference about how or whether to intervene in and end these conflicts.

The United States has found itself a part of this process, directly in several instances and less than directly in others. In the euphoria of the overwhelming success of Desert Storm, the United States sent troops into Somalia in December 1992 as part of an international effort to relieve massive suffering in that destitute east African country. Operation Restore Hope ended unhappily and caused the United States to rethink its attitude toward intervention. In 1994, the US sent troops into Haiti with the putative purpose to "uphold democracy" in a country that had never really known that political form (by reinstalling President Aristide to office). In Bosnia, the United States was part of the Operation Deliberate Force air campaign that convinced the participants to come to the negotiating table and agreed to participate in the Implementation (later Stabilization) Force (I/SFOR) whose job was to enforce the provisions of the Dayton Accords signed in December 1995; American forces remained stationed in Bosnia as part of that commitment as the new millennium dawned, with no agreed target for ending the mission. In 1999, the United States provided most of the muscle for Operation Allied Force in Kosovo and signed on as a participant in the Kosovo Force (KFOR) and the United Nations Interim Mission in Kosovo (UNMIK), commitments of indeterminant duration. In places like Rwanda, the United States was not sufficiently engaged in the situation to become involved and now is mired in a controversy about how much (if at all) American indifference contributed to the magnitude of the 1994 genocide in that small African land. There is a very different, very much more complicated environment now than the one to which we grew accustomed in the cold war.

This amounts to saying that, for the foreseeable future, it is unlikely that the United States will be engaged in military actions *of necessity*, where the situation or the circumstances give us no choice but to become involved; rather the kinds of situations where American fighting men are put at risk will be those in which we accept the risk more or less voluntarily—deployments *of choice*. In these circumstances, it will often be the case that the United States chooses to mount military action because of its position as the remaining superpower and the acknowledged military world power, not because the United States and the American people will be so adversely affected by any possible outcome.

This change in geopolitics has its military counterpart. The situations where force can be applied are not only more complex and less compelling politically, they are also more ambiguous militarily. As noted, the situations are often militarily chaotic and unfamiliar to armed forces trained and indoctrinated in conventional warfare. The role of outside (including American) forces in internal conflicts is often to pry and keep apart warring neighbors, a task that often resembles that of the policeman as much as the soldier. It is not clear what kinds of soldiers and what kinds of equipment, doctrine, and tactics fulfill this role. Moreover, a salient characteristic of involvement is its overtly political nature; what forces do on the ground can have an intimate effect on the political situation in ways to which we are scarcely accustomed.

In some ways, the situation is not so new. It can be argued that in most of the places where the United States was engaged in the cold war, there were minor actions of choice. Korea is the most arguable exception. Whether novel or not, the experience of the 1990s raises three questions that are the subject of this chapter. Two are: Where should the United States be willing to fight? Into what kinds of circumstances should we be willing to put Americans at risk, and where should we not? The experience of the 1990s in Somalia, Bosnia, and Kosovo offers incomplete and occasionally contradictory precedents. The third is: What can and should we do with American armed forces when the decision is made to become involved? The wars of the future will not much resemble those of the cold war past and before, at least not in the short run of the next decade or so. How do we prepare for new futures without throwing out the lessons of the past that remain valid guides to the future?

## Issues and Events

The issues that impel a country to engage in the use of armed force are, in large measure, the result of factors in the international environment that affect a country's interests in different ways. At the end of World War I the peace negotiated at Versailles helped create a poisonous international environment that precipitated the slide toward World War II. Similarly, after World War II the collapse of the prewar international order left only the United States and the Soviet Union capable of filling the vacuum and restructuring the peace. The result, of course, was the cold war and the military dictates that the geopolitical situation presented.

The situation in the 1990s was both similar and different. Its similarities included the collapse of the preexisting order and a transition period toward a restructured international order. The dissimiliarities include an evolving order in which the United States is clearly politically and militarily predominant, where this country apparently faces no serious, realistic military threat to its survival, and where the sources of violence and instability in the world are at the peripheries, far removed from traditional American national interests.

As already noted, most of the opportunities to engage force are now at the peripheries, where important, and especially vital, American interests are hardly engaged and in which, as a result, there is little positive guidance about when the political objectives the United States might put forward warrant the use of American force. The lens of the cold war paradigm, based in notions of vital interests, would suggest a great deal of American inaction, which has clearly not been the case during the 1990s. Rather, the United States debated the level of activism in which it should engage with American forces. Preeminence in the system meant we could not duck the question, and we came to learn that the American decision to be uninvolved probably often meant the system as a whole will not act.

If the international environment from which issues emerged was opaque and confusing, the proximate events that activated the US (and the rest of the system) were not. The triggering events in each of the instances where the United States chose to use force (and in a number of instances where it decided not to) were human emergencies, often man made. More precisely, involvements have been the result of widespread public awareness of human disasters, awareness normally provided by the mass media.

Neither the events nor responses have been entirely uniform or predictable, as a brief review demonstrates. The United States' first post–Desert Storm involvement came in December 1992, when American forces were sent into Somalia under Operation Restore Hope to support a United Nations effort. The precipitating event was widespread suffering and starvation within the Somali population that, if not alleviated, was projected to cost literally millions of Somali citizens their lives. The causes of the famine were both natural (a prolonged drought that was just beginning to break) and pilferage of international relief supplies by combatants in a multisided, clan-based civil war. Responding to this humanitarian disaster, the first goal of the United States (and others) was to restore the food distribution system and thus relieve the suffering. Beyond a humanitarian concern, there were no discernible American interests in the situation.

Although the military aspect was too limited to justify full treatment here, the United States acted again in 1994, leading an international force (that it largely created) into Haiti to restore the elected government of President Jean-Bertrand Aristide (which had been overthrown by a military junta) to power and to try to stabilize the Haitian situation sufficiently to permit the government to prosper. A secondary, though not officially acknowledged, event that aroused American interest was the flow of Haitian "boat people" from the island country to south Florida. It was hoped that improved conditions in Haiti would convince more Haitians to stay at home rather than to undertake the treacherous trip across the Caribbean Sea. Operation Uphold Democracy, as it was known, remained in the country for over four years before withdrawing.

The United States has also been drawn into the Balkans for two significant missions, both of which are ongoing. The precipitating event for all of these involvements, of course, was the breakup of Yugoslavia in 1991, in which all the states of that union except Serbia (of which Kosovo remained a part) and Montenegro seceded. The breakup initially precipitated a communal war in Bosnia and Herzegovina (hereafter Bosnia) between ethnic Serbs, Croats, and Muslims (who call themselves Bosniacs) for control of the new republic. After nearly four years of fighting in which the international community failed to take decisive action to end the killing, the United States took the lead in organizing a military response to help convince the parties, notably the Serbs, to negotiate and in convening the parties (except the leadership of the Bosnian Serbs, whose leaders were under indictment for war crimes) at Wright-Patterson Air Force Base in Ohio. Operation Deliberate Force was an allied air campaign which, in conjunction with ground activities discussed later in the chapter, demonstrated allied will for a ceasefire in the war. As part of the terms of the Dayton Accords restoring peace to Bosnia, the United States contributed forces to the 60,000-soldier Implementation (later Stabilization) Force (I/SFOR) that remains in place as of this writing (although the American contingency has been reduced in numbers).

Second, the United States took the leading role in the global reaction to suppression of attempted Serbian ethnic cleansing in Kosovo. Until 1987, Kosovo had been a semiautonomous province of Serbia, meaning its ethnic Albanian Muslim majority could practice their faith, use their language, and run their schools and the rest of their lives without much Serbian interference. Serbian President Slobadan Milosevic rescinded that autonomous status, and, after assuming the presidency of the reduced Yugoslavia in the early 1990s, he increased the extent of Serbian control. In 1996, the Kosovo Liberation Army (KLA) began operations against the central government in response to Serbian oppression. KLA actions escalated in 1998 and 1999, precipitating a concerted Serbian campaign (Operation Horseshoe) to drive Albanians from their homes and out of the province. NATO, led by the United States, responded with Operation Allied Force. The outcome was a NATO occupation of Kosovo (KFOR) including American troops as part of a United Nations mission (UN Interim Mission in Kosovo or UNMIK) that has an open-ended stay.

In contrast, the United States chose not to respond to similar situations elsewhere. In Rwanda, the United States joined the international community in officially ignoring the human rampage that left over 500,000 slaughtered and that certainly constituted a humanitarian disaster. Similarly, the international community virtually ignored Russian efforts against Chechen separatists in 1995 and 1999–2000, on the premise, vociferously maintained by the Russians, that the levelling of Grozny and other parts of Chechnya was an internal Russian matter. When the Indonesian province of East Timor voted overwhelmingly for secession and was attacked by mobs encouraged by elements of the Indonesian military, the United States was only too happy to allow the Australians to restore order.

What is striking about each instance where the United States has elected to respond to a human emergency (and for the matter when we have not) is the absence of traditional vital American interests in the situations and their outcomes. One can, for instance, argue it was in the interest of the United States (and certainly southern Floridians) to stop the flow of boat people from Haiti, but that was hardly a major national problem. Similarly, our excursions into former Yugoslavia can be justified as supporting the interests of our major European allies in European tranquility, although how much that tranquility was endangered is a matter of disagreement. It is hard to find any objective US interest in Somalia beyond humanitarian interests.

**Political Objective**

The absence of clear enemies and compelling interests unfocused the process of divining political objectives in the 1990s. Once again, the problem began with the fact that most conflict situations were outside the realm of traditionally important American interests. Indeed, it can be argued that a kind of "interest–threat mismatch" existed: important American interests were hardly threatened by events in the world, and the threats that did exist are, in geopolitical terms, less than compelling. If the realist paradigm criterion of vital interest engagement had been applied to the pattern of violence, then recent American uses of force could rarely have been justified.

The consequences of this situation for the formation of political objectives was obvious. If the remaining superpower must play an activist role in the international system and if part of that activism is regulating and ameliorating the violence and human suffering of war, then the definition of important American interests had to be expanded. The debate was (and remains) over so-called humanitarian interests, human conditions the violation of which are so important as to impel American military response. The problem was the development of concrete criteria to determine when the United States should and should not become involved at various levels in specific situations. Within the Clinton administration, Presidential Directive (PD) 25, issued in 1994, attempted to create such criteria, but the standards were too vague and general to provide a checklist. The debate continues into the new millennium.

The absence of situations where American vital interests were threatened provided another way to look at the process of forming political objectives. When vital interests are threatened, there is little choice about whether to act or not; responses are dictated by the threat, and usually the nature and purpose of needed efforts are fairly straightforward. That situation rarely held in the 1990s, where even the most tragic situations could be ignored without direct consequences to the United States or most Americans; we became engaged where we chose to become engaged, not where we were forced to by the situation.

The difficulty of confronting these situations was further complicated when one applied the two purposes the political objective is supposed to serve: providing guidance for the effort (defining the better state of the peace and assisting in forming military objectives and strategies) and providing a rallying cry to guarantee public support for the effort. The nature of contemporary situations makes achieving both, or even either, of these purposes difficult.

The strategy process as we have described it throughout this volume works best in discreet situations that conform to the peace-war-peace model of conflict (the normalcy of peace is interrupted by war, the purpose of which is to restore peace in some politically acceptable manner). Unfortunately, the internal conflicts of the 1990s have rarely been so simple, especially in terms of specifying end states toward which to aim efforts and which provide a guidepost that allows one to know the political objective has been achieved.

Contemporary internal wars often bedevil such orderly thinking. Often, they have been the result of longtime animosities that have deep-rooted causes (clan violence in Somalia, ethnic hatred in Bosnia and Kosovo). When these causes have overflowed into violence, two possible political objectives (beyond ignoring the problem) have been possible for an outsider like the United States: *conflict suppression* (ending the fighting by forcing the opponents the stop the violence and preventing its recurrence for as long as one is present) or *state-building* (engaging in efforts that will produce an atmosphere wherein the former antagonists accept the better state of the peace and do not want to resume fighting—normally entailing the building of popular political institutions and an economic infrastructure in which the people have a stake and support).

Choosing among these objectives has not been as easy as it might have seemed. Clearly, the desirable outcome in Bosnia or Kosovo was to achieve national reconciliation among the parties, so that at some point in time those intervening can leave with the prospect that the peace will be embraced by all concerned.

There is an irony here. Conflict suppression has proven to be a basically attainable objective (at least since Somalia): the process of imposing order by intimidating the population was first demonstrated in Haiti, was improved in Bosnia, and has been implemented—with some opposition—in Kosovo. Conflict suppression can be translated into a military objective and achieved. The irony, however, has been that achieving this modest objective does not alleviate the underlying animosities that gave rise to the violence in the first place. As evidence, there is virtually unanimous agreement that if foreign troops were removed from Bosnia or Kosovo, fighting would resume (as it did in Somalia). Clearly, the more desirable objective is state-building, but the problem is that we have little concrete idea of how to engage in it successfully (assuming it is possible to do so). The only agreement is that the process is long and arduous and threatens resources and public support for seemingly endless, open-ended commitments.

Until Kosovo, the United States made no explicit commitment to state-building as opposed to the more modest task of conflict suppression. The UNMIK mandate includes building (or rebuilding) civil and criminal authorities and procedures, crafting a democratic constitution, and economic development. No one knows whether this will result in a stable, free-standing Kosovo that can live in peace once KFOR leaves.

Since the Vietnam War, we have been particularly sensitive to how the public views potential military actions. A first question that political and military figures (the other two elements of the Clausewitzian trinity) ask is whether the public will support an action. In the contemporary setting, there is a widespread perception (accurate or not) that the chief limitation on possible involvements is the prospect of American casualties. Since Desert Storm, the precedent cited for this belief is the devastating effect the combat loss of 18 Rangers in Mogadishu had in forcing our abandonment of Somalia. Since Somalia, we have acted to minimize casualties and have succeeded in Haiti, Bosnia, and Kosovo. The most dramatic (some would say extreme) manifestation of this belief was the conduct of the air campaign in Operation Allied Force in Kosovo, where American pilots were instructed to fly above effective antiaircraft range to avoid the loss of pilots.

A major difficulty in forming political objectives is meeting the criteria, identified in Chapter 1, for a "good" objective. Historically in those instances where the criteria are unmet, the result has been a lack of public support for action, to the detriment of the operation. The three post–cold war operations of the US all suffer when measured according to the criteria.

The first criterion, of course, is that an objective be simple, straightforward, and unambiguous. In the murky circumstances surrounding involvements in third world internal wars, that criterion can seldom be met beyond the general goal of recreating order. But what kind of order? How, for instance, does one restore and promote democracy in a country like Haiti that has no real democratic tradition? Is there an American presence in Bosnia to support establishing another Muslim state in Europe? Or in Kosovo to support the vast majority of Muslims, who want a total divorce from the Yugoslav Serbs?

Moral and political loftiness, the second criterion, is difficult to establish as well. Restoring hope in Somalia meant, among other things, establishing a functioning government that could guarantee order. But which clan leader did we choose? On the surface, all the factions looked more or less equally corrupt and unworthy of support. How can one be morally superior anointing one thug over another? In Kosovo, we began by attempting to save the Kosovars from their Serb torturers. That seemed fine until the Kosovars turned on the remaining Serb population of the province, subjecting the Serbs to more or less the same treatment the Kosovars had previously suffered.

The third and fourth criteria, vitality to the United States and importance to at least some Americans, has already been addressed. There have been no objective interests of any kind in many of the places where the United States has intervened, and in each case, the country was one that is not represented by a sizable immigrant community in the United States, meaning an effective voice for the conflict was missing.

There is another difficulty attaching to the political objective. This problem, which we saw most dramatically in Vietnam, was one in which the objectives of the people in the country under duress did not match the objectives of those seeking to interrupt the violence. In Somalia, for instance, the United States first negotiated with Mohammed Farah Aidid, the clan leader whose forces controlled most of Mogadishu. Unfortunately our objective of Somali tranquility did not match his desire to rule, and the relationship cooled. The most dramatic instance of this is unfolding in Kosovo. The United Nations, including the United States, has as its ultimate objective the reformation of Kosovo to its former status as a semiautonomous region that is part of Yugoslavia. Neither partisan group shares this objective. The Albanian Kosovars want total independence from Serbian Yugoslavia, and the Serbs equally reject a Kosovo that is essentially independent of Serb rule. How can these objectives be reconciled?

## Military Objectives and Strategy

The military objectives of the three major American combat operations that followed Desert Storm in the last decade of the twentieth century were remarkably different from one another and from the struggle against Iraq. However, some fundamental elements of the strategies employed in each case that were remarkably similar. Furthermore, the success of Desert Storm and its meager cost in American lives had a direct influence on the way in which US forces pursued their objectives in subsequent contingencies.

### Somalia—Operation Restore Hope

In Somalia in late April 1992, the United Nations began humanitarian operations designed to alleviate mass starvation that resulted from terrible drought and several years of bloody, chaotic civil war. It was soon clear, however, that the small UN contingent known as UNOSOM (United Nations Operations in Somalia) could not provide a secure environment for aid workers or prevent the troops of the various Somali war lords from plundering relief supplies. In December 1992, 20 nations, led by the United States, intervened to provide the military muscle required to make the UN humanitarian relief effort a success. Known as Operation Restore Hope in the United States, the military force was designated UNITAF (Unified Task Force) and commanded by Marine Corps Gen Robert B. Johnston.

The UNITAF objective seemed straightforward initially: to provide a secure environment for the aid workers to perform their function and to secure land routes to the interior of Somalia to facilitate the orderly and timely distribution of relief supplies to isolated inland villages where the famine was at its worst. Much of the strategy to accomplish all of this was based on a variation of the theme used in Desert Storm, the so-called Powell corollary to the Weinberger doctrine. The doctrine articulated by then Secretary of Defense Caspar Weinberger during the 1980s identified the need for vital interests, wholehearted commitment, clear objectives, strong public support, and capable forces to be present before the United States committed its forces abroad. Later, Chairman of the Joint Chiefs of Staff General Colin Powell added that when forces are committed, they should be committed immediately as an overwhelming force. The result was that UNITAF was not the typically small and lightly armed UN peacekeeping force. Rather, it was a large (over 25,000 US troops alone), heavily armed combat force supported by air and sea power and a strong logistical effort. The objective was to awe the Somali warlords and their ragtag militias and to fight them if necessary. Ideally, the militias would be disarmed, but directions from Washington were unclear about attempting to disarm them. It was very clear, however, that force protection was uppermost in the minds of the policy makers. Minimal casualties were the expected norm, a policy clearly influenced by the incredibly low casualty rate in Desert Storm. Needless to say, unclear directives about disarming the militias and very clear objectives about friendly casualties had a very strong influence on operations, as will be seen in later sections.

Beyond the initial goal of getting food to the starving Somalis, it soon became clear that any lasting success would depend upon ending the civil strife and lifting Somalia out of utter chaos. Somalia had neither a national government nor any functioning regional governmental institutions. The only quasi-governments were those of the numerous regional warlords whose constant fighting had thoroughly destroyed the political, economic, and social fabric of the country. There were no schools, public utilities, transportation system, police, or judicial system. It seemed as if every teenager carried a gun; many of them were intoxicated by "khat," a narcotic in widespread use in Somalia. In the long run, a state-building effort would have to eliminate the power of the competing warlords. How this would be done was unclear as the humanitarian mission began. Missteps in the state-building effort would eventually doom the entire UN effort in Somalia.

### Bosnia—Operation Deliberate Force

Operation Deliberate Force, executed between 30 August and 14 September, 1995, was the final iteration of a series of US-led NATO air operations over Bosnia. The first, Operation Sharp Guard in 1992, attempted to enforce the arms embargo on the former Yugoslavia. Sharp Guard was followed in October 1992 by Operation Sky Watch, which observed and reported violations of the UN ban on military flight operations over Bosnia. At the end of March 1993, Operation Deny Flight replaced Sky Watch. Deny Flight was authorized to enforce the no-fly zone over Bosnia with force. As the situation on the ground in Bosnia continued to deteriorate, offensive missions were added to Deny Flight to protect threatened UN peacekeeping forces, punish factions violating UN Security Council resolutions, and suppress air defenses that might threaten NATO/UN air operations. Deliberate Force, which began on 30 August 1995 and concluded 16 days later, was an expanded version of Deny Flight designed to protect the so-called safe havens established by the UN and to coerce the Bosnian Serbs into accepting UN terms for a peace settlement in Bosnia.

Although offensive air strikes had been carried out under Deny Flight, they had been both timid and sporadic. Air attacks were limited to forces and weapons that were directly attacking UN peacekeepers. In a sense, retaliatory air attacks required a "smoking gun" for a target. Even if the smoking gun could be found, the strategy amounted to little more than a tit-for-tat exchange and gave the initiative to the forces opposing the UN. The Deliberate Force strategy was to seize the initiative, expand significantly the kinds of targets airpower would attack, greatly magnify the intensity of air operations, and where possible, coordinate air operations with the offensive capabilities (mainly artillery) of UN ground forces.

The expanded targeting scheme had been under development since the spring of 1993. The NATO planners developed three targeting options. The first supported the kind of air strikes that limited Deny Flight's effectiveness—that is, very limited strikes against the smoking guns directly attacking UN peacekeeping forces. Option two broadened the target list well beyond the smoking guns to include military targets throughout the immediate area surrounding a UN safe haven. The third option provided an even broader set of targets throughout the general area of operations, certainly all of Bosnia and perhaps further afield.

In crafting the strategy for Deliberate Force, the influence of Desert Storm is again obvious in at least two ways. First, although the forces assembled to execute Deliberate Force were not nearly as large as those assembled for Desert Storm—220 fighter-bomber aircraft plus about 70 supporting aircraft (primarily electronic warfare, AWACS, and reconnaissance aircraft)—the force was overwhelming relative to Bosnian Serb capabilities. The Bosnian Serbs could not begin to mount an effective challenge to NATO's dominance in the air. The second influence of Desert Storm concerned the attempts of the planners and commanders to limit the risks to noncombatants through collateral damage. After Desert Storm, observers in Iraq were surprised by the very low levels of collateral damage, a product principally of the use of precision-guided munitions. To a great degree, the low levels of collateral damage in Iraq became the acceptable standard for western military operations. When NATO executed Deliberate Force, US Air Force Lieut Gen Michael E. Ryan, the commander of Allied Forces Southern Command (AIRSOUTH) responsible for the operation, personally scrutinized every targeting decision to include exact aim points, weapons used, timing, and so forth. It was no accident that nearly 70 percent of all the weapons used in Deliberate Force were precision-guided munitions.

### Kosovo—Operation Allied Force

The clash between Serbs and ethnic Albanians in Kosovo led NATO to begin planning for air operations against the Serbs as early as July 1998. The need for a NATO ground attack on Serbia was regarded as unnecessary and believed to be politically impossible. The opinion was widely held throughout NATO that the Serbs would quickly crumble under NATO air attacks just as they had quickly caved in to NATO demands under the Deliberate Force air attacks in 1995. The initial air attack plan was quite robust. However, between July 1998 and the commencement of operations on 24 March 1999, the plan reportedly went through some 40 revisions as NATO members fretted over whether or not the alliance, which had always been defensive in nature, should undertake offensive action "out of area." Eventually, the plan evolved into a slowly escalating three-phased air attack. The plan provided NATO decision makers with the smallest possible escalation steps should the struggle go beyond the first-phase air strikes against Serbian air defenses and command centers. If the second phase was needed, NATO air strikes would attempt to isolate Serbian military forces by expanding attacks against command centers in Serbia and Kosovo and striking petroleum production, storage and distribution facilities as well as the road and bridge network. The third phase was designed to concentrate on fielded forces as well as electrical power and industrial targets north of the 44th parallel and in Belgrade itself. The North Atlantic Council, NATO's political arm, much to the chagrin of many military leaders, tightly held the levers of control over the campaign. As NATO planning and replanning continued, the Serbian assault against the ethnic Albanians in Kosovo also continued with predictably tragic results.

When operations commenced on 24 March 1999, the US Secretary of Defense and the Chairman of the Joint Chiefs of Staff announced to the American people that the intervention had four military objectives:

1. Deter the Serbs from further action against the Kosovars
2. Reduce the capabilities of the Serbian forces to attack the Kosovars
3. Attack the Serbian air defenses
4. Reduce the Serbian ability to wage war in the future, should near-term deterrence fail

Experiences in Deliberate Force, Somalia, and even Desert Storm significantly influenced the development of NATO's strategy for the Kosovo contingency. As already noted, the ease with which Deliberate Force had convinced the Serbs to cave in to NATO demands in 1995 clearly set the tone for campaign planning and initial preparations. From the outset, Allied Force would not be the kind of overwhelming air campaign seen in Desert Storm because such an enormous display of military might would not be required—or so said the common wisdom. Rather, a slowly graduated air campaign with both the escalation controls and target selection authority held by NATO political authorities would be the case. To American airmen, the NATO plan and its execution brought back bitter memories of the Rolling Thunder bombing campaign during the war in Vietnam.

Other memories, namely the memories of the bloody tragedy in Somalia, combined with ambivalence among its members about whether or not NATO should intervene, convinced NATO strategists that casualties had to be held to an absolute minimum. The perceived need to strictly limit casualties certainly played a role in the rejection of any plans for a ground assault by NATO forces. It also affected the air campaign in that NATO flyers were ordered to fly above 15,000 feet, out of range of most ground-based anti-aircraft artillery and out of the operating envelope of many smaller ground-to-air missiles. While flying at these altitudes limited NATO air casualties (two aircraft lost, no air crew members lost), flying at these altitudes also posed significant problems in target acquisition and identification.

Finally, the results and memories of both Desert Storm and Deliberate Force made NATO airpower the military instrument of choice. Airpower was widely perceived as the decisive element in both Desert Storm and Deliberate Force. The efficiency and limited collateral damage of air-delivered precision-guided munitions demonstrated in both Desert Storm and Deliberate Force were very appealing given the kind of political environment NATO planners faced. The low casualty rates for air crews in both Desert Storm and Deliberate Force were a perfect fit with NATO's requirement for minimal friendly casualties. Finally, NATO airpower was a force that the Serbs could not effectively challenge. The Serbian air force had about 140 relatively modern aircraft, but only 16 of those aircraft could challenge the enormous number of first-line aircraft that NATO could muster.

**Political Considerations**

Disagreement about what is important enough to justify the application of American force has extended to the purely political concerns that leaders face when attempting to assess the use of force in the environment of the 1990s. Since the need to use force in these situations is almost never mandatory or even overwhelmingly obvious (deployments of necessity), more subtle judgment about deployments of choice must be made. At the domestic level, the question has been public opinion: What forms of intervention will the American public initially support and in the long term sustain? Internationally, the problem is a matter of building an international consensus about the kinds of situations in which outside involvement is legitimate and necessary, a debate that has tended to center around the role of the United Nations both as legitimator (through Security Council Resolutions) and as organizer (through peacekeeping operations or PKOs).

The concern for public opinion is a direct artifact of the public's angry response to Vietnam and particularly of the fracture of the Clausewitzian trinity (the people, the government, and the Army) that many perceived as a fatal flaw in that operation. The Army's solution to that problem for post-Vietnam uses of American forces has been to integrate the reserves into all complex, extensive missions, such that missions cannot be dispatched without some reserve call-up. The reaction to activating the reserves, the Army reasoned and continues to believe, provides a kind of informal referendum on public support that hopefully guides the use of armed forces into situations where public support will be sustainable and avoids places where it will not. This approach was first tested successfully with the call-up of reserves for Operation Desert Storm. It has been repeated in subsequent deployments, particularly in areas such as civil action, which are delegated exclusively to the reserves.

The concern for public opinion is a limiting factor on the ability to mount and sustain operations, and it was framed in the dual, and quite different, experiences in Kuwait and Somalia. Operation Desert Storm was an enormous public-relations success (at least after initial fears of the toll in blood were quieted in fall 1990), beginning with detailed television coverage of the air campaign against the Iraqis and the smashing victory of the 100-hour ground campaign that ended the war in February 1991.

The success of Desert Storm created a kind of euphoria (false, as it turns out) about the use of force in the post–cold war era. When President Bush declared his intention to send American troops to Somalia on 4 December 1992 to help UN efforts to break the disruption of food supplies to that country, the reaction was overwhelmingly favorable, an example of what he trumpeted as the "new world order." As the Marines clambered onto the beaches of Mogadishu and began to patrol, the television airwaves were filled with images of Somali children (who were Muslim) interacting with American troops, including singing Christmas carols in exchange for candy bars. Operation Restore Hope looked like the glowing example of how American force could be used to alleviate human suffering in the new international environment.

And then the 18 Rangers were killed in a Mogadishu ambush, and the corpse of one of the victims was dragged through the dusty streets of the capital with the cameras rolling. Support quickly gave way to shock and disillusion at the horror of the event and the ingratitude it demonstrated. Public support was shown to be very thin and fickle; public opinion demanded an end to the mission, and the cry of "no more Somalias" (eerily reminiscent of Vietnam) was heard. The "people" leg of the trinity was once again severed; the question was how that could be avoided in the future.

The US government and the military took two lessons from the Somali experience that have guided subsequent operations in Haiti, Bosnia, and Kosovo. The first was that public support for this kind of mission was not likely to be deep or stable. The political objectives available and the rationales flowing from them (President Clinton's defense of involvement in Bosnia, for instance: "It's the right thing to do") were unlikely to create a firm base of support among the public. Second and relatedly, since the support base would continue to be very thin, it would not likely survive adversity, as it had not when the Rangers were gunned down in Mogadishu.

The lesson seemed clear enough: the American public would support (or at least not oppose) the interjection of American forces as long as that involvement did not entail American combat casualties. This assessment has been assiduously applied in subsequent operations. This approach was taken to the I/SFOR operation in Bosnia; once again, a plurality of the public opposed the deployment, but the lack of casualties has meant that there has been no real opposition to their continued (and continuing) presence there.

This assessment reached its logical conclusion (or absurdity) in Kosovo, where the pilots of Operation Allied Force were given the somewhat contradictory missions of protecting the Kosovars from ethnic cleansing and of avoiding combat losses. The latter requirement, of course, flowed directly from the assessment that the American public would turn rapidly against our involvement if the body bags began returning; it also meant that bombing had to occur from such high altitudes as to compromise the ability to discriminate and hit nonstationary targets and thus arguably compromised the ability to accomplish the first objective.

The assessment is arguably cynical. Is it in fact true that the American people have a zero tolerance for casualties, as the assumption about Kosovo suggested? Or, is the problem that the assessment is correct if little is done to convince the public that a mission is worthy of American sacrifice, but not true if the leadership goes to the trouble of mounting an adequate defense of the mission? There are certainly some disagreements in the professional community and notably among the military, who would argue that the failure of the Clausewitzian trinity in this regard really lies with the government, which has not done its job of adequately convincing the American public that our interests are sufficiently engaged in the Bosnias and Kosovos of this world to commit American forces, with all the risks entailed by such commitment.

The international political dimension aggravates this part of the problem. If there is no American consensus about when outside intervention in the internal tragedies of states is justified and appropriate, that disagreement has simply mirrored the greater international lack of consensus on the subject. The international dimension contains both legal and geopolitical areas of disagreement.

Part of the problem is one of legitimacy. Since nearly all these conflicts were internal wars with little if any interstate aspects, the laws of intervention in civil conflicts traditionally hold. (The conflict in the Democratic Republic of Congo, where there have been widespread accusations of outside intervention by neighboring states, is an exception.) Under international law, intervention in a civil war is prohibited except for limited purposes (such as evacuating your endangered nationals) even at the invitation of one or another party. In some cases (e.g., Somalia), there is no government to issue an invitation even if it wanted to, and in others power is so fractionalized that it is impossible to determine who is an official.

The "solution" to this problem is to use the imprimatur of the United Nations to legitimize proposed interventions—more specifically, chapter VII of the Charter, which authorizes the Security Council to "determine the existence of any threat to the peace, breach of the peace, or act of aggression and . . . make recommendation, or decide what measures shall be taken" to deal with these situations (Article 39). Thus, UN Security Council Resolutions (UNSCRs) have become a vehicle to legitimize international efforts and thus guarantee that the world body will have at least some role in almost any action (if not necessarily providing military leadership).

The geopolitical part of the problem is deciding the situations in which to act and not to act. Here international lack of consensus parallels American indecisiveness. When internal conflicts have broken out in Europe (Bosnia and Kosovo), there have been sufficient European interests to warrant intervention, and American interest in a tranquil Europe has proven adequate to support our intervention. Desert Storm–bred optimism nurtured an intervention in Somalia that traditional interests or spheres of interest would have advised against. The application of geopolitical principles dictated a hands-off approach to Rwanda and Sierra Leone and sent the Australians into the breach in East Timor.

## Military Technology and Technique

Desert Storm made clear that two decades of post-Vietnam investment in high-technology military systems had yielded an impressive harvest of capabilities. During the remainder of the 1990s, the US military would continue to capitalize on its technological advantage. In both Deliberate Force and Allied Force, US technology played a dominating, perhaps even decisive role. In Somalia, however, the US military found that high tech weaponry developed for one kind of warfare is not necessarily the key to success in a very different kind of struggle.

Of all the technological wonders put on display during Desert Storm, precision-guided munitions were perhaps the most awe inspiring. Day after day during the coalition air attacks on Iraq and Iraqi forces in Kuwait, gun camera tapes gleefully displayed at news conferences showed precision munitions striking even the smallest targets with almost unbelievable accuracy and reliability. Although precision munitions provided great theater during Desert Storm, 93 percent of all the bombs dropped during the war with Iraq were free-fall, unguided, "dumb" bombs. Four years later in the very short Deliberate Force campaign, NATO carefully *coerced* the Serbs to the negotiating table by making precision-guided munitions nearly 70 percent of all the bombs dropped. Still another four years later in Operation Allied Force, NATO's objective was to *compel* the Serbs to end their assault on the Albanian Kosovars and comply with NATO mandates. In this campaign, longer even than Desert Storm (although far less intense), a full 35 percent of all the bombs dropped by the NATO air forces were precision guided. Precision-guided munitions had become far more than the interesting technological gadgets providing great pictures for television news programs. By the end of the 1990s, precision munitions were the preferred "coin of the realm," particularly in those contingencies that required very careful controls on collateral damage.

One of the most important innovations in the field of precision munitions was the mating of the space-based global positioning system (GPS) with precision munitions guidance systems. Prior to the use of the GPS, precision munitions were guided to their targets by laser designators or self-contained miniature television cameras. Unfortunately, in bad weather conditions or when targets were obscured by smoke or low clouds, laser- and TV-guided munitions were often useless. However, precision munitions guided to specific coordinates by the GPS system transmissions from space satellites are unaffected by the kind of weather and smoke conditions that often blind other systems, although GPS systems are nominally a bit less accurate.

Stealth aircraft were also stars of the show in the war with Iraq. The F-117 stealthy fighter-bomber repeatedly flew into the most heavily defended areas of Iraq and returned unscathed. Nine years later, the stealthy "flying wing" B-2 had been added to the US long-range, heavy-bomber fleet. In its first operational use during Allied Force, it proved to be both successful and reliable, launching directly from Whiteman AFB in central Missouri on 30-hour, round-trip bombing missions to Serbia. The B-2 was the first manned aircraft to penetrate the Serbian air defenses. The B-2 carried GPS-guided munitions including large special-purpose weapons designed to attack super-hardened command and control targets. As in Desert Storm, the newest version of stealth technology worked well—the B-2s returned from all of their sorties without a scratch. However, the first generation stealth technology F-117s suffered their first loss, apparently to a Serbian surface-to-air missile. The pilot was rescued.

It is all too easy to think of the air campaigns of the late 1990s as high-tech showpieces. But amid all the high-tech gadgets that performed so well in Allied Force (including the widely used unmanned aerial vehicles and the B-1 bomber) the fact remains that 65 percent of the bombs dropped by NATO were free-fall, unguided bombs. Incredibly, most of these unguided munitions were delivered to their targets by venerable 1960s-vintage B-52 bombers. There was delicious irony in the fact that as some high-tech aircraft were seeing their first operational use, the youngest B-52 in the fleet had now seen action over enemy territory in four different decades. Moreover, B-52s dropped more tons of bombs during Allied force than any other weapon system.

While investments in high-technology weapon system development paid large dividends in Deliberate Force and Allied Force, the intervention in Somalia presented very different challenges. Much of the investment in technology had been focused on developing weaponry to counter other sophisticated military forces—primarily Warsaw Pact forces. Many of these weapons were optimized for use against maneuvering armored forces in relatively open terrain. In Somalia, the enemy did not possess sophisticated equipment. There were no maneuvering armored forces, and in Mogadishu, which was the center of US operations, the terrain was anything but open.

Built-up areas such as Mogadishu present thorny problems for any military force. Air power and artillery are difficult to use unless one does not care about collateral damage. Enemy soldiers are difficult to find in the jumble of buildings or the remains of buildings. The ability of military vehicles to maneuver is severely limited in narrow streets, and in many cases armored vehicles are at an extreme disadvantage to enemy light infantry. Area security becomes problematic as a soldier can often control only the few square feet of ground upon which he stands. The utility of helicopters in built-up areas is offset by their vulnerability to ground fire from every building in every quadrant. This was amply demonstrated in October 1993 when two Blackhawk helicopters were shot down and a third crippled during a disastrous raid in Mogadishu on warlord Mohammed Farah Aidid. Not only were the helicopters shot down by small-arms ground fire, Army Rangers on the raid were trapped in the narrow streets by Aidid's ragtag militia. By the time a relief column forced its way through narrow, blockaded streets and innumerable ambush points and arrived on the scene, 18 Americans had been killed and 84 wounded. American forces learned the bitter lesson that high-tech weapons developed under one set of assumptions about combat conditions often do not provide helpful solutions if the assumptions do not apply. In the wake of the tragedy in Mogadishu, "urban warfare" became a hot topic for research, doctrinal development, and training for US forces.

## Military Conduct

Considered as a group, the military operations in the three cases highlighted in this chapter began surreally and ended inconclusively. Consider, for example, that in the darkness of the very early morning hours of 9 December 1992, a US Navy Seal team, their faces blackened with camouflage paint, swam ashore near Mogadishu, Somalia, fully expecting a firefight with one of the heavily armed Somali clans. Instead, they came out of the surf and into the glare of television lights and the shouted questions of waiting newsmen. It was the first amphibious invasion broadcast on television around the world as it happened. Eight years later the defeated Serbians pulled their forces out of Kosovo and returned home to tote up the damage to their home-land. Meanwhile, the Albanian Kosovars began returning to Kosovo along with peacekeeping forces. It was not long before Serbian repression of the Albanian Kosovars was replaced by Albanian repression of the Serbian Kosovars. Meanwhile, in Serbia those responsible for the entire situation remained in power, even though Kosovo had been lost and much of the Serbian infrastructure and economy had been destroyed.

### Somalia—Operation Restore Hope

Although the military operation in Somalia began on a surrealistic note on the beaches, US forces quickly came ashore in strength and fanned out into Mogadishu. The airport and port were quickly secured. But there was confusion as to exactly what the troops were to do in order to provide a secure environment for the aid workers and how the troops were to get food supplies to the starving settlements inland. There were halfhearted and somewhat confused attempts to seize arms from the various militia groups, but little was accomplished. Rather, the operation focused very narrowly on moving food to the starving while leaving long range state-building efforts to the UN. Even in this narrowly focused effort the cautious approach of the US forces drew considerable criticism. It was, for example, six days before the first heavily armed food convoy (including some 700 Marines) left Mogadishu for Baidoa, one of the most important of the inland feeding centers.

In all, the US sent nearly 26,000 heavily armed troops to Somalia during the following five months. The large show of force had its intended effect. To a large extent the marauding militia units gave way and the food got through to the starving. Thousands of lives were certainly saved. To be sure there were some shooting incidents, some confrontations, and much frustration. By mid-May 1993, the US had pulled most of its troops out of Somalia, leaving behind a small rapid-reaction force and supporting logistics troops to assist the lightly armed UN peacekeeping force.

Emboldened by the departure of the heavily armed US forces and worried that his position of power was being undercut by UN actions, troops of Mohammed Farah Aidid struck a Pakistani peacekeeping contingent and killed 24 in early June. The US rapid reaction force took part in several attempts to capture or kill Aidid and his lieutenants. The last attempt ended tragically for the American contingent when they mounted a helicopter assault on the Olympic hotel and captured 19 of Aidid's aides on 3 October. As they waited for a relief column to arrive, two of their Black Hawk helicopters were shot down and a third badly damaged as Aidid's well-armed militia men swarmed over the area. In the ensuing firefight, the outnumbered and outgunned US force suffered over 100 casualties, including 18 killed. Tragically, pictures of celebrating Somalis dragging the nearly nude body of a dead American soldier through the streets of Mogadishu were broadcast on American television.

The upshot of this tragic incident was immediate reinforcement of the small remaining US force in Somalia, but only for self-protection. Within six months (1 April 1994) all US forces had been withdrawn from Somalia. The United States maintained it had successfully completed the mission it set out to accomplish. The actions of American forces had broken the cycle of starvation and had saved thousands of lives. In short, the United States declared victory as it abandoned the field.

### Bosnia—Operation Deliberate Force

Deliberate Force was by far the shortest of the military operations featured in this chapter. Nominally, the bombing campaign lasted 22 days from the first raid on 30 August 1995 until the campaign was officially declared completed on 20 September. However, combat operations actually took place on only 12 days. Operations were suspended after two days of bombing to encourage negotiations. Operations resumed on 5 September and were again suspended on 14 September when it was learned that the Serbs had agreed to NATO's terms.

As the situation for UN peacekeepers in Bosnia had deteriorated in the summer of 1995, the UN had very carefully returned many of its scattered peacekeeping units from the field to more secure and defensible positions. This was done quietly without any fanfare. At the same time, the NATO Rapid Reaction Force concentrated its units in the area around Sarajevo. Although there was some rush to complete the withdrawal of the peacekeeping units into secure areas, all was in readiness when the bombing commenced. The event that finally spurred NATO to commence bombing was the particularly bloody mortar attack on the crowded Mrkale marketplace in Sarajevo on 28 August. Nearly 40 people were killed, obviously an unacceptable situation for an area declared to be a UN safe haven. Perhaps worse for the Bosnian Serbs, because the attack was in Sarajevo the international press had rapid access to the devastation and quickly broadcast pictures of the grim scene throughout the world. The outrage in many quarters was palpable and pressure for NATO to take strong military action was overwhelming.

During the short campaign, 48 Bosnian Serb targets were hit with just over 1,000 munitions—nearly 70 percent of them precision-guided munitions. In total nearly 300 aircraft from nine countries took part in the campaign—220 of them were fighter aircraft. One US Navy ship also took part in the campaign, firing 13 cruise missiles on 10 September against Bosnian

Serb air defense installations. Finally, it should be noted that the NATO Rapid Reaction Force used its artillery to shell Bosnian Serb forces in the Sarajevo area. The aforementioned UN peacekeeping units did not take an active part in the campaign.

Although it appears in many US accounts that the Deliberate Force bombing was responsible for coercing the Bosnian Serbs to accept UN terms for the settlement of the strife in Bosnia, there is more to the story. The UN and NATO were very fortunate that two other military actions were putting great pressure on the Bosnian Serbs at the same time. First, Croatia had launched Operation Storm in late July to retake the Krajina area of Bosnia and to break the Bosnian Serb siege of the area around Bihac. Second, the rejuvenated Bosnian Federation, consisting of Bosnian Croat and Muslim factions, cooperated with the Croatian offensive by successfully attacking Bosnian Serb forces and driving them out of the central portion of Bosnia. By mid-September the Bosnian Serbs, who had once controlled 70 percent of Bosnia, had been pushed into headlong retreat and the area under their control had shrunk to just over 50 percent.

### *Kosovo—Operation Allied Force*

Allied Force, the final American military campaign of the 1990s, was far longer than Desert Storm, the first American military campaign of the decade. However, the bombing campaign against the Serbs in Kosovo and in Serbia proper was far less intense than the bombing campaign against the Iraqis eight years earlier. In military circles, at least, the lack of intensity in the campaign caused considerable outcry, as did a major strategy blunder—both of which probably prolonged the campaign.

As mentioned earlier, conventional wisdom in the West predicted that the Serbs would quickly cave in to UN and NATO demands after an almost symbolic air attack, repeating what had happened in 1995 during Operation Deliberate Force. That conventional wisdom combined with reluctance on the part of many NATO countries to undertake offensive out-of-area operations led to early strikes which were anything but robust. In accordance with the three-phased bombing campaign discussed in a previous section, the early air strikes concentrated on the Serbian air defense system. On 24 March 1999, the first night of combat operations, NATO forces struck using both sea- (submarine) and air- (B-52 bomber) launched cruise missiles as well as 400 aircraft sorties. However, only 120 of the aircraft sorties were strike sorties; the remaining sorties were flown to provide support and protection for the strike aircraft. The intensity of the attacks stayed at very low levels during the entire first week of the campaign, averaging only about 50 strike sorties per day.

It was soon clear that something more than a symbolic air campaign would be required to convince the Serbs to bend to UN and NATO demands. The North Atlantic Council approved an expansion of the campaign into phase two, which expanded attacks on fixed targets in Serbia and also approved the first attempts to strike Serbian fielded forces in Kosovo. The latter were moved up in the previously planned order of progression because the early air strikes, rather than acting as a deterrent, had caused the Serbs to increase the pace of their ethnic cleansing in Kosovo. Although the target list expanded, the intensity of the campaign did not significantly increase, in part due to poor flying weather. For the first three weeks of the campaign, NATO forces averaged only 80 strike sorties per day, and strike sorties averaged only 28 percent of the total sorties flown.

Beginning in week four, NATO began attacking phase-three targets in Belgrade, going after bridges over the Danube; radio and television stations; political headquarters; and businesses owned by Milosevic, his family and friends. On 3 May NATO attacked Belgrade's electrical power grid causing temporary power outages. The pounding continued throughout the remainder of the campaign, destroying much of the Serbian economic infrastructure. The campaign against the Serbian forces in Kosovo was more problematic. The Serb forces dispersed, hiding among the civilian population, and carried on the ethnic cleansing mission in small group operations. These actions made it very difficult for NATO airmen to acquire their targets, particularly since they had been ordered to fly at no less than 15,000 feet.* Much of the problem was solved in late May when the Kosovo Liberation Army (KLA) launched a counterattack that forced the Serbian forces to come out of hiding, reassemble, and defend themselves. The Serbs beat back the KLA advances, but in the process exposed themselves to NATO air attacks.

On 9 June, 78 days after the bombing began, the Serbs finally agreed to UN and NATO terms, and the bombing came to a halt as Serbian forces began evacuating Kosovo. Many who believe the campaign was far longer than it should have been contend that an intense Desert Storm-like campaign probably would have ended Serb resistance much sooner. Indeed, except for length, Allied Force paled in comparison with Desert Storm. In Desert Storm, Coalition air forces flew nearly four times the number of strike sorties flown in Allied Force and did so in just over half the time. In a sense, Desert Storm was seven to eight times as intense as Allied Force.

An additional factor contributed to the lengthy campaign against the Serbs.

---

*The minimum altitude was lowered somewhat in certain situations as the operation continued.

NATO committed a strategy blunder when it publicly announced at the beginning of the campaign that the alliance had no intention of mounting a ground campaign into Kosovo or Serbia. While the announcement was true, it was misguided. Without the threat of a ground invasion, Serb troops in Kosovo were able to avoid NATO air attacks by dispersing, which was exactly what they did. Second, in Serbia proper, without the threat of invasion the Serbs could "hunker down" and ride out the less than overwhelming air attacks in the hope that internal NATO policy disagreements would put an end to the campaign. As the campaign wore on, the alliance partners realized the error of their ways and several (led most notably by Great Britain) began openly talking about the need for a land campaign. The possibility of a NATO land campaign may have been the final straw in the Serb decision to accept the UN and NATO demands. One is left to wonder what might have happened had a ground attack been threatened from the beginning of Allied Force.

**The Broader Military Context**

Following the war with Iraq, the American military was engaged in many more operations in the 1990s than Restore Hope, Deliberate Force, and Allied Force. The Iraqis provided the most consistent problem throughout the decade in spite of their stunning defeat in Desert Storm. In a very real sense, the war with Iraq never ended as US forces continued throughout the decade to enforce Iraqi no-fly zones in Operations Northern Watch (designed to protect the Kurdish people living in Northern Iraq) and Southern Watch (designed to protect the Shiite Muslims living in Southern Iraq). Both operations were active every day from the end of Desert Storm to the end of the decade. The Iraqis raised US ire on repeated occasions by making aggressive troop movements toward Kuwait or resisting UN arms-control inspection teams. The US quickly moved forces to the Persian Gulf area when it appeared trouble was again brewing, and on one occasion the US launched Operation Desert Fox, a four-day bombing campaign against 100 Iraqi targets. Beyond Iraq, US forces were committed as peacekeepers and nation builders in Haiti in 1994 and remain as peacekeepers in both Bosnia, following Deliberate Force, and Kosovo, following Allied force. US forces have often been committed to provide logistical support to emergency humanitarian missions in far-flung corners of the world such as Rwanda and East Timor. Finally, a substantial US combat force commitment remains in South Korea, nearly 50 years after the conclusion of the Korean war. Ironically, the unending Korean commitment was a fitting precursor to the seemingly unending commitments that have typified the post–cold war military landscape.

## Better State of the Peace

One of the major ways in which the military involvements of the United States in the post–cold war era differ from our previous experience has been in the determination of the better state of the peace. In previous wars, the United States, its allies, and its adversaries have entered with well-defined political objectives for which the military instrument has served as the major means of attainment. Once one side or the other has achieved the postwar conditions for which it began fighting and the other either accepts—or cannot or will no longer resist—the victor's definition of the better state of the peace, then the conflict ends.

The internal conflicts highlighted in this chapter violate that model on several counts. The first is the "peace-war-peace" model that is implicit in formulating the better state of the peace. In contemporary conflicts, the period of gestation is generally long—sometimes even centuries—in development, and involvement from the outside does not begin at the commencement of conflict but only when a long, amorphous process boils over into some public atrocity that the international community cannot ignore and feels impelled to interrupt. If the political objective is no more than conflict suppression, that goal is normally attainable, as has been the case in Haiti, Bosnia, and Kosovo. Attaining that objective, however, has been inadequate to constitute either closure or the attainment of the better state of the peace for all participants, for at least two reasons.

The first reason is that conflict suppression may represent an interruption of the violence and the pursuit of the parties of opposing political objectives, but it is not an end to the process. Virtually by definition, stopping the violence short of some grisly outcome means neither side attains its objective— its image of the better state—and those goals remain in the minds of the combatants. The intervenors merely interrupt the pursuit of those objectives for as long as they are willing to remain on the site (a fact the intervenors quickly realized). Hostile ability may be suspended by conflict suppression; neither sense of hostile will is addressed.

The application of the peace-war-peace model presumes that some outcome can be reached with which the parties are reconciled. The act of suppression and remaining in place to prevent the recurrence of fighting means that neither side's hostile ability can be overcome, and in all likelihood, neither will either side's cost-tolerance. Instead, the only way to reach closure is through a reconciliatory peace in which both (or all) sides embrace the terms of the peace as preferable to the continuation of hostilities. The current method for trying to do so is state-building: the development of political and economic institutions and structures that will be superior to those that existed before and during the fighting and thus will be embraced by all sides. The analogy is the rebuilding of Germany and Japan in such a manner that they so clearly benefited that they could embrace the peace imposed by the allies. Anything less in contemporary situation is likely to be unacceptable to all sides.

But there is a problem here. In most of the involvements to date, there has been no real commitment to the kind of state-building this implies. In Kurdistan, the United States agreed to protect the Kurds but not to address their underlying problems with the Iraqi government, and Operations Northern and Southern Watch remain as apparently indefinite commitments the effects of which satisfy the long-term objectives of no one. Nothing like providing the necessary resources to build an infrastructure in Haiti that could provide the support for "upholding" democracy was even attempted, and the situation is not much better than it was before the intervention. Serious plans for rebuilding and developing Bosnia have never been formulated, much less implemented, and SFOR remains the perpetual bulwark against the return of violence.

Kosovo is the exception. In Kosovo, the UNMIK/KFOR structure has explicitly committed itself to building a Kosovar state that its citizens can embrace. It is a long-term commitment that UN Secretary General Kofi Annan estimated in 1999 could take a decade or more to complete. Our better state of the Kosovar peace is a strong, democratic, and prosperous Kosovo. Attaining that objective, however, is confronted with two major stumbling blocks.

The first and most obvious problem is that state-building is a rather new enterprise, and one for which there is not a well-developed history of success. The closest equivalent we have are the post–World War II reclamations of the defeated enemies, Germany and Japan, and the concentrated efforts over a period of time in places like South Korea and Taiwan. Trying to apply the lessons of those enterprises to Kosovo is difficult; Germany and Japan were well-developed states before the war, each with considerable intellectual and physical infrastructures that needed rebuilding and redirecting. South Korea may be more instructive, because it was developed from the ashes of decades of Japanese colonialism. Still, it took a lot of time and a great deal of resources to build the postwar Republic of Korea into the formidable regional power it now is.

The fact that we have little experience in state-building in a region where there are no institutions or political traditions in place and no economic infrastructure means that state-building is likely to be an arduous, time-consuming, and expensive adventure, and the outcome is going to be uncertain. Will the American public support an open-ended assistance program for

Kosovo, even if the Europeans are putting up much of the energy and resources? What will be the fate of state-building generally if it fails in Kosovo? If state-building cannot succeed (a possibility that cannot be dismissed), does that diminish the role of outside intervention in conflict suppression? Is success in prying the principals apart an adequately lofty objective to produce an acceptable better state of the peace?

There is another problem with achieving the better state of the peace that is manifested in Kosovo. The problem is incompatibility between the political objectives (and thus definition of the better state of the peace) of the intervening party or parties and those of the population on whose behalf the intervention occurs.

The situation in Kosovo illustrates the point. As suggested earlier, there are three possible final outcomes for the Kosovars: total independence from Yugoslavia (with or without union with Albania), total reunification back into Yugoslavia, and a return to the autonomous province position they enjoyed before Milosevic rescinded that status. Total independence is the overwhelming choice of the Albanian Muslim Kosovars and, of course, is equally strongly opposed by the Serbian Kosovars and Yugoslavians. Total reunion is the favored choice of Yugoslavia and the Serbian minority in Kosovo (what little is left of it) and is absolutely unacceptable to the Albanians. The intermediate position (return to autonomy within Yugoslavia) satisfies no one: the Albanian Kosovars do not trust Belgrade not to renege again on such an arrangement, and the Serbs see that status as a short step from secession.

Autonomy for Kosovo within Yugoslavia is precisely the better state of the peace that the United Nations mandate dictates. The apparent idea behind it is that at the end of the state-building process, an economically and politically healthy Kosovo will look across its borders at a Yugoslavia that has shorn itself of the Milosevic regime, has shed its image as a rogue state and joined the general prosperity of Europe, and is thus an attractive partner for Kosovo. All of this may happen; it also may not. If it does not, there may be no better state of the peace acceptable to all involved.

We have already experienced variations of this problem. In Somalia, the American interest was in restored order and the emergence of a stable government. To that end, we tried to find leaders who shared that objective; instead, we found clan leaders like Aidid who were willing to appear to cooperate with us, but only to the extent that the cooperation assisted in his personal claim to power. In Haiti, the local authorities went to some lengths to appear to cooperate with the Americans, but as the last Americans prepared to leave in January 2000, the situation was hardly improved from when we first arrived in 1994.

Crafting a better state of the peace in the internal wars of the post–cold war world is an elusive task, and one for which the historical American experience is only questionably relevant. Our past experience has been in situations that are finite in duration and where reasonably clear objectives could be drawn and translated into a postwar better state of the peace. As the contemporary experience of the country shows, it is not so easy now.

# 11

## The American Experience

The American experience with the use of military force is unique, shaped by history, geography, and a host of other factors, many of which have been discussed in previous chapters. Our task now is to sort through that experience to see what patterns may emerge and what may be learned that can enrich our understanding of the present and guide our encounters with the future. What, in other words, does examination of America's experience with military force tell us about the present and future prospects of employing military force to achieve national ends?

Certain general comments can be made as a preface to a systematic review of the framework that has been employed. The first is the great degree to which our understanding of American military history is enshrouded in mythology partially the result of our ahistoricism. Part of this mythology is our notion of Americans as a pacific people for whom peace is the norm and war is the exception. Rather than seeing peace as an interlude between wars (an attitude held by many Europeans whose history reflects such a view), we tend to look at war as a transgression of our normal circumstance.

The record, of course, does not fully support such a view. As the preceding chapters demonstrate, the United States has been involved in six major wars during its existence (including every major European conflict during our history), as well as three categorized in this work as minor, and a number of smaller recent employments of American force. Even that listing is not inclusive, as it omits actions like the taming of the Barbary pirates (Colonel Qadhafi is not the first Libyan with whom we have tangled), the Seminole War, unconventional engagements against Philippine insurgents, and the various campaigns against both the eastern and western Indians. An inventory of the number of years in which Americans have been at war all or part of the year is a lengthy list that does not comport with any sense of passivity. Yet partially as a result of this myth, Americans tend to treat war as a dirty business (which, of course, in significant ways it is). Americans believe war, when it is thrust upon us, is to be gotten over with as quickly as possible so that we can get back to the more normal business of peace.

There is a second element in the American mythology and that is the myth of our military invincibility. Americans may be slow to anger, so goes the myth, but when we are aroused we are winners. The watchword of the American military is "can do." When called to arms, Americans respond and prevail. The truth is that, although we have usually been militarily successful in the long run and have generally achieved those political purposes for which we have entered hostilities, our record is not unblemished. The United States has not always prevailed militarily (for example, the War of 1812). Realizing the falsity of this myth would help, among other things, to put the Vietnam experience into proper perspective.

Another part of the myth of invincibility is the belief that not only has the United States fought successfully, but that we have fought well in the process. Once again, this assertion does not bear up well under close examination. Rather, at least until the post–World War II period, we have entered wars unprepared to fight them and have either taken a long time to prepare to fight (World War I) or we have fought poorly early in the war while our green troops gained combat experience (the early North African campaign in World War II). Moreover, the American experience can hardly be described as one of great tactical or strategic brilliance. America has produced, after all, no universally recognized great strategist of land warfare, and our style usually has been that of using our superior manpower and weaponry to grind down our enemies' ability to resist. Although our style of warfare has not been pretty or subtle, it has been effective, at least against enemies who played by the same rules. To say these things is not to denigrate the tradition of the American military; it is simply to put it in proper perspective.

There is a second general strand that runs through the American experience, and it is a basic, underlying antimilitary bias. This antimilitarism expresses itself in a suspicion about military solutions to problems, a negative attitude toward maintaining military forces during peacetime, and an aversion to military spending when the country is not at war. The signs that one can occasionally find in New England antique shops that read "no dogs or soldiers allowed" are a part of our heritage.

Antimilitarism was born in the nation's formative days. As argued earlier, the stationing of British troops on American soil was an important link in the chain that led to the American Revolution, and the Continental Congress watched the Army suspiciously throughout the war, fearing it might be used to usurp congressional authority. (This led a frustrated George Washington to remark that he could understand why the Congress might worry about the existence of the Army during peace but not during war.) That fear and suspicion led to a quick disarmament immediately following the Revolution and the virtual absence of any military preparedness until the War of 1812.

The result, through most of American history, has been a pattern of a small professional military establishment during peacetime and rapid mobilization of forces when war occurs. Until World War I, this generally meant the calling of the militia, based on the notion that the "citizen-soldier," valued because he was more citizen than soldier, was an effective fighting man. The evidence, of course, does little to support this notion, which should have died conclusively on the battleground of First Manassas in 1861. The net effect has been that we have entered wars with neither the trained personnel nor equipment to begin hostilities rapidly and successfully.

This particular pattern has, of course, disappeared to some degree since World War II and especially the Korean conflict. For the past near half-century, the United States has maintained a substantial "force in being," prepared to assert itself in a timely fashion when called upon. This state of perpetual preparedness, in addition to being considerably more expensive than the earlier pattern, does represent a discontinuity from America's past.

Our suspicion of the military has influenced the American military as an institution as well. The implicit fear that the military might insert itself into politics has produced a military establishment that has been apolitical and even anti-political in some respects. The apolitical orientation has had both its beneficial and unfortunate consequences. On the positive side of the ledger, civil-military relations are based on the principle of civilian dominance of the military, and that tenet is firmly and fully accepted by the military. Members of the professional military can and often do question the competence of their civilian masters, but they almost never question their authority.

Apoliticism, however, has a price. To be certain that we will have no scheming "man on a white horse," our system has produced a professional officer corps whose background is in engineering (all three of the major service academies are essentially engineering schools). These technicians mechanically learn the so-called science of war (the tactical aspects of conducting combat). That training, however, has underemphasized instruction in military history and international politics that provides the context for military operations (the so-called art of war). The result is a lack of appreciation of the relationship between politics and war that has made the military a poor adviser to political authority on anything other than the technical side of military activity and fails to provide the base for dialogue between military and civilian authorities. (The latter, it might be added, usually have a corresponding ignorance of the science of war.) Part of the reaction within the military after Vietnam was to create a more geopolitically sophisticated officer corps, some of whose members' expertise rivals that of their civilian counterparts.

## Issues and Events

In attempting to generalize from the American experience at war, the central question that must be asked is: What kinds of issues have most and least galvanized the American people as they moved down the road to war? Although any generalization runs the risk of oversimplification and hence of raising the ire of the historian, American military history does suggest a criterion that divides the wars that have had great support from the wars that have not. That criterion is the high moral character that could (or could not) be attached to the issues leading us toward war.

The most popular American military adventures have sprung from issues that were perceived as both absolute and moral in nature. Although there was division within the body politic, the issues of British tyranny and American independence had an absolute and moral character, as did the protection of hearth, home, and way of life for Confederates during the Civil War. The other American wars that were unfailingly popular, the two world wars, were also of this nature. World War I, the "war to end all wars," was fought by Americans to make the world safe for democracy, thus serving the dual interests of ridding the earth of the scourge of war and promoting a morally superior political form. Destroying the total evil of Hitlerian fascism in World War II had a similarly lofty ring that was irresistible once Pearl Harbor had propelled us into that fray; a demonized Saddam Hussein or a vilified Slobadan Milosevic are contemporary cases in point.

By contrast, when issues were perceived as less important or of a lower moral content, there have been divisions in the public that have lessened support for wars. America's first unpopular conflict, the War of 1812, had impressment and de facto independence from Britain as underlying issues, and these issues were of such marginal appeal that New England, which would have benefited from the ending of impressment, actually opposed going to war. Territorial expansion in the Mexican War, tied as it was to the extension-of-slavery issue, generated support only in the West, and Lincoln was burdened throughout the Civil War (as well as the period leading to the war) by Northern apathy about union and emancipation. America's major adventures in Korea and Vietnam, where the issue was the containment (but not rollback and eradication) of communism, similarly had limited appeal.

This moral sense spills over when it comes to proximate events that bring about war. Although it is an arguably accurate self-depiction, we Americans view ourselves as a peace-loving, pacific people who cannot, by our nature, be the initiators of war. The government of Mexico and a number of Indian tribes might well take exception to such a characterization, but this perception does create a need to be attacked in order to produce the sense of moral outrage necessary to push the American people to war. In some cases, our leaders have recognized and even exploited this fact.

A quick review of the American past reinforces this typification. The British march out of Boston to Lexington and Concord (even if no one knows who shot first) became a rallying cry to begin the Revolution. President Lincoln, anxious to quell the rebellion but unwilling to appear to be engaging in aggressive action that would legitimize secession, was forced to wait patiently for the South Carolina militia to fire on Fort Sumter. Despite the war hysteria whipped up by the yellow press, it took the sinking of the USS *Maine* (by persons unknown) to engender the rallying cry in the war against Spain. The German sinking of the *Lusitania* provided impetus in 1916, and there is no better example than the Japanese attack on Pearl Harbor. In more contemporary times, the North Korean invasion of South Korea compelled the United States to enter that conflict; President Johnson used the Gulf of Tonkin incident as the excuse to prosecute the Vietnam War; and Iraq's invasion of Kuwait compelled an American response. Widespread atrocities against populations by their own governments has been a trigger since the end of the Cold War.

## Political Objective

The role of the political objective is absolutely critical in the conduct of war by a democracy, because the objective provides the rallying cry to generate and sustain the public support without which a democracy cannot long fight. The sweep of the American experience suggests that there are four criteria that define a "good" political objective, that is, an objective Americans will support. To the extent that an objective meets all these criteria, it is likely to develop and sustain public support. To the extent an objective violates one or more criteria, it is likely to lead to erosion of public support. The four criteria are: the objective must be simple, straightforward, and unambiguous; it must be morally and politically lofty; it must be overwhelmingly important; and it must be seen to be in the best interest of most Americans.

The first criterion says that a good political objective can be easily understood by everyone. Ideally, the objective should be reducible to a catchphrase or slogan that both captures the essence of the main objective and serves as a rallying cry (e.g., "Remember the *Maine*" as a way to simplify assumed

Spanish perfidy). The second criterion, following on the earlier discussion, suggests that a good objective can be turned into a crusade that appeals to our moral sense ("Make the world safe for democracy"). The third criterion means that the attainment of the objective must be vital to the United States and failure to attain it disastrous. This criterion would be best exemplified in the situation where losing a war would physically endanger the integrity of American soil, and the only example in our history was the Southern side in the Civil War (the British threat in 1814 was more limited). The fourth criterion, of most importance when there were still great sectional differences between Americans, refers to the need for a majority of groups to view the objective as important. In contemporary times, the third and fourth criteria can be merged into a single criterion of perceived self-interest.

The critical importance of an appropriate objective can be demonstrated by looking at which American wars violated which criteria. The criterion of simplicity is rather clearly violated in three instances: Vietnam, Korea, and the War of 1812. As argued earlier, the problem of the objective in Vietnam was, at least partially, that average Americans did not understand why their country was at war, and the various means that were used to try to convince them (the Munich analogy and the domino theory) provided neither clarity nor simplicity to aid understanding. In Korea, the problem was not in understanding objectives but in knowing which was operative at any point in time. Freeing South Korea was straightforward enough, as was liberating the entire Korean peninsula. What was not so clear was why and when the objectives changed. In the War of 1812, the agendas of impressment (an issue, of course, resolved before war was declared) and of annexing Canada (either as a "bargaining chip" to end naval harassment or to expand the United States) were similarly confusing.

The criterion of moral loftiness has been even more often abused, with at least five instances from the historical record when one could question the moral force of the objective. The first instance was the War of 1812, when the morality of seizing Canada was particularly questionable. In the Mexican War, manifest destiny was but a thin disguise for naked American aggression and seizure of sovereign Mexican territory. One of Lincoln's recurring difficulties was convincing his countrymen that forceful union and then union plus abolition were worthy of their support and blood. In the twentieth century, the principle has arguably been violated twice: in the Korean and Vietnam wars. In Korea, the problem was not associated with the original and eventual objective of containing North Korea but with not liberating it from "godless communism." If the evil was sufficiently dire to require the sacrifices of war, then it should be exorcised, not simply contained. In Vietnam, this sort of dilemma was combined with our support for a succession of either venal or incompetent South Vietnamese governments.

The third criterion reflects the importance (worth) to national security of attaining the objective. As pointed out, this kind of objective is always somewhat difficult for a government that fights primarily in an expeditionary manner, when the physical security of hearth and home is not directly in jeopardy and when threats to the homeland are abstract extrapolations from the situation at hand. In fact, the only American war experience in which territorial integrity was really at issue was the Confederate side in the Civil War. Support for the Rebel cause was quite high among Southerners throughout the long conflict.

The question of worth has been raised as a significant concern in four American wars—two in the nineteenth century and two in the twentieth. In the nineteenth century, the question was raised in both the War of 1812 and about Union conduct of the Civil War. Whatever its feasibility, annexing Canada was not a major priority for most Americans, and the naval harassment issue affected only a small slice of the population, mainly in New England. Much of Lincoln's problem in maintaining support for his war effort arose from the fact that many Northerners did not care whether the South seceded or not, or at least did not think preventing secession was worth fighting over.

The necessity of achieving the objective has been questioned significantly in the twentieth century during both the Korean and Vietnam wars. In the case of Korea, the importance of "merely" ridding South Korea of its North Korean invaders was widely questioned, but only the second time this objective was adopted. At that point, the war had become a static contest of attrition about the 38th parallel, and the war seemed increasingly pointless and worthless. In Vietnam, a principal burden of American officials was trying to convince the American people that there was something about the outcome worth our involvement and our sacrifice. Those attempts were ultimately unsuccessful, and it may be one of the ironies of Vietnam that our participation was truly not worthwhile, since it can be argued that US vital interests were hardly affected by the outcome. The emergence of "humanitarian interests" suggests a reassessment of what constitutes a worthy cause, but whether those interests justify much American sacrifice in blood remains an open question.

The final criterion is the perceived vitality of the objective to most Americans. In the nineteenth century, when this most often was a problem, the divisions of Americans tended to be along sectional lines that have largely disappeared as an important factor in US foreign policy. During the twentieth century Americans have been more divided by political philosophies, demographic classifications, or socioeconomic factors. Extended to cover these newer divisions, the fourth criterion is still valid.

Using this slightly extended definition, three wars immediately come to mind as violating the criterion. The first two were in the nineteenth century and involved sectional differences. In the War of 1812, the war was opposed by New Englanders because they feared the result would be to destroy New England's commerce with Europe. Support was greatest, ironically, in the South and along the frontier. These sections would not have benefited directly from the achievement of the war's objectives, but they nonetheless produced most of the War Hawks. Similarly, the Mexican War was popular only in the Midwest and the West. It was opposed in New England on the grounds that it was a ploy by Tennessean Polk to extend slave territories, and it was opposed in the South on the grounds that the additional territories were unsuited for the plantation system. The Vietnam War similarly divided Americans along political lines (liberals in general opposition, conservatives in support) and along demographic lines (the young, college-aged middle and upper-middle classes in greater opposition to the war than the lower, less-educated classes).

A pattern of the kinds of political objectives that the American people will and will not support for a sustained period of time emerges, especially if one adds two considerations—the limited or total nature of the objective and the physical duration of active fighting (and hence dying) by Americans. The latter distinction is made because the period of combat is a better indication of sacrifice and deprivation than is overall length of a war. World War I, when we were technically at war for over a year and a half but engaged in combat for less than six months, illustrates this point most dramatically.

These two criteria are added to make more explicit a hypothesis about the objective that has until now been somewhat implicit: political democracies support long wars entailing sacrifice better if they are total in purpose rather than limited. Hence if a limited purpose is to be pursued, the war should be relatively short and painless (which, in contemporary terms, appears to mean the absence of American casualties).

The reasons for this assertion follow from the statement of criteria for a good objective. Total objectives aimed at removing an evil regime (a Hitler) easily meet the criteria of simplicity, moral loftiness, worth, and general interest. Limited wars, on the other hand, do not seek to exorcise some overwhelming evil (hence being questionably lofty). They are generally fought for some geopolitical reason that is questionably important or straightforward (hence violating worth and simplicity) or which affects the average American to the extent that the dynastic wars of the eighteenth century affected the average French peasant (violating general interest).

These concerns suggest some observations about the role of the political objective. The first thing one notices is the sharp contrast between the wars of total and limited purpose. With the exception of the Union side in the

Civil War, all of the violations of the criteria occur in the justification of limited wars. Moreover, in general there appears to be no particular relationship between total and limited wars in terms of duration. In terms of actual combat, the total wars average out to a little over three years in duration, but so do the limited wars. Where duration is of interest is within the category of limited wars; the only one that violated none of the criteria (or at least where the salience of it all was not raised) was Teddy Roosevelt's splendid little war against Spain, the active military conduct of which spanned barely three months and which resulted in minor American casualties.

What is particularly striking about grouping the wars this way is the relationship of the criteria to the wars' popularity. The most popular of America's wars have been total, with the exception of the war with Spain. Certainly the world wars were the most popular in American history, followed closely by the Confederate side in the Civil War. One can argue that the majority of Americans were not steadfast in their support of the Revolution, but revolutions rarely have anything like majority support. There was opposition in the Union to the Civil War, but that may be at least partially the result of the shock of the consequences of modern total war and the ineptitude of early Union military leadership.

By contrast, America's least popular wars have been limited in purpose. The two most unpopular clearly were Vietnam and 1812, which also share the distinction of violating all the criteria for a successful objective. The Korean conflict comes in third on the list of violations, but it may also best illustrate the point about what kinds of wars the American public will and will not sustain.

As was argued at the time, the problem in Korea was the way the objective changed. The Korean adventure could, however, have been popular in one of two circumstances. The first, as already argued, would have been if UN forces had stopped at the 38th parallel the first time (in September 1950), dictated peace terms to a North Korea that would have had little choice but to accept them, declared the mission accomplished, and come home. Most troops (except for garrison defenders) would have been home by Christmas, and the war would have been short and victorious, to be remembered as something like the war with Spain. The other way would have been not to return to the original objective when the United Nations drove the North Koreans and Chinese back to the 38th parallel in disarray the second time. In that case, the objective would have been the total one of uniting the peninsula. Presuming that uniting the peninsula would not have aroused a further Chinese or Soviet military response, it might have been accomplished.

These two possible outcomes point to the kinds of wars Americans like to fight: either wars of total purpose or limited wars that are bounded in time and by the sacrifices associated with their conduct. If this is the case and Americans have had and will continue to have difficulty sustaining support for other kinds of wars, this has important implications for the future application of American military force.

## Military Objectives and Strategy

The military objectives sought by American armed forces have varied widely during the American experience, as have the strategies used to seek them. It was not until the Civil War that US forces fought for unlimited objectives, best described as destroying the enemy's ability to resist. Military objectives during the American Revolution were time dependent and limited, ranging from throwing the British out, to preventing the British return, to achieving a decisive battlefield victory, and finally to preserving the Continental army until the peace treaty was signed. The objectives in both the War of 1812 and the Mexican War were limited and circumscribed, as were the military and political objectives during the Spanish-American War.

Even in the Civil War, one set of Americans in that awful struggle was pursuing limited military and political objectives: the Confederates sought to convince the federal government that the price of union would be too high in blood and treasure. The political objective was not to destroy the government in Washington, but rather to end its authority in one part of the former Union. The Union's political and military objectives, on the other hand, were unlimited: the North had to destroy the Confederate ability to resist and the Confederacy itself if the Union was to endure.

It was out of this savage struggle to preserve the Union that an enduring American military tradition evolved. Since 1864 the favored American military strategy has followed the tradition of Ulysses S. Grant during his campaign in northern Virginia. Grant's method was simply to take advantage of the North's superior resources and overwhelm the Army of Northern Virginia. The strategy was to attack relentlessly, giving Robert E. Lee and his forces no rest. Grant could replace losses from his vast manpower pool for which the South had no equivalent.The Grant tradition was somewhat apparent in World War I but became predominant in World War II, when the United States figuratively drowned its enemies in a sea of men, firepower, superior technology, and logistics.

The unlimited objectives of the Union and overwhelming strategy of Grant dominated the memories of Americans. The total, brutal style of warfare begun by Grant and practiced in the world wars became the American way of war. Thus, when limited war took center stage during the cold war, Americans seemed to forget the much larger part of their military heritage—limited wars fought for limited purposes. The traditions of U.S. Grant did not apply well in Korea and Vietnam. With the shadow of nuclear weapons hanging over the battlefield, unlimited war came to mean potential nuclear holocausts. The world was no longer safe for conventional wars waged to total victory in the Grant tradition.

Frustration with the new era of limited war became very high in the US military, perhaps most dramatically exemplified by the confrontation between President Truman and Gen MacArthur during the Korean War. Frustration erupted again during the Vietnam War as the military cried out against being forced to fight with "one arm tied behind its back." From the end of the Vietnam conflict to the end of the cold war, the military continued to struggle to come to terms with this problem.

By 1991 the cold war was over and the threat of escalation to nuclear confrontation had receded. The stage was set for a return to the Grant tradition in the Gulf War. The trip back to that tradition seemed complete when the Iraqi forces were totally overwhelmed by US and Coalition numbers, firepower, technology, and logistics. The only thing that saved the Iraqi government was that the war was fought for limited political objectives. But even if the political outcome was not as overwhelming as some would have wished, it seemed that the tradition of US Grant had regained center stage in military operations.

But on the heel of Desert Storm came Somalia and the other instances of humanitarian intervention described in Chapter 10. In one sense the military clung to Grant; rather than deploying a small, lightly armed peacekeeping force, the American force was large and heavily armed. Otherwise, the operation in Somalia (and after) was anything but Grant-like. Little was done to disarm the militias and the top priority appeared to be the prevention of US casualties. Even this objective could not be sustained when the United States left and then returned to the country and suffered 18 dead in an ambush of Rangers in Mogadishu. In the angry public reaction to the corpse of an American serviceman being dragged through the streets of Mogadishu, it became clear that force protection would be a major priority in the future. This thread of strategy and objective continued through the rules of engagement for the air campaign in Kosovo (Operation Allied Force).

## Political Considerations

As the discussions in each chapter have tried to demonstrate, domestic and international concerns, which are primarily political in character, inevitably affect and are affected by the conduct of war. Although this statement is unexceptional and even self-evident, American military and civilian officials have often acted as if this Clausewitzian dictum did not exist. The problem is much more severe in limited-war situations than it is in instances of total war.

Total war tends to lessen the friction between the military and civilian authorities. This is so to some measure because a total war calls for maximum military effort, thereby lessening the politically defined shackles on the conduct of hostilities. At that, political considerations enter even into total-war situations. Grant, during the climactic 1864–65 campaign against Lee's Army of Northern Virginia, tried to obscure the reportage of the large number of casualties he was incurring for fear that public opinion would be adversely affected. In World War II, a central disagreement between the Americans and the British was whether the war should be fought against Germany primarily with an eye on the earliest possible destruction of the Nazi armies or whether the shape of the postwar political map should be the overriding concern.

These kinds of considerations are mild compared to military-civilian frictions during limited wars, and especially the limited wars of the second half of the twentieth century. As Clausewitz pointed out, war tends to feed on itself and thus expand and intensify. When military objectives, strategy, and resulting combat are constrained because political objectives are limited, the basis for friction exists. To some extent, a limited objective inevitably means that the military will fight with less than its total capacity, with "one arm tied behind its back." This is especially true as technology has increased the lethality of war machines. Political constraints against the military using all its resources are generally motivated by a fear of widening the war and transforming its objectives in the process. In a world where the ultimate transformation could be to total war with thermonuclear weapons, constraints are likely to be tight indeed.

Aspects of both Korea and Vietnam illustrate this problem and the frustration and friction that inevitably emerge. In retrospect the problem has at times been almost comical. An extreme instance is the instruction to US pilots during the Korean War to bomb only the southern half of bridges spanning the Yalu River to avoid attacking Chinese territory and consequently altering fundamentally the nature of the war. The instruction created an impossible task for the military, which became frustrated and angry because of this political "interference."

A more general and vexing problem that arose in both Korea and Vietnam was sanctuary. Sanctuaries were areas to which enemy forces could retire without danger of attack because the areas were off-limits to American military efforts. In the Korean War, the People's Republic of China was the sanctuary. It was not attacked for fear of starting a general Asiatic war that military wisdom said should be avoided and which would have tied down so many American forces as to invite Soviet activity in Europe. In the Vietnam War, the most important sanctuaries were those parts of North Vietnam on the proscribed list for American bombers during most of the struggle, especially Hanoi and Haiphong. The reason for making sanctuaries of Haiphong and Hanoi was to avoid sinking Soviet or Chinese ships and thus to avoid drawing either or both into the war. At the same time, placing these areas off-limits made it impossible to attack the conduit of war materiel that substituted for an industrial web in North Vietnam.

What these examples show is that political restrictions placed upon the military in limited wars make the effective prosecution of hostilities more difficult. Politically motivated constraints probably make such wars last longer and reduce the likelihood of winning by some degree, but one of the lessons of the American contemporary experience is that such dynamics are a fact of life.

Interference (if that is the proper term) of this kind is absolutely predictable. Anyone surprised that political authorities imposed limitations on the military in Vietnam was ignoring the Korean experience (which the military as an institution largely did, a process generally replicated over Vietnam). The sanctuary example may best make the point. Some observers of Vietnam have concluded that the American military should not allow itself to be placed in another combat situation where the enemy is unilaterally granted a sanctuary because the military task is too greatly compromised. From a military viewpoint, such a conclusion makes perfect sense. At the same time, a look at a world map does not reveal many places where American military assertion would not raise the possibility that sanctuaries would be granted for fear of broadening the war.

The other largely domestic political consideration, to which allusion was made in a previous section, is the question of public support for hostilities. Public support is absolutely necessary if a democracy is to conduct war. The problem is that there are influences that almost automatically erode the support for a war. Two of these are worth raising and considering.

The first has to do with the distinction between wars of total and limited purpose. As noted in the section on political objective, wars of total purpose have been generally more popular than limited wars because they arouse our moral zeal and seem to provide adequate reason for the sacrifices that war entails. The problem, of course, is that there is only one total war the United States could have fought since World War II, and that was a likely nuclear World War III against the former Soviet Union. Such a war rather clearly would have been unacceptable. Limited wars, on the other hand, are often ambiguous and debatable in merit and tend to lose support as they lengthen or as they exact increasing sacrifices, especially in American blood. Does that mean we can fight no more wars (is that the meaning of "no more Vietnams")? Or does it mean that future wars will have to be so short and decisive that the public will not have time to turn against them? Or does it mean the avoidance of casualties will become a major goal as it did in Kosovo?

The second influence is the news media, especially the electronic medium (television). The major effect of television was first felt in the Vietnam War, which was transformed into a "living-room war" that simply could not be avoided because it covered the screen every evening. Television, by bringing pictures into our living rooms, personalizes war in a way the printed word cannot. It is one thing, for instance, to read about how many casualties there were in a firefight; it is quite another to have the maimed bodies flashed on your television screen. Moreover, television specializes in the dramatic visual impression rather than contemplative, in-depth analysis (the ideal television spot is about 45 seconds long). Thus, television has difficulty depicting the complexity of what is going on in war. What it emphasizes are the dramatic aspects, especially acts of violence.

The impact of all this, and especially global television, on the conduct of war is not well known, and sadly, there is little definitive research in this area. At one level, at least, the effect is to deglamorize war by showing its most raw and most destructive manifestations. The result is to make electronic coverage of war at least implicitly pacifistic. War has always been most glamorous to those who have never seen it, and the television camera guarantees that everyone—not just the participants—sees what war looks like. The almost inevitable result is that television coverage erodes support for physical hostilities to the extent it is allowed unfettered coverage of combat. At the same time, publicity about great suffering in places such as Somalia, Bosnia, and Kosovo has made military action more appealing. It may also be that relentless coverage of carnage desensitizes us to it and increases our tolerance for atrocity. The jury is still out on the influence of the electronic media.

Two international considerations emerge from the American experience. The first of these is the interdependence of America with the rest of the world, especially Europe. Although Americans have thought of themselves as independent and aloof from the affairs of Europe, such clearly has not been the case. A critical element in the birth of this country was the direct alliance with France and the indirect alliance with Spain, the Netherlands, and Tsarist Russia (the latter two through the League of Armed Neutrality). In the case of each "ally," the motivation to aid the revolutionary cause was solely geopolitical in nature, an attempt to get even with Britain because of the outcome of the Seven Years' War. For that matter, the issue of taxation, which had its roots in the stationing of British troops in the colonies after the

French and Indian wars, was but an outgrowth of the war in Europe that had strained the British economy and forced Lord Richard Grenville to look for alternate sources of revenue.

American interdependence was also demonstrated during the Civil War. Until the battle of Antietam, the Confederacy conducted a lively courtship of Britain and France that was opposed by the US government, and the failure of the Confederate States of America to gain European recognition and succor may have been critical to the eventual Southern failure. Likewise, the government of the United States, despite its best efforts at neutrality, became involved in the European wars that punctuated the nineteenth and twentieth centuries. Our War of 1812 was nothing more than the New World theater of the Napoleonic Wars, and US involvement was made necessary by our commercial interests. Similarly, recognition that a German-dominated Europe would be intolerable for American commercial efforts made our attempts to remain neutral in World War I futile. When the second great conflagration came about, our instinct toward aloofness was rapidly drowned in the necessity of avoiding a permanent German victory on the continent.

After World War II, the United States recognized this interdependence by making the longest and most extensive and expensive peacetime military commitment in our history, the North Atlantic Treaty Organization (NATO). NATO remains the keystone of American defense posture, but its future outside Europe (e.g., in other than the Balkans) remains problematical. Maintaining the independence of Western Europe is clearly America's most vital defense interest, after the defense of the American homeland.

Problems of the alliance point to the second international political concern that has arisen in the twentieth century, the problem of coalition warfare. The United States has fought two real coalition wars—the world wars—in which there were significant contributions by several states, each of which had somewhat different political objectives. (Although Vietnam, Korea, and Desert Storm were technically coalition wars, the United States dominated to such an extent that our objectives were those of the coalition.) In both cases, objectives have been at least partially compromised. In World War I, Wilson's vision of the peace lost to Georges Clemenceau's punitive vision, with the detrimental effect of paving the way to the second global war. In World War II, the Americans overrode Churchill's greater concern for the postwar map, which allowed the Soviets to capture more territory than they might have otherwise. Both cases point to the historical deficiencies of Americans as geopoliticians. If these instances are a guide, one might hope for a more geopolitical orientation by Americans in a future where involvements in enterprises such as humanitarian interventions will almost always be coalition efforts.

## Military Technology and Technique

A constant trend throughout military history has been the increasing power and destructive efficiency of weapons. The change over 200 years of American history is stark, ranging from inaccurate and unreliable smoothbore muskets to highly accurate nuclear-tipped intercontinental ballistic missiles and laser-guided "smart bombs." Although these weapons represent extremes of the spectrum, advances in firepower, accuracy, and range can be found in every category of weapons.

The impact of increased lethality has been both dramatic and multifaceted. The most obvious and dramatic impact has been in the general destructiveness of war. In the American Revolution, damage was limited to the immediate battlefield, and total casualties to both sides were minimal. By World War II, casualties numbered in the tens of millions, many of whom were noncombatants killed and injured as whole cities were laid waste.

The fact that cities were destroyed in wholesale lots brings home the fact that traditional "home fronts" are now on the front lines because of the range and distinctiveness of modern weapons. Worse, perhaps, the home front has been rationalized as a legitimate military target because of the importance of industrial production to the prosecution of modern warfare. Although naval blockades have indirectly attacked the home front for centuries as a method of producing strife and inconvenience, modern strategists can directly target home front industrial capacity as a central part of the overall war effort.

Bombs falling from the sky, whether they fall on industrial plants or troops in the field, typify the impersonal nature of modern war caused by the increased range and firepower of weapons. Modern warfare is a far cry from battles of mounted knights in the Middle Ages. Modern warfare is also far different from eighteenth-century warfare, in which linear formations often fired one volley and then pressed the battle home with the bayonet. Hand-to-hand fighting still takes place in modern war, but the range and accuracy of modern weapons place most of the killing at a distance. Technology has eliminated "waiting until you see the whites of their eyes"; so also it has eliminated some of the perceived glory of combat. This trend reached an epitome of sorts in the electronic "shooting gallery" during the Persian Gulf War.

Although further increases in the range and accuracy of weapons can be expected, we may be near the end of useful increases in firepower, at least in terms of the largest and most dangerous of man's weapons. Many would argue that the firepower of thermonuclear weapons is so great that they are, in effect, unusable. Man's inventive genius has turned its attention to weapons whose energies are far more adaptable to precise and concentrated application, thus eliminating the unwanted "collateral damage" and dangerous side effects of multimegaton thermonuclear devices.

Whatever the future of weapons development, the increased lethality of today's weapons has been accompanied by several technological trends. The first is that increases in range, accuracy, and firepower have been paid for by increased complexity. Even today's most common weapon is an engineering marvel compared with earlier versions of the same type of weapon. As examples, compare the Revolutionary War musket with the modern infantry assault carbine or the biplane of World War I with the modern supersonic jet fighter.

Second, complex weapons are generally much more costly to produce than simple weapons. They are more expensive both in terms of absolute cost and in terms of the time required to design, perfect, and produce them. Combined with economic limitations, these cost factors result in a dilemma known in the United States as the "quality-versus-quantity" quandary. In short, the dilemma deals with the issue of whether it is more prudent to buy a small number of highly lethal but expensive weapons or a large number of less effective but cheaper weapons.

A third major technological trend in American military history has been the steady mechanization of warfare. Until the Civil War, the American military was powered by muscle and wind. In that great struggle, steam power began to replace both muscle and wind, and the trend in mechanization accelerated from that time to the present. The impact of mechanization has been staggering. Perhaps the greatest single effect has been to make warfare three-dimensional. The development of the internal combustion engine and its subsequent application to aircraft added a new dimension to warfare. The airplane added mobility and flexibility to armed forces, shrank distances, brought the home front to the front lines, and vastly complicated the problems of and increased the possibilities for military commanders.

Mechanization has also speeded the pace and scope of war. Armies on wheels and tracks move many miles a day and arrive ready for combat. Often the secret to survival in battle, whether on land, on the sea, or in the air is speed of movement. Thus, modern tanks can travel and shoot at 30 to 40 miles per hour, modern submarines travel submerged at speeds as fast as World War II surface combatants, and modern aircraft fly and fight at supersonic speeds. Mechanization has meant that military power can be projected within minutes over great ranges.

The fourth major technological trend is the most recent. The electronic age has come to the battlefield, a trend that gathered speed in the Vietnam War and has reached the point where weapon systems now rely on miniaturized solid-state electronics. "Smart" bombs, laser designators, infrared homing devices, beam-riding missiles, computerized fire control systems, and other sophisticated electronic devices have become commonplace in the arsenals of modern military powers. Computer-aided management systems have become the standard in personnel and logistic systems. Sophisticated computer-driven training devices allow realistic training even with the most expensive weapon systems, and computer-driven war games are used to educate and train military officers. In addition, electronic warfare in the form of intelligence gathering and communications jamming has become an important area of conflict. All of these capabilities were prominently displayed in the Persian Gulf War and to a less comprehensive extent, Operation Allied Force over Kosovo and Yugoslavia.

What conclusions can be drawn from advances in the technology of war during the American experience? Perhaps the most obvious conclusion is that modern warfare has become a very complex and expensive undertaking. War now emphasizes the importance of the economic base to national defense and, within the economy, the importance of the heavy industrial and technological bases. However, in spite of the importance of technological innovation in the conduct of America's wars, superior technology has never been the decisive factor in any American war. The struggle to use technology effectively and to cope with enemy technology has been much more important.

Until recently, superior technology on the battlefield has rarely been the decisive factor in war for at least four reasons. First, technological advantage is incremental, affecting the margins of combat capability. The technological gap between contending forces tends to be small and, although the gap can be important in a battle, it is generally not large enough to be the decisive factor in the outcome of a war. The gaps are also often quickly filled. Technological advances are based on known physical properties that can often be duplicated quickly by the enemy. As a result, any given technological advantage tends to be short lived.

Second, how technology is used is as important as the technology itself. Possession of superior technology does not mean that its advantages will be exploited effectively. The story of military technique is the story of attempting to use technology in the most effective manner. The rifled weapons of the Civil War caused significant changes in infantry tactics, but not until bloody lessons had been learned at such places as Fredericksburg. In World War I, it took more than two years to determine how to use the tank effectively. In World War II, the effectiveness of strategic bombing was hindered by our search for the vital industrial targets whose destruction would cripple Germany and by diversions of strategic bombing forces to nonstrategic roles.

Third, the side with the less developed technology seeks methods to negate the advantage of superior technology by obtaining weapons of equal power, by constructing effective defenses, and by using superior strategy and tactics. Perhaps this was best demonstrated in the Vietnam conflict. Guerrilla tactics tended to negate the effects of superior American firepower by eliminating lucrative targets for that firepower. At a different level, the North Vietnamese were able to obtain the ground-to-air missiles and antiaircraft artillery necessary to produce an effective defense against American air power. Finally, our Vietnamese enemies were able to obtain weapons equal to our own at least at the level of the combat infantryman.

The fourth reason that superior technology is often not decisive is that for political reasons it is not used to its full extent. This has become evident in the post–World War II era as American political leadership has attempted to prevent the spread and escalation of American wars. For example, in Korea and Vietnam we did not use all the weapons at our disposal, nuclear weapons being the most obvious example. For the same sorts of political reasons, the use of weapons that were employed has been circumscribed. In Korea and Vietnam, the enemy was provided sanctuary areas immune from the effects of our superior technology.

Desert Storm would appear to be, at first glance, an exception to the rule. The success of such high-technology weapons as precision-guided munitions, night vision devices, and low-observable technology (stealth) was important to the performance of Coalition forces in that struggle. It was a decisive factor in the sense that it made the conflict much shorter than it otherwise would have been, and undoubtedly spared the spilling of much Coalition blood in the desert. It was not decisive in the sense that without the high-technology weaponry, the Coalition in all probability still would have been successful. The Iraqis used their considerable arsenal of high-technology weaponry very poorly, reemphasizing the point that possession of such weapons does not mean that they will be exploited effectively.

The ability to produce and field sophisticated weapons that provide great firepower combined with the tradition of overwhelming our enemies has produced a significant trend in twentieth-century American military technique. Modern American strategists and tacticians have sought to substitute fire and steel for American blood. Strategic bombing in World War II was an attempt to find a way to victory that would minimize American bloodshed. Harry Truman's rationale for using nuclear weapons against Japan was based, at least in part, on the desire to save lives that would have been lost had American forces invaded the Japanese home islands. In Korea, and particularly in Vietnam, fire delivered by artillery and aircraft was constantly used to reduce our casualties in infantry operations. "Indirect fires" were used so extensively that some military analysts worry that the US Army became overly dependent on such capability. The Persian Gulf War, once again, is the most vivid example of this trend.

## Military Conduct

Numerous factors, the most important of which have been discussed in earlier sections of this chapter, affect the conduct of war. However, there are several subjects that should be addressed in terms of synthesizing the American experience in military conduct. Recent American experiences in war—Korea and Vietnam—have brought to light two major misconceptions about the American military experience and have led to considerable frustration and debate. The first of these misconceptions concerns the types of wars Americans have fought.

In both Korea and Vietnam, heated debate arose over political limitations placed on the military conduct of those wars. There was much hue and cry over forcing the military to "fight with one hand tied behind its back" and demands to "turn the military loose." Critics pointed to World War II as the traditional and proper model for American military conduct. However, part of the American tradition is one of war fought with limited means. Of the wars covered in this volume, only three—the Civil War and the two world wars—were conflicts in which the nation was mobilized and the military was "turned loose."

The second misconception centers on the involvement of civilian authorities in conducting warfare. Many critics have decried the tendency of the American civilian leadership to become directly involved in the details of conducting military campaigns, rather than leaving the conduct of the war to the military professionals. The most famous incident of this type was the confrontation between General MacArthur and President Truman during the Korean conflict. The debate reached its peak during the Vietnam War and centered around control of the aerial bombardment campaign by the White House.

To a large extent, the protests over civilian control are made in ignorance of American military tradition. As has been pointed out in this book, civilian control over military campaigns has been the rule rather than the exception in American military history. In the Mexican War, Polk ordered field commanders to start and stop their campaigns based on his personal political motives. In the Civil War, Lincoln played musical chairs with his generals and at one time took responsibility for the defense of Washington, D.C., during the Peninsular Campaign. In 1898 William McKinley took a personal hand in directing preparations for a war from a newly installed White House "war room." Of course, Korea and the confrontation between MacArthur and Truman provided an immediate foretaste of the close political control exercised in Vietnam. Only the two world wars seem to offer exception to the general trend. But even in World War II, political considerations determined the overall shape of the military effort and often overruled the desires of military leaders.

The trend toward close civilian control accelerated during the cold war. This acceleration was a product of traditional civilian control, of the fear of escalation to nuclear war, and of the increased capacity for close control provided by instantaneous worldwide communications. Korea and the MacArthur–Truman confrontation provided an immediate foretaste of the close political control exercised in Vietnam. The selection of bombing targets by the "Tuesday Lunch Group" in Washington, D.C., gradual escalation of the bombing campaign, and bombing pauses were typical of the close civilian control exercised during the Vietnam War. Desert Storm appeared, at first glance, to change the long-standing trend, because it appeared that the civilian leadership stayed out of the planning and conduct of the war. In reality, there was an enormous amount of interplay between the senior civilian and military leadership in Washington and the American forces in the Gulf region. Plans were presented, amended, and approved at the highest policy levels before they were implemented. During the actual campaign, overbearing civilian "interference" did not hamper Gulf War commanders, because potential problems were addressed and resolved before the fact.

By the time Allied Force was launched against Serbia in 1999, it was clear that in NATO operations, the political leadership was going to be firmly in charge. The North Atlantic Council maintained very tight control over target selection and the intensity of aerial attacks, much to the frustration of many military leaders, particularly airmen. Each of the 19 NATO countries could veto attacks on a given target, and some of the NATO states exercised that right. Some analysts might argue that the tight control in Allied Force was civilian control run amok (the argument made about Vietnam). Knowledgeable Americans, on the other hand, knew that for better or worse, the tight political controls in Allied Force fit well with the long-standing American tradition.

The "overwhelming" approach of U.S. Grant combined with a love of high technology defines the preferred American method for conducting military operations. An overwhelmingly high-tech military force is the American ideal. The combination of overwhelming force and technology produces a view of war somewhat akin to an engineering project and a resource management exercise. The secret to success, in this view, is to apply overwhelming resources (numbers and technology) efficiently. This engineering approach to war served the United States well when the enemy was a modern military power who fought in the same general style. But the Vietnam experience demonstrated that clever, asymmetrical strategies can negate the advantage of overwhelming resources and high technology. Part of that lesson included the corollary that victory on the battlefield does not necessarily translate into victory in war. Although American arms were nearly always victorious in battle and inflicted far more damage than the enemy was able to inflict, the outcome of the war was determined by a myriad of other factors, particularly the impact of the war on home front morale. War is a complex struggle between rival societies and battle is only its most obvious and deadly manifestation.

Finally, in the latter half of the 1990s, two military operations were conducted by American forces (with NATO allies) almost entirely through the use of airpower. Both Deliberate Force and Allied Force were aerial bombing campaigns, and in the case of Allied force political leaders ruled out a ground campaign even as the air campaign was getting underway. Some observers have extrapolated from these cases that airpower had become the preferred military instrument of American policy makers. While probably overstated, the advantages of airpower seemed obvious. Airpower was somehow more detached, less directly involved, and less likely to lead to large numbers of friendly casualties. Airpower did not signal the same depth of commitment as ground troops in harm's way. These qualities, it seemed, were especially beneficial for contingencies on the peripheries of American interests. If this were the case and airpower had become the preferred coin of the realm for actual combat operations by the United States, what would be the impact on the organization, structure, roles, and mission of American military services? What would be the impact on American allies in future conflicts, especially circumstances where "muddy boots" operations on the ground by *someone* are clearly necessary? Would air power reign in "target-poor" environments in the third world? Will future opponents learn how to negate the effects of airpower? These are all difficult politico-military questions rooted in the American conception of modern military conduct.

### Better State of the Peace

The period since the end of World War II and especially since the end of our involvement in Southeast Asia has been wrenching for Americans in terms of their relationship to armed violence. We entered the second world conflict as a geopolitical babe in arms and emerged as the world's most powerful state, with international responsibilities that simply could not be shirked. The United States was a superpower and had to learn to act like one. Part of the responsibility was learning to employ the military instrument of power in a way that would serve American national interests. We are still struggling with the problem.

Part of the reason for this difficulty, of course, is America's relative inexperience in the geopolitical game. Historically buffered from the realities of international power politics and having the luxury of never having to develop a tradition wherein the military played a prominent part, we have considered military force something of a novelty. For Americans war has been an abnormality that occasionally intruded on the more normal condition of peace, and it has not been viewed as just another instrument of political power.

Our learning process has been made more wrenching and difficult because of at least two other factors. On one hand, there is the radical transformation of the political power map of the world since 1945. The traditional European world powers have been relegated to regional status, and in their place only two military superpowers—the United States and the Soviet Union—could take their place. With the demise of the former Soviet Union, only one superpower remains. At the same time, the introversion of Europe has accelerated the processes of nationalism in former colonies in Africa and Asia. The international system of 1945 that consisted of about 60 states now encompasses more than 190, and many of these new states are sources of instability and competition between the East and the West. The role of the United States in this evolving environment remains in transition, as does the system itself.

On the other hand, technology—which has steadily expanded the range, accuracy, and firepower of weapons since the early nineteenth century—has transformed the means of war to the point that the ends may have been changed fundamentally as well. Nuclear weapons are the obvious apex of this process and raise the basic question of whether any political objective can be achieved by military means when nuclear weapons might be used. At a somewhat less dramatic level, so-called conventional weaponry has also changed so that making nonnuclear war is both considerably more dangerous (there are, for instance, chemical explosives whose effects are indistinguishable from those of a nuclear blast except for the absence of radiation) and more expensive to conduct.

The result of all this may be to transform the kinds of political objectives for which military force can be employed, forcing us back to an age of limited warfare and hence better states of the peace defined on a different model than that of the world wars. Warfare fought for total political purposes and employing total means may simply have gotten too dangerous and too expensive to wage.

There is a certain irony in all this. In earlier eras, political purposes had to be limited because the means available for conducting war were too modest for anything else. It may be that now the tables are turned: War may have to be limited in its purposes because the means are too great to be sensibly employed for anything but circumscribed ends. There will probably never be another amphibious assault of the nature and grandeur of Normandy, partly because the firepower available to the defenders would make the attempt suicidal but also partially because the objectives that would give rise to such an effort would probably result in escalation beyond any controllable and politically meaningful level.

There, of course, is the rub. We have, over the five and a half decades since the end of World War II, done a splendid job of preparing to fight the next total war, but our preparations have been so thorough and complete that we can no longer contemplate fighting that for which we are ready. Countless millions of dollars have gone into the preparation, but conducting the war would probably mean the end of civilization as we know it. The reemergence of ideology as the cause of war that began with the American Revolution has given us the motivation and issues for World War III; our means have gotten so far beyond those ends as to render the prospect meaningless.

Since it is difficult to envisage a better state of the peace after a future total war, one is faced with two possibilities. One is that the United States will not involve itself in future wars because those wars are unaffordable. Certainly there was, in the immediate wake of Vietnam, sentiment to this effect, but there is little evidence to suggest that the end of armed conflict is about to occur. And that leaves the second possibility: the military instrument of power will continue to be employed, but it will serve limited political objectives and involve the controlled application of violence at levels well below total war. Limited war, in other words, is the only likely possibility for gaining a better state of the peace militarily.

Such a prospect affects the way we think of better states of the peace and their attainment. Wars fought for limited purposes are not, by and large, wars of societies pitting their total resources against one another, although in cases such as Vietnam, when polarity was lacking, war may be total for one side but not the other (a possibility that American decision makers must clearly discern before committing forces in the future). In those circumstances, the questions of hostile ability and will are somewhat different than in previous times. In the case of combating an opponent seeking to achieve total political objectives, it may be necessary to overcome hostile ability. If both sides are fighting for limited objectives, destroying the enemy's armed forces (hostile ability) may not only be inappropriate, it might cause the nature of the war to change and expand, possibly beyond tolerable limits. Rather, the limited wars of the future may be fought with the purpose of overcoming hostile willingness to continue (cost-tolerance).

Future wars are likely to occur on the periphery of the East and West, which is to say, in the developing world, and are most likely in Asia (including the Middle East), Africa, and Latin America. They are likely to be limited in scope and purpose, at least as viewed from the outside. As the discussion in Chapter 10 indicated, many of these clashes will be quite passionate, even brutal, for the principals, but the efforts by which the United States and others will impose peace will be quite measured.

If this characterization is accurate, it will also be somewhat discomforting for Americans because wars so defined do not fit well into the American military self-image. What we are speaking of are potential uses of military force that bear some resemblance to Vietnam, but on a much more constrained scale. We are not envisioning great crusades against some monstrous Hitler figure; rather we are looking at carefully measured applications of force to accomplish a limited goal. Moreover, we are likely to be looking at situations where our adversaries view the whole thing as considerably more important than we do.

If this is the future, it will require some very real adjustments. Those charged with applying the military instrument—the professional military—will have to recognize these sorts of problems and plan for them, something that does not have high priority now. Part of that planning has to include a greater understanding of the international and domestic politics surrounding the types of situations in which the military might be asked to participate. The failure to do so is virtually to guarantee repeating the worst of Vietnam. Another aspect of that preparation is recognizing that such involvements, if they last long at all, will tend to become unpopular. (This recognition includes gaining some understanding of how the media affect support.) From the civilian side, there will have to be a massive education of the public about how, when, and why military force is applied. The Pollyannaish notions that Americans have of military force will simply not serve in a complex and changed world. We must become geopoliticians, whether it fits our predispositions or not.

# Selected Bibliography

Alexander, Bevin. *Korea: The First War We Lost*. Revised edition. New York: Hippocrene Books, 1998.

Ambrose, Stephen E. *Americans at War*. Jackson: University Press of Mississippi, 1997.

————. *Citizen Soldiers: The U.S. Army from the Normandy Beaches to the Bulge to the Surrender of Germany June 7, 1944–May 7, 1945*. New York: Simon and Schuster, 1997.

————. *D-Day, June 6, 1944*. New York: Simon and Schuster, 1994.

Atkinson, Rick. *Crusade: The Untold Story of the Persian Gulf War*. Boston: Houghton Mifflin, 1993.

Baldwin, Hanson. *Battles Lost and Won*. New York: Harper and Row, 1966.

Barnett, Coffelli. *The Swordbearers: Supreme Command in the First World War*. New York: William Morrow, 1975.

Bemis, Samuel Flagg. *The Diplomacy of the American Revolution*. Bloomington: Indiana University Press, 1957.

Blair, Clay Jr. *The Forgotten War: America in Korea, 1950–1953*. New York: Random House, 1987.

Bowman, John S. *The Vietnam War: An Almanac*. New York: World Almanac Publications, 1985.

Brands, H.W. *T.R.: A Life*. New York: HarperCollins, 1998.

Brodie, Bernard. *A Guide to Naval Strategy*. New York: Praeger, 1965.

————. *War and Politics*. New York: Macmillan, 1973.

Brodie, Bernard, and Fawn M. Brodie. *From Crossbow to H-Bomb: The Evolution of Weapons and Tactics of Warfare*. Revised and enlarged edition. Bloomington: Indiana University Press, 1973.

Brown, Harold. *Thinking About National Security: Defense and Foreign Policy in a Dangerous World*. Boulder, CO: Westview Press, 1983.

Burg, David F., and L. Edward Purcell. *Almanac of World War I*. Lexington: University Press of Kentucky, 1998.

Burg, Steven L., and Paul S. Shoup. *The War in Bosnia-Herzegovina: Ethnic Conflict and International Intervention*. Armonk, NY: M.E. Sharpe, 1999.

Calvocoressi, Peter, and Guy Wint. *Total War.* New York: Pantheon Books, 1972.

Carter, Samuel, III. *The Final Fortress: The Campaign for Vicksburg* 1862–1863. New York: St. Martin's Press, 1980.

Catton, Bruce. *The Civil War.* New York: Fairfax Press, 1980.

———. *Reflections on the Civil War.* Edited by John Leekly. Garden City, NY: Doubleday, 1981.

Chandler, David G. *Atlas of Military Strategy.* New York: Free Press, 1980.

Churchill, Winston S. *The Second World War.* Six volumes. Boston: Houghton Mifflin, 1948–1953.

Clausewitz, Carl von. *On War.* Revised edition translated and edited by Michael Howard and Peter Paret. Princeton: Princeton University Press, 1984.

Coddington, Edwin B. *The Gettysburg Campaign.* New York: Charles Scribner's Sons,1979.

Coffman, Edward M. *The War to End All Wars: The American Military Experience in World War I.* New Edition. Lexington: University Press of Kentucky, 1998.

Commager, Henry Steele. *The Blue and the Gray.* New York: Fairfax Press, 1982.

Cordesman, Anthony H. *The Lessons and Non-Lessons of the Air and Missile War in Kosovo.* Washington, DC: Center for Strategic and International Studies, July 1999.

Corry, John A. *Prelude to a Century.* New York: Fordham University Press, 1998.

Craven, Wesley F., and James L. Cate, eds. *The Army Air Forces in World War II.* Reprinted edition. Washington, DC: Office of Air Force History, 1983.

Davis, Burke. *Gray Fox: Robert E. Lee and the Civil War.* New York: Fairfax Press, 1981.

Donovan, Timothy H., Jr., Roy K. Flint, Arthur V. Grant, Jr., and Gerland P. Stadler. *The American Civil War.* West Point, NY: Department of History, United States Military Academy, 1980.

Dupuy, R. Ernest, and Trevor N. Depuy. *The Encyclopedia of Military History.* New York: Harper and Row, 1977.

Eisenhower, David. *Eisenhower: At War, 1943–1945.* New York: Random House, 1986.

Eisenhower, Dwight D. *Crusade in Europe.* New York: Doubleday, Inc., 1948.

Eisenhower, John S.D. *Agent of Destiny: The Life and Times of General Winfield Scott.* New York: Free Press, 1997.

———. *Intervention!: The United States and the Mexican Revolution, 1913–1917.* New York: Norton, 1993.

———. *So Far from God: The U.S. War with Mexico, 1846–1848.* New York: Random House, 1989.

Esposito, Vincent J. *The West Point Atlas of American Wars.* New York: Praeger, 1978.

Falls, Cyril. *The Great War.* New York: G.P. Putnam's Sons, 1959.

Farrell, Robert H. *American Diplomacy: A History.* New York: W.W. Norton and Sons, 1959.

Farwell, Byron. *Over There: The United States in the Great War, 1917–1918.* New York and London: Norton, 1999.

Ferguson, Niall. *The Pity of War: Explaining World War I.* New York: Basic Books, 1999.

Foote, Shelby. *The Civil War: A Narrative.* New York: Random House, 1958.

Frank, Richard B. *Downfall: The End of the Imperial Japanese Empire.* New York: Random House. 1999.

Freedman, Lawrence, and Efraim Karsh. *The Gulf Conflict 1990–1991*. Princeton: Princeton University Press, 1993.

Freeman, Douglas S. *Lee's Lieutenants*. New York: Charles Scribner's Sons, 1942.

Fromkin, David. *The Independence of Nations*. New York: Praeger Publishers, 1981.

Fuller, J.F.C. *The Conduct of War*. New Brunswick, NJ: Rutgers University Press, 1961.

Futrell, Robert F. *Ideas, Concepts, Doctrine: A History of Basic Thinking in the United States Air Force, 1907–1964*. Maxwell Air Force Base, AL: Air University, 1972.

———. *The United States Air Force in Korea, 1950–1953*. Revised edition. Washington, DC: Office of Air Force History, 1983.

Gaddis, John Lewis. *Strategies of Containment: A Critical Appraisal of Postwar American National Security Policy*. Oxford, UK: Oxford University Press, 1982.

Gilbert, Martin. *The First World War: A Complete History*. New York: Henry Holt, 1994.

Gold, Gerald et al., eds. *The Pentagon Papers. New York Times Edition*. New York: Bantam Books, 1971.

Gordon, Michael R., and General Bernard E. Trainor. *The General's War*. Boston: Little Brown, 1995.

Gray, Edwyn A. *The Killing Time*. New York: Charles Scribner's Sons, 1972.

Guernsey, Alfred H., and Henry M. Alden. *Harper's Pictorial History of the Civil War*. New York: Fairfax Press (originally published in 1866).

Gurr, Ted Robert. *Why Men Rebel*. Princeton: Princeton University Press, 1970.

Haass, Richard N. *Intervention: The Uses of American Military Force in the Post-Cold War World*. Washington, DC: Carnegie Endowment for International Peace, 1994.

Hallion, Richard P. *Storm Over Iraq*. Washington, DC: Smithsonian Institution Press, 1992.

Hansell, Haywood S., Jr. *The Air Plan That Defeated Hitler*. Atlanta: Higgins-McArthur/Longido and Porter, 1972.

Hartmann, Frederick H. *The Relations of Nations*. 6th edition. New York: Macmillan, 1983.

Hassler, Warren W., Jr. *With Shield and Sword: American Military Affairs, Colonial Times to the Present*. Ames: Iowa State University Press, 1984.

Hastings, Max. *D-Day and the Battle for Normandy*. New York: Simon and Schuster, 1984.

Herring, George. *Americas's Longest War: The United States and Vietnam, 1950–1975*. New York: McGraw-Hill ,1995.

Hickey, Donald R. *The War of 1812: A Forgotten Conflict*. Urbana and Chicago: University of Illinois Press, 1989.

Hillen, John. *Blue Helmets: The Strategy of UN Military Operations*. Washington, DC: Brassey's, 1998.

Holbrook, Richard. *To End a War*. New York: The Modern Library, 1999.

Hynes, Samuel. *The Soldiers' Tale: Bearing Witness to Modern War*. New York: Penguin, 1997.

Kahin, G.M., and John W. Lewis. *The United States in Vietnam*. New York: Dell, 1969.

Karnow, Stanley. *Vietnam: A History*. New York: Viking Press, 1983.

Kattenburg, Paul M. *The Vietnam Trauma in American Foreign Policy, 1945–1975*. New Brunswick, NJ: Transaction Books, 1980.

Keegan, John. *Fields of Battle: The Wars for North America*. New York: Knopf, 1996.
———. *A History of Warfare*. London: Hutchison, 1993.
———. *Six Armies in Normandy: From D-Day to the Liberation of Paris, June 6th–August 25th, 1944*. New York: Viking, 1982.
Keegan, John, and Andrew Wheatcroft. *Who's Who in Military History*. New York: William Morrow, 1976.
Knox, Donald. *The Korean War, Pusan to Chosin: An Oral History*. San Diego: Harcourt Brace, 1985.
Koenig, William J. *Americans at War: From the Colonial Wars to Vietnam*. New York: G.P. Putnam's Sons, 1980.
Krepinevich, Andrew F., Jr. *The Army and Vietnam*. Baltimore: Johns Hopkins University Press, 1986.
Lambeth, Benjamin S. *The Transformation of American Airpower*. Ithaca, NY: Cornell University Press, 2000.
Leckie, Robert. *The Wars of America*. Revised and updated edition. New York: Harper and Row, 1981.
Lewy, Guenter. *America in Vietnam*. New York: Oxford University Press, 1978.
Liddell Hart, B.H. *The Real War 1914–1918*. Boston: Little, Brown, 1964.
Linderman, Gerald F. *The World Within War: America's Combat Experience in World War II*. New York: Free Press, 1997.
Long, E.B. *Civil War Day by Day: An Almanac 1861–1865*. Garden City, NY: Doubleday, 1971.
Lyons, Terrence, and Ahmed I. Samatar. *Somalia: State Collapse, Multilateral Intervention, and Strategies for Political Reconstruction*. Washington, DC: The Brookings Institution, 1995.
MacIntyre, Donald. *The Naval War Against Hitler*. New York: Charles Scribner's Sons, 1971.
Maclear, Michael. *The Ten Thousand Day War*. New York: Avon Books, 1982.
Mao Tse-tung. *Mao Tse-tung on Guerrilla Warfare*. Translated by Samuel B. Griffith. New York: Praeger, 1961.
McCaffrey, James M. *Army of Manifest Destiny: The American Soldier in the Mexican War, 1846–1848*. New York: New York University Press, 1994,
Miller, David. *The Cold War: A Military History*. New York: St. Martin's Press, 1999.
Millett, Allan R., and Peter Maslowski. *For the Common Defense: A Military History of the United States of America*. New York: Free Press, 1984.
Millis, Walter. *Arms and Men*. New York: Capricorn Books, 1967.
Morgenthau, Hans J., and Kenneth J. Thompson. *Politics Among Nations: The Struggle for Power and Peace*. 6th edition. New York: Alfred A. Knopf, 1985.
Morrow, John H. Jr. *The Great War in the Air*. Washington, DC: Smithsonian Institution Press, 1993.
O'Ballance, Edgar. *The Wars in Vietnam 1954–1980*. New York: Hippocrene Books, 1981.
Olson, James S., and Randy Roberts. *Where the Dominos Fell: America and Vietnam, 1945–1990*. New York: St. Martin's Press, 1991.
Overy, R.J. *The Air War 1939–1945*. New York: Stein and Day, 1981.
———. *Why the Allies Won*. New York: W.W. Norton, 1996.
Owen, Colonel Robert C. *The Balkans Air Campaign Study*. Maxwell AFB, AL: Air University Press, 2000.
Palmer, Lt Col David. "American Strategy Reconsidered." In *Military History of the*

*American Revolution*, edited by S.J. Underal. Washington, DC: U.S. Government Printing Office, 1976.

Parrish, Thomas, ed. *The Simon and Schuster Encyclopedia of World War II*. New York: Simon and Schuster, 1978.

Pike, Douglas. *PAVN—People's Army of Vietnam*. Novato, CA: Presidio Press, 1986.

Porter, Gareth, ed. *Vietnam: A History in Documents*. New York: New American Library, 1981.

Preston, Richard A., and Sydney F. Wise. *Men in Arms*. New York: Praeger, 1970.

Record, Jeffrey. *Hollow Victory: A Contrary View of the Gulf War*. Washington, DC: Brassey's, 1993.

Remini, Robert V. *The Battle of New Orleans: Andrew Jackson and America's First Military Victory*. New York: Viking, 1999.

Richards, Denis. *The Hardest Victory: RAF Bomber Command in the Second World War*. New York: W.W. Norton, 1994.

Ropp, Theodore. *War in the Modern World*. New York: Collier Books, 1974.

Sandler, Stanley. *The Korean War: No Victors, No Vanquished*. Lexington: University Press of Kentucky, 1999.

Scales, Robert H., Jr. *Certain Victory: The U.S. Army in the Gulf War*. Washington, DC: Brassey's, 1994.

Schelling, Thomas C. *Arms and Influence*. New Haven: Yale University Press, 1966.

———. *The Strategy of Conflict*. Cambridge: Harvard University Press, 1960.

Sharp, U.S.G. *Strategy for Defeat: Vietnam in Retrospect*. San Rafael, CA: Presidio Press, 1978.

Singletary, Otis A. *The Mexican War*. Chicago: University of Chicago Press, 1964.

Snow, Donald M. *When America Fights: The Uses of American Military Force*. Washington, DC: CQ Press, 2000.

Spector, Ronald H. *Advice and Support: The Early Years of the United States Army in Vietnam, 1941–1960*. New York: Free Press, 1985.

———. *After Tet: The Bloodiest Year in Vietnam*. New York: Free Press, 1993.

Stevenson, Jonathan. *Losing Mogadishu: Testing U.S. Policy in Somalia*. Annapolis, MD: Naval Institute Press, 1995.

Stoessinger, John G. *Why Nations Go to War,* 7th edition. New York: St. Martin's Press, 1998.

Stokesbury, James L. *A Short History of World War I*. New York: William Morrow, 1981.

Stueck, William. *The Korean War: An International History*. Princeton: Princeton University Press, 1995.

Summers, Harry G., Jr. *On Strategy: A Critical Analysis of the Vietnam War*. Novato, CA: Presidio Press, 1982.

Tanner, Robert G. *Stonewall in the Valley: Thomas J. Stonewall Jackson's Shenandoah Valley Campaign Spring 1862*. Garden City, NY: Doubleday, 1976.

Trassok, Leonid, and Claude Blaiz, eds. *The Complete Encyclopedia of Arms and Weapons*. New York: Simon and Schuster, 1982.

Traxel, David. *1898: The Birth of the American Century*. New York: Random House, 1998.

Ulanoff, Stanley M., ed. *American Wars and Heroes: Revolutionary War Through Vietnam*. New York: Arco, 1985.

*United States–Vietnam Relations 1945–1967*. Washington, DC: U.S. Government Printing Office, 1971.

US Air Forces in Europe. *The Air War over Serbia: Aerospace Power in Operation Allied Force—Initial Report.* Washington, DC: Headquarters, United States Air Force, September 1999.

Ward, Christopher. *The War of the Revolution.* New York: Macmillan, 1952.

Weigley, Russell F. *The American Way of War.* New York: Macmillan, 1973.

Werrell, Kenneth P. *Blankets of Fire: U.S. Bombers over Japan during World War II.* Washington, DC: Smithsonian Institution Press, 1996.

Westmoreland, William C. *A Soldier Reports.* New York: Dell, 1980.

Williams, T. Harry. *A History of American Wars: From Colonial Times to World War II.* New York: Alfred A. Knopf, 1981.

Winders, Richard B. *Mr. Polk's Army: The American Experience in the Mexican War.* College Station: Texas A&M Press, 1997.

Wright, Quincy. *A Study of War: An Analysis of the Causes, Nature, and Control of War.* Abridged edition. Chicago: University of Chicago Press, 1964.

Young, Peter. *Atlas of the Second World War.* New York: Berkley, 1977.

Zook, David H., Jr., and Robin Higham. *A Short History of Warfare.* New York: Twayne, 1966.

# Index

# About the Authors

**Donald M. Snow** is professor of political science at the University of Alabama. He is the author or coauthor of over twenty-five books in the fields of foreign and defense policy and international relations. His most recent titles include *International Relations: The Changing Contours of Power* and *United States Foreign Policy: Politics Beyond the Water's Edge* (both with Eugene Brown), *The Shape of the Future: World Politics in a New Century*, and *When America Fights: The Uses of American Military Force*. Snow has held visiting appointments at the U.S. Naval War College, U.S. Army War College, U.S. Air War College, and U.S. Air Command and Staff College. He holds B.A. and M.A. degrees from the University of Colorado and a Ph. D. from Indiana University.

**Col. Dennis M. Drew** (USAF, retired) is professor of Military Theory, Strategy, and Doctrine at Air University, and serves as the Vice Commandant and Associate Dean of the university's School of Advanced Airpower Studies. Colonel Drew is the author, coauthor, or editor of five books, and the author of numerous book chapters, monographs, and journal articles concerning military affairs.